*Research Methods in
Educational Leadership
and Management*

2nd E

Research Methods in Educational Leadership and Management

2nd Edition

Edited by
Ann R.J. Briggs
and
Marianne Coleman

SAGE Publications
Los Angeles • London • New Delhi • Singapore

SAGE Publications Ltd
1 Oliver's Yard
55 City Road
London EC1Y 1SP

SAGE Publications Inc
2455 Teller Road
Thousand Oaks, California 91320

SAGE Publications India Pvt Ltd
B1/I1 Mohan Cooperative Industrial Area
Mathura Road, Post Bag 7
New Delhi 110 044

SAGE Publications Asia-Pacific Pte Ltd
33 Pekin Street #02-01
Far East Square
Singapore 048763

Library of Congress Control Number: 2006938389

A catalogue record for this book is available from the British Library

ISBN-978-1-4129-2353-8 (hbk)
ISBN-978-1-4129-2354-5 (pbk)

Typeset by Pantek Arts, Maidstone, Kent.
Printed in Great Britain by Athenaeum Press, Gateshead, Tyne & Wear.
Printed on paper from sustainable resources

Contents

Foreword

The first edition of this book, edited in 2002 by Marianne Coleman and Ann Briggs, has proved to be a world-wide success. It addressed the specific needs of researchers into educational leadership and management, particularly of new researchers, and has been adopted as a core text in many UK universities as well as in Canada, Australia and Hong Kong. One strength of this book is that it identifies a specialist niche in the field of research methods, namely a book that is required by researchers – including practitioner researchers – who are working in the field of educational leadership and management throughout the world. A second strength is that it contains specially commissioned pieces that are appropriate for the field of educational leadership and management, and addresses issues of concern to the experienced researcher, the new researcher and those engaged in practitioner research.

The second edition draws upon the strengths of the first. Responding to reader evaluations, Ann Briggs and Marianne Coleman have sought updated chapters from many of their authors, and new chapters from others, in response to the needs of the field. Subjects introduced in this second edition include: research design, life-history interviews, practitioner research and making use of existing data. The contributions provided by various authors demonstrate the rich range of methodologies that social scientists use when studying educational settings. As with any volume on research methodology, the authors indicate the 'different voices' in which research methodology can be discussed. The range of chapters provided within this second edition is indeed impressive. The philosophical issues that underpin our rationale for undertaking research, and our approaches to it are addressed; there are technical and moral appraisals of validity, reliability and research ethics, discussion of a wide range of research approaches, such as case studies and action research, as well as thought-provoking chapters about research tools. A particular feature of this book is the way in which it focuses on data analysis, writing and dissemination as well as some of the standard topics of research techniques and data collection.

This volume, like its predecessor, is an important contribution to the literature, which enables students to engage with the wide range of issues which affect and underpin their research, before consulting specialist texts on particular aspects of research methods. It is this facility that this collection provides. Overall, it is a volume that will be of great use to those engaged in teaching and learning about the research process and research methods. I am sure that this second edition will become essential reading for students engaged in the study of educational leadership and management.

Professor Robert G. Burgess
Vice-Chancellor
University of Leicester
September 2006

Notes on contributors

Michael Bassey is Emeritus Professor of Education of Nottingham Trent University and an Academician of the Academy of Learned Societies for the Social Sciences. Until October 2004 he was Academic Secretary of the British Educational Research Association and editor of its house journal *Research Intelligence*. His major claim to knowledge is offering a solution to the problem of generalisation in the form of fuzzy generalisation and best-estimate-of-trustworthiness.

Dr Judith Bell has worked as a college lecturer, head of department and vice principal; as a lecturer in several universities; a course team writer in the Open University and as one of Her Majesty's Inspectors specialising in further and higher education.

Ann Briggs is Professor of Educational Leadership at Newcastle University. Her principal research interests are: management of post-compulsory education, middle leadership in colleges, schools and universities, professional identities in educational settings and analytical modelling techniques. Before moving into higher education, Ann worked in secondary schools and further education colleges.

Professor Robert Burgess is Vice-Chancellor of the University of Leicester. His research interests include social research methodology and the sociology of education. He has researched and written extensively on research methodologies and the ways in which they can be used in the study of educational settings.

Tony Bush is Professor of Educational Leadership at the University of Warwick. He has written or edited 29 books and is the editor of the leading international journal, *Educational Management, Administration and Leadership*. His current international work involves collaboration with colleagues in Norway, South Africa and the Seychelles.

Dr Hugh Busher has supervised research projects for many years, focusing recently on the construction of inclusive school learning communities and participants' voices in them. A former member of BERA Council, he is co-editor of the journal *Improving Schools*. His most recent book is *Understanding Educational Leadership: People, Power and Culture* (Buckingham: Open University Press).

Dr Marianne Coleman is Reader in Educational Leadership and Management and Assistant Dean of Research at the Institute of Education, University of London. She has recently developed an on-line distance learning course for an MA in Applied Educational Leadership and Management and has written and researched extensively on leadership and management in education, particularly focusing on gender issues in relation to leadership.

Dr Chris Comber is a Senior Lecturer in Educational Research Methods at the School of Education, University of Leicester and has particular expertise in quantitative methodologies. His main research interest is the use of ICT in educational contexts. He has also written about the underachievement of boys and the impact of educational transitions on pupil attitude and attainment.

Shirley Dex is currently Professor of Longitudinal Social Research in the Bedford Group for Lifecourse and Statistical Studies at the Institute of Education, University of London and is an economist and sociologist. She is engaged in a programme of research using the longitudinal British Birth Cohort studies of babies followed up over their lifetime.

Clive Dimmock is Research Professor of Educational Leadership and Management in the School of Education, University of Leicester. He is particularly interested in the application of grounded theory and inductive analysis research methods to educational leadership and management and has published extensively in the areas of culture and leadership.

Dr Tanya Fitzgerald is Professor of Education at Unitec Institute of Technology, Auckland, New Zealand. Tanya's research spans the fields of history of education and educational leadership and management. Her current research project examines historical and contemporary perspectives of women professors in the educational, medical and legal professions.

Ken Fogelman was Professor of Education, Director of the School of Education and Dean of the Faculty of Education and Continuing Studies at the University of Leicester until his retirement in 2005. His previous career was as a full-time researcher, at the National Foundation for Educational Research, at the National Children's Bureau and at City University.

Dr David Frost is a member of the Educational Leadership and School Improvement team at the University of Cambridge Faculty of Education. He is co-ordinator of the HertsCam Network and editor of the journal *Teacher Leadership*. His research and writing focuses on teacher leadership, organisational capacity and school improvement.

Margaret Grogan is currently Professor and Chair, Department of Educational Leadership and Policy Analysis, University of Missouri–Columbia. She taught high school in Australia, and was a teacher and an administrator at an international school in Japan. Together with Cryss Brunner, she has a new book in press, *Women Leading School Systems: Uncommon Roads to Fulfillment* (Rowman & Littlefield Education).

Peter Gronn holds the newly established Chair in Public Service, Educational Leadership and Management at the University of Glasgow. Previously he held a personal professorial chair appointment in Faculty of Education, Monash University. His most recent book is *The New Work of Educational Leaders* (Sage, 2003). In 2004–5 Peter was the recipient of an Australian Research Council (ARC) funding for a Discovery Project to investigate principal recruitment in three Australian states.

Dr Nalita James is a lecturer in the Centre for Labour Market Studies, University of Leicester. Her research interests include work, learning and identity particularly in relation to higher education and young people's learning and social inclusion in non-school settings, and the development of online research methods.

Veronica James is Professor of Nursing Studies at the University of Nottingham. With an MA and PhD in sociology her research interests are in citizenship and the mixed economy of health, and the sociology of emotion. She has been teaching on cross-faculty research courses of education, health, sociology and social policy for fifteen years. She works as a Practice Nurse, and is co-leading a project on multi-disciplinary learning for student nurses and doctors.

Heather Keeble is Education Librarian at the University of Leicester and has a background of working in academic libraries. In recent years she has specialised in library provision for distance learning students and is particularly interested in methods of delivering information skills teaching to this group.

Roy Kirk was Education Librarian at the University of Leicester Education Library until his retirement in 2005. He has held the offices of Chair and Secretary for both the Library Association Education Librarians Group (ELG) and the Librarians of Institutes and Schools of

Education (LISE) group over the past decade. In 2002 Roy Kirk received the Honorary Fellowship of the Library Association.

Pamela Lomax was Professor of Educational Research at Kingston University until July 1999. Since then she has been working as an independent consultant for a number of universities, mainly supporting doctoral students who are using action research. She has published many books and papers in the field of action research.

Marlene Morrison is Professor of Education at Oxford Brookes University. Through her long involvement with Doctoral programmes, and her personal involvement in a range of research projects, her publications reflect her methodological and substantive interests in leadership for learning and social justice, equity issues, and post-compulsory and lifelong education.

Janet Moyles was Professor of Early Childhood Education and Research at Anglia Ruskin University, and is now a writer and consultant based in Leicester. She has led several research projects including the Study of Pedagogical Effectiveness in Early Learning (SPEEL, DfES, 2002) and Reinventing the Reception Year (ATL, 2004). She is author of numerous books and articles: her latest research-based book is *Effective Leadership and Management in the Early Years* (OUP/McGraw-Hill, 2006).

Dr Anthony Pell is a research associate at the University of Leicester. His research interests include the construction and use of attitude and psychological scales for quantitative research. He has been recently the research analyst for major projects on Transition and Transfer, Group Work and Teacher Status.

Peter Ribbins is Emeritus Professor of Educational Management at the University of Birmingham and Professor of Educational Leadership at the University of Lincoln. He has edited *Pastoral Care in Education* and *Educational Management and Administration* and published 25 books and 110 articles. He has extensive experience, in his own research and in supervising the work of many post graduate students, of the use of interviews in a wide variety of settings.

Juanita Cleaver Simmons is an assistant professor in the Department of Educational Leadership and Policy Analysis at the University of Missouri–Columbia. She is a graduate of the University of Texas at Austin where she earned a Ph.D. in Educational Administration, and a Master's of Educational Administration. She has several years' experience in urban public school administration and has worked at state and national levels. Her research focus is social and academic factors that impact high-poverty, minority students.

Dr Rob Watling has worked as an educational researcher at the Universities of Nottingham and Leicester. He specialises in social inclusion, urban policy and citizenship. He is currently an education consultant at the BBC World Service Trust, where he is developing innovative media programmes with marginalised diaspora communities in the UK and around the world.

Dr Anna Vignoles is a Reader in Economics of Education. She is a Deputy Director of the Centre for the Economics of Education (Institute of Education branch), and Research Associate at the Centre for Economic Performance at the London School of Economics. Her research interests include issues pertaining to equity in education, basic skills issues, the value of qualifications and the return to different types of curricula, the supply of and demand for particular skills, as well as various school management and performance issues.

1

Introduction

Ann R.J. Briggs and Marianne Coleman

This book offers insight and guidance concerning research paradigms, research methodology and research practice, guidance which is essential for any social science researcher. However, as the title indicates, the book focuses particularly upon the needs of a sub-set of researchers: those undertaking investigation into educational leadership and management. In this chapter we first consider why such research is undertaken, and what challenges it presents. This section draws strongly upon a special edition of *Educational Management, Administration and Leadership* (Vol. 33, 2), which focuses upon researching educational leadership and management and is recommended as further reading. Secondly, through introducing the four parts of the book and its various chapters, we encourage you to think about the process of research design, and what this means for your own research.

This book has been written for Masters and Doctoral students, and for the increasing range of practitioner researchers in education throughout the world. In this second edition, we have strengthened the international focus of the book, and drawn in new international writers. In many countries there is currently a strong focus upon school and college improvement being addressed through small-scale empirical research, potentially providing a direct link between research and practice. Our readers therefore have a range of research experience and levels of theoretical and practical knowledge, and we hope that the various sections and chapters provide a stimulus for thought and action across this spectrum of experience.

Why undertake research into educational leadership and management?

Educational leadership and management as a research field is relatively new, having been developed over the past 40 years (Bush, 1999). It draws upon theory and practice from the management field and from the social sciences. The fields of leadership and of management overlap to some extent, but educational management research may be taken to be a study of the organisational structures of educational institutions, and the roles and responsibilities of staff in organising and directing the work of the institution, including 'work activities, decision making, problem solving, resource allocation' (Heck and Hallinger, 2005: 230).

1

Educational leadership research involves analysing the concept of leadership itself, the types and styles of leadership and their relevance to educational settings. Ribbins and Gunter (2002) claim that two important areas of leadership research are under-represented. First, studies of *leading*: 'what individual leaders do and why they do it in a variety of specific circumstances, how and why others respond as they do, and with what outcomes' (Ribbins and Gunter, 2002: 362). Secondly, Ribbins and Gunter call for more studies of *leaders*: 'what leaders are, why and by whom they are shaped into what they are, and how they become leaders' (Ribbins and Gunter, 2002: 362). Empirical research into educational leadership and management, therefore, encompasses a wide range of types of investigation, undertaken for a variety of potential purposes.

Research activity seeks to extend our knowledge, and a typology for educational leadership research offered by Gunter (2005: 166) enables us to distinguish between different approaches to knowledge. She offers five such approaches:

- Technical – field members log the actualities of practice
- Illuminative – field members interpret the meaning of practice
- Critical – field members ask questions about power relations within and external to activity and actions
- Practical – field members devise strategies to secure improvements
- Positional – field members align their research with particular knowledge claims

The type of knowledge sought links closely with the purpose of the research. For example, a technical study could be undertaken with the purpose of producing a rich description of leadership or management practice, an illuminative study would seek to interpret meanings from the data collected, whilst the purpose of a practical study would be to use the knowledge gained in order to achieve organisational improvement. A critical approach would examine the power relations within the leadership or management activity, and a positional approach would assess practice against a particular theoretical framework. These different approaches to knowledge affect the type of data collected and the analysis to which the data are subjected.

Challenges in researching educational leadership and management

Research in this field presents challenges, and this short section introduces some of them. Educational research in general has been censured as lacking relevance, leaders and leadership relationships are difficult to define, causal factors associated with leadership and management practice are complex, presenting problems for the small-scale researcher, and the range of different types of research undertaken can make it difficult to draw upon previous findings.

The educational research field has been criticised for its lack of relevance to the work of educational organisations (see Gorard, 2005: 155 for a summary of these criticisms). One of the major themes that runs through this book, therefore, is that research in educational management and leadership is likely to be embedded in practice. In their book *Practitioner Research in Education: Making a Difference*, Middlewood et al. (1999) explore the premise that research in schools and colleges and in other educational settings will lead to change and improvement. At the very least, research will impact on the professional development of the individual, but it may also encourage small changes in practice, such as the development of a policy; it may even underpin a major change in the ethos that affects the whole institution, particularly where multiple research projects are involved.

The educational leadership researcher encounters difficulty, as Peter Gronn points out in Chapter 12, in defining who are leaders, who are 'followers' and what their relationship is. Is leadership a construct of the leader (or leaders), created by those whom they lead? And how do we take account of the intricacies of leadership and management of schools, colleges and universities, where an individual may be a leader in one context and a 'follower' or team member in another? It is important to acknowledge these complexities, and not to adopt simplistic definitions of leadership too readily.

A further problem encountered by researchers in the educational leadership and management field is the difficulty (especially for the small-scale researcher) of linking causal factors: for example, linking leadership or management activities to improvement in student learning. The meta-analyses undertaken by Hallinger and Heck (1998) and Witziers et al. (2004), which reviewed 40 and 37 research studies respectively, found only weak or indirect effects of leadership on student attainment in the studies reviewed. Levačić (2005: 201) offers a causal model for leadership effects upon student outcomes (see Figure 1.1), which identifies variables involved in direct, indirect and reciprocal causal effects. Having explored the possibilities for statistically based investigations, and for applying quasi-experimental design within the natural setting of an educational organisation, Levačić suggests that mixed methods 'hold most promise' (Levačić, 2005: 208) in identifying causal effects. She warns that considerable amounts of money and expertise would be needed for such investigations, with research involving large-scale longitudinal studies. Her cogent arguments should not deter the small-scale researcher from investigating the variables suggested in Figure 1.1, nor from using the model as a tool for research design; that is why we reproduce it here. However, the purpose of such research would probably be to understand more about particular aspects of the leader–learner/leading–learning relationship, rather than to establish specific causal effect.

Finally, as this book exemplifies, research in the educational leadership and management field encompasses a wide range of possible purposes and approaches. Heck and Hallinger (2005: 232) warn that:

> Researchers employing different conceptual and methodological approaches often seem to pass each other blindly in the night. They ask different questions and base their enquiry on widely differing epistemological assumptions. For the field as a whole, greater diversity has not added up to greater accumulation of knowledge.

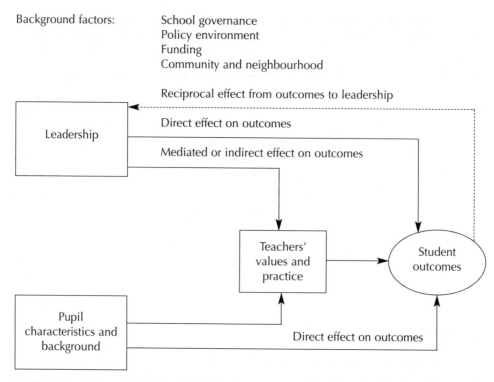

Figure 1.1 A simplified causal model of educational leadership and its effects on student outcomes (Levačić, 2005: 201; reproduced with permission)

In considering your own research design, therefore, do not limit your reading and thinking to researchers who 'think like you'. Through reading papers by investigators who have adopted a particular stance towards their research, or have collected and analysed data sets unlike your own, you will broaden your insight into your own investigation, its conceptual basis, purpose and methodology.

Designing your research: focus and purpose

Gunter (2005: 168) suggests the following interests which educational leadership and management researchers might have.

Learners: who are they, how do they experience learning, how do they progress, and why?

Staff: who are they, how do they experience their work, how are they developed, and why?

Organisation: what formal structures are there in the division of labour, how do they function, and why?

Culture: what informal structures are there, how do they function, and why?

Communities: what direct (parents, governors) and indirect (businesses, charities), participation is there by local people, how do they participate, and why?

State: what are the purposes of schools and schooling, and how is the school as a public institution interconnected with citizenship and democratic development?

Connections: how are local, regional, national and international communities interconnected, what impact does this have on learners and staff, and why?

This list provides a useful starting point in developing a research focus. A research focus could combine some of the interests outlined above, for example: how do staff create and experience culture? An interest in 'state' could investigate the impact of an educational policy, or the purposes of colleges or universities. When combined with Gunter's list (2005: 266) cited earlier of approaches to knowledge – technical, illuminative, critical, practical, positional – both the focus and the purpose of the research can be located. You do not have to use Gunter's terminology or classification, but you can use it to establish what you wish to investigate and why. If you wish to investigate how staff experience their work, do you wish your research outcomes to be a detailed description of staff roles and activities? Do you wish staff to evaluate their motivation to work, or their satisfaction with their working environment? Do you think that some staff (women or those from minority ethnic groups perhaps) may experience their work differently from others? Do you need to find out how staff could be better led, or how they could improve their own management of learning? Does your research purpose include the analysis of student perceptions of the staff who teach them? These various suggestions for research focus and purpose demand different research approaches, and different data.

From research problems to research questions: exploring the concept of research

The thinking above leads us to an important question: what is the research problem? It is important to define as carefully as possible the issue that is to be investigated, and the context within which it is set. The way that you frame the problem will both influence, and be influenced by, the research paradigm within which you work. Part A of this book (Chapters 2–7), 'The Concept of Research', challenges you to consider not only the research problem you are about to investigate, but how to think about it, how to see it in a research context. This will enable you to frame the research questions appropriately and choose research tools which support the purpose of your research.

Part A therefore considers the wider questions related to research which underpin our choice of research approach and research tool. In Chapter 2 of this book, Marlene Morrison refers to research as both an attitude and an activity. She comments that through a process of reflexivity, 'researchers come to understand how they are positioned in relation to the knowledge they are producing'. She introduces us to research paradigms, challenging us to think about the nature of knowledge and being, and how this relates to the methodological issues that will tax your mind as a researcher. Chapter 3 adds another layer to the process of reflexivity essential to research design: are you to adopt a particular stance towards your research, and the area of your investigation? You may see research as being a neutral, objective activity; however, Margaret Grogan and Juanita Simmons open our minds to critical stances adopted by social science researchers who are likely to operate at the subjective, interpretivist end of the research paradigm spectrum. It is important also to consider the context of your research. Much that has been written about research is based on an unthinking assumption that what applies in the Western world, particularly in the USA and the UK, will also apply elsewhere. In Chapter 4, Clive Dimmock shows clearly not only that research is seen differently in different cultures, but that the focus of any research can only be fully understood within its cultural context. Reflection upon these three chapters will lead you to consider deeply the nature and purpose of research, and the importance of its cultural context.

In order to establish the focus of your research, you will need to undertake a review of the literature to discover what has already been written in your chosen area. This includes an examination both of existing research and of the theoretical and conceptual areas that relate to your research focus. In Chapter 5, Heather Keeble and Roy Kirk show the importance of systematically making use of all available sources to provide a secure foundation for your work. As your research focus becomes clear, and you frame your research questions, two important issues need to be addressed: how can I ensure that this investigation is reliable and valid, and what are the ethical issues presented by this research? In Chapter 6 Tony Bush discusses reliability, validity and triangulation – what he calls the 'authenticity' of research – and in Chapter 7 Hugh Busher and Nalita James consider the ethics of research in education. These chapters deal with two of the book's most consistent themes. Virtually every chapter invites you to consider some aspect of validity, very often incorporating Michael Bassey's notion of the 'trustworthiness' of the data. Similarly, the desire to ensure that research is carried out with due regard to ethics, and that no one is damaged by your research, is a theme that most of the authors in this book take into consideration.

Framing your research questions and planning your own methodology will therefore include taking account of the methodology and conceptual frameworks of previous research in the field, constructing a research design which maximises the reliability, validity and trustworthiness of your own research, and ensuring that the ethical basis for the research is sound. It is useful at this point to consider the recommendations of the US National Research Council (Shavelson et al., 2003, referred to by Gorard, 2005: 160), which state that good research would:

- Pose important questions that it was possible to answer
- Relate research to available theory and seek to test that theory
- Use methods allowing direct investigation of the questions; therefore a range of methods are appropriate dependent upon the purpose
- Create a coherent, explicit chain of reasoning leading from the findings to the conclusion
- Be replicable and fit easily into syntheses
- Be disclosed to critique, rather than playing to a gallery of existing converts

From research questions to research methods: approaches to research

The advice offered above exhorts us to use research methods that allow direct investigation of the research questions: methods which are appropriate to purpose. This leads us to consider the methodological approaches available to researchers in educational leadership and management. Having used the first part of this book to consider the type of research you are to undertake – what its philosophical, ethical and conceptual basis is – the second part of the book will enable you to link those understandings to appropriate methodologies. Three broad approaches to research are discussed in Part B: surveys (Chapter 8), case studies (Chapter 9) and action and practitioner research (Chapters 10 and 11). Chapter 12 is concerned with some of the broad issues associated with interviewing of and about leaders. These five chapters discuss the basic choices to be made about your research, and the need to consider your own values and understanding in making those choices. In Chapter 8, Ken Fogelman and Chris Comber offer an introduction to survey and sampling, even dealing with thorny questions such as: 'How many questionnaires do I need?' They outline the ways in which a researcher can ensure that research outcomes are as generalisable as possible, whilst Michael Bassey makes the case for 'fuzzy' generalisations in Chapter 9. Here, he presents an authoritative account of an approach that will be taken by many insider researchers, that of the case study, and shows ways of achieving trustworthiness through the design and operation of the study. In Chapter 10, Pam Lomax shows how action research is truly embedded in values and practice and how those who use it set out to change a situation rather than to observe and record it, an approach which practitioner researchers in particular will need to consider. The theme of practitioner research is taken up and developed by David Frost in Chapter 11, where the reader is urged to consider carefully how research design is to be linked to research purpose. Finally, in Chapter 12, Peter Gronn discusses ways of investigating the phenomenon of leadership through conducting interviews with and about leaders.

Choosing your research tools

The train of thought which started with research paradigms – the philosophical underpinnings of the process of research – through to considering research purpose, research design and methodological approach, leads us through to the practical choice of the research tools themselves. Part C of this book (Chapters 13–15) is therefore concerned with the research tools that may be used within any of the wider approaches discussed above. Researchers into educational leadership and management are often seeking opinions, perceptions and evidence of day-to-day practice from active participants in the field. Chapter 13 by Peter Ribbins, provides valuable practical advice to complement the chapter by Peter Gronn which ended Part B. Both authors use their considerable experience in interviewing in the field of leadership and management in education to draw valuable lessons for the reader. In Chapters 13 and 14, Peter Ribbins and Judith Bell provide clear, practical guides to working with two of the most commonly used types of research tool: interviews and questionnaires. Both make links with the survey method, particularly with the issues of sampling discussed in Chapter 8, and also refer to validity and reliability and the ethics of research. Leadership and management in action may also be observed, and in Chapter 15, Janet Moyles draws on her own experience of using observation as a research tool to show how it can be used systematically in classrooms or in management settings such as meetings or, alternatively, in a more interpretive way through participant observation and the use of field notes. Her helpful thoughts on the analysis of data from observation provide a useful link to the work of Rob Watling and Veronica James in Chapter 20.

The final three chapters in Part C are concerned with text and with existing data sets. In the excitement of collecting 'fresh' data to explore a research theme, existing data may sometimes be overlooked. In the field of education, there is a rich seam of such data, both in the form of statistics and text documents. Whether they form the whole basis of the research, or are used to establish contextual factors for an investigation, these data should not be overlooked. In Chapter 16, Shirley Dex and Anna Vignoles discuss ways of making use of existing data which may be of particular interest to those who lead educational institutions, and to those who wish to conduct unobtrusive research. In Chapter 17, Tanya Fitzgerald invites us as educational leaders and practitioners to 'read between the lines' when using documents and documentary analysis. In Chapter 18, the final chapter in this section, Marlene Morrison draws on her extensive experience with the use of diaries as research instruments. In this chapter, diaries are seen as potentially useful to researchers in a variety of ways, whether as diaries kept by researchers themselves, as respondent diaries, or as diaries accompanied by interviews.

Whichever research tools you use, it is important to consider their fitness for purpose, and your own expertise in using them and analysing the ensuing data.

It is very important that the tools you use properly address the research purpose and the research questions. Consider your research questions carefully: what kind – and what range – of data do you need to elicit in order to pursue this enquiry? And how are you going to analyse your data? Although the part of this book which considers data analysis is placed last, its consideration should take place early in the research design process. The choice and design of your research tools are inextricably linked to the ways in which the data are to be analysed.

Making sense of your research: analysing and presenting data

The final section of the book (Part D: Chapters 19–21) considers the analysis of your data and the presentation and dissemination of your research. Although research is carried out sequentially, it is vital that you consider at the outset how your work is to be analysed and in particular whether you have the resources to undertake the sort of analysis that your data sets will require. Transcribing even one interview is a painstaking process and the extraction of themes from a number of transcriptions should develop as the work progresses rather than being left to the end. Similarly, inputting and analysing a large amount of quantitative data requires skills that may have to be learned and practised. In Chapter 19, Anthony Pell and Ken Fogelman outline some of the ways in which quantitative data can be analysed and presented, while in Chapter 20 Rob Watling and Veronica James show the steps that can be followed in the analysis of qualitative data, reinforcing the point that analysis is not necessarily something that you only consider towards the end of a research project.

Whilst research is seemingly a linear process, from considering the research problem and purpose, to considering research approaches and design, through to the collection and analysis of data, in practice these thought processes, choices and actions are all inter-dependent, and the researcher may move back and forth, considering analysis alongside research design, and ethical issues together with research outcomes. Moreover, although the research questions may have set out what the researcher wished to discover, the most important findings may have been unsought and unexpected. Research is, after all, an exploratory process: if the outcome could be predicted, there would be little point in undertaking the research.

Chapter 21, the final chapter, has been written by Ann Briggs with you, the practitioner/student/researcher/writer, very much in mind, as you write and disseminate your research findings. The book as a whole has been written for Masters and Doctoral students and for practitioner researchers of educational management and leadership. We hope that your research will lead not only to the achievement of your desired qualification, but also to the publication of research that will disseminate your findings, and add to the understanding and improvement of educational processes and their leadership and management. In this Introduction, we have taken you through the stages in thinking which underpin your research, and indicated some of the choices and understandings that are needed. We hope that you will read and re-read the various chapters as you progress in your research, and move on to consult the many associated texts recommended by the chapter authors. Above all, we hope that you enjoy your research, and that from it you gain both practical insight and personal growth.

References

Bush, T. (1999) 'Introduction: Setting the Scene', in Bush, T., Bell, L., Bolam, R., Glatter, R. and Ribbins, P. (eds) *Educational Management: Redefining Theory, Policy and Practice*. London: Paul Chapman.

Gorard, S. (2005) 'Current contexts for research in educational leadership and management', *Educational Management, Administration and Leadership*, 33 (2): 155–164.

Gunter, H.M. (2005) 'Conceptualizing research in educational leadership', *Educational Management, Administration and Leadership*, 33 (2): 165–180.

Hallinger, P. and Heck, R.H. (1998) 'Exploring the Principal's contribution to school effectiveness: 1980–1995', *School Effectiveness and School Improvement*, 9 (2): 157–191.

Heck, R.H. and Hallinger, P. (2005) 'The study of educational leadership and management: where does the field stand today?', *Educational Management, Administration and Leadership*, 33 (2): 229–244.

Levačić, R. (2005) 'Educational leadership as a causal factor: methodological issues in research on leadership "effects"', *Educational Management, Administration and Leadership*, 33 (2): 197–210.

Middlewood, D., Coleman, M. and Lumby, J. (1999) *Practitioner Research in Education: Making a Difference*. London: Paul Chapman.

Ribbins, P. and Gunter, H. M. (2002) 'Mapping leadership studies in education: towards a typology of knowledge domains', *Educational Management and Administration*, 30 (4): 359–386.

Shavelson, R., Phillips, D., Towne, L. and Feuer, M. (2003) 'On the science of education design studies', *Educational Researcher*, 32 (1): 25–28.

Witziers, B., Bosker, R. and Kruger, M. (2004) 'Educational leadership and student achievement: the elusive search for an association', *Educational Administration Quarterly*, 39 (3): 398–425.

Recommended reading

Educational Management, Administration and Leadership, Vol. 33 (2).

Wallace, M. and Poulson, L. (eds) (2003) *Learning to Read Critically in Educational Leadership and Management*. London: Sage.

Part A
The Concept of Research

2

What do we mean by educational research?

Marlene Morrison

Thinking about educational research

The aim of this chapter is ambitious though, on the surface, straightforward. It is to convey a sense of educational research as twin-focused – a systematic inquiry that is both a distinctive way of thinking about educational phenomena, that is, an *attitude*, and of investigating them, that is, an *action* or *activity*. This is a necessary starting point; educationists are living through times when research outputs have often received a hostile reaction, interestingly, if disturbingly, from both within the educational research community (Hargreaves, 1996; Tooley with Darby, 1998) and without (Barber, 1998; Woodhead, 1996). At first sight, such 'spats' may seem far removed from the world of the first-time or small-scale researcher in education leadership and management. Yet they remain critical because the published outcomes of educational research form the bedrock from which postgraduate researchers start their own research journeys. As importantly, at the macro-level they raise awareness about the extent of political manipulation in which research intentions and frameworks are bounded, and sound warnings at the micro-level, especially about what is 'researchable' and what is permitted or celebrated as research. Making visible the various debates that determine what constitutes educational research is complex and fruitful for *all* researchers, whether incoming or continuing.

My experience of conducting research over the past 18 years, and of encouraging others, would suggest that for leaders and managers of educational institutions, departments and classrooms, some but not all criticisms of educational research are well founded. Tendencies towards academic elitism, the inaccessibility of research outcomes and the perceived irrelevance of educational research may have left some education leaders, managers and teachers in 'a vacuum, with the so what? or what next? factors failing to be addressed' (Clipson-Boyles, 2000: 2–3). The growth of professional doctorates and research-focused postgraduate degrees is seen as a counterpoint to such tendencies. Educational leaders might now feel that they have an ownership of research knowledge and practice. Yet, becoming researchers rather than research recipients brings other challenges, described graphically by Brown and Dowling (1998) in terms of the emergence of 'all

13

singing/all dancing practitioner researcher[s]' (1998: 165), with attendant tendencies to deny the existence of 'research as a distinctive activity' and a 'plundering' of techniques which may lead to 'a fetishizing of methods' (1998: 165).

One manifestation of this tendency is training in educational research that is almost totally associated with the acquisition of research skills that enable individual small-scale researchers to collect, process and analyse research data. Asking important 'Why?' questions may be sacrificed upon the altar of immediacy and urgency in the rush to answer 'how to' questions, as if research were 'only' a matter of skills acquisition for a technical craft. If educational research *is* both an attitude and an activity, then the task of this chapter is to invite readers to consider and re-consider educational research not just as a 'rule-driven' means of 'finding out' what educators did not know before (even if they suspected!), but as an approach to skilful and intellectual inquiry that is rooted in, and shaped by a number of research traditions, and by multiple ways of viewing the educational worlds we inhabit.

Some, but not all of this discussion will focus upon the appropriateness of quantitative and qualitative approaches to educational research, and the extent to which earlier debates about usefulness have been superseded by more recent methodological debates about combining approaches. Consequently, the chapter includes a section on mixed methods, considering both epistemological and methodological implications. It is well understood that small-scale researchers need to balance the practicalities of doing research with the philosophies that underpin, sometimes implicitly, their engagement with it. Yet research in education leadership and management, whatever its primary concerns, makes claims about what counts as legitimate 'knowledge' and for whom. Traditionally, education researchers have justified those claims by pointing to the robustness of the methods that inform their research. Some may spend months, even years, convincing themselves and others that their research techniques are 'objective' whilst failing to recognise that the term 'objectivity' – being neutral, unbiased and making sure one's personal values do not enter the research – is *itself* a value-implicit position which assumes there is a world 'out there' to be studied that is 'independent of knowers' (see also Usher, 1997: Introduction).

So, in order to explore the meanings of educational research, we need to consider the range of intentions, claims and purposes that underpin it. Let us begin with definitions.

Exploring definitions

What do we mean by 'research'?

Bassey (1999: 38) provides readers with a useful starting point:

> Research is systematic, critical and self-critical enquiry which aims to contribute towards the advancement of knowledge and wisdom.

Some key terms are used here. 'Systematic' implies a sense of order and structure: whilst some research relies more on innovative design than others, the implication is that there is a connectedness about research which involves the planning and integration of design, process and outcomes. The terms 'critical' and 'self-critical' are clearly important: the assumption is that the research design, and in particular, its methodological integrity, should be open to the scrutiny and judgement of others, and that all aspects of research are subject to reflection and re-assessment by the researcher. The terms 'critical', 'self-critical' and 'advancement of knowledge and wisdom' are each value-laden. Research will bring 'more' knowledge and 'more' wisdom, though at this point of definition we might be less sure about who benefits.

So far, our definition seems to imply that research will make known – in terms of a new or different situation, location, or context – that which was not known before; for small-scale researchers, this might be to themselves *or* those colleagues with whom they work, or to a much wider audience if the outcomes are published. To explore this further, researchers need to look at the empirical and theoretical fields in which they operate. For Brown and Dowling (1998), research should always justify the claims it makes to knowledge 'in terms of reference to experience of the field to which these knowledge claims relate' (1998: 7). Specifically, 'it must justify those claims further in relation to the empirical settings, which is the local space in which the researcher is operating' (1998: 9). What is meant by the word 'justify'?

Let us consider the role of 'manager'. Researchers will not embark upon a study that has a management focus without having some idea about what management means to them, or indeed what they think it means to others. Though they may not always be fully conscious of the preconceptions they bring to their research, they need to make as overt as possible the conceptual structures that they bring to their projects. This is what Brown and Dowling (1998) have called 'the theoretical problem' and this is, in turn, embedded in a range of published literature that the researcher will investigate as part of 'the theoretical field' (1998: 10). But researchers do not, and probably could not, study all there is to know in their area of interest; theoretical development occurs as researchers progressively focus their areas of research. As we develop our understanding of the subject of the research, and the of fitness for purpose of the research design, we move between theoretical and empirical development. Depending upon the research questions asked, some aspects of the theoretical field become more relevant than others.

As an example, readers might wish to consider differences in the theoretical fields that writers like education management consultant Daphne Johnson and academic Professor Stephen Ball might bring to their investigation of management principles and practices, and of the relationship between those fields and the research questions addressed. For Johnson (1994: Preface):

15

The ethos of research into educational management is to assist the development of effective school and college management. Your research-based enquiry is meant to lead to professional reflection and, where appropriate, a commitment to change. The hope is that all concerned with your enquiry will be helped by it.

Links between effective management and professional reflection are assumed, and these are, in turn, linked to different aspects of management such as curriculum management or the management of staff (Johnson, 1994: 93–4).

For Ball (1999) a core educational 'myth' is the assumption that 'good management makes good schools'. He paints a 'grim picture' (1999: 88) that questions 'the social and moral costs' of an increasingly pervasive managerialism in which the headteacher, for example:

is the main carrier and embodiment of managerialism and is crucial to the transformation of the organisational regimes of schools. That is, the dismantling of professional organizational regimes and their replacement with market-entrepreneurial regimes ... Some heads have been aggrandized and others damaged by the requirements of managerial leadership and its attendant responsibilities. (Ball, 1999: 89)

Even if agreement can be reached about the overall purposes and intentions of research enquiry, the preceding extracts would suggest that as an attitude and an activity, research in education leadership and/or management (in themselves 'leadership' and 'management' are controversial concepts within the field) does not exist in an objective or neutral vacuum in which understandings about the term 'management', for example, remain uniform or uncontested.

What do we mean by 'education'?

The concerns of this book are to do with empirical research in the field of education leadership and management. All researchers, including first-time researchers, need, as Bassey (1999: 37) has pointed out, 'to be clear what he or she means by [the term]'. For Bassey, education is:

First, the experience and nurture of personal and social developments towards worthwhile living. Second, the acquisition, development, transmission, conservation, discovery, and renewal of worthwhile culture. (1999: 37)

A noteworthy feature of this definition is its open-endedness; 'worthwhile' and 'culture' include what others recommend or prescribe or denounce. Meanings that underpin research frameworks are therefore always imbued with values.

So, what is 'educational research'?

The study of education is both multi-disciplinary and inter-disciplinary. In part this is what makes educational studies exhilarating as well as challenging! A range of aims and purposes guides all educational research; decisions to 'settle upon' one research project rather than another are guided implicitly and explicitly by researchers' practical, personal, professional and/or disciplinary interests, even if, at the start of the research journey, such interests may lack the coherence of later stages. Bassey (1999: 39) is in no doubt about what constitutes educational research, and expresses this as:

> Critical enquiry aimed at informing educational judgements and decisions in order to improve educational action. This is the kind of value-laden research that should have immediate relevance to teachers and policy-makers, and is itself educational because of its stated intention to 'inform'. It is the kind of research in education that is carried out by educationists.

For others, research may be about *using* research for 'working towards justice, fairness, and openness in education' (Griffiths, 1998: 1). Although, for Griffiths, 'research into organizations – or into educational management – is not, routinely, described as "for social justice"' (1998: 19), educational management, she argues, does not need to be excluded:

> On the face of it, research related to organizational theory (and educational management) could be thought of as one of the less promising areas, since it has a history of being theorized to reflect the interests and needs of educational managers (Ball, 1987: 5) ... A closer look [at some examples of educational research output in the area] reveals the underlying concern with social justice. (1998: 19)

Stances advocated by Michael Bassey and Morwenna Griffiths show some similarity. Here are views that educational research 'can lay no claim to abstract neutrality or being a curiosity-driven quest for knowledge ... rather, in the short run and in the long run, it is action-orientated' (Griffiths,1998: 67). Whilst such an orientation implies no one particular methodological approach, educational action is foregrounded, and the making of knowledge claims, for the claim's sake, is relegated. Bassey (1999) distinguishes between action-oriented research, with its intentions to effect action, and what is described as 'discipline research', which is primarily concerned with *understanding* the phenomena of educational activities and actions.

> Discipline research in education aims critically to inform understandings of phenomena pertinent to the discipline in educational settings. (Bassey, 1999: 39)

Whilst readers of this book are likely to be researchers who will conduct research single-handedly and on a small scale, they will be joining an educational research community in which there is 'a lively and sometimes agitated debate within the traditions of educational studies about its status and forms of inquiry' (Ranson, 1996: 528). In trying to make sense of the world in which educational research operates, researchers work within a range of beliefs about the ways in which education and research are/can be understood as practice. Sometimes disputes about forms of enquiry appear to be conducted at the level of method or technique, with relatively little attention paid to issues of epistemology, ontology, or methodology. Yet, researchers need to consider how and why such issues matter, and to whom, and it is to those issues that the chapter now turns.

Epistemology, ontology and methodology

Why do we need to make connections?

Research enquiry is full of challenges and uncertainties. As researchers we want to know if the conclusions we reach are the 'right' ones; at the same time, our literature searches and reviews tell us that the history of published research into education leadership and management, as for other educational areas, is one in which a range of published authors appear to reach different as well as similar conclusions about the same or very similar phenomena. As McKenzie (1997: 9) points out, 'research is embedded in a churning vortex of constructive and destructive tensions in which old educational "certainties" are replaced by new "certainties"'. That tension is historical. For researchers, two questions are key:

> What is the relation between what we see and understand [our claims to 'know' and our theories of knowledge or *epistemology*] and that which is reality [our sense of being or *ontology*]?
> In other words, how do we go about creating knowledge about the world in which we live? (McKenzie, 1997: 9)

Epistemology, then, is central to research endeavour. All researchers ask questions about knowledge – how we find it, how we recognise it when we find it, how we use it and how it distinguishes truth from falsehood. In other words, researchers seek to 'know' the 'reality' they are describing. Educational researchers bring a wide range of theoretical perspectives to their work. Perhaps the widest of these is *ontology*. This consists of a range of perceptions about the nature of reality and is important because the latter affects the way in which researchers *can* 'know'. *Methodology* is also critical, since ontology and epistemology affect the methodologies that underpin researchers' work. As Scott and Morrison (2006: 153) explain:

Methodology is the theory (or set of ideas about the relationship between phenomena) of how researchers gain knowledge in research contexts and why. The 'why' question is critical since it is through methodological understanding that researchers and readers of research are provided with a rationale to explain the reasons for using specific strategies and methods in order to construct, collect, and develop particular kinds of knowledge about educational phenomena.

Crucially, then, methodology provides a rationale for the ways in which researchers conduct research activities.

From this perspective, methodology is much more than *methods* or *techniques* or *tools* for research, like 'conducting an interview' or 'keeping a research diary'. The methodological rationale provides researchers with underlying reasons for 'conducting an interview'; as importantly, in choosing to conduct serial life-history interviews with a secondary school head of science, for example, rather than a questionnaire survey with a number of heads of science, the researcher is arguing that interviews provide a 'more informed' way of claiming knowledge than a questionnaire could provide in order to address one or more of his/her specific research questions.

Epistemological and methodological concerns are implicated at every stage of the research process. There might be a tendency to think that the information collected by researchers is transformed into 'data' and then into 'knowledge' as if this were both automatic and linear. Not so. Information is transformed into data by the process of analysis; information is collected in a range of forms, as qualitative or quantitative information, or as combinations of both.

Paradigms

In making sense of research information and transforming it into data, researchers draw implicitly or explicitly upon a set of beliefs or epistemological assumptions called *paradigms*. In educational research these are sometimes called epistemes (following Foucault, 1972) or traditions (following MacIntyre, 1988) about how research evidence might be understood, patterned, reasoned and compiled. Researchers who adhere to a specific paradigm hold a kind of consensus about what does or should count as 'normal' research.

Bassey (1999: 42) describes a paradigm as:

a network of coherent ideas about the nature of the world and the function of researchers which, adhered to by a group of researchers, conditions the patterns of their thinking and underpins their research actions.

In the field of educational research a range of paradigms has been developed. Scott and Morrison (2006: 170) point to four of these:

19

- *Positivism/empiricism*, where it is accepted that facts can be collected about the world; language allows us to represent those facts unproblematically; and it is possible to develop correct methods for understanding educational processes, relations and institutions.
- *Phenomenology* as a form of *interpretivism*, where the emphasis is placed on the way human beings give meaning to their lives; reasons are accepted as legitimate causes of human behaviour; and agential perspectives are prioritised.
- *Critical theory*, where it is accepted that values are central to all research activities; describing and changing the world are elided; and the researcher does not adopt a neutral stance in relation to the world.
- *Postmodernism*, which rejects universalising modes of thought and global narratives; understands knowledge as localised; and seeks above all else to undermine the universal legitimacy of notions such as truth and legitimacy.

The ways of thinking which underpin such beliefs are often referred to in terms of philosophical positions. This means that all discussions about the methodology of educational research require researchers to familiarise themselves with philosophical debates about the meaning of education, the nature of educational enquiry, and whether that enquiry will be influenced by individual ontologies. In the following sections, discussion turns to the respective influences of positivism and interpretivism upon educational research activities and environments. The core aim here is to introduce readers to epistemological and methodological issues that are frequently reduced to matters of 'quantity' and 'quality'. Finally, arguing against a 'naive' use of any one paradigm, prospects for combination will be considered and implications for research practice summarised.

Introducing positivism

Positivism is a social theory. Its basic tenet is to view the natural science as *the* paradigm for educational inquiry. Four issues confront readers who wish to explore the term *positivism* for the first time:

1 As Bryman (1988) articulates, there is a range of definitions attributed to positivism.
2 The term is not always recognised by educational researchers, who may work implicitly within the paradigm. Especially with regard to first-time researchers, it is not always easy to discern whether the approach being used is seen 'simply' as the most appropriate or 'scientific' way of conducting research, and/or whether this reflects a cultural preference for one paradigm or methodology over another (see also Chapter 5 of this volume).
3 The term is sometimes used pejoratively, particularly by those who would reject this paradigm in favour of (an) alternative(s).
4 The educational community includes researchers who, for reasons that might be ideological, technical, or pragmatic, engage in 'mix-and-match' approaches

to research methodology and method. They may not perceive, or indeed value, the need for a specific distinctiveness in paradigmatic approaches to research activities.

Readers will be invited to consider 'combination' frameworks in the final sections of this chapter. (Meanwhile, 'mix-and-match' approaches may also be viewed as a research response to criticisms from research sponsors who berate the boldness or 'exaggeration' of research claims emanating from one paradigm, frequently but not always interpretive.)

The key point about positivist approaches to educational research is their adherence to the scientific method. The positivist tradition has a number of key features:

- People – pupils, students, heads of departments, principals and parents – are the *objects* of educational research, notwithstanding their uniqueness as one from another and from the other objects of the natural world.
- Only educational phenomena that are amenable to the researcher's senses, in other words, are *observable* through experience, can validly be considered as knowledge. 'Feelings' as the objects of educational research activity, therefore, need to be ruled out, unless they can be rendered observable and measurable.
- Scientific knowledge is obtained through the collection of verified 'facts'. Such facts can be observed 'out there' in an educational world that is distinct from the observer. These facts feed into theories about educational leadership and management, for example; theories, in turn, represent the accumulated findings of educational research. Theories are likely to have law-like characteristics because they are based upon empirically established *regularities*. The notion that a theory of educational management … or learning … or leadership can be built upon an edifice of empirically established facts is called *inductivism*.
- Theories also provide a backdrop to empirical research because *hypotheses* can be generated from them, usually in the form of postulated *causal connections*. This implies that educational research is also *deductive*.
- Positivists take a particular stance with regard to values. As Bryman (1988: 15) articulates, they do so in two senses. The first involves the need for educational researchers to 'purge' themselves of values that may impair their objectivity and undermine the validity of the research. The second is to draw a distinction between scientific statements and normative ones. Thus 'whilst positivists recognise that they can investigate the implications of a particular normative position, they cannot verify or falsify the position itself' (1988: 15). In such ways, factual statements can be separated from value statements, so that:

> Secure knowledge of the world can be obtained free from any type of values. Observations can be theory-free, and thus it is possible to construct a science of education, which consists of enduring law-like statements. (Scott and Morrison, 2006: 174)

- Human characteristics and attributes can be considered as *variables*. When combined, they can capture the essence of either human beings or the educational activities in which they are engaged. Discoveries about the relationship between variables should enable positivists to explain the world they have uncovered. Again, Scott and Morrison (2006) describe this in terms of 'atomism': 'generalizations refer to the constant conjunction of atomistic events ... these generalizations refer not to causal relations but to empirical regularities' (Scott and Morrison, 2006: 174). Because positivists do not consider themselves as 'inside' the research milieux they investigate, then it should not matter who does the research, provided that others are as 'expert' as they are in applying the scientific method. One would expect that other researchers handling similar data would come to similar conclusions.
- Positivists may predict, in the sense that observations in the past may enable them to predict what will happen in the future, given similar circumstances and significant associations between variables.

What is the relation between positivism and quantitative research?

Quantitative research as a rational, linear process has been heavily influenced by the application of the scientific method which has, in turn, been seen mainly in positivist terms. Bryman (1988) provides an 'idealised' model in which he reminds us that 'the truth' is often messier than the ideal, with theory playing a smaller role in quantitative research than is frequently assumed.

Quantitative research has a number of core features:

1 The relation between *concept formation*, observation and *measurement* is central. How we objectify, observe and measure 'leadership styles', 'intelligence', 'educational attainment', 'reading ages' and 'home–school partnerships', for example, are key concerns; with this comes the important notion of 'breaking down' the research problem into manageable 'bits' that can be observed and measured. The use of structured observation and questionnaires is common in educational research for measurement purposes (see Chapters 15 and 14 respectively).

2 Quantitative research is also interested in *causality*. So, quantitative researchers make frequent use of independent and dependent variables, frequently associated with experimental and cross-sectional survey design, and more recently, mathematical modelling. What makes a school 'effective'? How can we tell a 'good school' from a 'bad school'? How do we know that a school has 'improved'? By 'how much' and 'why'?

3 In cross-sectional studies, three conditions have to be met in order to establish causal relations (Bryman, 1988: 30–34). First, researchers need statistical techniques to show that there is a relationship between variables; second, they need to show that the relationship is non-spurious; third, the analyst needs to show that there is a temporal order to the data being studied.

4 Following the model of the natural sciences, quantitative researchers have a central interest in showing that their findings can be *generalised* beyond the location of their project. Hence the concern among such researchers about the representativeness of survey samples, or the extent to which the results of experiments can be generalised beyond the circumstances of the original experiment.

5 As suggested in the Introduction, few educational researchers, whether disposed towards qualitative or quantitative research, subscribe to the view that research can be *entirely* value-free. Therefore, the interest of the quantitative researcher turns more generally on whether the research can be (rather than is) replicated.

6 In quantitative research, the emphasis is very much upon the individual as the object of research; the aggregation of individualised data provides overall measures. Thus in a survey sample of 300 women managers and 300 male managers designed to ascertain a 'measure' of gendered leadership styles, individual responses may be aggregated in order to give a summative measurement. Following Bryman (1988), there may be a kind of perversity in reifying aggregated data on 'gendered management styles' on the one hand, and placing an emphasis upon individual, unconnected and discrete responses on the other.

Introducing interpretivism

Interpretivism has made an important impact upon education research. It is most strongly signalled in an approach to research that is called symbolic interactionism (see also below). The basis of the approach is expressed succinctly by Scott and Morrison (2006: 130) as one in which:

> Social actors negotiate meanings about their activity in the world. Social reality therefore consists of their attempts to interpret the world, and many other such attempts by those still living and those long since dead. These are real and constitute the world as it is. Thus interpretivists subscribe to a realist ontology. Educational researchers insert themselves into this continual process of meaning construction in order to understand it.

As with positivism, a range of issues confronts readers who may be exploring the term 'interpretivism' for the first time:

1 The term 'interpretivism' encompasses a number of philosophical traditions. The substitute term *anti-positivism* sets interpretivism in binary opposition to positivism. In the following section, the terms 'phenomenology', 'ethnomethodology', 'symbolic interactionism', 'naturalism' and 'ethogenics' are introduced; boundaries overlap and some traditions are excluded (see Silverman, 2001: 38–40 for additional terms and approaches, for example). For some, ethnography is also a branch of this paradigm, although it is not always clear that there is agreement about whether ethnography is a philosophy or a method (Pole and Morrison, 2003).

2 The term is not always recognised by educational researchers who work within the paradigm. Recognising the inter-subjectivity of educational research may be viewed as 'obviously' the most appropriate way of conducting research on, with or for human beings.

3 The educational community includes researchers who, for reasons that might be ideological, technical, or pragmatic, engage in 'mix-and-match' approaches to research methodology and method. Some researchers may not perceive, or indeed value a specific distinctiveness in paradigmatic approaches to research activities.

The starting point for interpretive researchers is to operate within a set of distinctive principles regarding what it means to conduct educational research *with* people. Thus the world of the educational researcher is different from the world of the natural science researcher – all educational research needs to be grounded in people's experience. For interpretivists, reality is not 'out there' as an amalgam of external phenomena waiting to be uncovered as 'facts', but a construct in which people understand reality in different ways. (It may be that some human groups perceive reality similarly, but this does not diminish the potential for reality to be construed differently.)

There are a number of implications that flow from this not least of which are the ways in which education researchers 'work' with and on their data. First, interpretive researchers recognise that they are part of, rather than separate from, the research topics they investigate. Not only does their work impact upon research participants but participants impact upon researchers. Secondly, for interpretivists, the core task is to view research participants as research subjects and to explore the 'meanings' of events and phenomena from the subjects' perspectives. Thirdly, a related issue for educational researchers is the extent to which it is possible to present the accounts that research participants give in a different language, namely those accounts contained in research reports and theses in education leadership and management as being accounts by them, and whether or not researchers' accounts represent or distort what research participants have said or written. How these issues are tackled shows some variation; in part these relate to the use of data as advocated by early proponents, such as the following:

• *Phenomenologists*. From the writings of the 'father' of *phenomenology*, Albert Schutz (1967), and from recent proponents, comes the view that 'the phenomenologist attempts to see things from the person's point of view' (Bogdan and Taylor, 1975: 14). The emphasis is upon how people in educational settings build understandings of their world by continually trying to interpret sense data. Reality is viewed as a social construction. In recent years, it is a research position inhabited most closely by those who follow critical and postmodernist schools of thought.

- *Ethnomethodologists* have also been influenced by the work of Schutz; early work drew largely upon participant observation, unstructured interviews and ethnographic studies in specific settings. More recently, emphases have been upon conversation analyses and breaching experiments. In the former, recordings of conversations with subjects are presented in as unadulterated a form as possible, with an emphasis upon how taken-for-granted conversations might be understood. In the latter, proponents such as Garfinkel (1988), with some notoriety, encouraged researchers to act in ways which violated everyday constructions of reality in order to shed light on how that reality was constructed.
- *Symbolic interactionists* view life as an unfolding process in which individuals interpret their environment and act upon it on the basis of that interpretation. Best-known proponents of this approach are G.H. Mead (1934) and Herbert Blumer (1969). Blumer (1969: 2) argued that symbolic interactionism rests upon three premises:

> The first premise is that human beings act towards things on the basis of the meanings that the things have for them …

> The second is that the meaning of such things is derived from, or arises out of, the social interaction one has with one's fellows [*sic*] …

> The third premise is that these meanings are handled in, and modified through an interpretative process used by the person in dealing with the things he [*sic*] encounters.

A key implication of this approach has been an emphasis upon participant observation, a common feature of school ethnographies of the 1980s (Ball, 1981; Burgess, 1983) in which the researcher becomes a participant in the activity he or she is observing.

- *Naturalism* implies reluctance among researchers to interfere 'artificially' in the world around them and in particular emphasises the need to record the educational world in a way that would be consistent with the images of the world that participants carry with them.
- A key aspect of *ethogenics* is the understanding of 'episodes' in social life. An early study by Marsh, Rosser and Harre (1978) of disorder in classrooms, and on football terraces, is cited by Bryman (1988: 61) as an example of the ways in which ethogenics provides a framework for the analysis of social action:

> The material collected on schools and football terraces reveals that the apparently disordered events that often occur in these milieux can be seen as 'conforming to a very distinct and orderly system of roles, rules, and meanings' (1978: 97); in other words, people's accounts of particular episodes and the observation of their acts … reveal a structure in the midst of apparent disorder.

Interpretivism and interpretation

As with positivism, interpretivism is subject to a number of criticisms, some of which reveal problems with the approach, especially in its purest form. The first issue is whether 'lay' accounts can ever be represented as 'reality'. In part, this is because reality is multi-perspectival and also because the way that humans create meanings is by offering accounts of what they do, and this is, in turn, affected by context. To give an example, the way a school headteacher describes his/her relationship with his/her senior management team might be described by him/her differently to members of that team, to an Ofsted inspector, to a researcher, or to a family member at home.

Second, it is still relatively unusual for humans to reflect in a structured manner upon their behaviour. Most often, behaviour is routinised. It is only when, for example, the researcher asks for reflection on an event or situation that it happens. So, descriptions of reality that are untainted by the process of the researcher asking are not possible – the best one can hope for is a re-description or a re-evaluation.

Third, it has been argued that people's accounts of themselves, of others, and of events, are incomplete in the sense that research participants may be unaware of the broader structures that govern the interpretations they give or of the conditions that underpin their actions. An illustrative example might be a mixed gender focus group of young people invited to respond to a researcher's question about how their behaviour is controlled in class. They note that, in the school attended by them, male and female teachers treat them differently in relation to discipline and tolerance of different kinds of behaviour. Much more difficult to unpack, because they are assumed, are the broader stereotypical assumptions that such young men and young women might have about what should or does constitute 'a male teacher' or 'a female teacher' and/or assumed distinctive characteristics of their behaviour. Such stereotypifications extend far beyond the confines of school to include socialisation that derives from broader familial, employment, economic and political structures.

Notwithstanding such problems, it is probably fair to point out that many educational researchers 'use interpretation as distinct from the interpretive paradigm' (Scott and Morrison, 2006: 132) in its purest form. This is especially common in qualitative forms of interviews, for example, when interviewees are asked to explain what they think about activities and actions: as, for example, in sequenced questions to a senior staff member in a school who has previously described collegiality as an aspect of how the school operates. Questions to follow might be: Why do you think that practices among staff in this school are based on collegial relations between them? Would you provide an example to illustrate practice that, in your view, derives from collegial relations? It is also a feature of biographical/autobiographical perspectives that might, for example, focus upon the career trajectory of a headteacher. Interpretive approaches are also used as part of first phase exploratory studies in order to understand educational processes and procedures; for example, how and why some students, rather than others, are formally excluded from school.

What is the relation between interpretivism and qualitative research?

What is apparent from the previous section is that there is an over-arching view that all human life is experienced and constructed from a subjective perspective. For an interpretivist there *cannot be* an objective reality which exists irrespective of the meanings human beings bring to it (though they may disagree about the extent to which reality is re-constructed by researchers). Therefore, the data collected and analysed have qualitative rather than quantitative significance.

Qualitative research has a number of key features:

1 Strategies that take the subject's perspective are central and draw heavily from the philosophical traditions introduced above. Understanding those perspectives is critical, regardless of whether the subjects are children or adults. Recent research, which emphasizes the importance of children's perspectives, as research 'with' and 'for' rather than 'on' children (for example, Mayall, 2000), reflects the need both to empathise with research subjects and to penetrate the meaning frames in which they operate. Researchers observing, for example, school management meetings are obliged therefore to acquire and understand a specialized language. The need to penetrate the subject's world suggests the need for lengthy immersion 'in the field'. The approach is replete with challenges, not least of which may be seeing 'through *whose* eyes' and the pressure to produce research outcomes over reduced time spans. Nonetheless, the aim is to investigate 'from the inside' through a process of *verstehen* or empathetic understanding.

2 Qualitative researchers pay much attention to detailed observation. Indeed, the essence of their work is 'rich' and 'deep' description. This provides contexts for description and interpretation when researchers ask, 'What is going on here?' Few details are excluded. Thus the layout of the chairs and tables in a principal's office in preparation for a senior management meeting, for example, can offer important descriptive insights about the ways a principal might construe the purposes and operation of such a meeting.

3 In qualitative research, detailed consideration is given to the holistic picture in which the research topic is embedded. This is more than attention to setting; the approach taken is that researchers can *only* make sense of the data collected if they are able to understand the data in a broader educational, social and historic context. For example, school improvement studies look at individual institutions 'as a whole' in order to understand the processes of change that have led to improvement in that school, but not necessarily in other schools.

4 Because qualitative research is frequently concerned with process(es) – of learning, adaptation, innovation, change, professional development etc. – there is often a longitudinal element to the research, and no shrinking from the commonplace, or what Miles and Huberman (1994: 6) describe as the 'banal':

> Qualitative research is conducted through an intense and/or prolonged contact with a 'field' or life situation. These situations are typical 'banal' or normal ones, reflective of the everyday life of individuals, groups, societies, and organizations.

5 There may be a reluctance on the part of qualitative researchers to impose prior structures on their investigation so as not to foreclose issues which may be invisible at the start of the research. Moreover, 'the researcher is the main "measurement device" of the study' (Miles and Huberman, 1994: 7). An absence of foreclosure should not be misconstrued as a reluctance to be systematic, and a case can be made for 'tight prestructured qualitative designs' (especially for those new to qualitative studies) as well as for 'loose, emergent ones' (1994: 17).

6 Linked to the previous point, there may be a reluctance to impose prior theoretical frameworks. Instead, notable writers in the field discuss the importance of 'sensitising concepts' (Blumer, 1954) and 'conceptual frameworks' (Miles and Huberman, 1994). 'Frameworks can be rudimentary or elaborate, theory-driven or commonsensical, descriptive or causal' (Miles and Huberman, 1994: 18).

7 In contrast to quantitative research, the emphasis in interpretivism is upon words rather than numbers. This should not, of course, be exaggerated from either perspective, but the key issue for qualitative researchers is that textual analysis predominates: 'Words can be broken into semiotic segments. They can be organised to permit the researcher to contrast, compare, analyse and bestow patterns upon them' (Miles and Huberman, 1994: 7). More recently, photographs and video images have complemented rather than replaced words (for example, Harrison, 1996).

What this chapter has sought to do so far is to encourage readers to think about the variety of ways in which researchers can investigate the educational world. In important respects 'qualitative' and 'quantitative' have been seen not only as different ways of researching education but also as if in competition with one another, or as 'largely uncontaminated "bundles" of epistemological assumptions, sufficiently divergent to constitute different ways of knowing and finding out about the social world' (Scott and Morrison, 2006: 155). More recently, arguments in support of combining approaches have been advocated, and draw on arguments that are both technical and epistemological. 'Combining approaches' has been likened to 'a third methodological movement' (Gorard with Taylor, 2004: Ch. 1). The position is best described in terms of four main points:

- Qualitative or quantitative represents only one way of classifying methods.
- Choice of method is determined by the needs of the investigation and not the personal preferences or fears of the investigator.
- All researchers need to be able to use a range of methods.
- Completely different methods can have the same research aim.
  (Adapted from Gorard with Taylor, 2004: 3)

Perhaps a key issue is the sense in which there is terminological slippage between 'combining approaches' and 'mixing methods'. It is therefore appropriate to consider the technical as well as epistemological arguments about 'combining approaches' and 'mixing methods'. These now will be considered.

Mixed methods

The technical argument in favour of mixed methods is primarily about practicality and appropriateness. Mixed methods may be used because in combination they provide the best opportunity to address the question set, or specific sub-facets of the research topic. The problem is essentially to find the best fit among methods in order to address the research topic. As Fraenkel and Wallen (2003: 443) comment:

> Can qualitative and quantitative research be used together? Of course. And often they should be ... The important thing is to know what questions can be best addressed by which method or combination of methods.

In other words, a careful and coherent research design that is fit for research purpose is critical. Creswell (1994: 564–568) describes at least three kinds of research design that use mixed methods; he describes these in terms of *design triangulation, explanatory design* and *exploratory design*:

> In a *design triangulation*, the researcher simultaneously collects qualitative and quantitative data. S/he then compares results and uses the findings to see if they validate one another. In the *explanatory design*, the researcher collects and analyses quantitative data and then obtains qualitative data to follow up and refine the quantitative findings. In the *exploratory design*, the researcher collects qualitative data and then uses the findings to give direction to quantitative data collection. This is then used to validate or extend the qualitative findings. (cited in Fraenkel and Wallen, 2003: 443–444; emphasis added)

From the mixed methods perspective, some writers view the researcher as someone who investigates all data that are potentially informative; Gorard with

Taylor's (2004) analogy is of the investigator 'hoovering' up all data by 'whatever means it takes … it is very difficult to imagine why anyone would want to do anything very different' (p. 5). However, their arguments extend beyond this; such research is better precisely because a 'routine combination of methods creates researchers with an increased ability to make appropriate criticisms of all kinds of research' (Gorard with Taylor, 2004: 7).

The epistemological argument in favour of mixed methods is usefully considered by Hammersley (1992), discussed by Scott (1996) and summarised in Scott and Morrison (2006: 156). Hammersley describes seven ways in which qualitative research has been distinguished from quantitative research in order to show that such distinctions can be both misleading and of limited value:

1 Both quantitative and qualitative researchers use numbers, and in either case, numbers may not be the best way of reflecting precision or accuracy.
2 Claims made by qualitative researchers about the ecological invalidity of quantitative research are misleading, first because valid and representative data can be collected in artificial settings, and second because artificiality is also a feature of participant observation, in which the researcher always affects, albeit, to varying degrees, the 'naturalness' of the research setting.
3 The distinctions between the focus on meanings in qualitative methods and upon behaviour in quantitative methods are thought to be exaggerated since investigations of both meanings and behaviour have applied both methods.
4 The concentration on the natural/social science divide is also considered to be exaggerated. Here, Hammersley argues that many educational researchers would not be unhappy to position themselves in both camps.
5 Furthermore, the inductive/deductive divide is similarly false. Hammersley cites the example of ethnographers who would argue that their studies are not merely descriptive but also draw upon the testing of previously formulated hypotheses.
6 The distinction that is made between qualitative and quantitative examinations of culture is also viewed as exaggerated.
7 Finally, the distinctions between the two Qs in terms of idealism and realism are considered similarly misleading. Here, Hammersley argues that researchers from both 'camps' usually accept that their accounts are constructed, but that, as researchers, they do not invent reality.

So, in terms of the prospects for mixing methods and combining approaches, there is a strengthening climate in favour of both, some ongoing disagreement about where mixing should begin or end (Scott and Morrison, 2006) and a limited number of textbooks about how it should take place (an exception being Gorard with Taylor, 2004). The strengths of mixed methods can be summarized as follows:

- Mixing enhances triangulation
- One method can be used to help the other, called 'facilitation' by Hammersley (1995)
- Mixed methods give a fuller overall research picture and allows the incorporation of 'insider' and 'outsider' perspectives
- Mixed methods helps to overcome the 'problem' of generalisability for qualitative research (depending of course upon whether or not generalisability is key to the aims and purposes of the study)
- A combination of methods may facilitate a better understanding of the relationship between variables
- Combination can encourage better links between micro- and macro-levels of analysis
- Combination allows appropriate emphases at different stages of the research process

But there are challenges; these can be usefully posed as questions:

- To what extent is combination 'really' possible when approaches start from different epistemological positions?
- Do researchers have the resources for combined approaches?
- Do published research accounts suggest that even when 'combination' occurs, it is, in reality, more a case of separate work proceeding in tandem rather than combination? (One consequence has been which conflict over which findings 'count' most, especially when one set of findings derived from one method appears to contradict those derived from another.)
- Do researchers have sufficient expertise and training to operate in this way? (This is not to deny the importance of better training in research skills.)
(Adapted from Scott and Morrison, 2006: 158)

For small-scale or first-time researchers perhaps the lessons to be drawn are: first, not to confuse method with methodology; and second, perhaps even more importantly, not to adopt non-reflective cook-book approaches to the use of mixed methods in the hope that 'more' methods will disguise or ignore underpinning weaknesses in research design, especially in relation to key research questions and the feasibility of the topic.

Elsewhere, Brown and Dowling (1998: 57) emphasise the importance for researchers to decide how to collect [their] data, and 'that the methods are consistent with the theoretical framework in which [they] are working'. Again, this begs the question of the extent to which the 'theoretical frameworks' in which researchers work are, in turn, nested in deeper epistemological frameworks that are concerned with what counts as worthwhile educational knowledge and how to get it. This brings us almost full circle to the starting points for this chapter: namely, the relationship between the nature of our research enquiry and the attitudes and activities of educational researchers. Almost, but not quite. One bridging point remains and that is known as reflexivity.

Reflexivity

Reflexivity is the process by which researchers come to understand how they are positioned in relation to the knowledge they are producing. At one level, reflexivity denies the possibility of researchers ever achieving an entirely objective position in relation to research, because they are part of the social, political and educational worlds they are studying. From the perspective of reflexivity, such awareness requires researchers to consider that 'the sense' they make of the world is reflected in, and affected by, the norms and values that have been absorbed as part of life experience.

In brief, reflexivity means two things: first, that all research orientations are shaped by and reflected in the social, political and educational worlds in which individual researchers operate; and second, that researchers need to be aware of the way such orientations affect all research aspects, including decisions about the selection of research topics. Such awareness is challenging since it may bring to the fore features of research that might otherwise have remained hidden, assumed, or denied.

Take, for example, naturalism. Naturalists share with positivists a commitment to accounts of 'other' educational phenomena, including people; research reports from both are supposedly untainted by the researcher. Positivism and naturalism show important similarities. Positivists want to eliminate the researcher (or distance him/her, sometimes physically, through postal questionnaires, for example) as much as possible from the research, and attempt to do this via statistical procedures. For naturalists, the key to their 'absence' from the research is to 'write' the other's actions and words, as if the other were unaffected by the researcher's presence, leaving research participants to 'tell it as it is'. Is this possible? Reflexive researchers appreciate that *it isn't*.

> Once we abandon the idea that the social character of research can be 'standardised out' or avoided by becoming a 'fly on the wall' or 'full participant', the role of the researcher as active participant in the research process becomes clear. He or she is the research instrument *par excellence*. (Hammersley and Atkinson, 1995: 19)

So, reflexivity is not exclusive to either positivist or interpretive research. I would want to argue that such awareness is empowering for researchers and those with whom they work. Researchers of education leadership and management are empowered to produce insightful, critical, systematic and skilful accounts without placing overwhelming 'emphasis upon futile appeals to naive empiricism of either the positivist or naturalistic variety' (Hammersley and Atkinson, 1995: 20–21). This allows researchers to reflect upon, and even celebrate, their key roles as contributors to, and participants in, the principles and practices of their educational research projects, and also 'denies the supremacy' (Hammersley and Atkinson, 1995) of qualitative or quantitative approaches.

Finally

In presenting the philosophical traditions that underpin *positivism* and *quantity*, *interpretivism* and *quality*, and of *combined* approaches in educational research, a tendency to under-estimate the degree of overlap, and indeed, similarity between them has been noted. In part, this is a consequence of establishing, for analytical purposes, a distinction between 'qualitative' and 'quantitative'; hopefully, evaluative distinctions between 'good' and 'bad' have been avoided.

This chapter has also considered mixed methods, the strengths as well as challenges in combining methods and/or methodologies, and the need to distinguish carefully between them. In the field of education leadership and management, there have been calls for change that include the incorporation of research perspectives from more disciplines and 'a wider range of methodologies, within qualitative and quantitative domains, and also ... mixed methodologies where appropriate' (Foskett et al., 2005: 251).

Perhaps the key issue for all educational researchers is to engage with research approaches knowingly and self-consciously as a counterpoint to naivety. According to Brown and Dowling (1998: 83):

> The naive use of quantitative methods imagines that statistical techniques themselves will guarantee the quality of the work. Correspondingly, naive qualitative research tends to substitute narrative for analysis. On the other hand, the adoption of a dual approach involving both qualitative and quantitative techniques can help in overcoming such tendencies to what we might refer to as naive empiricism. The qualitative imagination will tend to demand that quantitative analysis explains itself in terms of non-statistical concepts that it is claiming to measure. The quantitative imagination will demand a degree of precision in definition that qualitative work may want to slide away from.

Again, caution needs to be exercised in relation to the view that using a combined approach to educational research *necessarily* provides a balance between the shortcomings of one approach and the strengths of another. The critical issue for researchers is to choose the approach that best addresses the questions asked; and, as importantly, that researchers are aware of the implications of choosing one approach over another (or combining them), and its impact upon the things that researchers will find. Hammersley (1992: 172) evokes the image of the research journey:

> What is involved here is not a cross-roads where we go left or right. A better analogy is a complex maze where we are repeatedly faced with decisions, and where paths wind back on one another.

Such methodological awareness, I would argue, has seldom been more necessary. Researchers need to be very clear not only about *how* they are doing research about educational leadership and management but also '*why* this approach rather than another?' Such confidence and clarity about the robustness of our studies will relate to all approaches, including those that apply mixed methods.

References

Ball, S. (1981) *Beachside Comprehensive: A Case Study of Secondary Schooling*. Cambridge: Cambridge University Press.

Ball, S. (1987) *The Micro-Politics of the School: Towards a Theory of Social Organisation*. London: Routledge.

Ball, S. (1999) 'School management. Myth: good management makes good schools', in O'Hagan, B. (ed.) *Modern Educational Myths. The Future of Democratic Comprehensive Education*. London: Kogan Page.

Barber, M. (1996) *The Learning Game: Arguments for an Educational Revolution*. London: Victor Gollancz.

Bassey, M. (1999) *Case Study in Educational Settings*. Buckingham: Open University Press.

Blumer, H. (1954) 'What is wrong with social theory?', *American Sociological Review*, 19 (1): 3–10.

Blumer, H. (1969) *Symbolic Interactionism*. Englewood Cliffs, NJ: Prentice–Hall.

Bogdan, R. and Taylor, S.J. (1975) *Qualitative Research for Education. An Introduction to Theory and Methods*. Boston: Allyn and Bacon.

Brown, A. and Dowling, P. (1998) *Doing Research. Reading Research. A Mode of Interrogation for Education*. London: Falmer Press.

Bryman, A. (1988) *Quantity and Quality in Social Research*. London: Routledge.

Burgess, R.G. (1983) *Experiencing Comprehensive Education: A Study of Bishop McGregor School*. London: Methuen.

Clipson-Boyles, S. (2000) 'Introduction', in Clipson-Boyles, S. (ed.) *Putting Research into Practice in Primary Teaching and Learning*. London: David Fulton.

Foskett, N., Lumby, J. and Fidler, B. (2005) 'Evolution or extinction? reflections on the future in educational leadership and management', *Education Management Administration and Leadership*, 33 (2): 245–253.

Foucault, M. (1972) *The Archaeology of Knowledge*. London: Routledge.

Fraenkel, J.R. and Wallen, N. (2003) *How to Design and Evaluate Research in Education* (5th edn). New York: McGraw Hill Higher Education.

Garfinkel, H. (1988) 'Evidence for locally produced, naturally accountable phenomena of order, logic, reason, method, etc. in and as of the essential quiddity of immortal ordinary society (I of IV): an announcement of studies', *Sociological Theory*, 6: 103–109.

Gorard, S. with Taylor, C. (2004) *Combining Methods in Educational and Social Research*. Maidenhead: Open University Press.

Griffiths, M. (1998) *Educational Research for Social Justice. Getting off the Fence*. Buckingham: Open University Press.

Hammersley, M. (1992) *Deconstructing the Qualitative Divide: What's Wrong with Ethnography?* London: Routledge.

Hammersley, M. (1995) *The Politics of Social Research*. London: Sage.

Hammersley, M. and Atkinson, P. (1995) *Ethnography. Principles in Practice* (2nd edn). London: Routledge.

Hargreaves, D. (1996) 'Educational research and evidence-based educational research. A response to critics', *Research Intelligence*, 58: 12–16.

Harrison, B. (1996) 'Every picture "tells a story": uses of the visual in sociological research', in Lyons, E.S. and Busfield, J. (eds) *Methodological Imaginations*. London: Macmillan Press for the British Sociological Association. pp. 75–94.

Johnson, D. (1994) *Research Methods in Educational Management*. London: Pitman.

MacIntyre, D. (1988) *Whose Justice? Whose Rationality?* London: Duckworth.

McKenzie, G. (1997) 'The Age of Reason or the Age of Innocence?', in McKenzie, G., Powell, J. and Usher, R. (eds) *Understanding Social Research: Methodology and Practice*. London: Falmer Press.

Marsh, P., Rosser, E. and Harre, R. (1978) *The Rules of Disorder*. London: Routledge and Kegan Paul.

Mayall, B. (2000) 'Conversations with children: working with generational issues', in Christensen, P. and James, A. (eds) *Research with Children. Perspectives and Practices*. London: Falmer Press.

Mead, G.H. (1934) *Mind, Self and Society*. Chicago, IL: University of Chicago Press.

Miles, M.B. and Huberman, A.M. (1994) *Qualitative Data Analysis* (2nd edn). London: Sage.

Pole, C. and Morrison, M. (2003) *Ethnography for Education*. Buckingham: Open University Press.

Ranson, S. (1996) 'The future of educational research', *British Educational Research Association Journal*, 22 (5): 532–536.

Schutz, A. (1967) *The Phenomenology of the Social World*. Evanston, IL: Northwestern University Press.

Scott, D. (1996) 'Methods and data in educational research', in Scott, D. and Usher, R. (eds) *Understanding Educational Research*. London: Routledge.

Scott, D. and Morrison, M. (2006) *Key Ideas in Educational Research*. London: Continuum.

Silverman, D. (2001) *Interpreting Qualititative Data. Methods for Analysing Talk, Text, and Interaction* (2nd edn). London: Sage.

Tooley, J. with Darby, D.J. (1998) *Educational Research: A Critique*. London: Ofsted.

Usher, R. (1997) 'Introduction', in McKenzie, G., Powell, J. and Usher, R. (eds) *Understanding Social Research. Methodology and Practice*. London: Falmer Press.

Woodhead, C. (1998) 'Foreword', in Tooley, J. with Darby, D.J. *Educational Research: A Critique*. London: Ofsted.

Recommended reading

Brown, A. and Dowling, P. (1998) *Doing Research. Reading Research: A Mode of Interrogation for Education*. London: Falmer Press.

Bryman, A. (1988) *Quantity and Quality in Social Research*. London: Routledge.

Miles, M.B. and Huberman, A.M. (1994) *Qualitative Data Analysis* (2nd edn). London: Sage.

Ozga, J. (2000) *Policy Research in Educational Settings*. Buckingham: Open University Press.

Scott, D. and Morrison, M. (2006) *Key Ideas in Educational Research*. London: Continuum.

3

Taking a critical stance in research

Margaret Grogan and Juanita Simmons

As Marlene Morrison has made clear in Chapter 2, researchers carry certain philosophical assumptions about the world into their research even if such assumptions are not acknowledged or made explicit. Most scholars describe these ways of thinking as paradigms. Research paradigms in the human and social sciences range along a continuum from positivist to critical realist to interpretivist to postmodern to pragmatic, including action or applied research (see Grix, 2004; Heppner and Heppner, 2004; Mertens, 2005 among many others). Not everyone agrees on the terms for each paradigm or on the discrete nature of each. However, most would agree that taking a critical stance on research is embedded in paradigms at the opposite end of the continuum from the positivist paradigm. Within these paradigms researchers define the nature of the world subjectively and use methodologies that define knowledge from a subjectivist point of view. Researchers who take a stance on research are conscious of the relationship between the researcher and the object of the research. There is an acknowledgement of the researcher's belief systems and of the impact a researcher can have on the object of the research. Most important to all these critical stances on research is the desire to transform existing forms of social organization. The purpose of research conducted within the critical paradigms is not just to describe or understand social phenomena but also to change them. This is in contrast to the purposes of traditional research which are most often to explain or understand the social world.

In this chapter, we first situate the critical stance as applied to research within the context of traditional research paradigms to explain the ontological and epistemological foundations of such research. Then, we briefly outline the main concepts and tenets that have been used to characterize the most common critical stances today that are or can be employed in educational leadership/management studies. (In an effort to simplify terminology, we use the term educational leadership to encompass the notions of leadership, administration and management.) The most common critical stances include postmodernist, critical race-related, feminist, queer and postcolonial. We include in these outlines some examples of studies already conducted and/or ideas for studies that could be undertaken. Our purpose here is to introduce the reader to these ideas. Since we cannot do justice to the complexities, nuances or critiques of these theories in the space provided, we also try to include helpful references for further reading. Our overall aim is to place such research firmly within the traditions of the academy and to encourage research on educational leadership that has the potential of creating meaningful change for participants.

Foundations of research

It is generally acknowledged that a research paradigm includes three dimensions: an ontological perspective, an epistemological perspective and methodological approaches that are most often associated with the paradigm. The paradigms that are grounded in the critical perspectives or theories above are most often labelled transformative, postmodern, emancipatory or simply critical theorist (all hereafter referred to as transformative). Research continua that include action research often identify another paradigm labelled participatory or pragmatic that also includes transformative perspectives along with traditional perspectives. The ontological underpinnings of such paradigms address the question of what is the nature of reality. The epistemological foundation addresses the nature of knowledge and the relationship between the knower and what is to be known. Appropriate methodologies follow from the notion of how the knower can best learn the desired knowledge or understandings (Mertens, 2005).

Ontological foundations range from the belief that there is a reality out there that can be apprehended objectively to the belief that all realities are constructed by the perceiver. A critical stance embraces the latter. A critical perspective also takes the epistemological position that there is no knowledge that is value neutral in contrast to the belief that there is an objective truth. Thus, researchers operating under transformative paradigms accept that reality is shaped by conditions – historical, social, political, cultural, religious, economic, race- and/or gender-related, determined by sexual orientation, and ability-related. And unlike researchers who adopt a post-positivist or constructivist or interpretivist stance, transformative researchers create knowledge 'with' instead of 'for' powerless populations such as students, teachers, parents, custodial or secretarial staff. In particular, they investigate issues of marginalization that are related to gender, race, poverty, disability, sexual orientation, religious difference or other marginalizing structures.

As will become clear, there is no one philosophy or theory that characterizes transformative research paradigms. Theories labelled poststructuralist and, later, postmodern emerged in the late 1960s, 1970s and 1980s to challenge modernist notions of certainty and truth. Other critical theories that derived from the feminist movement at about the same time introduced another set of constructs that questioned patriarchy and its many outcomes, though not all feminist theories take a critical stance. More recently, individuals whose ethnicities separate them from the dominant white populations around the world have developed and tested critical race theories and postcolonial theories. In addition, there is a growing research tradition using queer theories to help challenge the heteronormative view of the world that has dominated modernity.

This is not an exhaustive list of critical stances. However, these stances can and do provide us with many useful insights into the practices and policies surrounding educational leadership. To date there are more examples available in English of research informed by feminist, postmodern, feminist postmodern/poststructural and critical race theories in educational leadership than of research using postcolonial or queer theories. Due to space limitations, we are unable to cite all the various ways in which the critical stances have been used in relevant research, but we will use examples and suggest possibilities.

Postmodernist/poststructuralist stances

French writers such as Michel Foucault, Louis Althusser, Jacques Derrida and Jean-François Lyotard, among others, introduced a critique of modernism that has gained considerable popularity in the latter part of the twentieth century and on into the twenty-first century. Although the meaning of the terms is contested and the way each writer conceptualized his ideas differs, postmodern and poststructural labels have been applied to their ideas (see English, 2004; Turner, 1990). For the most part postmodern and poststructural are used interchangeably in this chapter though the theories and constructs that characterize them are not entirely synonymous. An exception is the reference to feminist poststructualism (Weedon, 1997).

Central to most postmodern theories is an interest in language, subjectivity and meaning. They also share a suspicion of the 'grand narratives' or theories that are claimed as having universal application – such as functionalism, liberalism, Marxism, scientific theories, Western philosophy and so on. Therefore, researchers taking a postmodern stance would shy away from utilizing grand or formal theories in their work.

Postmodernism abandons the modernist tradition of seeking truth and objectivity in research. It also denies the idea of 'progress' that is accompanied by the steady 'enlightening' and 'civilizing' of human beings across the globe. '[P]ostmodernism has been distinguished by its distrust and rejection of such totalizing discourses of modernism in favor of limitless diversity and difference' (King, 1999: 475).

A postmodern stance on educational leadership questions the very notion of foundational knowledge of administration and management of schools. 'Indeed, such theories in management science represent attempts to solidify the power base of those presenting them' (Littrell and Foster, 1995: 36). Using the postmodern critique of who is best served by the way things are, it becomes clear that educational administration is dominated by the white, male, middle-class scholars who are in the business of defining knowledge in the field.

A knowledge base is unnecessary since postmodernism asserts that meanings of social phenomena are continually shifting and being re-assessed. This critique rejects the modernist approaches to organizational analysis that are based on positivist studies of management processes. Capper (1995) argues that from a poststructuralist perspective the very definition of leader would be contested since it has emerged from a rationalist, narrowly construed idea of top-down decision-making. Also suspect is the totalizing and de-personalizing experience of working and learning in organizations as modernist theories describe them. In the traditional scientific discourse of administration and management, 'social institutions come to control through language the very people who compose them' (Maxcy, 1994: 12).

Drawing on Foucault's (1977) concept of the Panopticon, researchers of educational leadership begin to understand in more complex terms the relations of power and discipline as they are played out in schools (McKinney and Garrison, 1994). These ideas provide some of the earliest critiques in the late 1980s of the narrow focus of accountability and the damage of high-stakes testing in the United States. The concept of technocratic education and its attendant instrumentality emerged (Foster, 1986).

Many of these themes are taken up and further complexified by the intersections of postmodern thought with the critical stances that follow. Further examples of postmodernist approaches to studies in educational leadership include English (2004) and Sugrue and Furlong (2002).

Critical feminist stances

Feminist theories have a common focus on gender inequities and women's rights. Two specific feminist theoretical approaches can be included in transformative paradigms as they have been defined here: feminist standpoint theories and feminist postmodern theories.

Standpoint

The basis of feminist standpoint theory is that all knowledge is dependent on the social and historical context of the individual knower. In other words, an individual's standpoint influences her knowledge of the world and her standpoint is shaped by the economic and political situation in which she is situated. As with most critical feminist theories, attention is paid to the question of power at the intersections of gender with race, class and sexuality. Nancy Hartsock (1983) and Sandra Harding (1991, 2004) are probably the best-known proponents of feminist standpoint theory. Harding (1993) states: 'Standpoint epistemology sets the relationship between knowledge and politics at the center of its account ...' (in Mertens, 2005: 21). Patricia Hill Collins (2000) problematizes the social and economic location of black women through standpoint theory arguing that they are better situated not only to understand their own lived experiences, but are also able to shed light on privileged others' views of the world. Consequently, standpoint theory provides an opportunity for black women to define themselves in a framework that includes their personal and cultural beliefs while suggesting transformative actions that might acknowledge and/or remediate the oppression. It provides 'conceptual, and representational tools that explicate deep meanings of the very bases of educational research and leadership, its ontologies, episte-mologies, pedagogies, and its ethical concerns' (Dillard, 2003: 131).

Feminist standpoint theorists encourage researchers to generate research questions that arise from the lives and experiences of marginalized people. The purpose of such research would be to help generate power for those without it (Mertens, 2005). Women's experiences, knowledge and subjectivities (their standpoints) ground their research (Hammers and Brown, 2004).

Postmodern

Many feminist researchers have found inspiration in postmodern ideas. One of the best-known examples is Chris Weedon (1997), who combined poststruc-turalist theories with feminism. Originally published in 1987, her book *Feminist Practice and Poststructuralist Theory* paved the way for researchers in many of the social sciences to use the critical tools of language, discourse, subjectivity and common sense (commonly held beliefs used to maintain the status quo) intro-duced by poststructuralism to studies of gender power relations. She posed an agenda for feminist poststructuralism which centred on an investigation into why women tolerated 'social relations which subordinate their interests to those of men, and mechanisms whereby women and men adopt particular discursive positions as representative of their interests' (Weedon, 1997: 12).

Postmodern feminist researchers are often interested in 'Textual analysis and the role of the text in sustaining the integration of power and oppression' (Mertens, 2005: 22). There is an emphasis on deconstructing binary categories such as leader/follower, light/dark, order/chaos, man/woman etc. The notion is that instead of seeing the world dichotomously, a more fluid, blurring of dis-tinctions is productive. Postmodernism also questions the implied privileging of the first of these binary oppositions. Moving out from the text, some researchers investigate the various institutional discourses within which women and other marginalized individuals are situated (see Davies, 1994; Grogan, 1996). The purpose of a focus on discourse is to discover how the discourse shapes participants' subject position. We are all situated in different discourses, but particularly for women and individuals of colour, the discourses often con-flict with each other. As Davies (1994: 26) explains:

My intention in elaborating feminist poststructuralist theory in relation to education … is to enable the participants to have a different way of seeing that does not necessarily replace other ways of seeing, but enables the stu-dent and the teacher to *position themselves differently* in relation to exist-ing discourses. (emphasis in the original)

Importance is placed on the understanding that the product of any research is a construction of reality not a representation of it. An effective tool that allows critical feminist researchers to attend to this point is reflexivity. A reflexive approach is one where the researcher critically reflects on her academic, race, class or other privileges, and on her methodologies to be sure that she is not creating knowledge from her own life (mind).

Both quantitative and qualitative methods are used in feminist research. Those who employ quantitative tools have been careful to use critical perspectives in framing questions and/ or in understanding data. Feminist researchers using quantitative methods have also departed from the positivist tradition by examining the impact on their research of their own values and social class or otherwise privileged positions. Fonow and Cook (2005) make the point that feminist researchers have sought to bridge the gap between quantitative and qualitative methods by doing collaborative research and by searching for more nuanced and sophisticated ways to measure complex issues. Qualitative tools allow the feminist researcher to probe social phenomena in depth and to hear participants' own accounts of their lived experiences. Good use has been made of mixed methods where a large enough sample has been surveyed to permit generalization, and in-depth interviews or observations have followed particular quantitative findings in order to enrich understanding. Ethnography has been often chosen by those wishing to study marginalized populations over time. In addition, participatory action research offers excellent opportunities for collaborative research with participants (see Lather and Smithies, 1997).

Examples of feminist standpoint or postmodern studies pertaining to educational leadership include: Ah-Nee-Benham, 2003; Blackmore, 1999; Brunner, 2002; Coleman, 2002; Dillard, 2006; Gardiner, Enomoto and Grogan, 2000; Grogan, 1996, 2000; Hall, 1996, 1997; Mendez-Morse, 2003; Scott, 2003; Skrla, 2003.

Critical race theory

Studies highlighting issues of race and racism in education that are informed by critical race theory (CRT) have been prominent in North America for the past decade or more and are now appearing in the UK. Many more scholars have employed this approach to research on education and educational leadership in the United States than have used the other critical stances discussed here. Therefore, we go into more depth on CRT to do justice to this growing body of research.

Gloria Ladson-Billings and William Tate (1995) published an article that first brought attention to the need for race-related critical analyses in education. CRT has its roots in critical legal studies in the United States, which critiqued American jurisprudence from a Marxist/postmodern perspective. But it did not go far enough. A growing number of scholars of colour realized the necessity of foregrounding and centring race. For instance, as Ladson-Billings and Tate argue, even though class and gender and their intersections with race are important categories contributing to our understanding of many school achievement issues, they still do not account for all inequalities between whites and students of colour. Many researchers of colour and others have begun to investigate educational issues through a CRT framework so as to question the dominant white causal conceptions and theories. Parker and Lynn (2002: 10) define three main goals for CRT:

(a) to present storytelling and narratives as valid approaches through which to examine race and racism in the law and society; (b) to argue for the eradication of racial subjugation while simultaneously recognizing that race is a social construct; and (c) to draw important relationships between race and other axes of domination.

The notion of institutionalized racism is a very important understanding brought to the fore by CRT. Scholars using the theory have argued that race is a permanent force in the United States, and that racism is not limited to individually perpetrated acts of discrimination, exclusion and/or violence. Influenced by postmodern critiques of societal structures, race and racism are seen as permeating laws and everyday policy and practice (see Young and Laible, 2000). Lopez (2003) argues that allowing racism to be defined as hateful acts or disparaging language encourages the idea that a decrease in those acts means a decrease in racism. This is essentially naïve because societal racism is far deeper and more systemic. Institutional racism is best understood when race is placed at the centre of research.

Another tenet of CRT is interest convergence, which emerges out of a Marxist view that the proletariat will only benefit from legal advances if the bourgeoisie stand to gain more power and privilege. Interest convergence is the understanding that changes in the law and in policies and practices that help to improve the social, economic or political situation of racial minorities only occur when such changes are also in the interests of the white, middle-class society (Kohn, 1998). For instance, during the Second World War, when it was in the interests of the country to mobilize as many troops as possible to fight foreign enemies, African-American men were readily accepted into the US military, and given some status even though segregation was alive and well in the South. Another example includes the landmark US Supreme Court decision *Brown* v. *The Board of Education* (1954). Using the framework of CRT, it becomes clear that it was politically important for the United States to be seen abroad as sensitive to the segregated conditions of schooling for African-Americans. The United States needed Third World allies in their Cold War struggle and they wanted to improve their racist image abroad (Bell, 1995; Lopez, 2003; Taylor, 2006).

The value of narratives and counter-stories is another key feature of CRT. Taylor (2006) argues that it is important to hear from non-white students, teachers, administrators and parents what their experiences of schools are. For instance, the practices of ability grouping and tracking in schools coincide with the racial identities of students – few African-American and Latino students are in the college preparatory classes in the United States. What happens when minority students read little about themselves that is positive in their texts? Pernicious stereotyping of children of colour (with the exception of some Asian-American groups) as less academically capable and uninterested in school affects teachers' expectations in the classroom. CRT urges researchers to provide students' stories that illustrate their experiences. A powerful example is DeCuir and Dixon's (2004) study of African-American high school students struggling in an elite private preparatory school.

Another critical stance taken by researchers who centre race is critical spiritualist (see Dantley, 2005; Dillard, 2006). Dantley argues that this approach is most important for African-American educational leaders in urban settings where the majority of students are students of colour. '[T]heir work is not only intellectual but can also be political and grounded in spirituality. … a spirituality that promotes dealing with pressing social issues through a mind-set that creates ways for leaders and the rest of the learning community to unravel and overcome obstacles they may face' (p. 662). He urges the inclusion of the idea of critical spiritualism in leadership preparation programmes.

Additional examples of CRT-informed research pertaining to educational leadership include: Fernandez (2002); Gillborn (2005); Lewis (2001); Solorzano and Delgado Bernal (2001) and Solorzano and Yosso (2002).

Queer theory

Queer theory is a fairly recent addition to the critical stances that have informed research and data analysis. Derived from a postmodernist deconstruction of the stable identity, queer theory calls into question and problematizes such binary constructions as straight/gay and male/female. That sexuality is naturally, as opposed to socially, produced is also critiqued. Just as feminist poststructuralists do, queer theorists abandon the notion of a fixed identity. Instead they use the idea of unstable and multiple subjectivities: 'Queer theory has established sexual identity as a central axis of contemporary critical discourse about personhood and agency' (Hostetler and Herdt, 1998: 250).

The origins of queer theory are thought to be in the gay and lesbian studies of the late 1980s and 1990s as gay and AIDs activists sought appropriate theoretical perspectives to counter the discrimination and violence associated with homosexuality and the disease (Hostetler and Herdt, 1998). Informed by poststructuralist and feminist theories, queer theory centres the notion of sexuality to challenge the restrictive and damaging heteronormative and homophobic social order. Hammers and Brown (2004) offer the insight that a feminist queer alliance can provide a very productive approach to research that aims to transform social constructions. They emphasize that such research should employ 'a reflexive and critical stance, praxis, and the use of participatory methods' (p. 100). By adopting sexuality as an analytic category, queer theory opens up a space for interrogating commonly held assumptions of sex, sexuality, pleasure, desire and how each of these intersects (Sumara and Davis, 1999). One key purpose in using queer theory in education is to provide an opportunity for resistance to the strongly heteronormative cultures of schools.

From a management perspective, Lugg (2003) observes that public school districts in the United States not only fail to address queer and gender issues, but they also make a conscious effort not to employ queer people. She uses queer legal theory to show how, historically, public schools have been particularly homophobic. This intersection between queer theory and critical legal studies, like the intersection that created CRT, provides an effective theoretical lens through which to understand discrimination and the abrogation of human rights in educational settings.

Critiquing pedagogy and curriculum through the lens of queer theory offers an opportunity to broaden the notions of what counts as knowledge. Sumara and Davis (1999) explain that in examining the forms of curriculum, researchers can identify what counts as difference or *other* within the prescribed texts, materials and teaching/administrative practices. And:

> Rather than defining queer identities in strict reference to particular bodily acts and aberrant or quirky lifestyles, queer theory asks that the continued construction of narratives supporting that unruly category 'heterosexual' be constantly interrupted and renarrated. (p. 192)

Qualitative methodologies have been most often used in studies informed by queer theory. Critical ethnography offers important transformative dimensions to such research. However, this is not in the traditional sense. Both queer theory and postmodern theory insist on researcher accountability and sensitivity to representation of participants. King (1999) insists that it is the duty of the ethnographer to shy away from deciding what and how change should occur. Instead, in the ethnographic account, the key is the opportunity for participant self-examination that may or may not be transformative.

Studies from a critical queer perspective have investigated different aspects of education. King (1998) studied male elementary school teachers to understand the gender and sexual identity issues that surrounded males teaching in an overwhelmingly female environment. With a group of self-identified gay, lesbian and transgendered teachers, Sumara (1996) conducted a study of literary texts written by and about authors who identified as queer. The purpose of the study was to learn from the group's identifications to, and interpretations of, the texts. And Koschoreck (2003) studied gay principals in American public schools.

Postcolonial theory

There is not much evidence of the use of postcolonial theory in the United States to inform studies of educational leadership yet. However, the theory offers interesting and important insights into the epistemological foundations of education, which have implications for educational leadership around the globe. Since the study of leadership and management in business and education has been and continues to be informed largely by Western concepts and ideas, it is appropriate to introduce a critical perspective that challenges the dominance of Western practice and policy (cf. the critique offered to Western concepts in Chapter 4 of this book).

As the name suggests, postcolonial theory emerged from a critique of the way Eurocentric colonial practices and policies shaped colonized societies. The theory has a historical dimension, referring to the Western colonialism that spread across the world in the wake of the industrial revolution. This modern Western colonialism (distinguishing it from the continuous conquest and colonization of earlier empires such as the Byzantine, Inca, Mongol, Roman etc.) is particularly powerful because: '[it] represents a unique constellation of complex and interrelated practices that sought to establish Western hegemony not only politically, militarily, and economically, but also culturally and ideologically' (Prasad, 2003: 5). As a critical stance, postcolonialism questions and explores the multiple and layered experiences of colonization and people's resistance to it both in the (former) colonies and in the West.

But the theory is not limited to a narrow interpretation of colonization. It includes the notions of neo-colonialism, which pertain to the continued economic dependence of independent nations on their former European power, and the newer forms of imperialism such as those associated with the US economic, political and cultural global dominance. In addition, it provides a powerful lens to study immigrant experiences in the West (Nguyễn, 2006). The theory offers researchers opportunities to understand more fully how Western culture, knowledge and epistemology profoundly affect non-Western societies, and how the complex dynamics of Western hegemony contributes to the continued international regime of exploitation and deprivation (Prasad and Prasad, 2003).

Postcolonial theory has had a significant impact on studies of literature in English. New understandings have emerged about language as English (capitalized to denote the language of the colonizer) becomes replaced and intertwined with english (small 'e' to denote the language enriched by local languages and usages). Important insights include: the expanded, contested, yet fluid sense of identity and thought english contributes, and the multi-layered concepts of place and displacement experienced by both colonizers and the colonized (Ashcroft et al., 2002). Nguyễn (2006) expands the lens of colonization in her interrogation of this same notion of place and displacement with the children of Vietnamese immigrants in a US school.

Like the other critical stances identified in this chapter, postcolonial theory offers epistemological and methodological approaches that question and challenge the traditional. Research that employs postcolonial theory often uses qualitative tools and designs. Postcolonialism exposes even more blatantly the challenge of representation with which critical feminism and queer theory are also concerned. When the researcher is an outsider or even an outsider 'within' a community, especially one bringing Western knowledge and practice, it becomes extremely important (a) that the researcher does not exploit the participants for her own academic purposes, and (b) that the researcher reflexively interrogates whose knowledge is being produced by the study. Echoing the cautions found in queer theory, postcolonial theory cautions that change must be owned by and be in the interests of the participants. Nagar (2003) explores these tensions as she writes about two studies in which she has been involved in North India. For instance, she makes the point that the women she has been studying must be trained as community researchers so that they can continue the research to solve their own problems without relying on outside experts.

Some examples of cross-cultural educational research that is informed by postcolonial theory are Johnson (2005) and Tikly (1999).

Conclusion

As stated earlier, there is not yet a large body of research in educational leadership using a critical stance. One textbook that provides good examples of how several of these lenses can be applied is Catherine Marshall and Maricela Oliva's (2005) *Leadership for Social Justice*. This is an edited collection of studies and essays on issues that affect various marginalized populations in the United States. The notion of leadership for social justice is clearly defined, offering researchers an excellent starting point for further research that is about changing educational processes to benefit those who have not been well served by current systems. School governance issues, curriculum content and pedagogies, drop-out rates, students' academic performance issues, recruiting, selection and hiring practices of teachers and administrators etc. all need to be interrogated from a critical perspective. In so doing, a new dynamic of possibilities in educational leadership may be allowed that includes reconsiderations, questions and debates about what we have taken for granted as knowledge.

When researchers adopt a critical stance in their research on educational leadership, they are contributing new knowledge. The vast majority of empirical studies conducted in educational leadership have been from traditional (non-transformative) perspectives. Most policies and practices in schools and districts today reflect this non-critical stance. Consequently, many students of poverty, and many non-white, non-mainstream students are failing to get an education in the United States and other rich Western democracies. We have the data to prove this, but we do not yet have the research base that will inform the necessary new leadership approaches that must be taken to challenge the status quo. Principals, superintendents, directors of curriculum and other leaders have the power to make these changes, but they must be guided by rigorous research. We hope that this chapter provides some ideas on how new and experienced researchers in this field can contribute to this vitally important conversation.

References

Ah-Nee-Benham, M. (2003). 'In our mother's voice: a native woman's knowing of leadership', in Young, M. and Skrla, L. (eds) *Reconsidering Feminist Research in Educational Leadership*. Albany, NY: State University of New York Press, pp. 223–246.

Ashcroft, B., Griffiths, G. and Tiffin, H. (2002) *The Empire Writes Back. Theory and Practice in Post-colonial Literatures* (2nd edn). New York: Routledge.

Bell, D.A. (1995) '*Brown v. Board of Education* and the interest convergence dilemma', in Crenshaw, K., Gotanda, N., Peller, G. and Thomas, K. (eds) *Critical Race Theory: The Key Writings that Formed the Movement*. New York: The New Press. pp. 20–29.

Blackmore, J. (1999) *Troubling Women: Feminism, Leadership and Educational Change*. Buckingham: Open University Press.

Brunner, C.C. (1999) *Principles of Power*. Albany, NY: State University of New York Press.

Brunner, C.C. (2002) 'A proposition for the reconception of the superintendency: reconsidering traditional and nontraditional discourses', *Educational Administration Quarterly*, 38 (3): 402–431.

Capper, C.A. (1995) 'An otherist poststructural perspective of the knowledge base in educational administration', in Donmoyer, R., Imber, M. and Scheurich, J.J. (eds) *The Knowledge Base in Educational Administration: Multiple Perspectives*. Albany, NY: State University of New York Press. pp. 285–299.

Coleman, M. (2002) *Women as Headteachers: Striking the Balance*. Stoke on Trent: Trentham Books.

Dantley, M.E. (2005) 'African American spirituality and Cornel West's notions of prophetic pragmatism: restructuring educational leadership in American Urban Schools', *Educational Administration Quarterly*, 41 (4): 651–674.

Davies, B. (1994) *Poststructuralist Theory and Classroom Practice*. Geelong: Deakin University.

DeCuir, J.T. and Dixon, A. (2004) '"So when it comes out, they aren't that surprised that it is there": using critical race theory as a tool of analysis of race and racism in education', *Education Researcher*, 33 (5): 26–31.

Dillard, C.B. (2003) 'The substance of things hoped for, the evidence of things not seen: examining an endarkened feminist epistemology in educational research and leadership', in Young, M.D. and Skrla, L. (eds) *Reconsidering*

Feminist Research in Educational Leadership. Albany, NY: State University of New York Press. pp. 131–159.

Dillard, C.B. (2006) *On Spiritual Strivings. Transforming an African-American Woman's Academic Life*. Albany, NY: State University of New York Press.

English, F.W. (2004) *Theory in Educational Administration*. New York: HarperCollins.

Fernandez, L. (2002) 'Telling stories about school: using critical race and Latino critical theories to document Latina/Latino education and resistance', *Qualitative Inquiry*, 8 (1): 45–65.

Fonow, M.M. and Cook, J.A. (2005) 'Feminist methodology: new applications in the academy and public policy', *Signs: Journal of Women in Culture and Society*, 30 (4): 2211–2236.

Foster, W. (1986) *Paradigms and Promises: New Approaches to Educational Administration*. Buffalo, NY: Prometheus Books.

Foucault, M. (1977) *Discipline and Punish: The Birth of the Prison*. New York: Pantheon.

Gardiner, M., Enomoto, E. and Grogan, M. (2000) *Coloring Outside the Lines: Mentoring Women into Educational Leadership*. Albany, NY: SUNY Press.

Gillborn, D. (2005) 'Education policy as an act of white supremacy: whiteness, critical race theory and education reform', *Journal of Education Policy*, 20 (4): 485–505.

Grix, J. (2004) *The Foundations of Research*. New York: Palgrave Macmillan.

Grogan, M. (1996) *Voices of Women in the Superintendency*. Albany, NY: State University of New York Press.

Grogan, M. (2000) 'The short tenure of a woman superintendent: a clash of gender and politics', *Journal of School Leadership*, 10 (2): 104–130.

Hall, V. (1996) *Dancing on the Ceiling: A Study of Women Managers in Education*. London: Paul Chapman.

Hall, V. (1997) 'Dusting off the phoenix: gender and educational management revisited', *Educational Management and Administration*, 25 (3): 309–324.

Hammers, C. and Brown, A.D. III. (2004) 'Towards a feminist-queer alliance: a paradigmatic shift in the research process', *Social Epistemology*, 18 (1), 85–101.

Harding, S.G. (1991) *Whose Science? Whose Knowledge? Thinking from Women's Lives*. Ithaca, NY: Cornell University Press.

Harding, S.G. (ed.) (2004) *The Feminist Standpoint Theory Reader: Intellectual and Political Controversies*. New York: Routledge.

Hartsock, N.C.M. (1983) 'The feminist standpoint: developing the ground for a specifically feminist historical materialism', in Harding, S. and Hintikka, M. (eds) *Discovering Reality: Feminist Perspectives on Epistemology, Metaphysics, Methodology, and Philosophy of Science*. Boston, MA: D. Reidel Publishing. pp. 283–310.

Heppner, P.P. and Heppner, M.J. (2004) *Writing and Publishing your Thesis, Dissertation and Research*. Belmont, CA: Brooks/Cole–Thompson Learning.

Hill Collins, P. (2000) *Black Feminist Thought: Knowledge, Consciousness and the Politics of Empowerment* (2nd edn). New York: Routledge.

Hostetler, A.J. and Herdt, G.H. (1998) 'Culture, sexual lifeways, and developmental subjectivities: rethinking sexual taxonomies', *Social Research*, 65 (2): 249–290.

Johnson, G.G. (2005) 'Resilience, a story: a postcolonial position from which to [re]view Indian education framed in "at-risk" ideology', *Education Studies*, 34 (2): 182–197.

King, J.R. (1998) *Uncommon Caring: Learning from Men who Teach Young Children*. New York: Teachers College Press.

King, J.R. (1999) 'Am not! Are too! Using queer standpoint in postmodern critical ethnography', *International Journal of Qualitative Studies in Education*, 12 (5): 473–490.

Kohn, A. (1998) 'Only for my kid: how privileged parents undermine school reform', *Phi Delta Kappan*, 79, 568–577.

Koschoreck, J.W. (2003) 'Easing the violence: transgressing heteronormativity in educational administration', *Journal of School Leadership*, 13 (1): 27–50.

Ladson-Billings, G. and Tate, W.F. IV. (1995) 'Toward a critical race theory of education', *Teachers College Record*, 97 (1), 47–68.

Lather, P. and Smithies, C. (1977) *Troubling the Angels: Women Living with HIV/AIDS*. Boulder, CO: Westview.

Lewis, A.E. (2001) 'There is no "race" in the schoolyard: color-blind ideology in an (almost) all-white school', *American Educational Research Journal*, 38 (4): 781–811.

Littrell, J. and Foster, W. (1995) 'The myth of a knowledge base in educational administration', in Donmoyer, R., Imber, M. and Scheurich, J.J. (eds) *The Knowledge Base in Educational Administration. Multiple perspectives*. Albany, NY: State University of New York Press. pp. 32–46.

Lopez, G.R. (2003) 'The (racially neutral) politics of education: a critical race theory perspective', *Educational Administration Quarterly*, 39 (1): 68–94.

Lugg, C.A. (2003) 'Sissies, faggots, lezzies, and dykes: gender, sexual orientation, and a new politics of education', *Educational Administration Quarterly*, 39 (1) 95–134.

Marshall, C. and Oliva, M. (2005) *Leadership for Social Justice*. Boston, MA: Allyn and Bacon.

Maxcy, S.J. (1994) 'Introduction', in Maxcy, S.J. (ed.) *Postmodern School Leadership: Meeting the Crisis in Educational Administration*. Westport, CT: Praeger. pp. 1–16.

McKinney, J.R. and Garrison, J.W. (1994) 'Postmodernism and educational leadership: the new and improved Panopticon', in Maxcy, S.J. (ed.) *Postmodern*

School Leadership: Meeting the Crisis in Educational Administration, Westport, CT: Praeger. pp. 71–84.

Mendez-Morse, S. (2003) 'Chicana feminism and educational leadership', in Young, M. and Skrla, L. (eds) *Reconsidering Feminist Research in Educational Leadership*. Albany, NY: State University of New York Press. pp. 161–178.

Mertens, D.M. (2005) *Research and Evaluation in Education and Psychology: Interpreting Diversity with Quantitative, Qualitative, and Mixed Methods.* Thousand Oaks, CA: Sage.

Nagar, R. (2003) 'Collaboration across borders: moving beyond positionality', *Singapore Journal of Tropical Geography*, 24 (3): 356–372.

Nguyễn, T.S.T. (2006) '"They don't even know what Vietnam is!": The production of space through hybrid place-making and performativity in an urban public elementary school'. Unpublished doctoral dissertation, University of Texas at Austin.

Parker, L. and Lynn, M. (2002) 'What's race got to do with it? Critical Race Theory's conflicts with and connections to qualitative research methodology and epistemology', *Qualitative Inquiry*, 8 (1): 7–22.

Prasad, A. (2003) 'The gaze of the other: postcolonial theory and organizational analysis', in Prasad, A. (ed.) *Postcolonial Theory and Organizational Analysis: A Critical Engagement*. New York: Palgrave Macmillan. pp. 3–46.

Prasad, A. and Prasad, P. (2003) 'The postcolonial imagination', in Prasad, A. (ed.) *Postcolonial Theory and Organizational Analysis: A Critical Engagement*. New York: Palgrave Macmillan. pp. 283–295.

Scott, J. (2003) 'The linguistic production of genderlessness in the superintendency', in Young, M. and Skrla, L. (eds) *Reconsidering Feminist Research in Educational Leadership*. Albany, NY: State University of New York Press. pp. 81–102.

Skrla, L. (2003) 'Mourning silence: women superintendents (and a researcher) rethink speaking up and speaking out', in Young, M. and Skrla, L. (eds) *Reconsidering Feminist Research in Educational Leadership*, Albany, NY: State University of New York Press. pp. 103–128.

Solorzano, D.G. and Delgado Bernal, D. (2001) 'Examining transformational resistance through a critical race and LatCrit theory framework: Chicana and Chicano students in an urban context', *Urban Education*, 36 (3): 308–342.

Solorzano, D.G. and Yosso, T.J. (2002) 'Critical race methodology: counter-storytelling as an analytic framework for educational research', *Qualitative Inquiry*, 8 (1): 23–44.

Sugrue, C. and Furlong, C. (2002) 'The cosmology of Irish primary principals' identities: between the modern and the postmodern', *International Journal of Leadership in Education*, 5 (3): 189–210.

Sumara, D.J. (1996) *Private Readings in Public: Schooling the Literary Imagination*. New York: Peter Lang.

Sumara, D. and Davis, B. (1999) Interrupting heteronormativity: toward a queer curriculum theory, *Curriculum Inquiry*, 29 (2): 191–208.

Taylor, E. (2006) 'A critical race analysis of the achievement gap in the United States: politics, reality and hope', *Leadership and Policy in Schools*, 5: 71–87.

Tikly, L. (1999) 'Postcolonialism and comparative education', *International Review of Education*, 45 (5/6): 603–621.

Turner, B.S. (Ed.) (1990) *Theories of Modernity and Postmodernity*. Newbury Park, CA: Sage.

Weedon, C. (1997) *Feminist Practice and Poststructuralist Theory* (2nd edn). Cambridge, MA: Blackwells.

Young, M.D. and Laible, J. (2000) 'White racism, anti-racism, and school leader preparation', *Journal of School Leadership*, 10 (5): 371–415.

Recommended reading

English, F.W. (2004) *Theory in Educational Administration*. New York: HarperCollins.

Marshall, C. and Oliva, M. (2005) *Leadership for Social Justice*. Boston, MA: Allyn and Bacon.

For recommended reading on critical feminist stances, critical race theory, queer theory and postcolonial theory, see the end of each section in the chapter.

4
Cross-cultural differences in interpreting and conducting research

Clive Dimmock

There is little doubt that research in different cultures, and the comparative study that often results, is rapidly assuming greater significance than at any time during the past century. Interest in cross-cultural research is a consequence of powerful trends acting at the macro-social level, in particular, the emergence of a global economy, and a cadre of policy-makers who increasingly 'sing from the same hymn sheet' (Lauder, 2000: 465).

For too long assumptions, policies and practices emanating from Western Europe and North America have been imposed on societies with very different cultures. As Broadfoot (1997: xii) puts it, 'There has been no shortage of individual researchers, government agencies and international aid organisations ready to define problems and prescribe solutions according to their own priorities and their own cultural assumptions'. (In this context, see also Chapter 3 of this book for discussion of postcolonial theory.)

More recently, however, a growing awareness of the need for cultural and contextual sensitivity when conducting empirical research and when drawing conclusions from comparative and cross-cultural studies, seems to be emerging (Dimmock, 2000). The need for raised sensitivity applies particularly to postgraduates and academics researching in at least one of the following three situations. First, it is pertinent to researchers wishing to conduct empirical and non-empirical research in cultures other than their own; secondly, it is applicable to those aiming to conduct studies in their own cultures while using methods, assumptions, models, theories and even conclusions drawn from elsewhere; and thirdly, it is relevant to researchers wishing to draw comparisons between the education systems of different societies.

While this chapter raises issues of relevance to academic researchers in general, it is primarily written with the interests and concerns of postgraduate students in mind. The chapter explores two main avenues of educational management research in different cultures. The first concerns the cultural effect of attributing different meanings or understandings to such research, and the second raises issues concerning the conduct of research in different cultures. Accordingly, the chapter is structured to reflect these two themes.

Societal culture and the implications for understanding the meaning of research

It is fitting to begin with words of caution to the novice researcher. A large part of the accumulated body of literature in educational leadership and management has been generated by a culturally homogeneous cadre of scholars from English-speaking backgrounds. These scholars represent societies that constitute no more than 8 per cent of the world's population yet they claim to speak for the vast majority. In many instances they fail to delimit the geo-cultural boundaries within which their models, theories, ideas, findings and conclusions apply. On other occasions, they advocate the transfer and adoption of policies and practices from one society to another with relative impunity and naivety. Policy-makers, too, are not slow to adopt policies that are culturally borrowed from elsewhere. We have come to expect this as part of the globalised world. Bajunid (1996) summarises the issues well in posing the following questions to non-Western societies:

- Is the wholesale acceptance of Western educational practices appropriate to their national goals?
- Are the educational practices they have adopted from the West consistent with and sustaining of their cultural heritage?
- What are their own intellectual traditions and indigenous approaches to education and cultural transmission?
- How does the indigenous knowledge embedded in their culture fit with the theories, assumptions and practices embedded in Western-derived educational programmes?

Paradoxically, the same questions apply equally well, but in reverse, to the USA and the UK, as they look to Japan, Taiwan and other Asian 'Tigers' for direction on how to improve teaching and student learning outcomes. For probably the first time, there is now reciprocal interest between East and West in each other's education systems.

The point to make, however, is not that such international cross-cultural awareness is negative and should cease. Indeed, quite the reverse. There is a strong case for encouraging more postgraduates and academics to research the influence of societal culture on schooling and educational management since relatively little is known about it. Through learning about other societies and cultures, each society can learn more about itself. A key issue is that successful policies and practices cannot simply be replicated and transplanted from one society to another, even with some adaptation. Before a particular policy or practice is adopted in a given system, there is a need to know why it is working in other societies and with what effects. This demands an understanding of the indigenous culture, its values, beliefs, customs and ways of life, all of which interact.

The problem is that our knowledge base for understanding culture and its intricate connections with policy and practice is extremely sketchy. Cultural variables mediate between society on the one hand and school policies and practices on the other. Orthodox school effectiveness and school improvement studies have generally failed to build cultural variables into their equations. This has repercussions for postgraduates and academics when designing future research proposals.

It is thus timely that research in educational leadership and management take more cognisance of societal culture. It is fair to claim that the cultural and cross-cultural dimension in the field has been ignored and neglected for too long. Among the reasons why societal culture and cross-cultural comparison are beginning to attract attention are the following:

- Narrow ethnocentrism of Anglo-American research
- International comparison of test results
- The work of international agencies
- Globalisation of policy and practice
- Increased mobility of ideas and people
- Internationalisation of schools, especially the private sector
- Internationalisation of higher education
- Multiculturalism within societies

This list may itself provide a framework of ideas for potential research proposals. A growing interest in cross-cultural research and in culture more generally in edu- cational management has a number of consequences. First, the foundation concept of 'culture' itself needs clarification. Second, to the extent that cultures differ, the meanings that societies impart to particular ideas, actions, behaviours, processes and structures may differ. Third, there is a need to develop more rigorous and sys- tematic methods of authentic comparison and measurement of cultural differences and their impact on educational management. The first two points are matters concerning the meanings attributed to research and will be discussed in this sec- tion, while the last relates to the following section on the conduct of research.

Clarifying the concept of culture

For the intending researcher in the field, a key early stage is to appreciate the different interpretations and nuances of the term 'culture'. The present argu- ment suggests that the concept of culture, and societal culture, in particular, is a promising base on which to build a comparative and international branch of educational leadership and management. Elsewhere, a justification for this approach has been provided (see, for example, Dimmock and Walker, 1998a, 1998b). However, the researcher should be mindful of potential difficulties.

Culture is an amorphous, ambivalent and contested concept (Brislin, 1993). Anthropologists and sociologists, 'culturalists' and 'modernists' tend to attribute different emphases, and meanings, to the term. Anthropological and 'culturalist' approaches dwell on the values, beliefs and customs of distinct groups of people, whether they be at national/regional level (societal culture), local level, or school level (organisational culture). From these perspectives, culture is based on the traditional values that have built up over a long period of time. Sociologists, on the other hand, adopt a more institutionalist position, viewing culture as an amalgam of values, institutional and structural arrangements, political and historical forces that together configure a society. 'Modernists' stress the world as a changing environment where traditional values are constantly eroded. They tend to see 'culture' as a mix of older and newer values, all in a state of flux.

While it is clear that culture does not account for all of the influences on schooling and educational management, it is difficult to know where exactly to draw its boundaries in delimiting it from say, history, politics, economics and religion. From a culturalist perspective, the latter may be considered part of, and certainly influential in shaping, culture. A further issue concerns the increasing phenomenon of multi-ethnic societies with distinctive sub-groups of people within a society, rendering the emergence of a homogeneous, typical and representative societal culture even more difficult.

The purpose of the present discussion is to encourage the postgraduate researcher to undertake studies in educational leadership and management from a cultural perspective, but to do so with insight and awareness of the complexities. There are many challenges confronting, as well as attractions enticing, the researcher when applying the concept of culture (for a full discussion, see Dimmock, 2000; Dimmock and Walker, 1998a, 1998b, 2005; Walker and Dimmock, 2002). It is not an easy concept to work with, but it is too important an influence to be ignored.

Examples of cultural context and differences of meaning

Since culture permeates all levels of society, it provides rich opportunities for researchers to explore the interrelationships between schools and their micro- and macro-environments. Studying the influence of societal culture is particularly rewarding at the level of the school, since it is here at the point of policy implementation that the macro- and micro-levels of culture interact.

'Culture' is a particularly useful analytical concept in situations where the characteristics of different organisations appear on the surface to possess similarity, but are, in fact, quite different in their actual *modus operandi*. For example, schools in different societies often appear to have similar, formal leadership hierarchies and organisational structures, while subtle differences in values, relationships and processes are hidden or disguised (Walker and Dimmock, 2000a). Likewise, while different societies may appear to adopt the same policy agenda and framework, the meanings and interpretations each attaches to the core ideas and concepts may vary dramatically. These are important considerations for researchers, as the following illustrations demonstrate.

A policy shift towards school-based management and devolution has been gathering momentum in very different cultures and societies for the past two decades. Associated with these reforms in the management and organisation of school systems are new configurations for curriculum, teaching and learning, as well as changes to assessment and evaluation. These are broad sweeping reform packages that are complex in affecting just about every part of an education system, including its rules, roles and relationships. They are thus attractive themes for postgraduate research.

In the global push to introduce such measures, a new educational lexicon has been invented based on core concepts such as 'school-based management', 'accountability', 'collaborative, shared and distributed decision-making', 'appraisal', 'national curriculum', 'curriculum frameworks', 'outcomes curriculum', 'student-centred learning', 'constructivism', 'league tables', 'performance indicators', 'creativity' and 'quality schools'. Educators across the world – policy-makers, practitioners and researchers alike – increasingly communicate by using this lexicon. The problem is that often, without realisation, educators in different cultures attribute different meanings and significance to the same core concepts and ideas. Put bluntly, distributed leadership in an English school context often means something quite different in a Hong Kong school. Researchers need to be alert not only to how globalisation spreads the same policy agenda across many societies, but how different cultures mediate the meanings and significance of these policies and practices.

This latter point is well illustrated by the current press in many societies for a national curriculum based on student-learning outcomes. In the UK, a national curriculum was introduced in 1988 to replace a situation where each school and local authority exercised considerable discretion as to what was taught and how much time was allocated to each subject. Teaching, especially in primary schools, had come to rely on so-called progressive, student-centred methods. The aim of the British government, therefore, was to establish a clear and detailed prescribed curriculum specifying learning outcomes, where none existed before, and to pare back the progressive methods by advocating direct whole-class teaching and testing. Contrast this with Hong Kong, which already had a prescribed curriculum for many decades, though not one framed in learning outcome terms. In Hong Kong, the problem – as perceived by the Special Administrative Region Government – was too great a reliance on direct whole-class teaching, too much standardisation, insufficient attention to individual student differences and too little variation of teaching methods. While the push in both societies is towards a national curriculum based on learning outcomes, the means of achieving the aims is very different. Each starts from a different position. Each culture attributes different importance and meanings to the same ideas.

Hong Kong, along with others of its Asian neighbours, aims to introduce more student-centred methods into their otherwise teacher-centred classrooms.

UK governments, fearing that student-centredness has gone too far, have sought to introduce more basic education and direct teaching. At the policy level, the tendency is for each to move towards the other. In practice, however, culture along with other factors, makes this global tendency difficult to achieve.

Continuing with this analysis, the practicality of student-centred methods is influenced by class size. Class sizes in Hong Kong are typically 40 or 45, while in mainland China, they can be upwards of 65 and 70. It is worth asking the question 'Is it possible for Hong Kong or mainland Chinese teachers to practise student-centred learning?' In addressing this question, Stevenson and Stigler (1992) show how Chinese teachers manage to combine both direct teaching and student-centredness in a uniquely Chinese style of teaching. They show convincingly that Chinese culture enables teachers to conduct lessons with very large classes and yet still attend to individual needs. Chinese culture is manifested in early childhood socialisation in the family, preparing children to conform more readily to school authority and traditional teaching, than do Western cultures, thus presenting few disruptive problems and enabling teachers to focus on learning. Home and school values seem to align more closely in Asian than Western societies, with ramifications for teaching and leadership.

Elsewhere, Watkins (2000) has argued that there are major cultural differences between Anglo-American and East Asian connotations of rote memorisation and learning. The Western view of rote learning and memorisation is derogatory, contrasting it with deep learning for understanding. In contrast, Watkins (2000) shows that for the Chinese student, memorisation is highly valued as a necessary prior step towards learning for understanding. Chinese students typically learn in a different way from their Western counterparts.

Many other examples are to be found of how culture imparts different meanings and connotations to the same concept. For example, in Singapore, 'creativity' is seen as a set of skills to be acquired, while in the UK and the United States it is viewed as the product of 'free' expression and original thought. Likewise, the notion of appraisal assumes a different connotation in Chinese societies such as Hong Kong, where the direct face-to-face exchange of views associated with Anglo-American cultures, is considered threatening (Walker and Dimmock, 2000b).

The foregoing discussion is not exhaustive. Rather, its purpose is to illustrate how researchers in educational leadership and management need to take cognisance of how apparently identical concepts, policies, ideas and behaviours may hide important differences in meaning and connotation, depending on their cultural context. Other important considerations for postgraduate and academic researchers, however, centre on the conduct of research in different cultural settings.

Differences in societal culture and the implications for conducting research

If, as this chapter suggests, postgraduate research in educational management is to take greater cognisance of societal culture, then there is a need to establish robust frameworks and rigorous methodologies. The field of cross-cultural comparative and international educational management is still in its infancy (Dimmock and Walker, 1998a, 1998b). Besides new frameworks and models, careful thought about the techniques and instruments to facilitate data collection and analysis is needed. Without this rigour, there is a danger that cross-cultural analysis and comparison will result in superficiality. This same pitfall awaits cross-cultural researchers of management problems within, as well as between, cultures. Failure to distinguish the part that culture plays may seriously weaken their thesis.

Postgraduate students, as well as academics, require a foundation for studying the influence of societal culture at school level and for making cross-cultural comparisons. In earlier work, a framework was presented for the systematic study of cross-cultural comparative educational leadership and management (see, for example, Dimmock, 2000; Dimmock and Walker 1998a, 1998b, 2000). This framework identifies four separate but interacting elements that make up a school:

- Organisational structures
- Leadership and management processes
- Curriculum
- Teaching and learning

In addition, the concept of culture is operationalised for research application. This entails identifying generic dimensions that are present in all cultures, but to different degrees. Since they are generic, they provide common reference points, thereby enabling more rigorous and systematic comparison. As an integral part of the framework, the dimensions of societal culture are as follows:

- Power-concentrated/power-dispersed
- Self-oriented/group-oriented
- Aggression/consideration
- Proactivism/fatalism
- Limited relationship/holistic relationship
- Long-term oriented/short-term oriented
- Male influence/female influence

Having identified the elements of schools and key dimensions of culture, the next stage in the development of a cross-cultural research agenda is to use both elements and dimensions as a source of generating instruments for data collection and analysis. The instruments developed to date reflect a mixed methodology, that is, both quantitative and qualitative. Through the process of administering the instruments and collecting cross-cultural data on school management and schooling in different cultures, the validity, reliability and 'trustworthiness' of the instruments can be tested and refined.

Ultimately, the research development process outlined above aims to build and test new theory. A fundamental assumption, however, is that the researcher will be able to gain access in different societal cultures to those cases and samples considered important for investigation Regrettably, this may not always be the case.

Difficulties of access

Conducting research in some cultures can present difficult if not insurmountable problems regarding access for even the most experienced academic researcher, let alone the postgraduate student. In some schools considered 'highly researchable', access might be difficult because many researchers wish to study them. They become 'over-researched' and access may be denied simply because of disruption to normal school life. There is always the need for researchers to cultivate good relationships with potential participants, and where possible, to offer benefits to the school in return for their willingness to participate.

These problems fade into insignificance, however, when compared with the challenges of researching in countries such as mainland China. There, research in school leadership and management is often seen as more difficult to execute if the researcher is from outside the country. School principals, in particular, are extremely sensitive to requests to collect data in their schools for fear of upsetting their superiors; teachers are equally sensitive for much the same reason. Normally, successful access to mainland Chinese schools requires the penetration of an elaborate bureaucratic network, highly trusted co-operative relationships with eminent local academics and bureaucrats, and even the payment of fees.

Undertaking research projects in some cultures – even if they are for Masters' or Doctoral theses – may require the permission of government authorities, as is the case in Singapore. Large bureaucracies are not the easiest of organisations to penetrate unless key people in prominent positions are known to the researcher. Even when government bureaucracies do respond positively by granting permission for a research study to proceed, they may insist on changes to the research design that fundamentally weaken it. For example, the authorities may insist that a large sample be reduced in size before it can proceed, with the effect that generalisation is rendered impossible.

Gaining the willing participation of subjects and respondents may also present a problem in cultures where power, influence and status are of great importance. In societies such as those of Arabia, Israel and China, participation is more likely if the researcher is perceived by the respondents to have power, standing and status. In such circumstances it is useful if postgraduate students can enlist allies in the system with some influence.

In general, it appears that the more democratic, open and liberal the society, the easier is access to the subjects to be researched. It also appears that a wider array of research paradigms and methodologies are tolerated and practised in such societies.

Preference for different paradigms and methodologies

A host of culturally related factors warrant consideration at the early stage of planning and designing a research study. For example, in certain societies there might be a tradition of using one research paradigm rather than another. Even within the same paradigm, some research methods might be more difficult to apply in certain cultures than others. For example, within the qualitative paradigm, the present author has in the past encouraged some of his postgraduate students in Hong Kong to adopt the life-history approach. These attempts have usually met with only partial success because of a reticence on the part of potential participants to talk openly about themselves, their life histories and the lives of others. Similarly, many subjects and respondents may be reluctant to participate in studies that involve their criticism of authority or government. In addition, cultural differences can account for why certain research paradigms or methodological approaches are particularly inappropriate in some settings. The adoption of a critical perspective or a feminist perspective in Singapore, for example, might be a case in point.

A further issue concerns the preference for a particular research methodology or paradigm that researchers in some cultures may tend to display. In many developing countries and some developed societies, such as Hong Kong, the preference for quantitative methods over qualitative is quite apparent. This phenomenon in the case of Hong Kong might simply be a reflection of the natural aptitude that Chinese students seem to have for mathematics and statistics, a characteristic borne out in their superior performance in international achievement tests at school. Some have even attributed this mathemetical gift to the Chinese language and its construction of characters based on symbols. Others account for it by recognising that the Chinese prefer to think synthetically and to gain the big picture (and hence, to undertake large sampling from which generalisations can be made), while Westerners tend to think analytically and creatively. With the recent expansion of higher education in Hong Kong, however, there is now a growing awareness of, and desire to learn more about, qualitative research methods in educational management.

Besides the marked preference for quantitative studies in such cultures, there is also a tendency to focus on policy and descriptive, system-wide studies, a phenomenon recognised by Vulliamy, Lewin and Stephens (1990). Comparative studies of a macro-system level in educational management typify this phenomenon. School-level and classroom-level research, especially of an empirical kind, is less prevalent and case studies of individual principals and teachers are a rarity. Consequently, there are many promising avenues for future research projects in these latter areas.

Overcoming cultural difference in conducting research: cross-cultural research teams

In conducting culturally sensitive or culturally based research in educational leadership, a key issue concerns the researcher's understanding of the particular culture(s) being studied. This is less of a problem where the culture of the researcher and the education system under investigation are the same. One would expect a native to possess a full appreciation of his or her own culture. Against this, however, is the view that people can be 'blind' to many aspects of their own culture since they are 'insiders.' They may take for granted many otherwise interesting characteristics, in the process failing to give them due recognition.

'Outsider' researchers, however, may also present problems in that they may lack intimate knowledge and appreciation of the indigenous culture. As Lauder asserts when describing comparative, cultural research in education:

> there is an experiential component necessary to good comparative research. It involves ... a range of cognitive and emotional understandings that enable individuals to get 'beneath the skin' of another culture. In turn, this raises all the problems about the difficulties of translation. (2000: 466)

On the other hand, 'outsiders' may bring a 'fresh' perspective, one which may not only highlight key aspects of a particular culture, but recognise salient differences between it and other cultures.

The methodological issues raised by cross-cultural research are potentially diverse, ranging from differences in how individuals and societies perceive larger macro-perspectives to how they respond to smaller, but no less important, issues concerning techniques and tools of data collection, analysis and interpretation. An important part of the research method process – especially in qualitative research – may involve the interaction of researcher and participant. A helpful illustration and reminder of the potential cross-cultural issues implicit when researcher and participant come together in the research interview are provided by Shah (2004) in the following example.

Research method issues posed by conducting cross-cultural interviewing

In an increasing number of research projects involving qualitative interviews, researchers/interviewers and participants are interacting across cultures. These situations, as Shah (2004: 552) points out, present conundrums:

> What the interviewee wishes to convey, what the interviewer learns, and how it is interpreted are influenced by the respective subjectivities of the participants and the complex forces present within that context. Face to face responses are not simply given to the questions, but to the researcher who poses those questions, in interplay with how the participants perceive the researcher and themselves in that social context.

Communication across cultures between interviewer and respondent can be 'loaded' with subjectivity, personal perception and experience. Consider for example, a British (Anglo-Saxon) researcher interviewing Muslim students in British secondary schools on the subject of how the September 2001 attack in the United States, the occupation of Iraq and Afghanistan in 2004, or the July 2005 bombings in London have affected their lives in general and their school lives in particular. If there is little or no basis for shared assumptions or meanings then communication and meaningful dialogue is likely to be seriously handicapped. Shah (2004) even goes on to question the relative power, control and influence that (Western) researchers/interviewers may assume they hold over participants, especially when the latter are from cultures that see power differently. For example, within particular cultures, the status differences attached to age, gender, wealth, religion, knowledge and socio-economic positioning can each play out differently. Indeed, access to potential participants might be difficult in some cross-cultural settings, severely handicapping the 'outsider' – compared with the 'insider' – researcher. In exchanging and sharing meaning, it is helpful to draw on common cultural ground rules of reciprocity and trust that are the foundation for communication within a culture, and establish a feeling of ease and comfort with the interview experience. Finally, Shah (2004) draws attention to the possibility of qualitative researchers being considered 'social intruders': 'This "unwelcome" and "uninvited" dimension of research for the researched is sharpened in cross-cultural contexts' (p. 565). Lacking appreciation of indigenous cultural norms and values, the researcher may lack cultural sensitivity; even the topic or phenomenon being researched may not be acceptable as a field of enquiry to the indigenous group.

How can the real difficulties of cross-cultural research posed above be overcome? One way is clearly to increase levels of cultural sensitivity and awareness before conducting such research. Training and educating researchers in cultural awareness, culturally matching the researchers and participants, and cross-cultural research teams are all ways of mitigating potential problems. Blending the strengths of both 'insider' and 'outsider' researchers in cross-cultural teams is a promising way forward. However, even here, there may be difficulties of language and communication in such teams, especially initially, but these may ease over the course of time . For individual Masters or Doctoral students, however, the possibility of forming teams is rare, unless the supervisor has a number of students investigating the same research themes cross-culturally.

Examples of contrasting cultures and the promotion of research in educational leadership and management

It was noted above that the conduct of research in some cultures may be inhibited for political and social reasons. In contrast, three countries with very different societal cultures – Papua New Guinea (PNG), Sierra Leone and the UK – provide examples of governmental encouragement of educational research. In the first two cases, independent research has been encouraged in order to reduce the dependence on expertise and funding from foreign agencies. Guthrie (1989) reports that PNG 'is a comparatively uncommon example of a developing country with an extensive, critical and readily available research literature which does inform educational policy and practice' (1989: 46). The country's Ministry of Education has supported educational research with a strong applied focus since the mid-1960s, when the *Papua New Guinea Journal of Education* was established. In the 1970s, the Educational Research Unit at the University of Papua New Guinea was established and since then research by foreigners has been encouraged.

The main reason underpinning the PNG government's enlightened policy with regard to research has been its avowed desire to improve educational practice. There is close cooperation between educational researchers, policy-makers and administrators at both national and provincial levels towards that end.

A rather different model of government sponsorship of educational research is provided by Sierra Leone. According to Vulliamy (1990: 23), research there has been 'more self-consciously national' and has been angled at influencing practitioners directly rather than through policy-makers and planners. Many projects begin with teachers who are encouraged to apply case study and action research methods in tackling their school-level problems. Although the government was initially sceptical, its policy has been to allow these projects to proceed.

Vulliamy (1990) goes on to draw three interesting conclusions from the successful examples of educational research in PNG and Sierra Leone. The first is the need for clear mechanisms whereby educational research can influence policy and practice; the second is the need for appropriate places to publish research findings; and the third is the benefit that can flow from cooperation between developed and developing countries. In PNG, this cooperation has been through the engagement of overseas researchers on locally defined projects and in Sierra Leone through the use of financial aid and external consultants to facilitate national research.

The recent UK experience provides a third example of government endorsement of research in education, more particularly in educational management and school leadership. Clearly, the British culture is very different from that of the developing societies of PNG and Sierra Leone. The Blair Labour government has made expenditure on education its top priority since taking office in 1997. A key government aim has been school improvement; that is, improvement in student-learning outcomes. Among the motivating forces for such a policy are the development of a globalised competitive world economy and its accompanying knowledge-based society, and the superior performance of East Asian and South-East Asian students on international achievement tests in maths and science. British students are seen as lagging behind their Asian counterparts in these subjects.

Consequently, a raft of policies has been introduced to secure improvement in the quality of teaching, learning and leadership. These include the establishment of national standards for all grades of teachers and headteachers; an elaborate system of school evaluation and inspection to affirm the standards; protected time each day for literacy and numeracy; and the establishment of a national college to promote school leadership. However, one of the most interesting initiatives, and one that is particularly relevant to this chapter, has been the focus on what is called 'evidence-informed policy and practice' (EIPP).

In the late 1990s, Hargreaves (1999) and others expressed concern that educational policy and practice was insufficiently grounded in research findings of what works. He challenged educators, somewhat contentiously, to identify a body of confirmatory research which would underpin a more robust set of practices for the profession to adopt. Only then could the teaching profession enjoy the level of rigour and credibility traditionally enjoyed by the legal and medical professions.

For some years, scholars, practitioners and policy-makers had made reference to 'best practice' as a set of standards and processes for schools to target. The meaning of the term 'best practice' was never clear either in the minds of those who used it, or those who tried to implement it. The term itself, as the present author has argued (Dimmock, 2000), was misleading in presuming that there was a clear-cut best way to practise education. For that reason, he coined the phrase 'informed practice' for teachers and school leaders (Dimmock, 2000: 21–23). The argument was much the same as that which Hargreaves (1999) had advanced, namely that teaching and leadership should, wherever possible, be founded on research evidence of effective practice.

Coincidentally, others in the UK had begun to use the phrase 'evidence-informed policy and practice', signalling an emphasis on the relationships between the three communities of researchers, policy-makers and practitioners. As Levačić and Glatter (2001) report, the government believes the lessons learnt from high-quality research can improve decision-making at all levels of education. Moreover, well-founded evidence on key issues is needed, and the newly formed Centre for Management and Policy Studies in the Cabinet Office is promoting strategies for knowledge-based policy-making. More recently, there has been a shift from 'evidence-based' to 'evidence-informed' policy and practice.

While these trends generate debate about the meaning of 'well-founded evidence', 'research' and the strategies by which evidence-based research informs policy and practice, the main point that emerges from the present discussion is the recent acknowledgement by the British government of the nexus between research, evidence and policy and practice as part of its effort to secure school improvement. It remains to be seen how this policy will in the future manifest itself in re-configuring institutional arrangements and relationships between the three communities of researchers, policy-makers and practitioners. A further complication for British educators centres on the issues discussed in this chapter. Further questions arise – such as: Will research evidence from certain parts of the world or specific cultures be given greater or lesser legitimacy than others? Will there be a status hierarchy of culturally related evidence-based knowledge? Or, perhaps more aptly, for research evidence from different cultures to be valid for the British or any other specific context, what processes of cultural sensitization and adaptation will need to be undertaken? There are many aspects to this development in the UK, as elsewhere, that will provide rich research opportunities for postgraduate students, and for academics.

Conclusion

This chapter has highlighted the relative neglect of societal culture as an influence in research on educational leadership and management. Many compelling forces account for the recent upsurge of interest in an international perspective in the field, particularly one that takes cognisance of societal culture. Among these are globalisation and the urge to borrow or import 'successful' ideas from other cultures. While a willingness to learn from other countries is desirable, drawing simplistic or superficial lessons from research or practice conducted in different cultures can be misleading as well as dangerous. The same lessons are as relevant for researchers conducting investigations in their own cultures – failure to bound their studies and to consider societal culture as an influence may seriously detract from their work and lead others to draw misleading conclusions.

At the same time, as this chapter has argued, there are rich research opportunities for postgraduate students wishing to examine educational leadership and management from a societal cultural perspective. The chapter has argued the case, first, for a more 'culture-sensitive' approach to study and research in educational leadership; and secondly, for a more systematic and robust approach to research involving culture and cultural difference in the field. Along the way, it has also highlighted methodological issues that will be of concern to postgraduate and academic researchers in what is bound to be an exciting and challenging avenue for future investigation. In this way, let us hope that a more sophisticated culture-sensitive field of educational leadership and management emerges in the future.

References

Bajunid, I.A. (1996) 'Preliminary explorations of indigenous perspectives of educational management: the evolving Malaysian experience', *Journal of Educational Administration*, 34 (5): 50–73.

Brislin, R. (1993) *Understanding Culture's Influence on Behavior*. Orlando, FL: Harcourt-Brace.

Broadfoot, P. (1997) Foreword in Crossley, M. and Vulliamy, G. (eds) *Qualitative Research in Developing Countries*. London: Garland Publishing.

Dimmock, C. (2000) *Designing the Learning-centred School: A Cross-cultural Perspective*. London: Falmer Press.

Dimmock, C. and Walker, A. (1998a) 'Towards comparative educational administration: building the case for a cross-cultural, school-based approach', *Journal of Educational Administration*, 36 (4): 379–401.

Dimmock, C. and Walker, A. (1998b) 'Comparative educational administration: developing a cross-cultural comparative framework', *Educational Administration Quarterly*, 34 (4): 558–595.

Dimmock, C. and Walker, A. (2000) 'Developing comparative and international educational leadership and management: a cross-cultural model', *School Leadership and Management*, 20 (2): 143–160.

Dimmock, C. and Walker, A. (2005) *Educational Leadership: Culture and Diversity*. London: Sage.

Guthrie, G. (1989) 'Higher degree theses and educational decision making in developing countries', *International Journal of Educational Development*, 9: 43–52.

Hargreaves, D. (1999) 'The knowledge-creating school', *British Journal of Educational Studies*, 47 (2): 122–144.

Levačić , R. and Glatter, R. (2001) '"Really good idea?": Evidence-informed policy and practice in educational leadership and management', *Educational Management and Administration*, 29 (1): 5–25.

Lauder, H. (2000) 'The dilemmas of comparative research and policy importation: an extended book review', *British Journal of Sociology of Education*, 21 (3): 465–475.

Shah, S. (2004) 'The researcher/interviewer in intercultural context: a social intruder!', *British Educational Research Journal*, 30 (4): 549–574.

Stevenson, H.W. and Stigler, J.W. (1992) *The Learning Gap: Why our Schools Are Failing and What We Can Learn from Japanese and Chinese education.* New York: Summit Books.

Vulliamy, G. (1990) 'The potential of qualitative educational research strategies in developing countries', in Vulliamy, G., Lewin, K. and Stephens, D. (eds) *Doing Educational Research in Developing Countries*. London: Falmer Press.

Vulliamy, G., Lewin, K. and Stephens, D. (1990) *Doing Educational Research in Developing Countries*. London: Falmer Press.

Walker, A. and Dimmock, C. (2000a) 'Leadership dilemmas of Hong Kong principals: sources, perceptions and outcomes', *Australian Journal of Education*, 44 (1): 5–25.

Walker, A. and Dimmock, C. (2000b) 'One size fits all? Teacher appraisal in a Chinese culture', *Journal of Personnel Evaluation in Education*, 14 (2): 155–178.

Walker, A. and Dimmock, C. (2002) 'Moving school leadership beyond its narrow boundaries: developing a cross-cultural approach', in Leithwood, K. and Hallinger, P. (eds) *The Second International Handbook of School Leadership*. Netherlands: Kluwer Academic Publishers. pp. 167–207.

Watkins, D. (2000) 'Learning and teaching: a cross-cultural perspective', *School Leadership and Management*, 20 (2): 161–174.

Recommended reading

Dimmock, C. and Walker, A. (2000) 'Developing comparative and international educational leadership and management: a cross-cultural model', *School Leadership and Management*, 20 (2): 143–160.

Shah, S. (2004) 'The researcher/interviewer in intercultural context: a social intruder!' *British Educational Research Journal*, 30 (4): 549–574.

Vulliamy, G. (1990) 'The potential of qualitative educational research strategies in developing countries', in Vulliamy, G., Lewin, K. and Stephens, D. (eds) *Doing Educational Research in Developing Countries*. London: Falmer Press.

Walker, A. and Dimmock, C. (2002) 'Moving school leadership beyond its narrow boundaries: developing a cross-cultural approach', in Leithwood, K. and Hallinger, P. (eds) *The Second International Handbook of School Leadership*. Netherlands: Kluwer Academic Publishers. pp. 167–207.

Watkins, D. (2000) 'Learning and teaching: a cross-cultural perspective', *School Leadership and Management*, 20 (2): 161–174.

5

Exploring the existing body of research

Heather Keeble and Roy Kirk

Recognising a need for information

'Knowledge doesn't exist in a vacuum, and your knowledge only has value in relation to other people's' (Jankowicz, 1991: 116). Your research is a contribution to existing knowledge in the field and should not be seen in isolation. Hence, conducting a review of the literature is one of the most important tasks that you will face.

There are several other reasons for spending time and effort on reviewing the field. Perhaps most obviously, a literature review helps to clarify what is already known, and what has been done so far and should therefore prevent duplication of work. The review itself does not present new primary scholarship (Lyons, 2005). It provides a context within which to interpret your findings.

Wisker (2001: 127) states that, 'Your work both engages with the known literature and adds something else', and the literature review should assist with this by revealing gaps in current knowledge and identifying what has yet to be researched. It could help to define the parameters of your research, including formulating and refining research questions. A review may also examine the methodology used in previous projects and therefore suggest which research methods you could employ.

Reading through the literature enables you to increase your breadth of subject knowledge. In the process, you will identify the seminal works in the field and place each work in the context of its contribution to the understanding of the subject. Remember that a literature review does not include a reference to everything ever published that is connected, however remotely, to your research interests. It should be driven by themes and trends related to your research questions. The review must be critical, going beyond a mere description of the items you have read, to demonstrate reflection and analysis. You may find new ways to interpret previous research, or provide some insight into the reasons for inconsistencies in past results (Harlen and Schlapp, 1998).

A literature review should also identify other people working in the same and related fields (Bourner, 2002). Building a network of contacts will enable you to engage with the research community, which is important for keeping abreast of the latest findings.

The key to finding and using information successfully for research is good planning, organisation and knowing where to go for help. A systematic approach can make the whole process less daunting and prevent information retrieval and management becoming an excuse not to start writing. To give some idea of the size of the exercise, there are on average some 33,000 academic books published each year in the UK alone. There are over 400 education journals published in the UK, and more than 1,000 in the United States. You will be principally looking for publications in educational leadership and management, but at research level, you may need to draw on other subject areas. The information you require may lie in sources which have no apparent relevance to your specific area of interest, making your task even more difficult.

It is likely that you will need to conduct more than just a literature review, that is, examining secondary sources. You may also need to acquire data from primary sources. In the area of educational management for example, statistical data, up-to-date government information and financial information may be essential.

Information retrieval is a rapidly changing field, as methods of information storage and dissemination develop. Although the names and interfaces, and even the types of resource may change, there are general guidelines that can be followed to help you through the literature-searching process. These principles can be followed regardless of the country you are in, and whether you are based on-campus, are researching independently, or studying as a distance learning student. This chapter aims to help you develop the information skills you need to carry out this task, and to carry it out efficiently, both in terms of time spent and results achieved.

Constructing a search strategy

A strategic approach to literature searching may, at first, seem time-consuming, but it is an efficient way of finding good quality, relevant material. Rather than browsing along bookshelves and trawling through runs of journals, or going straight to a computer and trying a few keywords that come to mind at the time, the strategic approach is an organised process that does not rely on serendipity. It requires some initial planning.

Mapping the concepts

The first step in the literature review process is to 'unpack' your research project. You may have identified one general question and perhaps several sub-questions that need to be addressed. Although it is tempting to try to narrow down the focus of your research it is useful at this early stage to gain an understanding of broader, and related areas that you may need to include. This will help identify areas that you already know well and those gaps in your knowledge that require more attention.

A visual map can help you to develop detailed thoughts around a central theme, with branches drawn out from the centre as related thoughts arise (Martin, 2002). It can encourage the discovery of links between subjects as well as helping to organise the structure of your research. These graphic diagrams are also called 'mind maps' or 'spider diagrams', and are intended to facilitate the thinking and planning process.

Example
Start with question/s that you have already identified as central to your research:

What is the role of middle managers in school improvement in secondary schools?

Important words and phrases should be highlighted and can be used as the basis of your brainstorm:

What is the <u>role</u> of <u>middle managers</u> in school <u>improvement</u> in <u>secondary schools?</u>

To ensure that you conduct as full a search as possible, you need to consider each of these concepts in turn and identify some of the following (examples of each are included in parentheses):

- Synonyms (improvement, achievement, gain, development, success)
- Alternative spellings (behaviour, behavior)
- Word variants (manage, manager, managing, management)
- Different cultural terminology (the United States uses 'high school' whilst the UK uses 'secondary school'.) Terminology within and across disciplines can vary according to the age, geographical location and personal preferences of the authors. Whilst you may have a clear idea of the terms you would use, it is important to identify alternative words that may also retrieve relevant information
- Broader (school improvement), narrower (exam results) and related (school culture) concepts
- Relationships between concepts (impact of senior management on the role of middle management)
- Key theories (distributed leadership, subject leadership)
- Appropriate research methodologies (case study, survey)

You may find it useful to use some of the following sources to help with this mapping exercise:

- Existing resources from previous research and references
- Supervisor or other researchers/colleagues
- Dictionaries, thesauruses and encyclopaedias

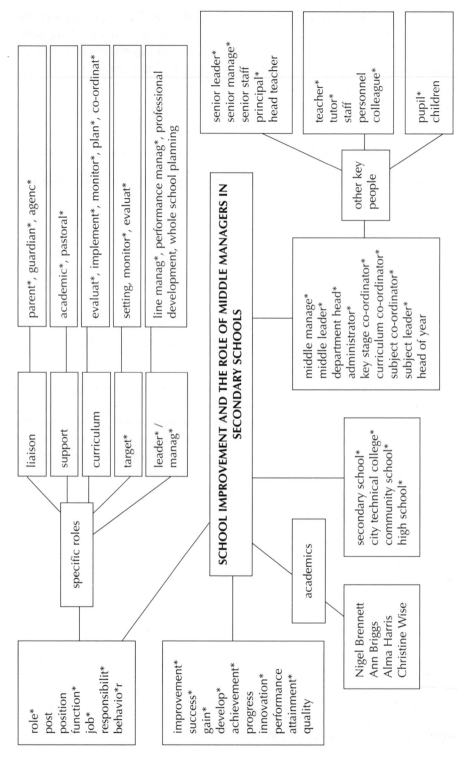

Figure 5.1 Mind map for 'School improvement and the role of middle managers in secondary schools'

The visual map in Figure 5.1 illustrates the range of ideas and concepts that can be produced from a single question.

If your main question is very broad, it may be helpful to produce several, more specific maps for each key area. This is a very individual process that will reflect your own approach to the subject and the way you organise information.

Keywords and phrases

The visual mapping exercise should have enabled you to translate your research question/s into keywords and phrases that will form the basis of your search strategy.

Developing a visual map is a continuing process. It will need to be amended as the research progresses and not all the terms you identify in the initial stages will be useful for your literature search. Experience during the searching process will provide you with a good idea of the most successful keywords or phrases for finding the most appropriate literature. New keywords may also become apparent as you read the literature.

Setting your limits

It is useful to have an idea of the limits you want to set on any enquiry, although at this stage they should not be too rigid. Some ways to limit searches are:

- Publication date – how far back do you need to go? Do you need an historical perspective, or are you principally concerned with recent research and theory?
- Geographical location – will you confine your research to a particular country or region?
- Language – some resources may only be available in one language. Are you prepared to get items translated?
- Time scale – are you focusing on a particular time period?

Most catalogues and databases have a 'limits' function on their search screen.

Sources of information

Information is available from a wide range of sources, in a variety of formats. An understanding of the different types of information and the publications in which these can be located, will help you identify the sources to search. To complicate the picture further, you will need to distinguish between published (formal) sources and unpublished (informal) sources (University of Leicester Library, 2005).

Formal sources are often published initially as conference papers or journal articles. Once accepted for publication, the information may be republished in reviews and textbooks and, in summarised form, in encyclopaedias. Literature reviews, therefore, may involve reviewing information contained in a number of different types of publications and in different formats. Everything mentioned in the lists below may be available in print, or electronically:

- Dictionaries give specific subject definitions and are, therefore, very specialised
- Directories contain useful information about organisations
- Encyclopaedias provide overviews of topics in specific areas and often give basic bibliographies of seminal titles in the field
- Statistical tables contain data representing local, national and international concerns
- Official publications are produced by the government of a country and include Acts, Command Papers, Committee reports, Statutory Instruments and debates from the legislative bodies
- Books contain accepted information, but they do become out of date
- Journals are primary sources of information based on current research. The most important journals are refereed or peer reviewed, which means that the articles are looked at critically by subject experts

Informal communication is not published in the usual sources listed above. Disseminating this information need not necessarily involve publication at all, as these examples show:

- *Grey literature*: in order to disseminate information quickly, the early results of research are published as reports, pamphlets or just information sheets
- *Academic colleagues*: research conclusions and themes need to be disseminated; researchers and academics communicate informally with each other by talking at conferences, by telephone or by email
- *Theses and dissertations*: these are not published in the conventional sense, but are made available within the libraries of the institutions awarding the qualifications

It may be worth talking to your tutor or librarian about accessing the most appropriate sources of information.

Searching

Searching library catalogues

Although the interface (what you see on the computer screen) may differ, most library catalogues are basically the same. They allow you to search a library's holdings by author name, title, keyword or subject heading. At research level, you will want to go beyond your own library's collection, but this task has been made easier now that most academic libraries have an online catalogue. Some university and research libraries have put their holdings together to form union catalogues. An example of this is COPAC (www.copac.ac.uk), which comprises the holdings of 24 of the largest research libraries in the UK, including the British Library and the National Library of Scotland. You can search millions of titles by inputting just one search. There may also be other libraries that are known to hold a strong collection in your subject, which are not part of a consortium, and will need to be searched individually.

Searching electronic databases

Databases are a vital resource for researchers as they pull together academic research on a particular topic. It is worth remembering that there are different types of database. Bibliographic databases only provide the basic details of an item (sometimes with an abstract). Others provide links to the whole journal article and are known as full-text databases. Some are a mixture of both.

Most databases are only accessible to those registered with a university or higher education institution and require a username and password to get in. The most common authentication system is called ATHENS. You will need to ask your 'home' library or computer centre for details of how to register for a username and password.

Here are some considerations for choosing which databases to search:

- Check the subject coverage of the database. Some are very specific, such as the 'British Education Index', whilst others cover a broad subject area, such as 'ISI Web of Science', which will include education.
- What does the database include in terms of publications? Does it only contain journal articles, or does it also have other documents, such as conference proceedings, reports, theses and books?
- What time period does the database cover? For example, the online version of the British Education Index (BEI) only covers 1976 to the present day, whilst the paper version goes back to 1954.
- How frequently is the database updated?

The following databases will be of particular use for researching educational leadership and management.

BEI (British Education Index)
This is produced by the University of Leeds and provides references to journal articles, book chapters, reports, Internet resources and conference literature, from 1976 onwards. It covers 350 British journals and selected European English-language titles.

ERIC (Educational Resources Information Center)
ERIC is sponsored by the US Department of Education and covers from 1966. Although produced in the United States, its coverage is international. It indexes over 775 journals but also includes a large number of reports, many of which are unpublished.

ISI Web of Science
This is a citation index from Manchester Information and Associated Services (MIMAS). For each article found it lists the articles cited in the found article, together with where that found article has been cited. The Social Science Citation Index fully indexes 1,700 major social science journals, from 1970. Abstracts are available from 1992 onwards.

EUDISED database

EUDISED (European Documentation and Information System for Education) is an educational research database, produced by the Council of Europe in collaboration with national agencies. Together with the *European Education Thesaurus*, its aim is 'to extract from the large amount of educational research in progress, data of interest to educational policy and practice'. About 2,000 project descriptions are added to the database each year, which is available in 18 languages (http://culture.coe.fr/her/eng/esused.html).

Australian Education Index database

The Australian Education Index is Australia's largest source of educational information. It indexes over 100 Australian journals comprehensively and regularly scans more than 500 Australian and international journals for relevant articles on Australian education. It covers the period 1976 to the present.

CBCA Full Text Education database

Formerly the Canadian Education Index, this database provides indexing from 1976 and selected full text access from 1996, to the principal education literature published in Canada.

CEPM (Clearinghouse on Educational Policy and Management)

This database is part of the US National Educational Resources Information Center network. Its scope includes 'all aspects of the governance, leadership, administration and structure of public and private educational organizations at the primary and secondary levels' (http://eric.uoregon.edu/).

ERA (Educational Research Abstracts)

This database gives access to seven leading international abstracting journals, including *Educational Management Abstracts*, from 1995 onwards (www.tandf.co.uk/era/)

Although most databases utilise the same general searching concepts and methods, the user interfaces can vary considerably. All databases provide a 'Help' option and it is worth looking at this before you start searching, as it provides tips and information to get the best out of that resource.

The visual mapping exercise should have generated several keywords and phrases. It is worth bearing in mind that searching using individual keywords, for example, 'school' and 'improvement', will find many results, but as the words may not be related to each other, not all results will be relevant. Therefore it is important to understand how to combine search terms to best effect.

Searching for phrases

Searching using phrases, for example, 'school improvement', will produce fewer, more relevant results. Some databases allow you to identify a phrase with the use of speech marks, such as **"school improvement"**. Others may provide you with a code to identify words that should be next to each other in the text, such as **school adj improvement**.

Different spellings/plurals

Searching for the word 'organisation' will only retrieve articles that use this exact word. During the visual mapping exercise you should have identified any alternative spellings, that is, 'organization'. Most databases allow you to use a symbol, or wildcard, which can represent any letter. This is often an asterisk or a question mark and will be identified on the Help screen for each database. Typing in **organi*ation** will retrieve articles with either spelling.

Symbols can also be used at the end of a word to allow retrieval of several word endings. This is called 'truncation'. Searching with the term **manag*** will retrieve articles with the terms: manage, manager, managing, management etc.

Combining terms and phrases

Most databases use the same method for combining separate keywords into a statement for searching. This is known as 'Boolean logic' and it allows you to broaden, narrow or limit a search depending on the coverage of your subject in a database. The three basic methods to combine terms are **AND, OR** and **NOT**.

AND finds items which contain all of the terms. Any number of words can be used, although it is advisable to start with a few key terms and narrow down with further terms if too many results are found. Examples are: **secondary school* AND middle manag***, or **school improvement* AND middle manag***.

OR finds items which contain either of the terms and is, therefore, a much broader search than using AND. This is a useful method to use at the start of a search to produce a large set of results that you can later refine using AND or NOT. Examples are: **secondary school* OR high school***, or **improvement* OR gain***.

NOT limits the search by excluding terms that you know not to be useful. Examples are: **leader* NOT senior manag***.

Figure 5.2 shows a sample search in the database International ERIC to illustrate the use of phrase searching, truncation and combining search terms using Boolean operators. This search is made up of several elements. The first set of results (1) is a broad search using the OR operator to find any items with **school improvement OR gain OR success**. Note that the code ADJ is used for phrase searching and the symbol $ is used to find alternative word endings.

The second set of results (2) is a truncation search for all items in the database with the phrase **middle manage ... .**

The third set of results (3) uses the AND operator to retrieve only those from set 1 which also have the terms from set 2. This narrows the number of results to 65 records, which would be considered a reasonable number for a final result.

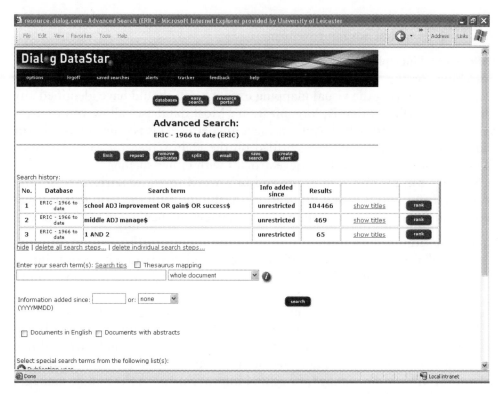

Figure 5.2   Screen shot of a search in the International ERIC database provided by Dialog (reproduced by permission of The Dialog Corporation/Thomson)

Searching by author

Many researchers will already be familiar with authoritative writers in their field. Most electronic databases allow searching by the author's name, which enables you to find anything in that database produced by that author. In Figure 5.3 an author search in the British Education Index database for anything written by Alma Harris produced 60 results.

It may, however, be important to find articles written by other authors about Alma Harris's work. A search for her name as a keyword anywhere in the record produced 10 results. After removing the duplicate records there were 67 results.

Citations searching

Some databases identify references to other research cited in an article. This can lead to the discovery of other authors in the field and key articles on the main subject or related topics. These databases may also identify which other articles cited the work you are looking at. This is an excellent way to ensure that your searching is as comprehensive as possible.

Figure 5.4 shows a list of citations for an article on school improvement.

Figure 5.3 Screen shot of a search in the British Educational Index database provided by Dialog (reproduced by permission of The Dialog Corporation/Thomson)

Controlled vocabulary searching

Most databases allow you to search using controlled vocabulary, that is, by using words selected from their online thesaurus. If you are finding very few results, it is always worth checking the preferred way of expressing the concept you are searching for, on that database. For example, a search for 'school improvement' on the ERIC database produces 4,104 results. The thesaurus also suggests the term 'educational improvement', which gives 15,374 results. Depending on the database, thesaurus terms may be called any of the following: 'authority file', 'concepts', 'controlled terms', 'descriptors', 'index terms', 'subject headings', 'identifiers'.

It is very unlikely that you will have the perfect searching strategy straight away. A reflective approach to literature searching will enable you to adjust and amend your strategy as you go along. Once you have done a search, look at the results. Are they what you really wanted? How can you change your search to find the results you need?

It is advisable to keep a record of the searches you have tried. Noting, for example, that one database produces better results with the term 'secondary school' and another with 'high school' can be an important time-saving factor

79

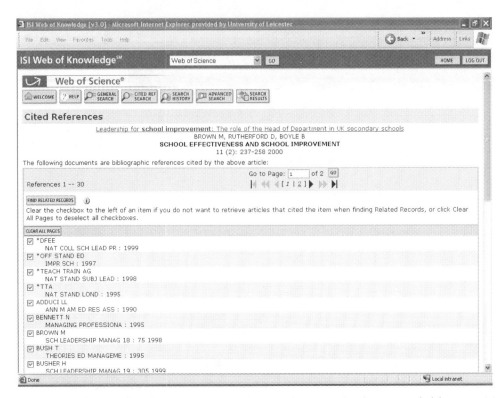

Figure 5.4 Screen shot of a search in the ISI Web of Science database provided by MIMAS (reproduced by permission of Thomson Scientific)

if you repeat a search further on in your research. One excellent feature of many databases is a function which allows you to save a search and re-run it at a later date. This is particularly useful if you carry out a successful search with a number of elements, as it prevents you re-inventing and re-typing the terms. The Help screens of individual databases will provide details of how to do this.

Searching the Internet

The Internet can contain information about your subject (data), for example an electronic journal, or have pages that point you towards the information you want (metadata), for example library catalogues and electronic databases. Catalogues and databases available through your own institution's library can be relied upon to provide information of high academic quality, so why then, should you consider using the Internet beyond this?

The Internet is the most prolific source of information available to us. Its federal nature means that anyone, anywhere in the world, can create their own web pages, although the information on these pages cannot always be relied upon to be accurate, up-to-date or of high quality. The Internet is dynamic, with regular changes to content. This can be a positive thing, in relation to 'up-to-the minute' research, but it can also cause problems with the relatively short life of some links, or when a researcher inadvertently accesses an outdated website. Even established websites of large institutions change the way they organise information on a regular basis.

The Internet can provide access to information not available through any other means. Unpublished research and 'research in progress' are two good examples. Many academics may disseminate their findings on their web pages before they are published in peer reviewed publications. Conference papers are also often available on the Internet before publication. These sources can help you become aware of recent developments in the field and identify current issues of debate.

Many organisations use the Internet as a platform to publicise their activities. For example:

BELMAS (British Educational Leadership, Management and Administration Society) www.shu.ac.uk/belmas
This society aims to 'advance the practice, teaching and study of educational management, administration and leadership in the UK, and to contribute to international developments in these areas'.

BERA (British Educational Research Association) www.bera.ac.uk
BERA supports educational research in the UK through publications, events and by linking organisations. It includes several special interest groups, such as Leading and Managing Schools and Colleges, and School Improvement.

CEPM (Clearinghouse on Educational Policy and Management) eric.uoregon.edu/directory/index.html
This contains a Directory of Organizations, 'to guide users to sources of information on a wide range of topics related to educational policy, management, leadership and organization in K12 (3–18-year-olds)'.

CERI (Centre for Educational Research and Innovation) www.oecd.org/cer
Established in 1968, CERI works with all member countries of the OECD and undertakes research particularly concerned with 'emerging trends and issues, futures thinking in schools and universities'.

NFER (National Foundation for Educational Research) www.nfer.ac.uk
The foundation undertakes around 200 research projects every year, spanning all sectors of education, listed under headings such as Educational Leadership and Educational Policy.

Official publications and statistics is another area that is well served by the Internet. Governments and other official bodies in many countries now make their documents available in full text, online. For example:

DfES (Department for Education and Skills) www.dfes.gov.uk
This is the starting point for UK government information on education.

Office of Public Sector Information www.opsi.gov.uk
This includes the full text of UK public Acts since 1988 and local Acts since 1991.

Europa europa.eu
The gateway to the European Union, including full text reports, legislation and statistics.

UNESCO www.unesco.org/education
This website has full text reports and statistics, including its annual international education survey.

Accessing information on the Internet is often time-consuming but there are several ways to eliminate some of the less useful, inaccurate or poor quality information. (For further useful sources, and how to use them, see Chapter 16 of this book.)

Using gateways and portals

Gateways and portals are usually established by subject experts and can be relied upon to provide access to accurate, up-to-date and legitimate academic sources. For example:

BUBL Information Service bubl.ac.uk
Education Virtual Library www.csu.edu.au/education/library.html

You can often browse their content following subject links, or search using keywords and phrases.

Using search engines

Perhaps the most common method for finding information on the web is to use a search engine. Most people have their own favourite, but it is important to consider the coverage of each search engine. Some well-established search engines are very effective but do not include as wide a range of pages as others. The Google search engine is one of the most comprehensive services available at the time of writing: www.google.com or www.google.co.uk

The problem most cited when using a search engine is the vast number of results it returns, but there are some very effective methods for eliminating thousands of irrelevant, commercial or dubious websites.

Example

If you type the words **middle management secondary school** into the Google search box (you do not need to use the AND Boolean operator) and search the whole web you will retrieve almost 25,000,000 results. Google attempts to list the most relevant hits first, but most people do not browse through more than three pages of results. Google has looked for these words anywhere in the web page, not necessarily related to each other.

A more focused search would be to add quotation marks: **"middle management" "secondary school"** instructs the search engine to only find these words when they appear as set phrases, and will retrieve over 84,000 results.

If you click on the 'Advanced search' link you will be able to specify which domain to search in. The domain informs you of the type of 'body' that has produced the web page, that is, commercial, governmental, charitable organisation etc.

If you want to locate academic material you would type in **.ac** in the domain box. You could be even more specific and restrict this by also using a country code, for example, **.ac.uk** would limit the search to higher education institutions in the UK. This retrieves about 300 results.

Other domains include:

.org = organisations
.gov = governmental
.co = commercial

Only the United States does not use a country code. It has its own set of domain names, for example **.edu** represents educational institutions and **.com** is commercial.

Google Scholar

Google has obviously realised that there is a demand for finding academic information on the Internet and so they have developed Google Scholar (http://scholar.google.com), which claims that it 'helps you identify the most relevant research across the world of scholarly research'. It searches for books, peer reviewed papers, theses, abstracts and articles from academic publishers, professional societies, reprint repositories, universities and other scholarly organisations.

A search for **"middle management" "secondary school"** retrieves 1,100 results (compared to the 84,000 in Google) ranked according to the number of times cited, by author and the publication the item appears in. Google Scholar will therefore be a useful tool for quickly finding some types of information but you may also need to continue to use the original Google. Not all government web pages are included in Google Scholar, for example.

If you do find something of interest, you will not automatically get the full text. In the majority of cases, you will need to check through your own institution's library, whether they can provide access to the whole item. The full text can often be accessed by using your ATHENS password.

Google Scholar is currently at the BETA stage of testing, which means that it is still in development and its appearance and functionality may change in the future. The main thing to bear in mind is that Google Scholar should only be used in conjunction with, and not as a replacement for, the sources of information mentioned in this chapter.

Searching for dissertations and theses

Theses completed for higher degrees will undoubtedly be of interest to anyone conducting their own research, and with Internet technology it has become a lot easier to identify, locate and purchase copies of theses.

Theses from your own institution

If you are studying with a university, you might want to check what has been written at that university. Usually the best method is to use the library catalogue. The terminology used can be confusing. In the UK a 'thesis' is research done at PhD (Doctoral) level, whilst Masters level research is written up as a 'dissertation'. In the United States the terminology is reversed, that is, you would be searching for a Doctoral dissertation and a Masters thesis.

Theses from the UK

The most comprehensive source of references to UK theses is a database called 'Index to Theses' (the electronic version of the Index to Theses accepted for Higher Degrees by the Universities of Great Britain and Ireland). The database goes back to 1716 with abstracts from 1970 and is available at http://theses.com

Theses worldwide

The main source of worldwide theses (although largely from North America) has always been Dissertation Abstracts International (DAI). This has recently been converted to an electronic format, under the name Proquest at www.lib.umi.com/dissertations/ Proquest allows you to search the last two years of theses and will supply an abstract. You can then purchase a hard copy of the theses online, using a credit card.

Another service available through Proquest is called Dissertation Express. This includes theses going back to 1952, but you can only search by author, DAI number or keywords in the title. No abstracts are supplied so it is harder to judge whether the item is of use to you.

Obtaining a copy of the literature

Once you have identified literature that is possibly relevant, you then have the task of finding a copy of the text. If you are lucky, the full text of a journal article may be available from the database you are searching, or the library may have purchased the journal electronically through another supplier. Many academic libraries are now buying e-books, whereby the entire text of a book can be accessed online (although you will not be able to download or print the whole text as copyright restrictions apply). It is likely that you will have to log in with a username and password to access an e-book.

If the item you seek is not available electronically, then you will have to find a hard copy (that is, a printed version). The first place to check is the library at your own institution, but if it has been ascertained that the item is not in stock, there are a couple of options.

It may be useful to investigate the possibility of accessing other libraries. Some provide reference and study facilities to researchers from other academic institutions, whilst others may allow you to borrow items. If you are considering using another library, it is always worth asking at your own institution's library first, for advice on how to gain access. They may be part of a reciprocal scheme or act on your behalf to negotiate access. Most academic libraries now have an online catalogue so that you can check what they have in stock before making a visit.

Another alternative is to ask your own library about any national inter-library loan facility. In the UK, the British Library Document Supply Centre operates through most public and academic libraries across the country and deals with more than 4 million requests a year. Many of these requests come from outside the UK, so even if the material you require is likely to come from another country, it is still worth enquiring whether this is possible. Other countries may lend you books and send photocopies of journal articles through a national inter-library loan scheme.

Evaluating information

It can be a challenge for the researcher to decide which information is relevant enough to include in the literature review. Items found even from a recognised database may vary in their value and reliability. As previously mentioned, information found on the web can be even more problematic.

Here are some questions to consider, most of which are applicable for both printed and electronic sources:

- Who is the intended audience?
- Have you heard of the author before? Can you check their credentials?
- Does the author work for an academic institution or commercial organisation? When using websites, this may mean checking the domain name, as described above, to see what sort of body has produced the information.
- Is there a bibliography or list of references at the end of the item? If not, how do you know that their conclusions are properly grounded?
- What methodologies have been used in the research? Are these accepted methods within your field of study?

- When was the information written (or the website updated?) Is it still accurate?
- Is the journal peer reviewed? If so, it will have been strictly scrutinised by experts in the field and can be considered a reliable source of information.
- Is the journal linked to a major professional institution?

If you are doubtful about the validity of a source, it may be better to omit it from your research.

Keeping up to date

As research, particularly at Doctorate level, can take several years, the literature review process does not stop after the initial search. You need to continue to review the literature throughout the research programme, to take account of developments in the field.

Current awareness services

Perhaps the most obvious way of keeping up to date with recently published research is to read current issues of key journals. This may mean a regular visit to the library to browse through the current journals shelf. Alternatively, some electronic resource providers offer an updating facility whereby you are automatically sent an e-mail to alert you to new articles of relevance.

The ZETOC database (http://zetoc.mimas.ac.uk) from the British Library is a good example of such a service. It allows you to set up alerts for the table of contents from particular journal titles, by keyword or by author. With 20,000 current journal titles and 16,000 conference proceedings each year, you will be able to cover a far wider range of journals than by manually searching print copies.

A similar service is provided by the Taylor and Francis Group, delivering table of contents for any of the journals they publish. These journals are all academic, peer reviewed and cover a variety of disciplines, including education. The SARA (Scholarly Articles Research Alerting) service is available at tandf.co.uk/sara/ and is free of charge.

Mailing lists

One method of keeping abreast of developments and current debate is to engage with other researchers and practitioners. Electronic mailing lists allow you to do this on the Internet, with discussion arriving straight into your e-mail inbox. Here are two examples for educational management and leadership. Both can be found on Catalist, a directory of public LISTSERV lists on the Internet, at www.lsoft.com/lists/lstref.html.

> EDPOLICY – Education Policy Discussion Forum
> EDPOLYAN – Education Policy Analysis Forum

Conferences

Conferences are another route for disseminating new information, so it is worth being aware of forthcoming events. There are several websites that provide these details.

HERO (Higher Education and Research Opportunites in the United Kingdom) www.hero.ac.uk/inside_he/conferences3888.cfm
This has the calendar of events of various special interest groups in education and related fields.

BEI (British Education Index) at Leeds University Library www.leeds.ac.uk/bei/
This has an Education Conference Listings Service, which is a calendar of education events. The Conferences listed will take place in the UK or will be non-UK events which invite significant and specific participation from UK education and training professionals. They also have a Conference Programme Service which allows you to search the content of conference programmes for particular themes and speakers.

Conference Alerts www.conferencealerts.com
This covers academic conferences worldwide, divided into subject areas (not just education). You can set up an alerting service for conferences that match your interests, available dates and destinations.

Managing information

Effective management of the bibliographic information is essential, as this will eventually become your own list of references and bibliography. You need to make decisions on how to manage this information at the beginning of your research. It will be a lot harder to establish a system once you have done a considerable amount of reading from lots of different documents. Managing the information throughout should also allow you to structure and map the bibliography in relation to the main themes of your research. It follows that one key to success is to make sure that you record all the publication details whilst you have the document in your possession. If you have borrowed a book either in person or through inter-library loan, or if you misplace a journal article or a website, it may be costly or even impossible to look at it again.

Many people use index cards, or create a cumulative list or table in Word to organise this information, but there are now several bibliographic software packages available, including Pro Cite, EndNote, Reference Manager and Refworks. These enable you to cut and paste bibliographic references saved in files or e-mails, and some databases allow you to download references directly into the software. You can then order the references as you wish, cite the documents in your writing and ultimately produce a bibliography using a reference style of your choice.

Communicatng your findings to others

Depending on the piece of work you are doing, you may be asked to include a bibliography (a list of all relevant sources you have used in your research), a reference list (details of those items that you directly refer to in your text) or both. A bibliography illustrates what you have read but should also enable other readers to find the same items again if necessary. Hence it is very important to choose a referencing style and stick with it – you must be consistent. You will probably be guided by your tutor on which style to use, but some of the more popular styles include:

- The Harvard system
- The Vancouver system
- The American Psychological Association (APA) guidelines system

Even if you are familiar with using a referencing style, it will be worth refreshing your memory, particularly with the growing number of e-resources (e-books, e-journals etc.) as these are referenced in a slightly different way to their print counterparts. For example, using the Harvard system:

A printed book:
> Begley, P.T. and Johansson, O. (eds) (2003) *The Ethical Dimensions of School Leadership*. Boston: Kluwer Academic

The electronic version:
> Begley, P.T. and Johansson, O. (eds) (2003) *The Ethical Dimensions of School Leadership*. Boston: Kluwer Academic. [online] Available from: NetLibrary. http://www.netlibrary.com [Accessed 7th August 2006]

A printed journal article:
> Meacham, J. and Gaff, J.G. (2006) Learning goals in mission statements: implications for educational leadership. *Liberal Education* **92** (1) pp. 6-13.

The electronic version:
> Meacham, J. and Gaff, J.G. (2006) Learning goals in mission statements: implications for educational leadership. *Liberal Education* **92** (1) pp. 6–13. [online] Available from: Expanded Academic ASAP, Thomson Gale. http://find.galegroup.com/itx/infomark.do?andcontentSet=IAC-Documentsandtype=retrieveandtabID=T002andprodId=EAIManddocId=A142684286andsource=galeandsrcprod=EAIManduserGroupName=leicesterandversion=1.0 [Accessed 7th August 2006]

Legal issues

Copyright

When you are attempting to gather all the literature for your review, you need to bear in mind copyright. Legislation in most countries forbids the copying of another author's work. The 1988 Copyright, Designs and Patents Act is the enforcing legislation in the UK. Photocopiers and online printing may encourage you to make copies of everything you need, regardless of the amount or where it is from, but rather than risk breaking the law, check exactly what you can and cannot copy. Electronic material also has legal restrictions.

Plagiarism

Plagiarism, when you deliberately copy someone else's work and pass it off as your own, is a serious offence. As with copyright, technology has made it easier to break the law, with electronic communication and a computer's 'Cut and Paste' facility. This has become a major concern in the academic world and in response software has been developed that can help to detect plagiarism. As a precaution, it is essential to ensure that when note-taking, you clearly mark which parts you have copied verbatim, which are paraphrased and which are your own ideas. Extracts from other people's work should be placed inside quotation marks or separated and indented from the rest of your text. For each extract, you need to state the page numbers in the in-text citation and fully reference the item in the reference list.

Conclusions

Exploring the existing body of research is a vital first step in any research project. As a researcher, the ability to search the literature effectively and efficiently is a core transferable skill (Hart, 2001: 21). This chapter has tried to demonstrate that there are fundamental steps which need to be followed if a literature review is to be carried out effectively. Clearly, there will always be advances in how information is disseminated and stored, but equally, there will always be over-arching guideline steps, no matter how easily bibliographical sources can be accessed. The following steps have been identified as being the most important to follow.

- Prepare your search thoroughly before you do anything else. This may involve producing some form of visual map of your ideas. The keyword list you construct from this exercise will, more than anything else, determine the success and efficiency of your search.
- Think through the various sources that you will need to consult, be they in paper or electronic form. Try to think beyond strictly 'education' resources.
- Don't attempt to narrow down the scope of your research project during the initial stages of your search.

- As you retrieve information, check the quality of your results. As the literature review is a critical piece of work, you cannot include an item simply because you found it.
- You also need to evaluate your searching technique. Are you finding the results you need? You may need to amend your approach to the search.
- Always make sure that you keep an accurate bibliographic record of the sources you have consulted. Do this when you have the document *in your hand*, or *on the screen*. Trying to remember it later invariably fails.
- Use one of the standard referencing styles or the one chosen by your institution and consider using bibliographic software to manage your references.
- Keep up to date by regularly checking what is published and announced during your research so that you do not miss vital information.
- Above all, consult with your institution's librarian at all times. He or she will be delighted to advise you and their experience could save hours of your time.

References

Bourner, T. (2002) 'The Research Journey: four steps to success', in Greenfield, T. (ed.) *Research Methods for Postgraduates*. London: Arnold.

Copyright, Designs and Patents Act 1988 (c. 48). London: HMSO.

Harlen, W. and Schlapp, U. (1998) *Literature Reviews*. Edinburgh: Scottish Council for Research in Education. www.scre.ac.uk/pdf/spotlight/spotlight71.pdf (accessed 26th April 2006).

Hart, C. (2001) *Doing a Literature Search: A Comprehensive Guide for the Social Sciences*. London: Sage.

Jankowicz, A.D. (1991) *Business Research Projects for Students*. London: Chapman and Hall.

Lyons, K. (2005) *How to Write a Literature Review*. Santa Cruz: University of California. http://library.ucsc.edu/ref/howto/literaturereview.html (accessed 26 April 2006).

Martin, V. (2002) 'Documenting your work', in Greenfield, T. (ed.) *Research Methods for Postgraduates*. London: Arnold.

University of Leicester Library (2005) Information Retrieval Skills Tutorial. http//le.ac.uk/li/sources/training/irs/irscontents.htm

Wisker, G. (2001) *The Postgraduate Research Handbook: Succeed with Your MA, MPhil, EdD and PhD*. Basingstoke: Palgrave.

6

Authenticity in research – reliability, validity and triangulation

Tony Bush

The purpose of this chapter is to examine different ways in which the authenticity and quality of educational research may be assessed. This is important for researchers of educational leadership and management for two reasons:

- It helps in assessing the quality of studies undertaken by other researchers
- It helps in determining their research approach and methodology

Although research methods should be determined largely by the aims and context of the research, they should also have regard to quality criteria. This enables the researcher to respond with confidence when explaining methodology at a conference, seminar or viva voce examination. This notion of scrutiny is important: can the researcher defend and explain decisions about methodology to peers, professionals and examiners? This concept may be particularly important for research on school leadership and management. Given the global significance of this field, and the strong belief in the role of leadership in determining institutional and student outcomes, there is a temptation for researchers to place the best possible gloss on their findings. A full and open explanation of the methods used by researchers is essential if their results and interpretations are to be accepted by policy-makers, practitioners and other researchers.

The authenticity of educational and social research can be judged by the procedures used to address validity, reliability and triangulation. These are all important and complex terms whose meaning and salience varies according to the stance of the researcher. These concepts were originally developed for use in positivist, or quantitative, research (see Chapter 2). As Easterby-Smith et al. (1994: 89) note, 'there has been some reluctance to apply these ideas to phenomenological ... research because they might imply acceptance of one absolute (positivist) reality'.

Hammersley (1987: 73) responds to this proposition by pointing to the increasing use of these notions by researchers from both positive and interpretive traditions. '[Use of] the concepts of validity and reliability ... is more frequent in "quantitative" than in "qualitative" research, but the basic issues apply to both'. Brock-Utne (1996) takes a similar view and asserts that they are equally important in both traditions:

> The questions of validity and reliability within research are just as important within qualitative as within quantitative methods though they may have to be treated somewhat differently. The commonly held assumption that qualitative methods pay attention to validity and not to reliability is false. (Brock-Utne, 1996: 612)

Reliability

Definition

Hammersley (1987: 73) claims that there is no widely accepted definition of reliability or validity: 'One finds not a clear set of definitions but a confusing diversity of ideas. There are substantial divergencies among different authors' definitions.' Despite this claim, there is wide support for the view that reliability relates to the probability that repeating a research procedure or method would produce identical or similar results. It provides a degree of confidence that replicating the process would ensure consistency. These notions underpin definitions of this concept:

> [Reliability demonstrates] that the operations of a study – such as the data collection procedures – can be repeated, with the same results. (Yin, 1994: 144)

> A measure is reliable if it provides the same results on two or more occasions, when the assumption is made that the object being measured has not changed … if a measure, or indeed a series of measures when repeated give a similar result, it is possible to say that it has high reliability. (Scott and Morrison, 2006: 208)

Reliability in surveys

A survey aims to collect a substantial amount of data in order to draw conclusions about the phenomenon under investigation. Johnson (1994: 13) describes it as 'eliciting equivalent information from an identified population'. Reliability in survey research requires standard instruments, such as questionnaires and structured interviews, and meticulous instrument design and testing, for example through piloting. One of the main ways of assessing reliability is through the 'test–retest' procedure. A reliable instrument should give more or less the same results each time it is used with the same person or group. 'When tests are developed, they are typically tested for reliability by giving them to a group of people then calling back those same people a week later to take the test again' (Bernard, 2000: 49).

Youngman (1994: 263) refers to the notion of reliability in questionnaire research and suggests ways in which it might be checked:

- Comparing findings with other sources, e.g. school records
- Direct questioning of respondents to see if personal responses match previous answers
- Cross-checking findings with the pilot study

The first of these approaches links to the notion of methodological triangulation, which is discussed later in this chapter. The second might occur through interviewing a sample of those surveyed by questionnaire and repeating certain questions. In the author's research on black and minority ethnic leaders in England (Bush, Glover and Sood, 2006), many of those responding to the research team's e-survey were also interviewed to obtain more depth and detail. This provided a helpful reliability check.

Wragg (2002: 156) asks two important questions in applying the concept of reliability to interviews:

- Would two interviewers using the schedule or procedure get similar results?
- Would an interviewer obtain a similar picture using the procedures on different occasions?

Fowler (1993) emphasises the need to ensure that all interviewees are asked the same questions in the same way if the procedure is to be reliable. This can work only if the interview schedule is tightly structured, with the properties of a questionnaire.

A survey data collection is an interaction between a researcher and a respondent. In a self-administered survey, the researcher speaks directly to the respondent through a written questionnaire. In other surveys, an interviewer *reads* the researcher's words to the respondent. In either case, the questionnaire is the protocol for one side of the interaction. (Fowler, 1993: 71; emphasis added)

Of course, in single-handed research such as postgraduate dissertations and theses, the interviewer and the researcher are the same person but the key point is that reliability depends on a highly structured instrument. When the researcher wants to modify the instrument to probe or prompt respondents, using a semi-structured approach, reliability may be compromised. However, Kitwood (1977) and Cohen and Manion (1994) express reservations about an over-emphasis on reliability for interviews because this may have implications for validity. Because reliability requires a standardized approach, it may limit validity. Validity is likely to require a friendly, human approach that allows respondents to answer in their own way, expressing their thoughts and feelings, and not to be restricted by the artificiality of a standard instrument. 'In proportion to the extent to which "reliability" is enhanced ..., "validity" would decrease' (Kitwood, 1977, cited in Cohen et al., 2000: 124).

This argument goes to the heart of the earlier discussion about research paradigms. Structured interviews are similar to questionnaires in their design and both may be regarded as methods within the positivist tradition. They both provide potential for 'reliability'. However, unstructured or semi-structured interviews are often used by interpretive researchers and assume greater diversity in both the design and use of the research instrument and in the nature of responses from participants. This may limit the scope for reliability while enhancing validity. We shall return to this debate later.

Reliability in case study research

Johnson (1994: 20) defines a case study as 'an enquiry which uses multiple sources of evidence. It investigates a contemporary phenomenon within its real-life context when the boundaries between phenomenon and context are not clearly evident.'

Yin applies the concept of reliability to case study research:

> The objective is to be sure that, if a later investigator followed exactly the same procedures as described by an earlier investigator and conducted the same case study all over again, the later investigator should arrive at the same findings and conclusions. ... The goal of reliability is to minimise the errors and biases in a study. One prerequisite ... is the need to document the procedures followed in the earlier case. ... The general way of approaching the reliability problem is to conduct research as if someone were always looking over your shoulder. (1994: 146)

As Johnson (1994) implies, case study research involves several different methods. The main approaches are usually interviews, observation and documentary analysis (Bassey, 1999: 81). We shall examine reliability issues in relation to each of these methods.

Interviews

Cohen et al. (2000: 268) suggest that 'the interview ... may be used as the principal means of gathering information having direct bearing on the research objectives'. The nature and applicability of reliability procedures depend on the type of interview utilised by the researcher. In structured interviews, where the questions are predetermined, the approach to reliability is similar to that of a questionnaire survey. When interviews are undertaken as part of case study research, they may be semi-structured or unstructured, allowing each participant to respond in their own way. Such interviews differ from the structured approach in that the interviewee contributes to shaping the conversation. What they want to say becomes as important as what the researcher wants to ask. As we noted earlier, it is more difficult to ensure reliability using unstructured or semi-structured interviews because of the deliberate strategy of treating each participant as a potentially unique respondent.

The increasing recognition that each school provides a distinctive context for practising school leadership increases the difficulties involved in seeking reliability in interview research. The author's evaluation of the *New Visions: Induction to Headship* programme (Bush and Glover, 2005; Bush et al., 2006), for the English National College for School Leadership (NCSL), illustrates this point. The research involved interviewing a large number of new headteachers about their experience of the programme and about its in-school effects. The evaluation team's semi-structured interviews covered the common experience of the participants, with some scope for reliability, but the application of the programme's ideas within schools inevitably varied significantly, leading to a response shaped by the unique context of the school. In this dimension of the research, reliability was unattainable and may not have been desirable.

Observation

Observation can be powerful, flexible and 'real' (Moyles, 2002: 172). It may be the basic tool in classroom research and can also be significant for studies of leadership and management issues, notably in observing meetings. The author's evaluation of the NCSL's *Working Together for Success* programme for school leadership teams (Bush et al., 2005) involved observation of SLT meetings to assess whether and how the programme's ideas were being implemented.

Brock-Utne (1996) applies the concept of reliability to participant observation and asks three questions 'of great relevance':

- Would we have seen the same and interpreted what we saw in the same way if we had happened to have made the observation at a different time? This question deals with the stability of the observations.
- Would we have seen the same and interpreted what we saw in the same way if we had happened to pay attention to other phenomena during observation? We may here speak of parallel form reliability.
- Would a second observer with the same theoretical framework have seen and interpreted the observations in the same way? We may speak here of objectivity or intra-judge subjectivity. (Brock-Utne, 1996: 614–615)

These questions illustrate in stark form the difficulties involved in achieving reliability in observational research. If the observation had been made at a different time, the phenomenon itself would have changed. Different people may be present, there may be an alternative agenda, and participants may bring different thoughts and feelings to the meeting. Predetermining the purpose and focus of the observation helps to avoid being distracted by other phenomena but this can only be partly successful.

In the author's evaluation of the 'New Visions' programme (Bush et al., 2006), observations were conducted by two or more researchers who recorded events separately, using the same structured framework. This is an example of inter-observer reliability (Scott and Morrison, 2006: 208). The researchers' independent records of the event were compared and an overview report prepared. Although most events were identified by both observers, a few points were noted by one researcher and missed or omitted by the other(s). This example illustrates the precarious nature of reliability in observational research, even where procedures are specifically adopted to address this issue.

Documentary analysis

Documentary analysis is an indispensable element in most case studies. Levačić's (1995: 86) research on the local management of schools, for example, involved both school and LEA documents, including 'budgets, minutes of meetings and supporting papers'.

The concept of reliability can be applied to documentary analysis, particularly when the approach is based on content analysis, a method which often involves counting words or terms found in the text (Cohen and Manion, 1994: 55). Robson (1994: 243) regards reliability as one of the advantages of content analysis using documents. 'The data are in permanent form and hence can be subject to re-analysis, allowing reliability checks and replication studies.' He recommends that two people are involved in coding text to improve reliability, although this is difficult for single-handed researchers such as postgraduate students.

It is evident from this brief account that applying the concept of reliability to case study research is problematic, notably in semi-structured or unstructured interviews and in observation. This is unsurprising as reliability is a notion associated with positivist rather than interpretive research. This leads Bassey (1999) to dismiss it for case studies and to substitute the concept of 'trustworthiness' put forward by Lincoln and Guba (1985).

Reliability and validity

Aspinwall et al. (1994) regard reliability, along with validity and relevance, as one of the key tests in judging the adequacy of research:

> Is it reliable? Would similar conclusions be drawn if the information was obtained by somebody else or by some other method? This is a tricky area. Again, quantitative indicators are often more reliable than more qualitative ones [but] their reliability may be bought at the expense of their validity. Where reliability is a problem, there is advantage in using more than one kind or source of data in relation to a particular criterion: [i.e.] triangulation. (Aspinwall et al., 1994: 218)

Scott and Morrison (2006: 208) note that a research finding might be reliable but not valid and 'thus of no worth to the researcher'. The tension between reliability and validity in qualitative research is noted by Brock-Utne (1996: 614), who questions:

> whether we need the concept of reliability at all as an independent concept since the question of reliability has little relevance except in connection with the question of validity. Reliability ... only has relevance because it is a necessary precondition for attaining validity.

As we noted earlier, reliability may be achieved only by reducing validity. We turn now to consider this latter concept.

Validity

Definition

The concept of validity is used to judge whether the research accurately describes the phenomenon that it is intended to describe. The research design, the methodology and the conclusions of the research all need to have regard to the validity of the process.

> Validity ... tells us whether an item measures or describes what it is supposed to measure or describe. If an item is unreliable, then it must also lack validity, but a reliable item is not necessarily also valid. It could produce the same or similar responses on all occasions, but not be measuring what it is supposed to measure. (Bell, 1999: 104)

Validity, like reliability, is a notion primarily associated with positivist research and has been questioned by those who favour qualitative, or interpretive, approaches. Denzin and Lincoln (1998) emphasise the central importance of validity within positivist paradigms and claim that it is inappropriate for other perspectives. Kincheloe and McLaren (1998) reject 'traditional' validity as unhelpful for 'critical' qualitative research and join Bassey (1999) in advocating the alternative concept of 'trustworthiness':

> Where traditional verifiability rests on a rational proof built upon literal intended meaning, a critical qualitative perspective always involves a less certain approach characterised by participant reaction and emotional involvement. Some analysts argue that validity may be an inappropriate term in a critical research context, as it simply reflects a concern for acceptance within a positivist concept of research rigour. ... Trustworthiness ... is a more appropriate word to use in the context of critical research. (Kincheloe and McLaren, 1998: 287)

Types of validity

Several different types of validity have been identified by writers on research methods in education. The main distinction is between internal and external validity. *Internal* validity relates to the extent that research findings accurately represent the phenomenon under investigation, as the following definitions suggest:

> The degree to which findings correctly map the phenomenon in question. (Denzin and Lincoln, 1998: 186)

> The accuracy or authenticity of the description being made ... [it is] a measure of accuracy and whether it matches reality. (Scott and Morrison, 2006: 253)

Cohen and Manion (1994: 99–101) apply the notion of internal validity to several different research methods. In relation to survey research, they point to two potential causes of invalidity:

- Respondents may not complete questionnaires accurately. They suggest that validity may be checked by interviewing respondents. This is an example of methodological triangulation.
- Those who fail to return questionnaires might have responded differently to those who did so. They suggest follow-up contact with non-respondents by trained interviewers to establish their views. This is an expensive strategy, which is likely to be prohibitive for many single-handed researchers, including postgraduate students. This problem may be reduced if the survey produces a substantial response. The greater the response rate, the smaller the risk of invalidity.

The main potential source of invalidity in interviews is bias. 'The sources of bias are the characteristics of the interviewer, the characteristics of the respondent, and the substantive content of the questions' (Cohen and Manion, 1994: 282). They suggest careful formulation of questions and interviewer training as possible solutions but bias is likely to be endemic, particularly in semi-structured and unstructured interviews, and is difficult to eliminate.

The risk of bias may be reduced through respondent validation (Scott and Morrison, 2006: 252), where transcripts or the researcher's notes are returned to the interviewee for confirmation or amendment. The author consistently uses this approach following interviews (see, for example, Bush et al., 2006 and Bush, Glover and Sood, 2006).

Similar problems arise in participant observation, where the researcher's 'judgement [may] be affected by their close involvement in the group' (Cohen and Manion, 1994: 111). As we noted earlier, the concept of validity may be rejected as a positivist construct, which cannot easily be applied to qualitative methods, including observation and most types of interview.

Silverman (2000: 176–177) refers to another problem, which may compromise validity in qualitative research. He says that researchers must avoid the 'special temptation' of 'anecdotalism', where 'a few well-chosen examples' are used to illustrate the findings. He argues that triangulation provides a way of addressing this problem (see below).

External validity relates to the extent that findings may be generalised to the wider population, which the sample represents, or to other similar settings:

> External validity refers to the extent to which findings from research can be usefully generalised. In positivist research traditions, and especially in social survey analysis, this problem has been seen largely in terms of sampling strategies in order to ensure that the people studied are representative of the wider population to which generalisations are desired. (Brock-Utne, 1996: 617)

> External validity ... is a measure of generalisability. (Scott and Morrison, 2006: 253)

As Brock-Utne (1996) notes, external validity is usually applied in positivist research and she is sceptical about applying this notion to qualitative methods. Case study research, for example, may be criticised because it does not match the survey approach in terms of generalisation. Indeed, Yin (1994: 147) claims that the unique case often provides the rationale for single case studies. Here, the potential for generalization is necessarily limited.

Bassey (1999) addresses this issue by distinguishing between statistical and 'fuzzy' generalisations and linking these notions to quantitative and qualitative approaches:

> The statistical generalisation arises from samples of populations and typically claims that there is an *x* per cent or *y* per cent chance that what was found in the sample will also be found throughout the population: it is a quantitative measure. The fuzzy generalisation arises from studies of singularities and typically claims that it is possible, or likely, or unlikely, that what was found in the singularity will be found in similar situations elsewhere: it is a qualitative measure. (Bassey, 1999: 12)

Bassey (1999) refers to 'singularities' but generalisation may become less 'fuzzy' if several similar case studies are undertaken. Yin (1994) says that the problem of generalisation can be minimised by replicating the study in another similar setting. This process should lead to wider acceptance of the external validity of the findings:

> The investigator is striving to generalise a particular set of results to some broader theory ... the theory that led to a case study in the first place is the same theory that will help to identify the other cases to which the results

are generalisable. ... A theory must be tested through replication of the findings in a second or even third [case], where the theory has specified that the same results should occur. Once such replication has been made, the results might be accepted for a larger number of similar [cases], even though further replications have not been performed. (Yin, 1994: 145)

Triangulation

Triangulation means comparing many sources of evidence in order to determine the accuracy of information or phenomena. It is essentially a means of cross-checking data to establish its validity:

> Triangulation may be defined as the use of two or more methods of data collection in the study of some aspect of human behaviour. ... The use of multiple methods, or the multi-method approach, as it is sometimes called, contrasts with the ubiquitous but generally more vulnerable single-method approach that characterises so much of research in the social sciences ... triangular techniques in the social sciences attempt to map out, or explain more fully, the richness and complexity of human behaviour by studying it from more than one standpoint. (Cohen and Manion, 1994: 233)

This definition links the notion of triangulation to a multi-methods approach. This is known as *methodological triangulation*, using several methods to explore the same issue. An alternative, or additional, approach is *respondent triangulation*, asking the same questions of many different participants. McFee (1992) clarifies these two different approaches to triangulation:

> Triangulation *between* methods employs two or more approaches to a single problem ... triangulation between methods compares (at least) two research 'solutions' to a single problem in an effort to 'validate' the outcomes of one approach in terms of the outcomes of another. (McFee, 1992: 215)

> Triangulation *within* a method takes as its starting point the claim that the 'reality' of a situation is not to be apprehended from a single viewpoint. Thus it brings to bear two or more viewpoints on a particular occasion (say those of teacher, pupil and observer), with a view to characterising the occasion so as to accommodate, or account for, all these viewpoints. (McFee, 1992: 216)

The author's research into management development and governor training in the Gauteng province of South Africa (Bush and Heystek, 2006) adopted both types of triangulation. A 100% sample survey of all principals was complemented by case studies of 30 schools identified by stratified sampling (methodological triangulation). Within each case study school, interviews were held with up to six different individuals: the principal, the chairperson of the school governing body (SGB), a teacher governor, a teacher who was not a member of the SGB, a non-teaching staff member and, in secondary schools, a student governor (respondent triangulation).

Cohen et al. (2000: 113) say that triangulation may be used in either positivist or interpretive research but it is particularly valuable in case study research when multiple methods are often employed (Bassey, 1999: 81). In policy-related research, for example, the aims of the policy may be stated in documents. Interviews and/or observation may then be undertaken to establish whether these aims were realised or if the policy has had certain unintended consequences. Conducting such interviews with different user groups (for example teachers and school leaders) may lead to the conclusion that the policy impacted differentially on each group. In both these examples, data are checked across different methods and sources.

Robson (2002) points to the value of using interviews and observations for triangulation in a study primarily based on content analysis of documents:

> The documents have been written for some purpose other than for the research, and it is difficult or impossible to allow for the biases or distortions that this introduces ... [There is a] need for triangulation with other accounts [and] data sources to address this problem. (Robson, 2002: 358)

Levačić's (1995) research on local management of schools in England provided for methodological triangulation through documents, observation and interviews, as did the author's evaluation of the NCSL's 'New Visions' programme (Bush and Glover, 2005; Bush et al., 2006).

Triangulation is fundamentally a device for improving validity by checking data, either by using mixed methods or by involving a range of participants. While contributing to validity, its use is not a panacea. As McFee (1992: 215) suggests, 'its value is easy to overestimate'. The assumption that 'true' fixes on 'reality' can be obtained separately from different ways of looking at it (Silverman, 2000: 177) may be incompatible with certain approaches to qualitative research that value and celebrate individual or subjective ways of seeing and interpreting phenomena.

Conclusion

Research has the potential to influence policy and practice and its importance for educational leadership and management has grown since the inception of the English National College for School Leadership (NCSL), and similar bodies for higher education and the learning and skills sector. The NCSL, in particular, strongly emphasises practitioner research as well as funding about half of all school leadership research in England (Weindling, 2004). Both new and experienced researchers need to ensure that research findings are authentic. Reliability and validity are the two main issues to address when seeking to ensure authenticity while triangulation is one important way in which validity may be sought.

We noted earlier that reliability and validity may be regarded as constructs within the positivist research tradition. However, authenticity remains an important issue for qualitative researchers. It may be achieved through alternative concepts such as trustworthiness (Lincoln and Guba, 1985) or through a modification of the positivist concepts to enhance their applicability to interpretive, or phenomenological, research. Easterby-Smith et al. (1994), for example, apply reliability and validity to both research traditions (see Table 6.1).

Easterby-Smith et al. (1994) acknowledge the many reservations about applying these concepts to interpretive research but assert that these notions are valuable for all researchers:

> Provided the researcher is committed to providing a faithful description of others' understandings and perceptions, then ideas such as validity and reliability can provide a very useful discipline. (Easterby-Smith et al., 1994: 89)

Table 6.1 Reliability and validity in different research traditions

Concept	Positivist viewpoint	Phenomenological viewpoint
Validity	Does an instrument measure what it is supposed to measure?	Has the researcher gained full access to the knowledge and meanings of informants?
Reliability	Will the same measure yield the same results on different occasions (assuming no real change in what is to be measured)?	Will similar observations be made by different researchers on different occasions?

Source: Adapted from Easterby-Smith et al., 1994: 90

Lincoln and Denzin (1998) go beyond the debate about positivist and interpretive research to point out that validity is not an absolute concept:

> Validity represents the always just out of reach, but answerable, claim a text makes for its own authority ... the research could always have been better grounded, the subjects more representative, the researcher more knowledgeable, the research instruments better formulated, and so on ... validity is the researcher's mask of authority, which allows a particular regime of truth ... to work its way on the world. (Lincoln and Denzin, 1998: 415)

Authenticity may be an elusive target, but it is an important objective for educational management researchers. While there is no perfect truth, a focus on reliability, validity and triangulation should contribute to an acceptable level of authenticity sufficient to satisfy both researcher and reader that the study is meaningful and worthwhile.

References

Aspinwall, K., Simkins, T., Wilkinson, J. and McAuley, J. (1994) 'Using success criteria', in Bennett, N., Glatter, R. and Levačić, R. (eds), *Improving Educational Management Through Research and Consultancy*. London: Paul Chapman with the Open University.

Bassey, M. (1999) *Case Study Research in Educational Settings*. Buckingham: Open University Press.

Bell, J. (1987) *Doing Your Research Project* (3rd edn). Buckingham: Open University Press.

Bernard, H. (2000) *Social Research Methods: Qualitative and Quantitative Approaches*. Thousand Oaks, CA: Sage.

Brock-Utne, B. (1996) 'Reliability and validity in qualitative research within education in Africa', *International Review of Education*, 42 (6): 605–621.

Bush, T. and Glover, D. (2005) 'Leadership for early headship: the New Visions experience', *School Leadership and Management*, 25 (3): 217–239.

Bush, T. and Heystek, J. (in press) 'School leadership and management in South Africa: Principals' perceptions', *International Studies in Educational Administration*, 34 (2).

Bush, T., Briggs, A.R.J. and Middlewood, D. (2006) 'The impact of school leadership development: evidence from the 'New Visions' programme for early headship', *Journal of In-service Education*, 32 (2): 185–200.

Bush, T., Morrison, M., Glover, D., Lumby, J. and Middlewood, D. (2005) *Working Together for Success: Final Evaluation Report to the NCSL*. Lincoln: University of Lincoln.

Bush, T., Glover, D. and Sood, K. (2006) 'Black and minority ethnic leaders in England: a portrait', *School Leadership and Management*, 26 (4): 289–305.

Cohen, L. and Manion, L. (1994) *Research Methods in Education*. London: Routledge.

Cohen, L., Manion, L. and Morrison, K. (2000) *Research Methods in Education* (5th edn). London: Routledge.

Denzin, N. and Lincoln, Y. (1998) *The Landscape of Qualitative Research*. Thousand Oaks, CA: Sage.

Easterby-Smith, M., Thorpe, R. and Lowe, A. (1994) 'The philosophy of research design', in Bennett, N., Glatter, R. and Levačić, R. (eds), *Improving Educational Management through Research and Consultancy*. London: Paul Chapman with the Open University.

Fowler, F. (1993) *Survey Research Methods*. Newbury Park, CA: Sage.

Hammersley, M. (1987) 'Some notes on the terms "validity" and "reliability"', *British Educational Research Journal*, 13 (1): 73–81.

Johnson, D. (1994) *Research Methods in Educational Management*. Harlow: Longman.

Kincheloe, J. and McLaren, P. (1998) 'Rethinking critical theory and qualitative research', in Denzin, N. and Lincoln, Y. (eds), *The Landscape of Qualitative Research*. Thousand Oaks, CA: Sage.

Kitwood, T. (1977) 'Values in adolescent life: towards a critical description', Unpublished PhD thesis, University of Bradford.

Levačić, R. (1995) *Local Management of Schools: Analysis and Practice*. Buckingham: Open University Press.

Lincoln, Y. and Denzin, N. (1998) 'The fifth moment', in Denzin, N. and Lincoln, Y. (eds), *The Landscape of Qualitative Research*. Thousand Oaks, CA: Sage.

Lincoln, Y. and Guba, E. (1985) *Naturalistic Inquiry*. Newbury Park, CA: Sage.

McFee, G. (1992) 'Triangulation in research: two confusions', *Educational Research*, 34 (3): 215–219.

Moyles, J. (2002) 'Observation as a research tool', in Coleman, M. and Briggs, A.R.J (eds), *Research Methods in Educational Leadership and Management*. London: Paul Chapman.

Robson, C. (1994) 'Analysing documents and records', in Bennett, N., Glatter, R. and Levačić, R. (eds) *Improving Educational Management through Research and Consultancy*. London: Paul Chapman.

Robson, C. (2002) *Real World Research* (2nd edn). Oxford: Blackwell.

Scott, D. and Morrison, M. (2006) *Key Ideas in Educational Research*. London: Continuum.

Silverman, D. (2000) *Doing Qualitative Research: A Practical Handbook*. London: Sage.

Weindling, D. (2004) *Funding for Research in School Leadership*. Nottingham: NCSL.

Wragg, E. (2002) 'Interviewing', in Coleman, M. and Briggs, A.R.J (eds) *Research Methods in Educational Leadership and Management*. London: Paul Chapman.

Yin, R. (1994) 'Designing single and multiple case studies', in Bennett, N., Glatter, R. and Levačić, R. (eds), *Improving Educational Management through Research and Consultancy*. London: Paul Chapman with the Open University.

Youngman, M. (1994) 'Designing and using questionnaires', in Bennett, N., Glatter, R. and Levačić, R. (eds), *Improving Educational Management through Research and Consultancy*. London: Paul Chapman with the Open University.

Recommended reading

Aspinwall, K., Simkins, T., Wilkinson, J. and McAuley, J. (1994) 'Using success criteria', in Bennett, N., Glatter, R. and Levačić, R. (eds), *Improving Educational Management through Research and Consultancy*. London: Paul Chapman with the Open University.

Denzin, N. and Lincoln, Y. (1998) *The Landscape of Qualitative Research*. Thousand Oaks, CA: Sage.

Easterby-Smith, M., Thorpe, R. and Lowe, A. (1994) 'The philosophy of research Design', in Bennett, N., Glatter, R. and Levačić, R. (eds), *Improving Educational Management through Research and Consultancy*. London: Paul Chapman with the Open University.

Hammersley, M. (1987) 'Some notes on the terms "validity" and "reliability"', *British Educational Research Journal*, 13 (1): 73–81.

Silverman, D. (2000) *Doing Qualitative Research: A Practical Handbook*. London: Sage.

7

Ethics of research in education

Hugh Busher and Nalita James

In whichever paradigm researchers choose to locate their work, they try to ensure the trustworthiness or validity of its outcomes by enacting it within a rigorous framework that addresses the epistemological complexities of a study's methodological process and intellectual focus. Research is a form of disciplined inquiry that holds at its core certain principles, and aims to contribute to a body of knowledge or theory 'as carefully and accurately as possible [to] develop knowledge for, in and of society' (Pring, 2000: 143).

Linked to that process of enquiry is a framework of procedures and practices that is intended to ensure that research is carried out properly. These have been variously described as a commitment to honesty (Sammons, 1989) and 'respect for the dignity and privacy of those people who are the subjects of research ... the pursuit of truth ... the right of society to know' Pring (2000: 143). In addition, the Economic and Social Research Council of the UK (ESRC, 2005: 25) asserts that 'the independence and impartiality of researchers must be clear and any conflicts of interest must be explicit' and that 'research should be conducted so as to ensure the professional integrity of its design, the generation and analysis of data, and the publication of results, while the direct and indirect contributions of colleagues, collaborators and others should also be acknowledged' (ESRC, 2005: 23).

Central to this framework are understandings of ethical conduct by researchers.

> Ethics embody individual and communal codes of conduct based upon adherence to a set of principles which may be explicit and codified or implicit, and which may be abstract and impersonal or concrete and personal. Zimbardo (1984, cited in Cohen et al., 2000: 58)

Whilst it is important to recognise the need for 'codes' or 'rules of conduct' (Simons, 1995) that allow researchers in the social sciences to defend their work in various educational, social and political contexts, this chapter goes beyond merely explicating such technicist solutions, not least because the rapid growth of research using Internet data sources such as email, chatrooms and discussion boards, means that researchers face a range of ethical issues 'in their efforts to acquire new knowledge about many of the behaviours and practices that arise in these new venues' (Ess, 2004: 253). This has led to discussions about what ethical research practice online entails (Mann and Stewart, 2000), as well as to a greater convergence between ethical practice for online and face-to-face research.

Ethical issues can arise at any stage of a research project (Cohen et al., 2000: 49) and are particularly acute when dealing with human subjects, defined very broadly by ESRC (2005: 7), especially those who might be defined as 'vulnerable' (ESRC, 2005: 8; AoIR, 2002), as occurs frequently in educational research, or when research might be deemed to generate greater risk of harm to participants (see Table 7.1).

Table 7.1 Research likely to cause greater risk of harm to participants

Vulnerable groups – e.g. children and young people, those with a learning disability or cognitive impairment, or individuals in a dependent relationship

Sensitive topics – e.g. participants' illegal or political behaviour, their experience of violence, their abuse or exploitation, their mental health, their gender or ethnic status

A gatekeeper normally permits initial access to members – e.g. ethnic or cultural groups, members of the armed forces or inmates and other members of custodial or health and welfare institutions

Deception or research conducted without participants' full and informed consent at the time the study is started

Access to records of personal or confidential information, including genetic or other biological information

Inducing psychological stress, anxiety or humiliation or causing more than minimal pain

Intrusive interventions – e.g. the administration of drugs or other substances, vigorous physical exercise, that participants would not normally encounter in their everyday life

Source: Abridged from ESRC, 2005: 8

The application of ethics in education research is situated in particular circumstances, including the researcher's disciplinary background, ideological background, socio-cultural contexts and interpretations (Madge, 2006; Simons and Usher, 2000). As Thomas (2004: 199) indicates, '[researchers'] views of ethics may reflect the class, race or ethnocentric biases of our own location in the social hierarchy'. However, they also have to reflect the individuality and autonomy of the researched (United Nations, 1989), for whom researchers have a duty of care (Glenn, 2000). This suggests the need to distinguish between general principles for guiding action in research and the views of particular researchers and other participants, such as research sponsors and respondents, while not denying society the value of the information and conceptualisation that can be gained from the research (Cohen et al., 2000). Carrying out research, then, involves a series of emergent or immanent ethical moments (Usher, 2000: 162) that require more than a mechanistic application of ethical codes of practice throughout the life of a research project.

Ethical principles and moral codes for carrying out educational research

Definitions of professional ethical practice are enshrined in codes to guide the decisions of researchers. Such codes have been developed by, for example, the British Educational Research Association (2004), the British Psychological Society (2006) and the British Sociological Association (2002). These codes have a common core of ethical issues providing 'a basis for discipline among social researchers and prescribe acceptable practice on the assumption of a professional consensus (Homan, 1991: 20). Moral and ethical codes apply equally to quantitative research methods (e.g. American Statistical Association, 1999) as to research based on qualitative data.

Major funding bodies for social science research in the UK, such as the ESRC, an extension of central government, and charitable bodies such as Nuffield and Rowntree, define how projects funded by them may spend money and on what they may focus their research. The ESRC's Research Ethics Framework (2005), which all universities in the UK are required to implement if they want to gain funding from this and associated research funding bodies, enshrines various principles that researchers have to implement to protect the privacy, anonymity and confidentiality of participants in research. As part of their conditions of funding research, such bodies can demand control over the outcomes of the research, for example, reading reports before they are published to ensure that there is no material in them that may be detrimental to the interests of the sponsors as well as to other participants.

Central government also regulates the processes of research. For example, in the UK the Data Protection Act (1998) only allows information on individuals to be held for lawful reasons and appropriate security measures must be taken to guard against people gaining access to it who have not had permission from the participants to access it. Government codes of practice limit how statistical data collected for government departments can be used (Raffe et al., 1989).

The advent of online research, where studies can span several distinct cultural boundaries each with their own approach to what might constitute ethical research, and the distinctive nature of virtual reality have raised the need for developing understandings of what might constitute ethical Internet research. As Ess (2002: 181–184) recognizes, there exists an 'ethical pluralism' in the world as well as on the Internet in which there is a continuum of legitimate ethical choices available to the online researcher. The different ethical philosophical frameworks (deontological, utilitarian, virtue) that exist (Ess, 2004: 254) mean that ambiguity, uncertainty and disagreement about practice will be inevitable (Madge, 2006). The Association of Internet Researchers (AoIR), based in the United States, has begun to address these issues, making recommendations for the proper conduct of research on the Internet by researchers, funding bodies and students, as well as exploring fundamental differences of approach to research ethics in the United States and the European Union (AoIR, 2002: 20). It points out that, 'the issues raised by Internet research are *ethical* problems precisely because they evoke more than one ethically defensible response to a specific dilemma or problem' (AoIR, 2002: 4).

The contexts of the research

The contexts in which research is conducted mean researchers need to think about the implications of the choices they make as part of their ethical practice and how that choice may impact on the ways in which researchers engage with other participants. Walford (2001) has argued that insufficient consideration is often given to the appropriateness of the context or site in which research is to be conducted, and often such contexts will be chosen because they are convenient to the research(er) rather than thinking through the implications of such choices. Such contexts can include both virtual venues (online communities) as well as onsite research (institutions and organisations). Whichever context is chosen, researchers need to be sensitive to the socio-political contexts in which individuals live out their lives, as members of overlapping communities as well as of a particular community or institution. This is because these communities form the context of a research study as well as shape how research and researchers are perceived and how participants respond to invitations to take part in research. Researchers need to be aware of their part in that process, since it may lead to distortion in the views of other participants in the study. Such distortions can affect the validity of a study.

Whilst the conduct of research in the virtual environment may reflect many of the ethical principles of onsite (face-to-face) research, there are many ethical issues that are specific to conducting research online (Madge, 2006). As the AoIR (2002: 2) points out, 'online [sic] research ... raises critical issues of risk and safety to the human subject. Hence, online researchers may encounter conflicts between the requirements of research and its possible benefits, on the one hand, and human subjects' rights to and *expectations* of autonomy, privacy, informed consent, etc.'. None the less, it also points out that, 'the Internet has opened up a wide range of new ways to examine human inter/actions in new contexts, and from a variety of disciplinary and interdisciplinary approaches' (2002: 2), offering researchers new means of engaging with research agenda which might not be possible or so easy using face to face, telephonic or postal means of communications.

Another context is that of the 'personal', especially in qualitative research where researcher and participants meet onsite (face-to-face). Shah (2004) points out that when an interviewer is a member of the opposite sex to the participants or of a different ethnic group or cultural community, this may make interviewing or observation more problematic, since such attributes may make some of the participants feel uncomfortable and unwilling to share their views openly. This risks distorting the outcomes of research conversations or observations so that researchers do not collect as truthfully and accurately as possible the range of views of participants in a situation. Riddell (1989) argues that it raises questions about the social characteristics of both the researcher and participants and how this influences the research process as people interpret the social characteristics of the other, such as age, race, gender as well as socio-economic and organisational status, to shape their responses to fit whatever pattern of sense-making they think is expected of them (Mann and Stewart, 2000). Participants construct these expectations from researchers' perceived social characteristics and their non-verbal and verbal cues.

If the presence of social signals is problematic for participants and researchers in face-to-face research, so is their absence in online research interviews. The non-verbal and contextual elements that are seen as essential to the interviewing process are absent online, giving participants no social framework in which to locate their interactions or space to construct or reconstruct themselves in all manner of ways (Anderson and Kanuka, 2003). Orgad (2005: 62) reflects that, in face-to-face interviews, her way of knowing the research participants was biased towards the *visual* and 'embedded in *embodied* ways of expression'. Online, she relied on participants' textual self-presentation. Moving between online and offline contexts means that researchers have to reflect upon 'the indeterminancy of the Internet and the complexity of the relationship between online and offline experiences' (2005: 63).

Participating in research: choosing to be a participant

A key principle for constructing ethical research is that of voluntarism by the participants when engaging with research. This is manifested by them giving their informed and explicit consent, free from coercion or bribery, to take part in a study (ESRC, 2005: 7) This emphasis on informed consent arises from fundamental democratic rights to freedom and self-determination (Cohen et al., 2000). Explanatory letters, or pre-interview explanations are some means by which researchers try to gain informed consent from potential participants.

This deontological stance to research is deliberately chosen to emphasise the rights of participants in research who are likely to be in a less powerful position than researchers to shape the agenda and outcomes of research. However, as the ESRC (2005: 25) admits:

there is no simple rule for getting right the balance between potential risks to participants and benefits of the research to a wider community. There may be exceptional circumstances in some fields of research when, with the consent of the participants, some short-term and minimal degree of harm which causes no lasting effects or prolonged personal discomfort might be acceptable.

Participating in any research involves risk to the individuals concerned (Chadwick, 2001). Inviting individuals to participate in research, means that the researcher must protect participants from harm and violation of privacy, whilst at the same time maintaining the integrity of the research and its ethical standards. As Baez (2002: 41) reflects: 'At the core of these concerns is the notion of the sanctity and sovereignty of the individual.' Such concerns are critical in research that involves gathering data about personal experiences, whether research is conducted onsite or online (O'Connor, 2006). What is at issue is how those risks can be minimised by researchers to ensure that participants are made fully aware of what risks they may face so that their choice of whether or not to participate constitutes fully informed consent.

Gaining informed consent is problematic, not least because of what might be construed by that term. Reasonably informed consent by participants is usually taken to mean that they have understood sufficiently well the purposes, processes and intended outcomes of the research to be able to give a consent that reflects their reasoned judgement to participate. For example, gaining children's consent can be problematic since they may not understand what are the consequences to them or significant others in their lives (Aubrey et al., 2000) of taking part in research. Researchers sometimes have to take uncomfortable decisions about what might constitute informed consent in particular circumstances, especially where they have to use proxies or gatekeepers to gain that consent. Although asking proxies for the participants – parents or teachers for children, for example – for permission to participate is sometimes perceived as a means of addressing this problem, ESRC (2005) point out that parents may not be the most suitable proxies to give permission for their children to participate in research as they stand in powerful social positions compared to the former and may not fully understand the implications of their children being involved in research. Similarly proxies may have to be used when participants do not speak fluently the same language as the researchers and so might not be aware nor fully understand what they are being asked to disclose.

Online researchers need to be clear about the nature of the environment in which they are working in order to gain informed consent and ensure security of that environment. Whereas some of these reflect conventional parameters of ethical research, for example, whether the participants are vulnerable persons (ESRC, 2005), others reflect the particularities of research that might spread across cultural and political boundaries and have to meet the requirements of participants' different legal and cultural systems (AoIR, 2002: 3). In online research, virtual space is dominated by the English language, which raises issues when carrying out research with non-native speakers of English about how clearly they are informed of the nature of a research project, as well as what the risks might be of being involved (Mann and Stewart, 2000). Where participants are engaged in a secure or private environment, for example, a discussion board within a VLE (virtual learning environment), or a password-protected sector of a website, there is likely to be less of a threat to their privacy and so less risk of harm to them than if they are engaged in a more open environment such as email or a public chat room, or a blog (AoIR, 2002: 7). However, elements of the environment are potentially revelatory of participants' identities. For example, email automatically sends participants' addresses along with their responses, so users are instantly visible. Explicit guidelines about how research will be conducted online will not always assuage putative participants' fears about protecting their privacy (James and Busher, 2006).

Researchers have a duty of care to ensure that they do not deliberately mislead participants as to the nature of the researcher or the research. One aspect of this is whether a researcher should use information that is available for private use in a group for research purposes without the explicit permission of all the members of a group. This dilemma is often faced by insider researchers wanting to use information for research that was originally collected for other purposes. Hewson et al. (2003) have suggested that data put into the public Internet arena should be made available to researchers provided that anonymity is assured. In online research, deception can be especially problematic as it is possible for participants to be unaware of the social characteristics or attitudes of a researcher as well as being able to deceive researchers about themselves. In some virtual situations, such as ongoing online discussion groups that have fluctuating populations, Kleinman (2004) notes that people, such as researchers, can join without the knowledge or consent of their other members. This is sometimes described as 'lurking'. Chen et al. (2004) view this as an important research act for understanding the topics and tones of exchanges of a group prior to a researcher gaining informed consent from its members to join. However, Madge (2006) views the practice as unethical as it allows 'lurkers' access to information about members of a group without the knowledge or permission of them. It might be conceived as equivalent to covert research.

Researchers have a duty to avoid causing both physical and psychological harm to participants and to the socio-political environments in which and with which they work, although feminist and critical researchers (e.g. Usher, 2000) might argue the importance of intervention to raise consciousness of power differentials, whether or not gendered. Cohen et al. (2000: 50) argue that this is a matter of protecting the rights of the participants: maintaining privacy, anonymity and confidentiality, and avoiding harm, betrayal and deception. In part this emphasis on avoiding harm is in the self-interest of the research community. Questions that raise uncomfortable issues about the participant to themselves, or invite participants to be revelatory about themselves to a stranger (the researcher) (ESRC, 2005), may raise the need for researchers to offer counselling to ensure no harm remains after the end of the discussion or observation. If environments and participants have been harmed by some researchers, they may choose not to cooperate with future researchers. In major part, however, this concern is altruistic. It leads researchers to seek those approaches that risk least harm to participants, although such choices are not absolute but dependent on the situations in which a study is being undertaken – including such factors as the location of the study, the age, gender, ethnic and socio-economic groups of the participants, as well as time, financial and personal costs involved (Walford, 2006).

In both virtual and physical worlds, researchers are ethically bound to maintain the privacy of participants, including confidentiality for any information they give and anonymity for their identity, because probing into areas that constitute participants' private space may have damaging consequences for participants (Baez, 2002; Kelman, 1977). Research that requires insider research, or that uses elements of deception or covert research raises particular ethical issues of breach of privacy and informed consent (Beynon, 1988). This can be further heightened when researchers are formally powerful people in an organisation. It raises questions about the nature of the consent that participants have given when asked to take part in research, and the quality of the data they feel able to reveal without, in their eyes, harming themselves within the micro-political processes of their organisation.

One approach to maintaining privacy is by fictionalising or codifying names and places, and even dates. In onsite research, Beynon (1988) suggests that researchers should always maintain the anonymity of the firm, but small groups of people within a firm may still be able to guess at the identities of participants or of the organisation. The fundamental difficulty here is that people involved with any institution that is the site of research will eventually get to know the identity of the researcher and of the participants (Walford, 2006). In research with school children for example, the headteacher, teachers, parents and pupils should know what research is taking place, by whom and why. With so many people knowing about the research, it would be very difficult to guarantee the privacy and anonymity of both the school and those participating in the research, especially once a report has been published (Walford, 2006: 88).

In conducting online research, expectations of privacy become complicated because of different sites having differing expectations of the ways in which participants should interact. Secure or private environments pose less of a threat to participants' privacy than more open environments (AoIR, 2002: 7). In the latter, researchers need to take much greater care to protect the privacy of participants if they are to gain and keep their explicit informed consent. For example, individuals need to be made aware that their conversations may not be taking place in a private setting (Barnes, 2004). Most Internet-based communication addresses contain part or all of their users' real names (Bruckman, 2004), making it possible in public sites to retrieve messages (Eysenbach and Till, 2001). Thus the records of participants' online conversations, even if carefully processed, may make participants' views instantly visible, depriving participants of confidentiality and anonymity.

Trustworthiness and voice: ethical dilemmas in data collection and analysis

To be ethical, a research project needs to be designed to create trustworthy (valid) outcomes if it is to be believed to be pursuing truth. Flick (2002) argues that qualitative researchers need to be as vigilant as positivist researchers about ensuring the validity and reliability of their studies, even if they choose to use other terms such as credibility and authenticity, to describe the qualities that establish the trustworthiness of their studies. Research that is untrustworthy is unethical because it is of no benefit in developing a society's knowledge base and wastes the resources of researchers and other participants. In positivist research, ethical principles emerge frequently around the relationship of the researchers to the resource-providers for permission to carry out research; to the data-providers (subjects); and to the public who want to know the outcomes (Raffe et al., 1989: 16), as well as around statistical processes used to analyse data (Jones, 2000).

Questionnaire surveys, like interviews, are intrusive, and their questions can be distressing for participants if they are requested to confront aspects of their work or their lives which they find uncomfortable. However, unlike their researcher counterparts using interviews, survey researchers are often unaware of the problem and not in a position to reduce levels of distress, as various ethical codes of research suggest they should. This is in order to leave the participants and the research field no worse off (not more harmed) at the end of a research intervention than when the research began.

The ethical principle not to cause harm and to capture truthful views of events faces researchers with questions about what data need to be gathered. Unnecessary data are not only a waste of time for researcher and participants, so causing harm to the participants, but can also be regarded as an unnecessary invasion of privacy. These issues emerge particularly in visual research, since the people whose images are captured by video or camera are forever revealed – the privacy and anonymity of participants is breached – unless some very sophisticated and expensive techniques are used. There is also a problem about the authenticity of the actions which the images claim to reveal – the extent to which participants are acting up for the camera – or the actions are reconstructed by the researcher (Prosser, 2000). Further, still, film and video images often only partially capture action because of the nature of their technology thereby giving an incomplete view of that action that is under the control of the researchers who direct the instruments, not of the other participants. This raises questions about how accurately such perspectives reflect those of the other participants.

Conventional approaches to interview-based qualitative research tend to use either semi-structured or unstructured interviews or conversations. The iterative process of qualitative research interviews – that constantly critical reflective process that Hammersley (1998) commends as a safeguard for qualitative researchers against the risk that they might unwittingly fall short of the rigorous standards of probity that are required – also guards against aspects of the interviews remaining under-developed. Asking participants in a study to reflect critically on their narratives helps researchers not only to authenticate participants' accounts but also to develop a greater understanding of the phenomena being studied (Seale, 1999). This is further enhanced by building research relationships that, as Oakley (1981) describes, go beyond stereotypical roles of question-asking and question-answering, and developing collaborative approaches (Lebesco, 2004). James and Busher (2006) found that as their online interviews progressed the participants began to take greater ownership of the processes of narrative construction. For them, the participants' lack of inhibition and frankness reinforced their belief that what emerged online was the material selves of the participants engaged in email conversations, as it did for Mann and Stewart (2000). It would have been very difficult for participants to sustain such conversations had they been fictitious, unless they were gifted story tellers. However, on the Internet there is also the potential for individuals to construct identities different from their embodied selves because they are hidden by the 'smoked-mirror' of the Internet. Lebesco (2004: 575) describes this as an 'act of identification' because 'disembodiment and anonymity allows users to take on many new identities that may have little connection to their off-line selves' (Hardey, 2004: 195).

Retaining the records of conversations and checking their veracity with participants is a key means for qualitative researchers gaining evidence of the authenticity and credibility of their data to meet the ethical requirement of constructing trustworthy research that may be of some benefit to society. In online interviews, so long as the record of the textual exchange is not deleted, the records of conversations are constantly under review and being authenticated as each new question and its responses are added to the existing record (James and Busher, 2006). It also enables participants and researchers to reflect in an iterative manner on their developing conversations and, in due course, to consider the accuracy of the texts of their conversations. Retaining evidence of participants' voices is central to the process of establishing authentic research records. As Flicker et al. (2004: 131) note: 'By stripping the data of voices and threads of conversation, the danger becomes losing some or even the entire context.'

Choosing the people to participate in research is ethically problematic. The number and identity of those invited to participate have to meet the requirements of the research design to strengthen the trustworthiness of the study but this is often constrained by the resources available to record and transcribe interviews. Choice is often further limited to those people who volunteer to take part, raising questions about the partial nature of the evidence that is collected (and not collected) and the extent to which it reflects the views, generally, of the people involved in the setting.

The generalisability of findings from one situation to another is also dependent on research being carried out ethically. Attempting to answer questions from an inappropriate sample or data set, or choosing an inappropriate unit of analysis, may lead to misleading findings, undermining their transferability (Bassey, 1998). Although, such research boundaries may be arbitrary (Usher, 2000), the more they are so, the more it is incumbent on researchers to explore every possible meaning emerging from their research and present this to readers. Sammons (1989) argues the importance of choosing appropriate statistical techniques and not using them to over-analyse or inappropriately analyse data. She also argues that statistical indicators chosen to represent the underlying concepts of a research project have to be appropriate (have construct validity).

Critical approaches to research particularly raise ethical issues around the engaged role of the researcher. For example, in action research researchers are reflecting on their own practices (see, for example, Lomax, 1994) and seeking to bring about change. To do this ethically, researchers have to be morally committed to enacting declared values which are participatory and emancipatory, by engaging other participants on an equal footing with the researcher in validating the research. This generates ethically informed practice in and through research since the findings of the researcher are moderated by the perceptions of other participants engaged in or related to the action under scrutiny. Similarly in online research, self-identification and self-presentation of the researcher will be critical, as participants will form their opinion about the credibility of the research and the researcher based on this (Markham, 2004).

Document-based research that writers such as Johnson (1994) regard as low-key or non-invasive itself contains a range of ethical dilemmas for researchers. These emerge particularly when documents written for one purpose or for a particular audience are used for other purposes by a researcher. In such cases it is not at all clear to what extent, if at all, informed consent has been given for the documents to be used for research purposes. Certainly documents allow researchers to invade the lives of the participants in research, giving insights into their views, values and attitudes which may not have been intended. It leaves researchers with a moral responsibility to protect the privacy and anonymity of the research participants. In the same way diary studies intrude on and reveal the private lives of research participants (Burgess, 1994), raising similar questions to other forms of document-based research.

Storing and disseminating research findings and outcomes

There is an underlying ethical principle that participants have a right to know some of the outcomes of a study. It is founded on their knowledge product, be that questionnaire answers or observed actions. Sammons (1989: 55) suggests that participants should always have an account of the findings of the research.

Other stakeholders also have an interest in the intellectual property rights of the research outcomes, for example researchers who have invested time, effort and thought, and sponsors who have invested funds or permitted access to research sites. Such rights can be in tension, particularly where sponsors are concerned to have particular points of view conveyed through the research, whatever the findings, as Osler et al. (2000) found out in a year-long wrangle with the DfEE as to whether their research on managing school exclusions showed evidence of institutionalised racism. Bulmer (1988) argues that it is important for researchers to protect their right to publish, so long as the identity of other stakeholders is protected by anonymity, and so should beware of giving organisations the right of veto over what is published about them, even if they have been a willing host to a study.

Writing up research has to be carried out ethically, too, so that the presentation of the data both respects participants' right to privacy and sustains the right of society to know about the research (Burgess, 1989; Cohen et al., 2000). It raises questions about what readers need to know about participants and about their contexts if they are fully to understand the outcomes of the research. It implies that all the results from a study should be published, whether positive or negative. Further, research reports should be explicit about the underlying ethical, social and political values held by researchers, participants and sponsors in a study, if they are to be as truthful as possible in presenting their findings (Usher, 2000).

Statistical outcomes, Sammons (1989) argues, should be presented in such a way that they are not misleading and are comprehensible to lay people who do not understand statistics. The publication of raw score data on school performance is probably unethical since it is open to misinterpretation when not set in the contexts of other performance indicators of a school, and so is likely to cause harm to a school as an institution and to its members. Statistical outcomes to research should consider the impact of:

- Sampling error
- Alternative interpretations to and discrepancies between interpretations of findings
- The impact of other variables on the findings (internal validity)
- The appropriateness of the sample to the interpretations made (external validity)
- The appropriateness of the level of analysis to the questions researched

The storage or curation of data after the end of a research project, particularly when linked to the personal data of participants, at least raises the possibility of harm being done to the participants (ESRC, 2005; Raffe et al., 1989), especially if those data are used for purposes other than the original research, and perhaps without the express permission of the original participants. Where the data are in the form of video records the problem is particularly acute and raises questions as to whether the data should be retained at all. It makes problematic ethically the holding of large data sets in the public domain, such as those requested by the DfES in England and Wales. In storing online data, complete anonymity is almost impossible to guarantee, as information about the origin of a computer-transmitted message will be difficult to remove (Stewart and Williams, 2005). Guaranteeing participant confidentiality is more difficult to achieve, especially in online focus groups, where postings and group discussions cannot prevent identification of the author of the message by others in the group.

Coda

There is no solution (Burgess, 1989: 8)! Fully ethical research is impossible (Busher and Clarke, 1990). De Laine (2000: 205) argues that 'fieldwork is inherently problematic by virtue of the conditions that make knowledge production possible ... where personal relations and social interactions are the context for unearthing meaning'. Further, Baez (2002: 53) argues that 'harm is inherent to all research, and the uncertainty over whether any action will cause harm is a fact of all qualitative research'. These arguments illustrate that in the end researchers have to take decisions about how to carry out research that make the process as ethical as possible within the frameworks of the project, including budgets of time and finance available to them. These include considering whether it is worthwhile undertaking a piece of research by weighing up the balance of harm and benefit that arise to participants and to society from carrying it out. Researchers are not always 'autonomous self-directing actors' but mediators between two or more audiences (De Laine, 2000: 205).

Online research does not diminish these conundrums but creates a further set of ethical challenges, in trying to ensure the truthfulness and trustworthiness of data collected by researchers. These challenges, alongside the absence of a commonly agreed set of guidelines, also suggest that there are many ethical issues which need to be resolved (Madge, 2006). No doubt as computer-mediated communication becomes more sophisticated so too will the ethical and methodological research practices.

Whatever context or site, whether online or face-to-face, the extent to which participants are likely to be open and honest with researchers in constructions of their perceptions of social and personal life will depend on the research focus, the approach it takes and the actual context being studied. It will also heavily depend upon the extent to which the researchers have been able to construct an ethical environment for the research which allows participants to feel confident that their privacy is protected and the risk of harm to them or their communities and families is minimised to a level acceptable to them.

References

AoIR (Association of Internet Researchers) (2002) *Ethical decision-making and Internet research*. www.aoir.org/reports/ethics.pdf (accessed April 2006).

American Statistical Association (1999) *Ethical Guidelines for Statistical Practice* (revised edn). Alexandria, VA: American Statistical Association.

Anderson, T. and Kanuka, H. (2003) *e-Research: Methods, Strategies and Issues*. Boston, MA: Ablongman.

Aubrey, C., David, T., Godfrey, R. and Thompson, L. (2000) *Early Childhood Educational Research: Issues in Methodology and Ethics*. London: RoutledgeFalmer

Baez, B. (2002) Confidentiality in qualitative research: reflections on secrets, power and agency. *Qualitative Research*, 2 (1): 35–58.

Barnes, S. (2004) Issues of attribution and identification in social research, in Johns, M.D., Chen, S.S. and Hall, G.J. (eds) *Online Social Research: Methods, Issues and Ethics*. New York: Peter Lang Publishing.

Bassey, M. (1998) 'Fuzzy generalisation: an approach to building educational theory'. Paper given at the British Educational Research Association Annual Conference, Belfast, The Queen's University, 1998.

Beynon, H. (1988) 'Regulating research: politics and decision making in industrial organisations', in Bryman, A. (ed.) *Doing Research in Organisations*. London: Routledge.

British Educational Research Association (2004) *Revised Ethical Guidelines for Educational Research*. Southwell: BERA

British Psychological Society (2006) 'Ethical Principles for Conducting Research with Human Participants'. www.bps.org.uk/the-society/ethics-rules-charter-code-of-conduct/code-of-conduct/ethical-principles-for-conducting-research-with-human-participants.cfm (accessed 4 July 2006).

British Sociological Association (2002) Statement of Ethical Practice for the British Sociological Association. www.britsoc.co.uk/equality/63.htm (accessed 4 July 2006).

Bruckman, A.S. (2004) Introduction: opportunities and challenges in methodology and ethics, in Johns, M.D., Chen, S.S. and Hall, G.J. (eds) *Online Social Research. Methods, Issues and Ethics*. New York: Peter Lang Publishing.

Bulmer, H. (1988) 'Some reflections on research in organisations', in Bryman, A. (ed.) *Doing Research in Organisations*. London: Routledge.

Burgess, R.G. (1989) Ethics and educational research: an introduction, in Burgess, R.G. (ed.) *The Ethics of Educational Research*. London: Falmer Press.

Burgess, R. (1994) On diaries and diary keeping, in Bennett, N., Glatter, R. and Levačić, R. (eds) *Improving Educational Management through Research and Consultancy*. London: Paul Chapman with the Open University.

Busher, H. and Clarke, S. (1990) The ethics of using video in educational research, and in Anning, A., Broadhead, P., Busher, H., Clarke, S., Dodgson, H., Taggart, L., White, S. and Wilson, R. (eds) *Using Video Recordings for Teacher Professional Development*. Leeds: University of Leeds, School of Education.

Chadwick, R. (2001) Ethical assessment and the human genome issues, in Shipley, P. and Moir, D. (eds) 'Ethics in Practice in the 21st Century', *Proceedings of the Interdisciplinary Conference of the Society for the Furtherance of Critical Philosophy*, Eynsham Hall, Oxon, October 1999.

Chen, S.S., Hall, G.J. and Johns, M.D. (2004) 'Research paparazzi in cyberspace: the voices of the researched', in Johns, M.D., Chen, S.S. and Hall, G.J. (eds) (2004) *Online Social Research. Methods, Issues and Ethics*. New York: Peter Lang Publishing

Cohen, L., Manion, L. and Morrison, K. (2000) *Research Methods in Education* (5th edn). RoutledgeFalmer.

De Laine, M. (2000) *Fieldwork, Participation and Practice: Ethics and Dilemmas in Qualitative Research*. London: Sage.

ESRC (Economic and Social Research Council) (2005) *Research Ethics Framework*. Swindon: ESRC.

Ess, C. (2002) Introduction. *Ethics and Information Technology* 4: 177–188.

Ess, C. (2004) 'Epilogue: are we there yet? Emerging ethical guidelines for online research', in Johns, M.D., Chen, S.S. and Hall, G.J. (eds), *Online Social Research. Methods, Issues and Ethics*. New York: Peter Lang Publishing.

Eysenbach, G. and Till, J.E. (2001) Ethical issues in qualitative research on internet communities. *British Medical Journal*, 323: 1103–1105.

Flick, U. (2002) *An Introduction to Qualitative Research* (2nd edn). London: Sage.

Flicker, S., Hans, D. and Skinner, H. (2004) 'Ethical dilemmas in research on internet communities', *Qualitative Health Research*, 14 (1): 124–134.

Glenn, S. (2000) The darkside of purity or the virtues of double-mindedness, in Simons, H. and Usher, R. (eds) *Situated Ethics in Educational Research*. London: RoutledgeFalmer

Hammersley, M. (1998) *Reading Ethnographic Research: An Ethical Guide*. London: Longman.

Hammersley, M. and Atkinson, P. (1983) *Ethnography: Principles in Practice*. London: Tavistock Publications.

Hardey, M. (2004) 'Digital life stories: auto/biography in the information age', *Auto/Biography*, 12: 183–200.

Hewson, C., Yule, P., Laurent, D. and Vogel, C. (2003) *Internet Research Methods*. London: Sage.

Homan, R. (1991) *The Ethics of Social Research*. London and New York: Longman.

James, N. and Busher, H. (2006) 'Credibility, authenticity and voice: dilemmas in online interviewing', *Qualitative Research*, 6 (3): 403–420.

Johnson, D. (1994) *Research Methods in Educational Management*. Harlow: Longman.

Jones, K. (2000) 'A regrettable oversight or a significant omission? Ethical considerations in quantitative research in education', in Simons, H. and Usher, R. (eds) *Situated Ethics in Educational Research*. London: RoutledgeFalmer.

Kelman, H.C. (1977) 'Privacy and research with human beings', *Journal of Social Issues*, 33: 169–195.

Kleinman, S.S. (2004) 'Researching OURNET: a case study of a multiple methods approaches', in Johns, M.D., Chen, S.S. and Hall, G.J. (eds) *Online Social Research: Methods, Issues and Ethics*. New York: Peter Lang Publishing.

Lebesco, K. (2004) 'Managing visibility, intimacy, and focus in online critical ethnography', in Johns, M.D., Chen, S.S. and Hall, G.J. (eds) *Online Social Research: Methods, Issues and Ethics*. Oxford: Peter Lang Publishing.

Lomax, P. (1994) 'Action research for managing change', in Bennett, N., Glatter, R. and Levačić, R. (eds) *Improving Educational Management through Research and Consultancy*. London: Paul Chapman with the Open University.

Madge, C. (2006) 'Online research ethics'. Available from www.geog.le.ac.uk/ORM/ethics/ethcontents.htm (accessed 6th July 2006).

Mann, C. and Stewart, F. (2000) *Internet Communication and Qualitative Research: A Handbook for Research Online*. London: Sage.

Markham, A.N. (2004) 'Representation in Online Ethnography', in M.D. Johns, S.L.S. Chen, and G.J. Hall (eds) *Online Social Research: Methods, Issues and Ethics*, Oxford: Peter Lang Publishing, pp. 141–157.

Oakley, A. (1981) 'Interviewing women: a contradiction in terms', in H. Roberts (ed.) *Doing Feminist Research*. London: Routledge. pp. 30–61.

O'Connor, H. (2006) 'Online interviews'. Available from www.geog.le.ac.uk/ORM/interviews/intcontents.htm (accessed 6 July 2006).

Orgad, S. (2005) 'From online to offline and back: moving from online to offline relationships with research participants', in Hines, C. (ed.) *Virtual Methods: Issues in Social Research on the Internet*. Oxford: Berg.

Osler, A., Watling, R. and Busher, H. (2000) *Reasons for Exclusion from School: Report to the DfEE*. London: DfEE.

Pring, R. (2000) *Philosophy of Educational Research*. London: Continuum.

Prosser, J. (2000) 'The moral maze of image ethics', in Simons, H. and Usher, R. (eds) *Situated Ethics in Educational Research*. London: RoutledgeFalmer.

Raffe, D., Blundell, I. and Bibby, J. (1989) 'Issues arising from an educational survey', in Burgess, R.G. (ed.) *The ethics of Educational Research*. London: Falmer Press.

Riddell, S. (1989) 'Exploiting the exploited? The ethics of feminist educational research', in Burgess, R.G. (ed.) *The Ethics of Educational Research*. London: Falmer Press.

Sammons, P. (1989) 'Ethical issues and statistical work', in Burgess, R.G. (ed.) *The Ethics of Educational Research*. London: Falmer Press.

Seale, C. (1999) 'Quality in qualitative research', *Qualitative Inquiry*, 5 (4): 465–478.

Shah, S. (2004) 'The researcher/interviewer in intercultural context: a social intruder!', *British Educational Research Journal*, 30 (4): 549–575.

Simons, H. (1995) 'The politics and ethics of educational research in England: contemporary issues', *British Educational Research Journal*, 21 (4): 435–449.

Simons, H. and Usher, R. (2000) 'Introduction: ethics in the practice of research', in Simons, H. and Usher, R. (eds) *Situated Ethics in Educational Research*. London: RoutledgeFalmer.

Stewart, K. and Williams, M. (2005) 'Researching online populations: the use of online focus groups for social research', *Qualitative Research*, 5 (4) 395–416.

Thomas, J. (2004) 'Reexamining the ethics of internet research: facing the challenges of overzealous oversight', in Johns, M.D., Chen, S.S. and Hall, G.J. (eds) *Online Social Research: Methods, Issues and Ethics*. Oxford: Peter Lang Publishing.

United Nations (1989) *Convention on the Rights of the Child*. New York: United Nations.

Usher, P. (2000) 'Feminist approaches to situated ethics', in Simons, H. and Usher, R. (eds) *Situated Ethics in Educational Research*. London: RoutledgeFalmer.

Usher, R (2000) 'Deconstructive happening, ethical moment', in Simons, H. and Usher, R. (eds) *Situated Ethics in Educational Research*. London: RoutledgeFalmer.

Walford, G. (2001) 'Site selection within comparative case study and ethnographic research', *Compare*, 31 (2): 151–164.

Walford, G. (2006) 'Research ethical guidelines and anonymity', *International Journal of Research and Method in Education*, 28 (1): 83–93.

Zimbardo, P. (1984) 'On the ethics of intervention in human psychological research with specific reference to the "Stanford Prison Experiment"', in Cohen, L., Manion, L. and Morrison, K. (2000) *Research Methods in Education* (5th edn). London: RoutledgeFalmer.

Part B
Approaches to research

8

Surveys and sampling

Ken Fogelman and Chris Comber

It is commonplace for discussions of survey research in education to start by describing it as the most frequently used research method. In the first edition of this book a rapid review of the contents of the journal *Educational Management, Administration and Leadership* over a two-year period revealed that this was equally true of research related to educational management or leadership. Of the 33 papers published in the journal in that period that were based on original empirical work, 19 reported on a survey of some kind, although for several this research method was combined with another method. By contrast, the second most popular method, the case study method, featured in 12 of these articles.

But these bare figures conceal considerable variety in the research activities being carried out under the heading of 'survey'. Indeed in some cases it is not clear whether a particular piece of research is more appropriately described as a survey or as a small number of individual case studies, when, for example, the research consists of interviews with a number of headteachers.

It is therefore extremely difficult to arrive at a straightforward and uncontested definition of what exactly a survey is. Many have tried nevertheless. Hutton (1990), for example, wrote:

> Survey research is the method of collecting information by asking a set of preformulated questions in a predetermined sequence in a structured questionnaire to a sample of individuals drawn so as to be representative of a defined population. (1990: 8)

Whilst this accurately describes a common form of survey, most would feel that as a definition it is far too narrow. Many surveys use methods of data collection other than questionnaires, including interviews, which may also be 'preformulated and sequenced', as is common in opinion polling for example. On the other hand, interview surveys may be semi-structured or even unstructured, and therefore may include questions which are neither pre-prepared nor in a pre-defined order. Again some surveys, such as a national census, are carried out on an entire population rather than a sample. Nor, as discussed further below, would one want to exclude from a definition surveys based on a sample which may not be able to demonstrate representativeness. For such reasons more tentative statements are preferable. Cohen et al. (2000), for example, wrote:

> Typically, surveys gather data at a particular point in time with the intention of describing the nature of existing conditions, or identifying standards against which existing conditions can be compared, or determining the relationships that exist between specific events. (2000: 169)

Even here, one would want to interpret some of the terms used, such as 'conditions' and 'events', as broadly as possible; and note the writer's use of the word 'typically', which allows for exceptions.

Denscombe (2003) is even more inclusive, and his discussion is replete with terms such as 'generally' and 'in principle'. He writes of the typical characteristics of surveys and that they are about 'an approach in which there is empirical research pertaining to a given point in time which aims to incorporate as wide and as inclusive data as possible'. As he rightly goes on to emphasise, 'The survey approach is a research strategy, not a research method.'

Varieties of surveys

As the above is beginning to illustrate, surveys can vary on several dimensions. They can vary in size or scope, instrumentation, structure and purpose.

Size or scope

At one extreme are surveys in which the number of respondents is extremely small. This might be where, for example, a questionnaire is being used as one source of data within a case study of a single institution and is distributed only to staff (students, governors, etc.) within that institution. In such studies the respondents may form a population (for example, a survey of an entire senior management team of a school) rather than a sample.

Equally, small numbers of respondents may arise where data are to be obtained through, for example, unstructured interviews. Here the balance that has to be struck between depth and richness of data and the resources available imposes practical constraints on the number of interviews that can take place. This is typical of small-scale research such as that conducted by Masters or Doctoral students, where opportunities to conduct wider-ranging surveys are often limited.

At the other extreme, the number of respondents can be very large indeed. A national census, for instance, involves many millions of respondents, again an example of a survey of a complete population rather than a representative sample. In the field of educational research, the most dramatic examples are probably those international comparative studies of educational achievement that study several thousand students in each of many countries (for example, Martin et al., 2004).

Instrumentation

The questionnaire, the most common method of data collection in a survey, is used to obtain factual information, attitudinal information or a mixture of both. However, as already noted, also common are interviews, which in turn can vary as to how structured they are and whether they are carried out face-to-face or by other means such as telephone or, increasingly, via electronic means such as email or videoconferencing. As mentioned above in relation to the international surveys of achievement, standardised tests can be used. The term 'survey' is also occasionally applied to studies which obtain data through observation.

Structure

Most surveys, and certainly the majority of those carried out by an individual researcher, are cross-sectional, obtaining data at a single point in time, and use just one questionnaire or other means of data collection. Some small-scale (usually quasi-experimental) studies may employ pre- and post-test questionnaires, collecting data at two separate points to determine the impact of an intervention strategy, for example a new management structure.

However, more complex designs are possible. Most obviously there are longitudinal studies (or panel studies as they are more commonly called in the American literature) which follow up individuals over a longer period of time, typically involving successive stages of data collection. These too can range from small studies of the growth and development of individuals to major projects such as national cohort studies that follow several thousand individuals over a long period ('from cradle to grave' in some cases) and draw upon many different sources of data. Examples in the UK include the National Child Development Study (NCDS) and the British Cohort Study (BCS), which aim to follow the lives of all those living in Great Britain who were born in a single week in 1958 and 1970 respectively (see, for example, Dearden et al., 2004).

Longitudinal studies provide opportunities for particular kinds of analysis and therefore for answering some particular kinds of research questions (Fogelman, 1985), but they can also give rise to additional issues of sample attrition, response rates (see, for example, Laurie et al., 1999; Shepherd, 1993) and expense.

More complex survey designs are also possible by, for example, combining cross-sectional surveys of part of a sample with longitudinal surveys of the remainder. Time series, or trend, studies, which obtain data at several points in time but usually drawing a new sample on each occasion rather than following up the same individuals, are also possible.

Purpose

Given the variety found in survey research, in terms of scale, methods of data collection and complexity of design, it is not surprising that surveys can be used for many different purposes and to answer many different kinds of research question. Most of the issues of fitness of purpose of whether a survey – of whatever kind – is appropriate, relate to the choice of the method of data collection. Such issues are discussed in other chapters in this book. However, some more general points relate to the nature of the analysis to be carried out once the data have been collected. At the simplest level, a survey may have been carried out to do no more than frequency counts: to discover, for example, what proportion of headteachers have a certain qualification; or the proportion of heads of departments who agree with a particular managerial policy.

At the next level are questions which can be addressed by two-way tables or simple correlations such as: 'Do the attitudes of heads of departments vary according to how long they have been in post?' or 'What is the relationship between size of school and examination performance?' In exploring such relationships, the researcher often hopes to uncover cause and effect relationships. Then more complex, multi-variate analysis (see Chapter 19) may be required to take account of intervening or confounding variables; for example: 'What is the relationship between size of school and examination results after the socio-economic characteristics of schools' student intakes have been taken into account?' The researcher may also be interested in examining the effect of group differences, for example: 'Are there differences in the leadership styles of men and women headteachers?' or the combined effect of two variables, such as gender and length of service on job attitudes. Statistical analysis – both simple and sophisticated – can be used to explore these relationships and differences.

Thus, because of the variety of methods and design that the survey as a research method encompasses, it is an approach which can be used to investigate a wide range of research questions and allows for a broad spectrum of analytic approaches.

Practical issues

Paramount in the early stages of preparation for any study is the need to identify clear, relevant and manageable research questions and then to decide on the most appropriate research strategy and method(s) for obtaining answers to those questions. As noted above, while surveys are often discussed in terms of the generalisability of their findings, it is quite common in small-scale research to use a survey for mainly descriptive purposes.

In broad terms then, the survey is the appropriate approach to use when systematically collected and comparable data are needed which can be obtained directly from a (relatively) large number of individuals. More specifically, a survey is the most advisable methodology where the research objective is to gather general information about attitudes, opinions or characteristics, where data are required in a standardised form and are not available from other sources and where the researcher wishes to explore quantifiable differences between groups or relationships between variables.

Although appropriateness for answering the research question(s) is the most important criterion for deciding which approach to use, resource issues should also be considered at the design stage. What direct costs, such as postage, stationery or travel, for example, will be incurred? What are the (financial or human) costs of identifying a sample and contacting and getting the agreement of potential respondents (often a time-consuming process where busy school personnel are involved)? How much of the researcher's own time (and skills) will be needed for data coding, input and analysis once the completed surveys have been returned? Such considerations are often overlooked by new researchers who assume that the survey is a 'quick and easy' means of data collection.

Other issues which can be particularly relevant to the use of surveys are those relating to access. Is it necessary to obtain permission to distribute questionnaires or conduct interviews; for example from a local authority, the head of an institution or from parents? Once access is agreed, other issues arise which need to be taken into account. Where and when might a headteacher be available for interview? What time of year would be least disruptive when asking teachers to find time to complete a questionnaire? And so on.

Ethical issues

Such practical concerns can also have an ethical component. For any research strategy or method it is the researcher's responsibility to ensure that their instruments or methods of data collection are of as high a quality as possible both in terms of design and content, and as unobtrusive and inoffensive as possible. Similarly, as with any educational research, the concept of informed consent of respondents is crucial (see Chapter 7). This can arise for the survey researcher in a particularly acute form in relation to anonymity and/or confidentiality, especially where potentially sensitive or controversial issues are under investigation.

In surveys in education, it is often difficult to ensure the anonymity of the respondent. Where postal questionnaires are used, for example, the researcher will usually want to maximise response rate by following up and sending reminders to those who have not returned them. This can only be done if you can identify who has and has not returned the questionnaire. This also applies if follow-up interviews with selected respondents are required. One strategy for maximising response rate without breaching anonymity is to send a reminder to everyone in the sample, with a statement similar to that found on official 'reminders' thanking those who have already replied. This approach can be costly, however, although email reminders can sometimes be an inexpensive and simple means of achieving this.

Researchers are sometimes tempted to get round the problem of anonymity by using a numbering system to link a response to the respondent's identity while telling respondents that the information they provide will be provided anonymously, since their name does not appear on the questionnaire. Not only is this unethical, but it is unlikely to fool the respondent. On the contrary, it may well irritate them and result in a reduction in the survey response rate or in the quality of information obtained from the survey.

On the other hand, it is usually possible to guarantee confidentiality that individual answers will be seen by no one other than the researcher (though if quotations from interviews are likely to be included in a thesis or report, even if they are anonymised, respondents should be made aware of this). The golden rule is to tell the truth and to explain the reasons for the procedures adopted. The potential respondent is then in a position to make an informed decision about whether or not to participate.

Equally important is to ensure that whatever is promised does actually happen. Some years ago one of the authors was involved in a study of school attitudes which distributed questionnaires to students. Teachers, who agreed to administer the survey, were given clear instructions to place the completed questionnaires in a sealable envelope in sight of the students. The students, meanwhile, were informed that this was the procedure to be followed by their teacher. In this way, confidentiality was, if not guaranteed, certainly much more 'visible' to the participants.

Piloting

Finally, the importance of piloting cannot be overstated. A poorly designed questionnaire will yield unusable data which no amount of manipulation using the most sophisticated analytic procedures can rescue. Careful and appropriate piloting of research instruments will weed out inappropriate, poorly worded or irrelevant items, highlight design problems and provide feedback on how easy or difficult the questionnaire was to complete. Although students on research methods courses are routinely reminded of the need to pilot their questionnaire (or whatever research instrument they choose to use), too often neglected is the equally important need to pilot administrative procedures and guidance to participants to ensure that these too work efficiently and in the way intended by the researcher. A failure to trial such processes (for example, systems for distribution and collection; information on when and how to return completed questionnaires) may lead to extra work for the researcher, uncertainty (and possible non-response) on the part of the participant, or both.

Sampling

Issues of, and decisions about, sampling need to be considered in a number of stages. The first crucial concept is that of *generalisation*. In many cases, the researcher will wish to argue that his or her findings have wider application and that they have relevance and implications beyond those particular individuals (schools, organisations, etc.), that is they will want to generalise their research findings to some extent. This introduces the second important concept, the *population*, that is, the entire group in which we are interested and which we wish to describe or draw conclusions about.

Thus identifying the relevant population is an important part of developing the research question. The researcher needs to decide about whom or what s/he wishes to be able to draw conclusions at the end of the research. This might be, for example, all teachers (or heads or schools) in England; those in a more limited geographical or administrative area (such as a local authority – LA); those in schools or colleges of a particular 'type' (such as state-supported or independent); those in a particular post or who teach a particular subject, and so on.

As already mentioned, there are examples of surveys where the 'sample' is in practice the population, such as a national census at one extreme, or a survey of the teachers in a single institution (perhaps as part of a case study) at the other. The purpose of a census is simply to provide information on the characteristics of the relevant population and not beyond, although the data may of course be used to make comparisons with census data from other populations. There are examples in the education management literature of surveys of entire populations. Harper (2000), for example, reports a study of organisational structures in further education colleges in which she requested data, in the form of organisational charts, from all 452 institutions funded by the Further Education Funding Council in England and Wales. Wilson and McPake (2000), in a study of management styles in small (fewer than 120 pupils) Scottish primary schools, combined a small number of case studies with a postal questionnaire to all 863 such schools.

Much more commonly, limited resources and other practical constraints (particularly those which apply to the lone researcher) on obtaining access to or information about the whole population, mean that we are obliged to collect data from a sub-set. In other words we must study a *sample* of that population, preferably one that can be shown to be *representative* of the larger group and which therefore allows us to be reasonably confident about the validity of whatever generalisations we make.

Methods of sampling

Samples can be created in one of two ways: through *probability* sampling and *non-probability* sampling. Specific methods are described in more detail below, but in essence, in a probability sample the researcher must have access to each individual person or 'unit' (such as a school) in the population from which the sample is being drawn and each member of that population should have exactly the same chance of being selected as every other member. Thus what various probability methods have in common is that the researcher can determine the statistical likelihood (probability) of any individual case in the population appearing in the sample. For example, in a 10 per cent sample drawn randomly from a population of 1,000 (that is, a sample of 100), the probability of any individual member of that population being selected is 1/10. With non-probability methods where the researcher does not have access to the whole population, the researcher cannot state the likelihood of an individual being selected for the sample in this way.

In principle, probability samples are much to be preferred, both because they are more likely to result in a sample which is representative of the population studied as a whole, but also because they are more likely to satisfy the mathematical assumptions which underlie many kinds of statistical analysis and inferential testing (see Chapter 19). In reality, as we shall see, it may not be possible to create a true probability sample for various practical reasons, so the previous statement may be seen as something of a counsel of perfection.

What is important, therefore, is that first we should use the best (most representative) sample we can within the resources and possibilities available, and secondly, where this sample falls short of what might have been ideal, then we should acknowledge this shortcoming and also recognise the implications it may have for the confidence with which we are able to generalise from our findings.

Probability sampling

Probability samples depend on the availability and accessibility of a *sampling frame*. This is a list of all the individual members of our population, providing at least 'theoretical access' to each and every member of that population. The electoral register is an example of a sampling frame commonly used in social and market research, at least where surveys concern the adult population. For market researchers conducting telephone surveys, the phone directory acts as a convenient sampling frame. Possible examples in education would be a list of all the primary or secondary schools in a local authority or of the headteachers of those schools. However, this immediately demonstrates why probability sampling may be difficult or impossible if an appropriate sampling frame does not exist or is not available to the researcher. This will often be the case if the population and the proposed sample is of teachers or students, for example.

However, if an appropriate sampling frame is available then it, and one of the following probabilistic methods of sampling, should be used.

Random sampling

This is where the sample members are selected literally at random from the sampling frame. Before this can be done another important decision has to be taken: that is, how big the sample will be. This determines the *sampling fraction*, that is, what proportion of the population is to be selected in order to provide a sample of the desired size. The issue of sample size is discussed below, but for now we need to note that this is the point at which this decision has to be taken. Once the sampling fraction has been decided then we can proceed with the random selection.

While it is common to explain simple random sampling with examples such as 'picking names from a hat' or 'sticking a pin' in a list, in practice we need to be more thorough than this. Most commonly this involves the use of a table of random numbers or a random number generator such as can be found in statistical packages such as SPSS or the many examples available online.

Systematic sampling

This is very similar to random sampling, except that the sample members are selected systematically rather than randomly. Again, the sampling fraction has to be decided first and then names/units selected on a systematic basis. For example, if the sampling fraction is one in ten, then we select every tenth name from our list. Of course, the starting point, the first name or institution in our sample, must be chosen randomly from the sampling frame, otherwise 'Mr Aardvark' or the 'A1 Academy' would be included in every survey. Helpfully, most population lists are organised in some already random way, where there is less danger of this being related to the other characteristics of its members and so systematic sampling should not introduce any bias and affect the representativeness of the sample. However, it should always be checked that this is the case for a particular sampling frame which you intend to use in this way.

Stratified sampling

For some research questions there might be a reason to judge that some particular characteristic of your population is of such importance that you want to impose further control over how it is distributed or represented in your sample. For example, in a study carried out to compare female and male headteachers, we might feel that there was a risk that random or systematic sampling might not generate enough heads of one gender or the other to make possible the kind of analysis needed. This is especially likely to be the case where your sample is relatively small. In this case you should divide your sampling frame into two (that is, stratified by gender) before proceeding to draw separate random or systematic samples from each group.

In stratified sampling, then, we first re-organise the sampling frame into groups whose members have a common characteristic, and then sample separately from these groups. Of course, this pre-supposes that we have the information that will enable us to do this (that is, that we know whether each of the heads is male or female). If you do not, compromises may have to be made and you may have to settle for a non-probability method of sampling.

Stratified sampling is most likely to be used for one of two reasons which, interestingly, are opposed to one another. The first reason is where we are convinced that a particular variable is of such importance that we want to ensure that it is represented as it would be in the population. The second reason is the opposite one, where we want to ensure that in a certain respect the sample contains different proportions to what would be found in the population. For example, if we wished to compare the experiences of children with a relatively rare disability with those of the general population of children, then we would probably need to use different sampling fractions for the two groups. In this way we could ensure that the minority group is large enough within our sample to make that analysis possible. Another example is provided by Newcombe and McCormick (2001) in their study of teachers' participation in financial decision-making in schools. They distributed questionnaires to 141 government schools in New South Wales, a sample which was stratified by school type, that is, primary, secondary and schools for specific purposes, making it possible to compare results for these different types of school.

Cluster sampling

In order either to reduce time and costs, particularly if interviews are used, or to increase the researcher's control over administrative procedures, it can be helpful if the individuals or institutions in a sample are grouped together geographically. Cluster sampling achieves this. It entails a two-stage procedure. The first stage is to select a sample of what Denscombe (2003) refers to as 'naturally occurring clusters', for example geographical or administrative areas such as an LA. A school or organisation is another example of a naturally occurring cluster. The second stage is to select a final sample, for example schools from within an LA or teaching staff from within a school. Strictly speaking, random, systematic or stratified sampling should be used at both stages, but it is common for the first stage to use purposive or judgemental methods (see below) rather than randomly selecting the LA or school from a sampling frame.

Cluster sampling can also be helpful when a sampling frame for the relevant population is not readily available but can be obtained at the lower level. For example, a list of all schools in a country might not be readily available but a list of schools for each area might be more easily obtainable.

Cluster samples are very common in survey research in education. Wilson (2001), for example, surveyed special needs provision in 203 comprehensive schools in five Local Education Authorities (LEAs) in the North of England. Similarly, Wise (2001), studying middle managers, sent questionnaires to heads and middle managers in all 94 schools in three authorities in the Midlands.

Stage sampling

Stage sampling is simply an extension of cluster sampling, where more than two stages are involved. For example, to create a national sample of school students we might first sample geographical areas, then schools within those, then classes within those schools, and finally students within those classes.

Non-probability sampling

Where we do not have access to a sampling frame or where for practical reasons we are unable to or cannot contact all members of a given population, we are not able to use probability methods. In such cases, we need have recourse to *non-probability* methods of determining our research sample. There are a number of non-probability sampling techniques, the most commonly used examples of which are discussed below.

Convenience sampling

This method is sometimes also known as *accidental* or *opportunity sampling*. A convenience sample is one composed of members most easily available to the researcher who does not – and certainly should not – attempt to claim it as being representative of a wider population. Although frequently used in student and other small-scale research on the grounds of pragmatism, in practice convenience sampling should thus be avoided if at all possible if sound claims for generalisation are to be made. Where there really is no alternative, it is essential that as much information as possible is reported about the sample and how it was selected. Was it composed of the researcher's friends, colleagues or people who were geographically convenient, or teachers who were on a course, for example? What was the distribution within the sample of age, gender or other characteristics relevant to the study? And so on. Armed with this information, readers can form their own judgement as to how such factors may affect any conclusions that are drawn from the research, and the potential for generalising from sample data to a wider population.

Purposive or judgemental sampling

Purposive or judgemental sampling is an improvement on convenience sampling in that the researcher applies his/her experience to select cases which are – in the researcher's judgement – representative or typical. Again this strategy must be clearly explained and justified to the reader by the researcher. As already mentioned, this can be a reasonable approach in the course of cluster or stage sampling, particularly if the number of cases at an early stage is small. Blandford and Squire (2000: 23), for example, report a study of training provision for newly appointed heads, in which they approached a sample of LEAs which was 'representative of LEAs nationwide', geographically, in terms of 'whether [they are] county, metropolitan or London boroughs and in size'.

Quota sampling

Quota sampling attempts to impose greater control and can be seen as a non-probability equivalent of stratified sampling. As with stratified sampling, the first stage is to identify a particular variable of importance. Once the sample size has been determined, then quotas can be set for the numbers to be included in the final sample for each category of that variable. This might be of male and female headteachers or of schools of different types, for example. Usually, the researcher's intention here is to ensure that members of category groups are represented in the final sample in the same proportions as they would be in the population as a whole.

Quota sampling is frequently used in commercial research such as opinion polling. For example, an interviewer might be required to interview certain numbers of people from particular occupational groups. The interviewer would then use convenience sampling (knocking on doors or stopping people in the street) to identify relevant individuals and fill those quotas. Once a given quota is filled (the required number of professional people have been surveyed, for example), the researcher stops looking for further cases.

There is a lively debate within the research community as to the merits of quota sampling, with the battle lines mainly drawn up at the academic–commercial frontier (see, for example, Curtice and Sparrow, 1997; Marsh and Scarborough, 1990). What is beyond doubt, however, is that quota sampling is a definite improvement on convenience sampling.

Dimensional sampling

This is an extension of quota sampling, but where the quotas are set in relation to a combination of two or more variables. So rather than quotas being selected on the basis of (say) occupational group alone, an interviewer might be set a quota consisting of a pre-determined number for each possible combination of occupation, gender, age group and so on.

Snowball sampling

This technique can be used to generate a sample where potential sample members are particularly difficult or potentially dangerous to identify. Here, a researcher first has to identify and interview one or two people with relevant characteristics. Those people are then asked to identify others with the same characteristic whom the researcher could contact. They in turn would be asked to identify further sample members. In this way the sample is built up, like a rolling snowball.

Although examples are relatively rare in the field of educational research (it is more common in areas of social research such as studies of drug cultures or football hooliganism), Busher (2005: 141) describes how its use in a study of middle leaders' professional identities 'minimised ethical problems of talking with people about others without permission'.

Sample size

Almost always, one of the first questions a student researcher embarking on a survey asks is, 'How big should my sample be?' (By this they sometimes mean 'What size of sample will be acceptable to my examiners?'). Although there is no single, straightforward answer to this question, guidance can be given at several levels.

The first point is that while sample size does matter, of at least equal importance is the way that the sample is drawn. A small probability sample free of bias is preferable to a larger sample that is biased and unrepresentative or whose lack of bias cannot be demonstrated.

The next answer is that your sample should be as big as you can manage within the practical constraints and the resources available to you. In common sense terms, if your sample is well drawn, then the larger it is the more confidence you can have in generalising the results of your research.

Some writers on survey research rather arbitrarily suggest that 30 is the minimum acceptable size for any survey and this is generally acceptable for a small-scale, exploratory study. However, this also assumes that the intended statistical analysis of survey results will be simple. If the research questions entail making comparisons between sub-groups, then each of the groups must be large enough to give reasonable confidence in the findings. A study of gender differences for example, should – on the basis of this yardstick – include at least 30 males and 30 females. If age is also a factor, then this would require 30 participants of each gender in each age group, and so on. Thus the more complex the proposed analysis, the larger the study sample would need to be.

The final answer is a longer and more technical version of the statement that the larger the sample is, the more confidence we can have in generalising the findings. For this, we first need to imagine a situation where we draw a very large number of probability samples from a particular population. If we then selected a variable of particular interest (for this example, a continuous variable such as test scores) and calculated the mean on that variable for each of those samples and plotted those graphically, we would get the distribution shown in Figure 8.1. This is the familiar normal or bell-shaped curve.

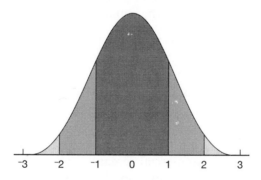

Figure 8.1 Hypothetical distribution of sample means

What this distribution shows is that we would obtain a large number of *sample means* that are close to the *population mean*, rather fewer numbers of sample means which are more distant from (above or below) the population mean, and a much smaller number of sample means at the extremes of the distribution which are very distant from the population mean. Just as a normal distribution of individual values can be described by the standard deviation, so can this distribution of means be described by a closely related statistic, the *standard error of the mean* (or simply 'standard error'), the formula for which is:

Standard deviation (SD) divided by the square root of n (i.e. the sample size)

In Figure 8.1, the numbers on the horizontal axis represent the distance from the mean in terms of the number of standard errors. Exactly as for the standard deviation in relation to the normal distribution of individual scores, we know the proportion of sample means which can be expected to fall within certain ranges, that is, two-thirds of the means will fall within one standard error either side of the population mean and 95 per cent of them will fall within two standard errors either side of the population mean. We now have moved a little closer to the answer to our original question, in that for a given result for which we know the standard deviation and the sample size, we can say that we are 95 per cent confident that the true population mean is within the range two standard errors either side of the sample mean (and this range is known as the 95 per cent *confidence interval* around the mean).

Where the variable of interest is categorical (for example gender, age group, school type) rather than continuous, we would report the result as a percentage or proportion rather than a mean (for example, 40 per cent of male voters interviewed say they will vote Labour in the next election compared with 37 per cent of females). Exactly comparable calculations are possible, except that the formula for the *standard error of a proportion* is:

Square root of (the proportion multiplied by one minus the proportion) divided by the square root of *n*

In theory, we can use these concepts to help us to decide in advance our desired sample size, in that we can decide on the level of uncertainty we are willing to live with, or what range of possible difference from the true population result we can tolerate. Provided we know the likely standard deviation or proportion for the population we can then use the above formulae to calculate the desired sample size. In reality, this is rarely done in educational research (mainly because the relevant information is not available in advance). It is more frequently encountered in commercial research, where a survey company may well say to a potential customer something like: 'Give me this much money and we will be able to carry out this many interviews and you will be able to be 95 per cent *confident* that the result we give you will be no more than this amount different from the figure for the total population,' or 'Give us this much more money and we will be able to carry out this larger number of interviews and provide a result which is 95 per cent *certain* to be within this smaller range of the population figure.'

What we *can* do in educational research, and certainly should do more frequently than we do, is make these calculations once we have our data. In this case we have to use the standard deviation (or proportion) from our sample as our best estimate of the population figure. We can then enter this, and our value for *n*, into the appropriate formula, calculate the standard error of the sample mean or proportion, and report the resultant confidence intervals for our results. In this way the researcher, and others interested in the findings, can see and evaluate the level of precision with which the results can be interpreted.

These concepts also relate very directly to those which underlie inferential statistical tests (see Chapter 19).

Response

So far, the discussion in the latter part of this chapter has focused on the intended sample of those to whom we wish to send our questionnaire or those we wish to interview. However, we must also consider our *achieved* sample, those who actually complete and return the questionnaire or agree to be (and are) interviewed. Obviously we hope that the number of those invited to respond will equal the number of those who do so (that is, that we obtain a 100 per cent *response rate*), but that will rarely be the case, especially with questionnaire surveys.

There is little point in our having taken great care to have drawn as large and representative a sample as possible if the actual number of respondents is small or if they form a very biased sub-group of the intended sample. Therefore, we must take every possible step to maximise our response rate. The first requirement, as always, is to ensure that our research instruments are of high quality, as clear, simple and easy to complete as possible and seen as relevant by potential respondents. Instructions to potential respondents must also be clear. The contents of a covering letter, or any other means of contacting potential respondents, are also important. Again this should be clear and engage the interest of the potential responder but the researcher should also use it to introduce himself/herself and the purpose of his/her research as well as describing the uses to which data will be put and any relevant information relating to confidentiality. Seemingly obvious, but frequently overlooked, is that instructions as to what to do with a completed questionnaire (for example, when and where to return it) should be on the instrument itself, not only in a covering letter which may (and frequently does) become separated from it and lost.

You should also consider what is the best time to carry out your fieldwork. For example do not expect a good response from primary teachers in English schools to a questionnaire sent to them during or close to an Ofsted inspection, at 'SATs' time or shortly before the end of term. Offering some kind of incentive to respond is an option, but a potentially risky one, with the possibility of 'skewing' the sample and should therefore be used with caution. If inducements are considered, the researcher needs to be confident that they would appeal equally to all respondents, such as an offer to provide participating headteachers with a summary of the findings of the study. These aspects and other research-based guidance on improving response rate are discussed more fully in Lewis-Beck (1994) and Kent (2001).

However hard we try, however, we will rarely achieve a response rate that approaches 100 per cent. Because of increasing pressures on schools and teachers, a 60 per cent response rate to a postal survey is now considered to be quite acceptable. However, with any response rate of less than 100 per cent there is still the possibility that respondents will be unrepresentative of our intended sample (and therefore of our population). Experience suggests that non-respondents may well be atypical in some way: teachers working in more pressured circumstances, individuals with more negative attitudes, students who are more frequently absent from school are just some of the possibilities.

It is therefore important to check, if possible, the characteristics of the achieved sample against those of known (and relevant to the study) characteristics of the intended sample or population. It goes without saying that it is necessary, therefore, to include in the survey questions about such features. Here is where longitudinal studies can have an advantage as they have the possibility of comparing the characteristics of those included and those omitted at one stage of the study using data from an earlier stage.

For more common cross-sectional studies this is not possible. However it is often the case that something can be known about the expected characteristics of the sample or population, even if this is only for one or two basic demographic variables such as gender, geographical distribution and/or type of school. These may be available from published national or regional statistics or from previous research, for example. Wherever possible, this should be explored and some simple checking analysis carried out. If this shows that your sample is close to representing what it was expected to represent, then you will have that much more confidence in any conclusions you draw from your survey. If the results of this analysis are more disappointing, at least you now know that and can be properly cautious in your discussion. Alternatively, if resources allow, you might consider a further reminder or some replacement sampling.

No researcher will be penalised for having had to accept the inevitable limitations and practical problems which arise in studying real life situations. What will be frowned upon is if you have not taken reasonable steps to avoid these as far as possible and can be shown to have failed to take sensible decisions; or if you do not recognise any limitations in your research; or if you do not take these into account in your discussion of your findings and any claims you may make as to their generalisability.

References

Blandford, S. and Squire, L. (2000) 'An evaluation of the Teacher Training Agency headteacher leadership and management programme (HEADLAMP)', *Educational Management and Administration*, 28 (1): 21–32.

Busher, H. (2005) 'Being a middle leader: exploring professional identities', *School Leadership and Management*, 25 (2): 137–153.

Cohen, L., Manion, L. and Morrison, K. (2000) *Research Methods in Education*. London: Routledge.

Curtice, J. and Sparrow, N. (1997) 'How accurate are traditional quota opinion polls?', *Journal of Market Research Society*. 39 (3): 433–448.

Dearden, L., McGranahan, L. and Sianesi, B. (2004) 'The role of credit constraints in educational choices: evidence from NCDS and BCS70', *Centre for the Economics of Education Working Paper*. London: LSE.

Denscombe, M. (2003) *The Good Research Guide*. Buckingham: Open University Press.

Fogelman, K. (1985) 'Exploiting longitudinal data: examples from the National Child Development Study', in Nicol, A.R. (ed.) *Longitudinal Studies in Child Psychology and Psychiatry*. Chichester: Wiley.

Harper, H. (2000) 'New college hierarchies? Towards an examination of organisational structures in further education in England and Wales', *Educational Management and Administration*, 28 (4): 433–435.

Hutton, P. (1990) *Survey Research for Managers: How to Use Surveys in Management Decision Making*. Basingstoke: Macmillan.

Kent, R. (2001) *Data Construction and Data Analysis for Survey Research*. London: Palgrave Macmillan.

Laurie, H., Smith, R. and Scott, L. (1999), 'Strategies for reducing nonresponse in a longitudinal panel survey', *Journal of Official Statistics*, 15 (2): 269–282.

Lewis-Beck, M. (ed.) (1994) 'Research practice', *International Handbooks of Quantitative Applications in the Social Sciences* (Volume 6). London: Sage.

Marsh, C. and Scarbrough, E. (1990) 'Testing nine hypotheses about quota sampling', *Journal of the Market Research Society*, 32 (4).

Martin, M., Mullis, I., Gonzalez, E. and Chrostowski, S. (2004) *TIMSS 2003 International Science Report: Findings from IEA's Trends in International Mathematics and Science Study at the Eighth and Fourth Grades*. Chestnut Hill, MA: Boston College.

Newcombe, B. and McCormick, J. (2001) 'Trust and teacher participation in school based financial decision making', *Educational Management and Administration*, 29 (2): 181–195.

Shepherd, P. (1993) 'Analysis of response bias', in Ferri, E. (ed.) *Life at 33: the Fifth Follow up of the National Child Development Study*. London: National Children's Bureau.

Wilson, M. (2001) 'Comprehensive school governance and special educational needs provision: policy, practice and future priorities', *Educational Management and Administration*, 29 (1): 49–62.

Wilson, V. and McPake, J. (2000) 'Managing change in a small Scottish primary school: is there a small school management style?', *Educational Management and Administration*, 28 (2): 119–132.

Wise, C. (2001) 'The monitoring role of the academic middle manager in secondary schools', *Educational Management and Administration*, 29 (3): 333–341.

Recommended reading

Cohen, L., Manion, L. and Morrison, K. (2000) *Research Methods in Education*. London: Routledge.

Denscombe, M. (2003) *The Good Research Guide*. Buckingham: Open University Press.

Lewis-Beck, M. (ed.) (1994) 'Research practice', *International Handbooks of Quantitative Applications in the Social Sciences* (Volume 6). London: Sage.

9

Case studies

Michael Bassey

Recently I heard an American educational researcher start a lecture by saying, 'There are three kinds of researcher: those that count things and those that don't.' She paused, we waited. She continued, 'I do not belong to the first kind'; laughter slowly moved around the hall. Her lecture was based on qualitative research. Case study is usually a form of qualitative research – and so doesn't involve counting!

Because this book is for educational managers and students I must make clear that I am writing about case study as a form of enquiry, as exploration of the unknown and not as a learning tool in the form that often features in management classes. It is, of course, true that cases as used in classes have arisen from systematic and thorough enquiry, but they are usually written up with pedagogic intentions rather than with research criteria in mind.

A prescriptive definition of research case study

Several years ago I had the opportunity of examining carefully the concept of case study as a research approach (Bassey, 1999), and I came to the conclusion that it needed pulling into shape! Figure 9.1 presents a definition that I believe gives a useful prescriptive account of what constitutes a worthwhile educational case study. Others provide different definitions: Yin (1994), Stake (1995) and Gillham (2000); see also Stake in Denzin and Lincoln (2000).

The terms in italics within Figure 9.1 inevitably entail value judgements being made by the researcher. It is worth elaborating on some of these and other terms contained in the statement the Figure makes.

An educational case study ...

'Educational' locates this definition in the field of educational research (including educational management research), as opposed to discipline research in educational settings. I define educational research as critical enquiry aimed at informing educational judgements and decisions in order to improve educational action, whereas discipline research in education I see as critical enquiry aimed at informing understandings of phenomena (in educational settings) which are pertinent to the discipline. (The term 'discipline' includes psychology, sociology, history, economics,

---

An educational case study is an empirical enquiry which is:

- conducted within a localised boundary of space and time (i.e. a singularity)
- into *interesting* aspects of an educational activity, or programme, or institution, or system
- mainly in its natural context and within an ethic of respect for persons
- in order to inform the judgements and decisions of practitioners or policy-makers
- or of theoreticians who are working to these ends, and
- such that sufficient data are collected for the researcher to be able:
    - (a) to explore *significant* features of the case
    - (b) to create *plausible* interpretations of what is found
    - (c) to test for the trustworthiness of these interpretations
    - (d) to construct a *worthwhile* argument or story
    - (e) to relate the argument or story to any relevant research in the literature
    - (f) to convey *convincingly* to an audience this argument or story
    - (g) to provide an audit trail by which other researchers may validate or challenge the findings, or construct alternative arguments

---

Figure 9.1   Prescriptive definition of research case study

philosophy, etc.) Educational research is more concerned with improving action through theoretical understanding, and discipline research with increasing theoretical knowledge of the discipline. The boundary between them is not clear-cut.

... an empirical enquiry ...
This means that the starting point is the collection of data – usually by asking questions, observing actions or extracting evidence from documents.

... conducted within a localised boundary of space and time ...
Most writers agree about this. When the report of the case study is written it focuses on a location and a defined period of time.

... (i.e., a singularity) ...
This is a term meaning that a particular set of events, or programme, institution, classroom, etc. is the focus of the case study research.

... into interesting aspects ...
Why spend time on it if the subject is not interesting? There should be something about the set of events, or programme, institution, classroom, etc. that is judged worth systematically describing to others, or there should be some feature or issue of it that deserves to be explored in order to try to understand what is happening.

... mainly in its natural context ...
This is one of the strengths of case study research, and again is something on which most writers agree. Case study research entails being where the action is, taking testimony from and observing the actors first hand.

... and within an ethic of respect for persons ...
Research bodies such as the British Educational Research Association (BERA) insist that all educational research should be conducted within an ethic of respect for persons (and of respect for truth and for democratic values). The closer one comes to the people being studied the more important it is to ensure that they are willing to be studied and that what they say or do is reported in such a way that it is not prejudicial to their best interests (see Chapter 5).

... in order to inform the judgements and decisions of practitioners or policy-makers ...
Case study is arduous and demanding of both researchers and researched. It should not be wasted on trivial pursuits but should aim to contribute to some aspect of what educationalists (in the widest sense) actually do.

... or of theoreticians who are working to these ends ...
We should not expect that all educational research will immediately inform the concerns of practitioners or policy-makers. It is essential that researchers also build scaffolds for other researchers to climb – with the hope that ultimately the climbers will be able to inform those who follow them. Case study research can contribute to this.

... in such a way that sufficient data are collected ...
Case study means that the researcher needs to collect sufficient data to allow him/her to explore features, create interpretations and test for trustworthiness. But 'sufficient' is a two-edged word meaning 'not too little, not too much'. There is no point in the case study researcher collecting more data than can be handled successfully in the time available – and that entails exercising considerable insight and judgement.

... to explore significant features of the case and to create plausible interpretations of what is found ...
It is only of limited value for a researcher to conclude 'if teachers do x then y may happen'. It is much better to go beyond this and try to discover why this may happen for this may contribute to a theoretical understanding that illuminates other events.

... to test for the trustworthiness of these interpretations ...
The critical approach should be ubiquitous in research. The question 'Does this really mean what we claim it means?' should always be in mind. Some tests of trustworthiness are given at the end of this chapter. In common with some other writers on case study I prefer the term 'trustworthiness' to the terms 'validity' and 'reliability' (for an elaboration of this concept see Lincoln and Guba (1985: 218)). 'Reliability' is an impractical concept for case study since by its nature a case study is a one-off event and therefore not open to exact replication.

... to relate the argument or story to any relevant research in the literature ...

If research is compared to a giant jigsaw puzzle then finding a new piece of the puzzle is of limited value unless it can be fitted into an area of the picture or at least stored with related pieces of the picture, ready to be slotted into it. The 'conceptual background' is an important section of most research papers, but the literature cited should be rigorously restricted to items judged pertinent to the enquiry.

... to construct a worthwhile argument or story and to convey convincingly to an audience this argument or story...

Unless research outcomes are expressed in a readable way for the intended audience they are likely to be ignored and the enterprise wasted. This is a particular problem for case study researchers for their accounts, in trying to do justice to their data, tend to be lengthy. Some answers to this are given later.

... to provide an audit trail by which other researchers may validate or challenge the findings, or construct alternative arguments

This idea is not widely practised today but I commend it. The audit trail is a flow chart of the data, and of its analysis and interpretation, that enables others to examine the evidence for the trustworthiness of the study and also enables them to exercise their own creativity in finding alternative interpretations. The idea is to invite a colleague to conduct an audit of one's research and to comment on its perceived trustworthiness.

Different end-points for research case study

The comedian Peter Cook, playing a clergyman in the pulpit, told how he left the railway station by 'the way you're meant to go in and was hailed by a railwayman, "Hey, mate! Where do you think you are going?" – or at least that was the gist of his remark.' He went on: 'But I was grateful to that man, for he put me in mind of the kind of question that I want to ask you, "Where do you think you are going?"' As researchers, you must ask yourselves the same question.

In my attempt to reconstruct the concept of case study (Bassey, 1999), I identified at least three different end-points (see Figure 9.2).

- Story-telling and picture-drawing case study
- Evaluative case study
- Theory-seeking/theory-testing case study linked to fuzzy general predictions

---

Figure 9.2 Three different end-points for case study research

Story-telling and picture-drawing case studies

Story-telling and picture-drawing case studies are both analytical accounts of educational events, projects, programmes or systems aimed at illuminating theory. Story-telling is predominantly a *narrative account* of the exploration and

145

analysis of the case, with a strong sense of a time line. For example, a story-telling case study might be an account of how a particular school responded over a period of time to the introduction of school development planning. Picture-drawing is predominantly a descriptive account, drawing together the results of the exploration and analysis of the case. For example, a picture-drawing case study might be an account of the system of school development planning operating in a particular school at a point in time. In both of these examples the research expectation would be that a case study attempted to contribute to theoretical ideas about school development planning. Often this entails the bringing together of a number of case studies, as will shortly be illustrated.

An example of a story-telling case study is one that I wrote recently about events that took place over ten years earlier: 'The Nottinghamshire staff development project 1985–1987' (Bassey, 1999: Ch. 8). It is a 21-page account that draws on the 250-page case record prepared at the time. Drawing on interviews, questionnaires, documents and transcripts of group discussions, it describes how the project started and what steps I took to find out what was happening in my role as an illuminative evaluator to the project. It shows how I tried to tease out the ideology of the project, then tested it (I later found that the project sponsors did not accept that that they had an ideology!). I interviewed people who were heavily involved in the project and others who only knew of it at second or third hand. Eventually I was able to describe the enthusiasm for it that the project generated in its key participants but also to show that the less people were involved in it the more they were inclined to treat it with cynicism. I finished this story-telling case study with this somewhat polemical statement:

> Perhaps the story has not ended yet. There are important messages for the national government ... classrooms are being seen as units of production and teachers as technicians carrying out tightly defined functions. I believe it is time that the banner be raised again to assert the essentiality of teachers being recognised as professionals, fundamentally working for the effective education of young people, and striving to enhance their practice through the shared process of structured reflective action. Only when they are free to exercise their own judgements and make their own decisions can they provide that enthusiasm, insight and enlightenment [that] young people need from their teachers if they are to grow up responding creatively and happily to a changing and challenging world. (Bassey, 1999: 115)

McMahon et al. (1997) provide an example of a picture-drawing case study:

> This is a study of a primary school in Bristol, a school which has a vibrant, exciting atmosphere, where pupils and teachers work hard and effectively. A school described by governors, parents and teachers as 'marvellous', 'absolutely brilliant', 'exciting', 'inviting' and about which the chair of gov-

ernors said 'it's all buzzing in the school now'. The classrooms and corridors are filled with displays of children's work, there is a school choir which has sung in Bristol Cathedral, children study the violin, participate in workshops with artists in residence, enter and win competitions, put on excellent, high-standard performances for their parents at Christmas, look after an area of woodland as part of an environmental project, enjoy and experience success with their academic work and above all are valued as individuals.

Teachers in schools like this can be justifiably proud of their work, but the achievements here are greater, since this is a school that can accurately be described as one which is succeeding against the odds. (1997: 271)

This case study is based on interviews with governors, headteacher, teachers and parents, observation and study of school documents. The case study is largely descriptive, but clearly, throughout the data collection, the researchers have kept asking the question: 'How has this school been transformed from one that was struggling?' They offer this explanation:

... hard work must be seen as a major explanatory variable. However, it is also important to note that this work and effort has had a clear focus and has been carefully planned by the headteacher in consultation with her staff. ... The headteacher has been able to build her staff into a strong team, help them develop a clear sense of direction and purpose, and together they have turned the school around. It is for these reasons that the school is succeeding against the odds. (1997: 280)

Theory-seeking and theory-testing case studies leading to fuzzy general predictions

This type of case study is best described by an example. MacGilchrist et al. (1997) carried out nine picture-drawing case studies in primary schools in England in the mid-1990s of systems of school development planning. They looked at questions such as: 'Who participates in preparing the plan?', 'Who acts on it?' and 'How is its success monitored?' Analysis of this data led them to ask further questions such as: 'Who has ownership of the plan, and how broad are its purposes?'. They were seeking a theoretical structure and they discovered that their findings could be interpreted in terms of four types of school development planning, which they termed the rhetorical plan, the singular plan, the co-operative plan and the corporate plan. Using their data they put to the test the 'assumption, made particularly by policy-makers, that school development planners (SDPs) will improve schools, [that] they are the answer to self-management and as such will make schools more effective'. We can categorise their work in the nine schools as a multi-site theory-testing case study. They expressed the outcome as what I have called a 'fuzzy prediction'. It is 'fuzzy' (Bassey, 2001)

147

because, instead of trying to state 'what works', it states 'what may work': in other words it has built in tentativeness or fuzziness (for an account of the concept of fuzziness in logical systems see Kosko, (1994)). MacGilchrist et al. said:

> This study … has shown that school development planning can be used as a school improvement strategy … Of the four types identified, only one [the corporate plan] was found to have a positive impact on student, teacher and school-wide improvements. (1997: 246)

Evaluative case studies

These are enquiries which set out to explore some educational programme, system, project or event in order to focus on its worthwhileness. The case may be tightly structured as an examination of the extent to which the programme's stated objectives have been achieved, or it may be illuminative in the phrase coined by Parlett and Hamilton (1977). It may be formative (in helping the development of the programme) or summative (in assessing it after the event). It draws on theoretical notions but is not necessarily intended to contribute to the development of theory – and in that sense is different from the other kinds of educational case study described above.

Multiple-site case studies

As noted, the study described above by MacGilchrist et al. (1997) illustrates the idea of multiple-site case studies. According to how the study is viewed this was either nine case studies in nine primary schools (each conducted along the same lines of enquiry into their development planning), or one case study into school development planning, carried out on nine sites. The distinction is, of course, unimportant. But the reason for the nine studies is very significant. These researchers were trying to say something significant about development planning and in order to do this they cast their net widely. As a result they came up with a four-fold typology. Perhaps they might have added to their typology had they studied more schools – but there is always a limit to what is possible. It is important to realise that in such a study there is an attempt to include as many varieties of practice as can be found, but no attempt to quantify them. If we wanted to know how prevalent these types of planning are, survey techniques would be needed. In this way sometimes case study and survey methods work in tandem, the case study informing the design of the survey.

Stages in conducting case study research

It is helpful to see the conduct of case study research as a stage-by-stage process (see Figure 9.3), but the reader must recognise that the procedures described here will only rarely be in complete accord with the processes of actual studies. Research is a creative activity and every enquiry has its own unique character.

Stage 1:	Identifying the research purpose
Stage 2:	Asking research questions
Stage 3:	Drawing up ethical guidelines
Stage 4:	Collecting and storing data
Stage 5:	Generating and testing analytical statements
Stage 6:	Interpreting or explaining the analytical statements
Stage 7:	Deciding on the outcome and writing the case report (publishing)

Figure 9.3 Possible stages in conducting case study

Stage 1: Identifying the research purpose

Going back to first principles, the purpose of research is trying to make a claim to knowledge, or wisdom, on the basis of systematic, creative and critical enquiry. It is about trying to discover something that was not known before and then communicating that finding to others. A helpful way of thinking about that 'something' is to see it as a research hypothesis to be tested, or as a research problem to be tackled, or as a research issue to be explored. Deciding initially on one of these provides a platform for asking research questions.

This is not a rigid classification. Often a research purpose can be expressed under more than one of these headings. Although one of the three may be judged to be the most suitable way of describing the research at a particular stage of enquiry, this may change and another of the three headings may be seen as a more apt way of describing the purpose of the research.

A *research hypothesis* is a tentative statement or conjecture that is in a form which can be tested. For example:

> That the introduction of performance management in this school will within three years have made a step-change in our examination results.

It enables clear research questions to be asked which should provide evidence that either supports the hypothesis or refutes it. The research purpose is to test the hypothesis.

A *research problem* identifies a difficulty which often can be expressed as a contradiction between what is happening and what someone would like to happen. For example:

> The introduction of performance management in this school is welcomed by the senior management team (SMT) as a means of raising standards in

examinations, but most staff believe it will damage senior/junior staff relationships and hence have a deleterious effect on results.

The popular idea that where there is a problem the job of the researcher is to
find a solution, is usually unrealistic. The research is more likely to formulate
and try out ways in which the problem may be better understood and so be alle-
viated or the difficulty reduced, and it is to this end that appropriate research
questions need to be asked.

A *research issue* is the least defined purpose of research. It describes an area
for enquiry where no problems or hypotheses have yet been clearly expressed
that can direct the enquiry. For example:

How will the introduction of performance management affect our school?

The research in this case will strive to focus the issue through asking pertinent
research questions. Later the research can be reformulated as a problem or a
hypothesis.

Early on in a research programme the question should be asked: 'What kind
of report is it envisaged will eventually be written?' Will it, for example, be a
story-telling or picture-drawing study, or an evaluative study, or a theory-seek-
ing/theory-testing study? The last of these obviously links with the idea of a
hypothesis, while story-telling, picture-drawing and evaluation tend to be linked
to either issues or problems.

As an example, consider an investigation pursuing the above research issue.
Suppose that it is refocused as an over-arching question:

What are the current perceptions of performance management of school staff?

This is the question that defines the claim to knowledge the enquiry is intended
to make when the first stage of the research is done, and hopefully will lead to
a more focused enquiry that endeavours to move the school forward. It is not a
research question in a technical sense because it does not set the agenda for data
collection and analysis. The end-point of this stage of the research is likely to be
a picture-drawing case study.

Stage 2: Asking research questions

Research questions drive enquiry. They should be formulated in a way that:

- sets the immediate agenda for research
- establishes how data are to be collected
- limits the boundaries of space and time within which it will operate
- facilitates the drawing up of ethical guidelines
- suggests how analysis can start

Thus, in terms of the above example, these might be posed as research questions:

- What documents have come into school that influence staff perceptions? (Collect documents and news cuttings.)
- What is the understanding and expectation of each member of the school management team (SMT) of performance management? (Conduct 10-minute interviews based on four main questions.)
- What is the understanding and expectation of a 10 per cent sample of non-SMT teaching staff of performance management? (Conduct 10-minute interviews based on the same four main questions.)

It will next be necessary, of course, to decide what the 'four main questions' are. Interview time is limited in recognition of the fact that everybody concerned is very busy and may well see the conduct of this research as unnecessary.

Stage 3: Drawing up ethical guidelines

Parallel to devising research questions should be the drawing up of ethical guidelines for the project. Ethical issues are discussed in Chapter 5. In the above example, the researcher and head (as senior member of the school) may agree the following guidelines:

- Interviews will not be tape-recorded but notes will be made and written up as brief reports. These will be shown to the interviewees as soon as possible after the events and will only be included in the case record in a form agreed by the interviewees, and with pseudonyms. Inclusion in the 'case record' (see below) will mean that the researcher may cite the evidence in the case report.
- The case report will require the agreement of the headteacher before it is made available to school staff.
- The case report will not be published outside the school unless permission is given by the headteacher and chair of governors.

Stage 4: Collecting and storing data

Case study research has no methods of data collection or of analysis that are unique to it. In other chapters some data-collecting methods are discussed in detail; here it is worth stating two rules which, although superficially obvious, are ones that from time to time we all fail to observe. First, be systematic in recording data by, for example, noting date and time and place of collection, and keeping back-up files. Secondly, do not collect more data than you have the time and energy to analyse. You may want to consider analysing data as they come in, rather than waiting until they are all collected.

As part of a systematic approach, it can be valuable to number each piece of data as it is stored, for ease of future reference. For example, each interview report may be given a reference number, with decimal points for answers to each of the key questions.

I commend the following terminology for data storage and data processing. The *archive* is the total collection of rough notes, tidied-up notes, draft reports and final reports. It needs a running index and probably resides in cardboard boxes or the drawer of a filing cabinet. The *case record* includes agreed interview transcripts and agreed observation reports, the final versions of analytical statements, the interpretive writings and the day-by-day journal of the research, and other documents. (It is a sub-set of the archive.) These are the papers, polished in format, that will eventually be approved for public access, but which are likely to be too voluminous for the sustained attention of all but the most dedicated reader. They are the researcher's source for the writing of the case report and are likely to be stored as a set of files on the researcher's computer. The *case report* – the end-point (perhaps one of several) of the case study – is written in one of the formats described earlier, drawing on the case record and citing it systematically as the source of data.

One essential feature of sound research is the application of a system for ensuring that in terms of data taken from people, only those which have been agreed in terms of the ethical guidelines are transferred from the archive to the case record.

The idea of *annotations* to data as they are stored can be helpful. Ideas often begin to develop during data handling and it is worthwhile having a systematic procedure for recording these changes – perhaps by using a different font on the computer.

It is helpful to keep on the computer a day-by-day journal of the researcher's activities – with entries showing who was seen, when, where and why, and recording when analytical work was done, etc.

Stage 5: Generating and testing analytical statements

Case study work usually produces a great deal of data and analysis is needed to condense everything collected into meaningful statements. These analytical statements need to be firmly based on the data and indeed may suggest the need for more specific data to be collected.

For example, a concise answer to the research question:

What is the understanding and expectation of a 10 per cent sample of non-SMT teaching staff of performance management?

will require careful re-reading of the interview notes, the formulation of draft statements (that is to say, hypotheses) and the systematic testing of these (and amendment where necessary) against the data. The outcome should be one or more statements which are in accord with the data.

When this has been done for the other research questions it may be appropriate to look for deeper analytical statements. They will arise from reading and reflecting on the first round of statements, and going back to the data: they may be stimulated by the annotations that have been made. For example, it could be that this analytical statement is posited:

In this school the less staff know about how performance management will operate the stronger are their objections to it.

The result of testing analytical statements is that some of them stand and some need modifying, while others lack verity and are rejected. Analysis and data testing is an iterative process which continues until the researcher feels confident that the analytical statements he/she produces are trustworthy.

It is quite possible that the first round of enquiry will stop at this point and the central purpose of the research be refocused. Thus, if the analytical statement above is thought to be trustworthy the next move should be a management imperative, such as:

Spend a training day briefing everybody about management performance.

In a large school this might be a useful outcome from a research case study – but we might hope that not too much time has been invested in producing it. What would be much more deserving of time would be a case study investigation into how performance management could enhance student achievements – an enquiry that might need research on a departmental basis.

Stage 6: Interpreting or explaining the analytical statements

This is where 'How?' and 'Why?' questions are brought to bear on the analytical statements in an attempt to provide understanding of the way things are. Interpretations tend to be associated with particular individuals or groups of people, while explanations tend to be attempts at expressing cause-and-effect relationships, within the boundary of the study.

Stage 7: Deciding on the outcome and writing the case report (publishing)

Before deciding that work on a case study is finished it is worth getting a colleague, as a critical friend, to conduct an audit; in other words, ask your colleague to read through the data and its analysis and judge whether your understanding of what has been found is reasonable.

It may be that publication amounts to no more than distributing a few sheets of report reproduced on a photocopier, or speaking about the case at a staff meeting. If your research seems to have wider implications it may be appropriate to submit it for publication in a printed journal; in this case it may be possible to link the case report in the form of a narrative story or descriptive picture with a fuzzy prediction of what may be found elsewhere.

Tests of probity

It is important for any form of research to be subject to tests of probity. In terms of the ethics of respect for truth and respect for persons, I find the 12 tests listed in Figure 9.4 helpful.

Tests of trustworthiness

1. Has there been prolonged engagement with data sources?
2. Has there been persistent observation of emerging issues?
3. Have data been adequately checked with their sources?
4. Has there been sufficient triangulation of data leading to analytical statements?
5. Has the working hypothesis, or evaluation, or emerging story been systematically tested against the analytical statements?
6. Has a critical friend tried to challenge your findings thoroughly?
7. Is the account of the research sufficiently detailed to give the reader confidence?
8. Does the case record provide an adequate audit trail?

Tests of respect for persons

1. Initially has permission been given to you by an appropriate manager to conduct the research in terms of the identification of an issue, problem, or hypothesis, in this particular setting?
2. What arrangements have been agreed for transferring the ownership of the record of utterances and actions to the researcher, thus enabling the latter to use them in compiling the case record?
3. What arrangements have been agreed for either identifying or concealing the contributing individuals and the particular setting of the research in the case report?
4. What arrangements have been agreed for giving permission to publish the case report and in what form?

Figure 9.4   Tests of probity in case study research

Envoi

Case study research into issues of educational leadership and management is vitally needed today because of the intense political scrutiny to which heads are subjected. For example, we need studies that highlight the impossible: cases where, however good the leader is, other factors prevent the national 'expected' level of achievement being reached (and so sacking the leader is both unjust and a stupid waste). We need case studies of good practice and bad, of the competent and the mediocre – not simply of the story-telling or picture-drawing kind, but theory-seeking/theory-testing studies which try to tease out why a situation is good, bad or mediocre. This is the contribution case study can make to educational leadership, which surveys cannot touch.

References

Bassey, M. (1999) *Case Study Research in Educational Settings*. Buckingham: Open University Press.

Bassey, M. (2001) 'A solution to the problem of generalisation in educational research: fuzzy prediction', *Oxford Review of Education*, 27 (1): 5–22.

Denzin, N.K. and Lincoln, Y.S. (eds) (2000) *Handbook of Qualitative Research* (2nd edn.). London: Sage.

Gillham, B. (2000) *Case Study Research Methods*. London: Continuum.

Kosko, B. (1994) *Fuzzy Thinking: The New Science of Fuzzy Logic*. London: HarperCollins.

Lincoln, Y.S. and Guba, E.G. (1985) *Naturalistic Inquiry*. Newbury Park, CA: Sage.

MacGilchrist, B., Mortimore, P., Savage, J. and Beresford, C. (1997) 'The impact of development planning in primary schools', in Preedy, M., Glatter, R. and Levačić, R. (eds) *Educational Management: Strategy, Quality and Resources*. Buckingham: Open University Press.

McMahon, A., Bishop, J., Carroll, R. and McInally, B. (1997) 'Fair Furlong Primary School', in Harris, A., Bennett, N. and Preedy, M. (eds) *Organisational Effectiveness and Improvement in Education*. Buckingham: Open University Press.

Parlett, M. and Hamilton, D. (1977) 'Evaluation as illumination: a new approach to the study of innovatory programmes', in Hamilton, D., Jenkins, D., King, C., McDonald, B. and Parlett, M. (eds) *Beyond the Numbers Game: A Reader in Educational Evaluation*. London: Macmillan.

Stake, R.E. (1995) *The Art of Case Study Research*. London: Sage.

Stake, R.E. (2000) 'Case studies', in Denzin, N.K. and Lincoln, Y.S. (eds) *Handbook of Qualitative Research* (2nd edn). London: Sage.

Yin, R.K. (1994) *Case Study Research*. London: Sage.

Recommended reading

Bassey, M. (1999) *Case Study Research in Educational Settings*. Buckingham: Open University Press.

Stake, R.E. (1995) *The Art of Case Study Research*. London: Sage.

Yin, R.K. (2003) *Case Study Research* (3rd edn). London: Sage.

Yin, R.K. (2005) *Introducing the World of Education: A Case Study Reader*. London: Sage.

10

Action research

Pamela Lomax

The linking of the terms 'action' and 'research' highlights the essential feature of action research: trying out ideas in practice as a means of improvement and as a means of increasing knowledge about educational management and leadership. Indeed, action research can be used to improve educational leadership and management, addressing issues raised in Chapter 1 of this book. For example, Kekale and Pirttila (2006: 251) show how participatory action research was used to develop: 'leadership and management, fluency and division of academic work, well-being, and the health of academic staff' at two universities. Some writers have argued that action research is about improving practice rather than producing knowledge (Elliott, 1991), while others say that action research is a means of creating 'living educational theories', that contribute individual epistemologies of practice, which taken together contribute to knowledge more generally (Whitehead, 1993). What is clear is that action research, although rigorous, is a very eclectic form of research. It builds upon educational practitioners' existing skills and experiences as reflective practitioners (Middlewood et al., 1999, see also Chapter 11 on practitioner research). It utilises many traditional research skills and most of the tools discussed in Part B of this book are used in action research.

I have adapted my preferred definition of action research from Carr and Kemmis (1986):

> Action research is a self-reflective, self-critical and critical enquiry undertaken by professionals to improve the rationality and justice of their own practices, their understanding of these practices and the wider contexts of practice.

This definition suggests the following approach to action research for educational practitioners, managers and leaders, that they:

- Are thoughtful and the enquiry intentional (self-reflective)
- Are willing to have their ideas challenged (self-critical)
- Will challenge existing knowledge and practice (critical)
- Start with open minds and not with prior knowledge of the results (enquiry)
- See themselves as educational professionals
- Seek to change practice in line with identified values (to improve)

- Are committed to effective practice (the rationality)
- Are committed to fairer practice (and justice)
- Are willing to change their current working practice if necessary (of their practices)
- Are willing to reframe their current knowledge if necessary (their understanding of these practices)
- Are willing to attempt to influence other managers, institutional practices and policies (the contexts in which they operate)

This is a big task and the most important advice for the novice action-researching educational practitioner or leader is to *Think small*. Put ambitious schemes on hold and identify a small aspect of practice as a beginning. It will grow.

This chapter is about establishing the principles of action research so that you can design your own enquiry to suit your particular aims and context. Action research is usually seen as a cyclical activity where you make a plan, carry it through, monitor what goes on, reflect on events critically (using the monitoring data) and move forward. This is an extremely simplistic idea and in my experience one that has never operated as smoothly as this description implies. However, the cycle of action research is generally thought to follow these stages:

1 The identification of an issue or problem area
2 Auditing the situation (reconnaissance)
3 Taking an action
4 Observing and monitoring the effects
5 Discussing and reflecting
6 Evaluating
7 Taking further action etc. leading to another 'round' of action research and moving the situation forward

In stages 2 and 4 and in subsequent rounds of auditing and monitoring those participating will make use of a range of research instruments and approaches that are appropriate to the issue of problem area identified. There are many publications which give practical guidance on 'how to do' action research. Two more recent publications that you might find useful are Koshy (2005) and McNiff and Whitehead (2005).

Establishing the principles of action research

It is important to be clear that educational action research is different from traditional positivistic educational research, because the latter was based on scientific premises that do not hold for action research or qualitative research. The most important difference between positivistic and action research is that in traditional research the researcher was required not to influence the situation being studied; in action research, the researcher intentionally sets out to change the situation being studied. This one difference means that the cultures of the two types of research activity are very different and, to some extent, aligns action research with the more critical approaches to research discussed in Chapters 2 and 3. It is important that researchers are comfortable with the culture of action research if they want to use it. It might be that researchers in some societies will find that action research is not for them. For example, there is a requirement to be clear about your value position because your values will be the yardsticks against which you can measure success. Another requirement is to draw upon a critical community (critical friends) to help move your thinking forward and this usually means exposing the more vulnerable sides of your practice as you deliberate and reflect on the best way forward. Both these requirements are incompatible with managerial requirements to meet targets and to compete in an educational marketplace. These requirements may also be more easily followed in specific cultural conditions such as the Western European and North American contexts (see Chapter 4 of this volume).

The following questions might be useful in deciding if a first project is manageable. If you are unable to answer these questions openly and honestly, you will probably need to select a different approach to your research.

Purpose
Action for improvement (to do with effectiveness and justice):

- Can I improve my practice so that it is more effective?
- Can I improve my understanding of this practice so as to make it more just?
- Can I use my knowledge and influence to improve the situation?

Focus
Participatory research (doing it oneself, on oneself):

- Can I take responsibility for my own action?
- Can I look objectively and critically at the part I play?
- Can I learn from my own practice and change if necessary?

Relations
Democratic (involving others as partners):

- Can I involve others in the action research process?
- Can I involve them in setting the agenda of the research and in interpreting the outcomes?
- Can I incorporate their (possibly different) perspectives into my explanation?

Method
Critical, rigorous and iterative:

- Can I monitor what is happening effectively?
- Can I collect rigorous data that provide evidence to support my claims about action?
- Can I make good professional judgements that will inform subsequent action?

Validation

Peer (testing outcomes with other professionals):

- Will the data provide evidence to support the claims?
- Will the data provide evidence that I have improved the practice?
- Can I convince my professional peers with my argument?

Action research by educational managers

I have drawn the following examples of action research from three educational leaders with whom I have worked in the UK. All the examples come from schools in the south of England, where the culture of education was conducive to the form of action research described in this chapter. The first two examples come from secondary schools and the third from a primary school. My purpose in describing this work is to show the centrality of the following ideas in the type of action research I am describing:

- Educational values
- Educational professionalism
- Reflection and critical community

Educational values and a deputy headteacher's management of staff development

> Good quality educational research for me is practitioner research. It is about me changing as a result of my research and striving to live my values more consistently in my practice as an educational manager. This means that I need to identify and recognise these values, and to face up to contradictions in my practice, acting to overcome them. (Evans quoted in Lomax et al., 1996: 10)

Moyra Evans is a successful educational leader. Action research was the means through which, as deputy headteacher of a large comprehensive school, she improved staff development, which was one of her main leadership responsibilities. She began by monitoring her weekly meetings as she supported a group of teachers who wanted to improve the exam results of children in a particular subject. She planned the meetings and the subjects to be addressed, recorded what happened, discussed her data with her critical friends and adapted her practice. In due course she could demonstrate that she had substantial and valid data about what had happened and how she had acted. She was able to offer some convincing explanations, drawing evidence from the data and refining her explanations as she shared her interpretations with critical audiences. She was able to develop theories about how to support teachers in school-based staff development and how to deal with the ethical issues that could arise (Evans, 1995).

I have used Evans's quotation to start this section because I think it gives a clue to the contribution that action research can make to the theory and practice of educational management and leadership. Her work highlights the importance of values in educational leadership (see, for example, Begley, 2003) as opposed to leadership in business and industry which will tend to be driven by market-related motives. Educators have a responsibility for their students' development that is different from the treatment of, for example, customers in the retail trade.

Evans's opening statement points to an action research that incorporates a value dimension in its theory and method. She is guided by a moral commitment to appropriate educational action rather than to solely technical solutions (Wildman, 1995). Values are qualities that provide meaning and purpose; they can be used as the explanatory principles for why people make the judgements they do. This is why the clarification of values takes a high priority in action research. Values are questioned, modified, clarified and sometimes changed as the research proceeds. Where this kind of critical engagement with values is not possible for personal or cultural reasons, action research is pointless and, if continued, the activity becomes a management tool for manipulating people rather than action research.

Moyra Evans's ideas about effective staff development changed drastically through her research. She changed her own practice as a school leader and was able to influence school policy and practice and teachers' expectations of staff development. One of the reasons why her understanding of the practice of staff development changed was that she was forced to reflect on her own values and how she put them into practice in her action. At the start of her research, Evans believed in the emancipatory potential of action research, yet it took some time for her to realise that some of the school's staff development initiatives were not emancipatory. Her action research led her to see this. At the end of her first year of supporting the staff development of teachers, she was confronted with some evaluation data that showed teachers' complicity in accepting the school's agenda for staff development even though they did not see this as improving their teaching. She realised that as a deputy head teacher, she had provided a hierarchical learning situation in a 'done to' model of in-service education in which the teachers felt no ownership. This was not what she had wanted to happen. She was clear about her values. She had wanted the teachers to be engaged in open access, self-identified, professional development rather than training to resolve needs identified elsewhere.

Her action altered radically from this point. She changed her model so that the professional development of teachers in her school was predicated on their perceived needs not those determined by her.

Evans's formula for success included a number of factors: teachers connecting their knowledge to the communities they teach in terms of content and relationships (Belenkey et al., 1986: 221); teachers being part of supportive networks; teachers empathising with other teachers' experiences in order to support them in their learning; teachers pushing the boundaries of what they know through the process of reframing (Schon, 1983: 140); teachers' excitement at seeing their students learning more effectively and being more successful; and teachers learning about themselves so they understand their own values and the forces that drive them to reflect and reconstruct their knowledge. The history of this action research and the part played by the university to support its work is well documented in Evans et al. (2000). The title of the paper, 'Closing the circle', makes the point that a successful action research community permeates the whole school and can include students.

At the beginning of this chapter I suggested that cultural difference is an important variable in achieving success through action research. Evans was clearly aware of the risk that she took in conducting her research. It involved a senior member of the school giving up her control over teachers' learning. Leaders in such schools are often seen as knowing the answers to problems, and to be responsible for directing teachers in pursuit of the solutions (Evans, 1997). This is a factor in Western European and North American cultures that needs to be overcome if action research is to flourish. Moyra Evans was able to change the culture of her school and so move it towards being the school it is today through an action research process that took five years initially and has been supported for another six years subsequently. Where action research has significant impact, it clearly takes time for the impact to be made.

I believe that it is possible for very different cultures and societies to adopt an action research approach. Hong Kong is a case in point. There, action research is supported by a number of initiatives at Department of Education and university level but has not taken root in schools in the way it has in the UK. Wai Shing Li et al. (1999), writing about the lack of action research in Hong Kong, suggest a number of factors at the professional level that militate against its adoption. These factors – the isolated culture of teaching, the 'deskilled' nature of teaching, and the dichotomy between theory and practice – work in a similar fashion in both Hong Kong and the UK. They are factors that discourage the open communication and discussion necessary for successful action research. Wai Shing Li et al. (1999) argue that:

> a special system with its own culture and characteristics survives and blossoms hindering the development of professionals, teacher reflectivity, action research, school improvement, educational innovation and democratisation of the workplace.

The reason given for this is the cultural heritage associated with paternalism (from both Chinese and colonial sources) that has led to a cluster of phenomena that is counter-productive to action research. Wai Shing Li et al. (1999) list these as the professional–bureaucratic divide, the tendency for administrators to know what's best for teachers and the practice of supervising to ensure standardisation. These factors exist also in the UK. It is arguable that it is global characteristics of education systems such as these that prevent action research in Hong Kong rather than more personal cultural values.

I maintain that educational values are not absolute qualities that necessarily remain unchanged. Clarifying personal educational values is crucial in Western Europe and North America today, because single prescribed ways of thinking and acting no longer exist. Clarifying personal educational values across cultures is even more important. It is one of the strengths of action research as a cross-cultural tool that the research starts with the researcher's own values. It is the task of the action researcher to clarify these educational values so that they can be used as clear yardsticks for measuring the success of the action. It is the responsibility of the action researcher's professional peers, people from the same cultural milieu, to judge whether the desired outcome is achieved.

Educational professionalism and a teacher-governor's management of teacher–governor relations

> … time for research is always limited, since the primary responsibilities of the action researcher are those of a working practitioner. … It is precisely for these reasons that I believe that those who engage in action research demonstrate the ultimate expression of professionalism. (Linter, 2001)

There has been a general trend in recent years in the UK for the autonomy of educational managers and leaders to be reduced as quality has become identified with bureaucratic procedures and institutional practices for monitoring the effectiveness of schools and colleges. Educational managers throughout the world will recognise this scenario. In the UK it has been associated with the changing role of the headteacher towards a more administrative or chief executive role, the prescriptions resulting from the national curriculum and assessment and the narrowing of the syllabus in teacher education.

Educational action research demands a critical approach, in which the leader is expected to challenge educationally inappropriate ends as well as inefficient means. I recognise that this is difficult in many contexts. In Hong Kong, for example, the Chinese community values conformity and hierarchy and individuals would expect to adapt their action to the community to which they belong (Wai Shing Li et al., 1999).

Teachers in the UK may feel that they have little control over the issues that concern them as professionals and there can be an apparent choice between passively implementing directives and being more innovative and adapting them to suit local conditions. Rod Linter is a good example of an educational leader who decided to be proactive when faced with what he saw as the damaging effects of too much change imposed on schools. He says he became a teacher-governor as a personal and political response to what he saw as the de-professionalisation of the teaching profession in the 1980s and 1990s.

Linter spent six years researching his practice. He used action research as an independent and critical form of enquiry to confront the value contradictions that he faced. He says that his thesis is an evidence-based, generative response, which is an authentic expression of his professionalism (Linter, 2001). At the start, his action research was aimed at influencing the school's governors who had been given increased powers over the school's practice by the recent legislation. He determined that governors needed to be better informed, more visible and active within the school if the new powers were to be used to the benefit of the school and in line with 'educational' rather than 'market' values. When he started his research, there was no interaction between governors and teachers and he determined to change this.

His success in generating meaningful interaction between staff and governors is reported in three action cycles. In the first cycle he persuaded individual governors to spend time in school and visit classrooms and observe lessons. He found that enabling governors to experience the daily workings of the school early in their term of office capitalised on their enthusiasm as new governors. The new governors also benefited because they could talk about their classroom experiences in the governors' meetings, where otherwise they would have remained silent.

A second cycle was the result of being asked to deliver school-based in-service training (INSET). Linter encouraged the governors to attend and even repeated the session for ten governors who could not attend the initial meeting. The INSET session was set up with the aim of getting the staff and governors to work together. Linter wanted to ensure that the governors were seen and saw themselves on the side of local practice; he wanted their support to interpret national policy so as to best fit the local context. The title of the session, 'Setting our own agenda', was intended to spell out the message that the development agenda was one for the whole school to decide and that staff and governors were partners in the enterprise.

His last cycle described his work chairing a working party that was set up by the headteacher to examine the nature of the changes that had taken place within the school over the previous five years and make practical recommendations that would bring about a better working ethos within the school. He determined to involve governors in this and set about designing and conducting a survey of teachers', students' and governors' views on the matter. This widened the scope of professional dialogue and secured a whole-school mandate for change. The working party process revealed a school that desired to learn and to seek change. It provided evidence that the separation of teachers and governors was historical and that the broad foundations for a collaborative learning culture that included school governors had been laid. Linter believes that the generative outcome of the three cycles of research enabled the school to undertake changes that would not have been possible at the beginning.

Rod Linter argued that researching one's practice is the ultimate expression of what it is to be professional. This is in line with those ideas that see action research as a social process and not simply a research method. I think his work demonstrates a new professionalism in education, which rests on a democratic knowledge-base that includes educators' theories, which have been generated through relevant experience and validated through systematic research (Lomax,

1999). This new professionalism is premised on a process of continuous professional development. It would be an evidence-based profession, but with an open mind about what could constitute evidence, recognising that evidence may reflect situational differences embodied in the different ways in which particular communities work. This view of professionalism and the role of action research has global application.

Reflection, critical community and an infant headteacher's attempt to make sense of her practice

> [We need to create a] 'collective professional confidence that can help teachers resist the tendency to become dependent on false scientific certainties ... by replacing them ... with the situated certainties of collective professional wisdom among particular communities of teachers'.
> (Hargreaves, 1995: 153)

Action research adds a self-conscious discipline to good reflective professional practice. There are two important aspects of this discipline. The first, an inward-looking dimension, puts emphasis on the researcher as a learner, committed to personal development through improving their understanding of their own practice (reflection). The second, an outward-looking dimension, puts emphasis on the researcher as a collaborator, actively seeking the validation of their practice and knowledge (reflexivity). Both elements depend on the fact that we are able to represent meaning in a concrete, objective form.

Margaret Follows was a headteacher of an infant school for ten years. Now no longer in post, she is engaged in an action research enquiry which uses her previous school experience as a focus for developing ideas about a fair(er) assessment. Her intention is to explore, critically, some of her own tacit knowledge by focusing on her past practice, which she represents in a fictionalised form. To do this she has involved professional colleagues to help her to deconstruct and reconstruct the past events so that they can learn from them together.

As part of her enquiry she constructed a story book, *All About Ourselves*, by Polly and Robert (Follows, 2000). The story book was based on the work of two children who had very different achievements, abilities, learning styles, personalities, interests and life experiences, and whose routes to learning and the implications for teaching would also have been different. The story book was based on data taken from: school learning and assessment policies; assessment records; children's personal portfolios of work; class teachers' formative assessment records; individual records of achievement and baseline assessment; curriculum plans; and annual and mid-term topic planners which provided a framework for teaching over time. Follows's aim was to provide a picture of the children's learning, development and attainment during the three-year period, 1994–7. The story book was a means of representing the concrete data to provide a picture of the whole child in a form that was in tune with the reality of infant classrooms; the story book was also her own construction, containing her tacit knowledge about infant education.

Because Follows was using action research to look at historical events, she needed to adapt the methodology to suit its purpose. She used what Van Manen (1995) has called retrospective reflection (done after the act), which is different to contemporaneous reflection (done during the act) and anticipatory reflection (done before the act). Van Manen argues that contemporaneous reflection or reflection in action is not possible because 'the active practice of teaching is too busy to be truly reflective' (1995: 35). Follows used a form of retrospective reflection called memory work that has been developed as a critical group activity to deconstruct events from the past in order to promote a better understanding of them (Hang, 1987; Lomax and Evans, 1996; Scratz and Scratz-Hadwich, 1995). Memory work enabled her to put in place the critical debate necessary to promote reflexivity, where the affirming or questioning response of others to our communicated meaning challenges us to see something else. In action research, critical community is encouraged through the formation of critical friendships and co-researching practices (Lomax, 1994a), and through the requirement that the claims emerging from the research must be critically validated against evidence, and that the research should go into the public domain.

Sharing action research with 'critical' others also demands a subtle use of representation. Follows used the story book as a representation of her past practice. It became the focus for a number of group sessions in which she hoped that others could help her to deconstruct and reconstruct her past practice *vis-à-vis* assessment. Following these sessions she re-edited the story book so that its final form emerged from the critical research process in which she was engaged. Before each session she thought long and hard about her purpose in presenting the material. When she presented the children's drawings and their emergent writing, she intended to present their learning and attainment through showing their developing language skills. In this way she believed that she was demonstrating the children's ongoing learning and development without reference to their attainment in national curriculum assessment. She wanted to generate discussion about the developmental and conceptual stages of learning, as seen through the drawings, and not about what she defined as the narrow and linear measurement of numerical scores.

In the first session she learned that she had not taken account of how much her considerable experience and knowledge of events had structured her understanding of the story book material. This tacit knowledge was not available to the other members of the group.

She decided to rewrite the story book and to try to clarify the essential knowledge that teachers possess about the children they teach. She was able to involve two teacher colleagues who had a personal knowledge of the research context. The two teachers had been members of the school staff when Follows was headteacher. They agreed to act as her research collaborators. They had first-hand knowledge of the two children, having been their class teachers for two out of the children's four years at the school. They could help Follows to explore this insider knowledge and its relation to the judgements that they had made about Polly's and Robert's work and the criteria and standards of assessment they had used at the time. They had three meetings. They used the technique of memory work to focus back together. They had concrete examples of the children's work before them and they addressed the questions, 'What, When, How and Why did we do this?' so that they could triangulate their memories.

Follows has used the results of these meetings in the most recent editing of the story book. Now it provides a fuller description and explanation of the children's learning, development and attainment in relation to curriculum planning, classroom organisation, the context of each activity related to each child's piece of work, assessment records and the possible next steps in the learning for each child. It includes a series of pictures and writing done by two children over a three-year period with captions written by her. Following each pair of pictures she has answered three questions about the children's work: 'What is there to see?' 'How best can we understand what we see?' and 'How can we put our understanding to good use?'. There is an introduction, which sets the context and provides background information about the children, and a conclusion which draws together the analysis provided after each picture. The footnotes that support this analysis show the evidential source of her conclusions, clearly distinguishing between objective data and constructed data. A more holistic picture is beginning to emerge.

I have included an account of Follows's research because it clearly demonstrates the importance of different forms of representation in supporting reflection and critical community. The more usual forms of representation used in action research have been through reflective journal writing or capturing action on video. The former has been used quite widely across different cultures. Moyra Evans used fictionalised story in order to share her perceptions of staff development with the teachers in a less threatening way than the use of video might have been. Most of the teachers at her school found this method acceptable and began writing fictionalised accounts themselves for the purpose of sharing with the group. Writing and discussing these fictionalised accounts frequently led to the teachers seeing connections that had previously been invisible to them. Rod Linter also used a more unusual form to represent his work in a series of 'rich' pictures. He says that the act of constructing the pictures revealed new connections within the data that were previously invisible to him and also enabled him to generate purposeful statements in which he could share his feelings with others. It facilitated an understanding of the painful and emotional conditions he had experienced and allowed an exploration of possibilities even in a humorous vein.

Eisner (1993, 1997) has argued that new forms of representation 'are rooted in an expanding conception of the nature of knowledge' and can lead to new ways of seeing things. He says they encourage empathy and recognition of the place of human feeling in understanding. They provide a sense of particularity that suggests authenticity and are evocative in that they encourage multiple interpretations. Finally, they support the exploitation of individual aptitudes that have tended to be ignored as research skills. New forms of representation may also be a way of encouraging cross-cultural ideas to flow more easily.

Conclusion

The new categories of scholarly activity must take the form of action research. What else could they be? They will not consist in laboratory experimentation or statistical analysis of variance, nor will they consist only or primarily in the reflective criticism and speculation familiar to the humanities. (Schon, 1995: 31)

I like the definition of action research provided by Carr and Kemmis (1986), in which they describe a self-reflective enquiry undertaken by practitioners to improve the rationality and justice of their educational practices, their understanding of these practices and the situations in which these practices occurred. I particularly like their emphasis on the social justice of practice and I think this parallels the emphasis that I have put on values. My dispute with them might be that they seem to imply that social justice is an absolute principle whereas I prefer the more tentative construction of working towards implementing personal and professional values.

Jack Whitehead is an exponent of the value of recognising the creative and critical capacities of each individual to create their own theories from within their own personal and professional perspectives. Alongside its theoretical implications, Whitehead's approach stresses the importance of sustaining enquiry by being open to the possibilities, which our values and life itself permits. This means valuing the humanity of others in one's relations with them (Whitehead, 1999a, 1999b). In this context he cites the writing of Fukuyama (1992), who wrote about the quality of valuing the humanity of the other (isothymia), and the destructive quality in which individuals seek to demonstrate that they are superior to others (megalothymia). Whitehead sees action research as a value-laden form of enquiry, which we use in giving some meaning and purpose to our lives as educators. In this sense the imagined solution, the practical outcome, the improved practice, the contribution to a better life, lead both methodology and theory (Whitehead, 1993).

Whitehead's ideas strongly support my view that research should be done by educational practitioners and leaders themselves. I like the way that Gurney (1989) argues that the researcher should be both innovator and implementer; the one who poses the questions and the one who investigates the solutions. I value this way of empowering professionals. This also relates to what I see as an ethical-professional dimension. I think educational research has to include in its doing an educational outcome; it has to address the issue of its own motives and explain what is meant by improvement in immediate professional terms (Lomax and Whitehead, 1998). This is one reason why I characterise educational research as insider research. It implies that the researcher will engage in a continuing critique of their own educational management values as part of the research process as answers are sought to the questions that educational leadership and management practices pose.

Being an insider to the research is crucially significant if one accepts the existence of 'situational' rather than 'scientific' certainty (Hargreaves, 1995). As insiders, we have the opportunity to transform our own understanding through self-reflective strategies that recognise other dimensions of the human condition besides the scientific, rational ones. This opens up the possibility of using moral, spiritual, political, aesthetic, emotional, affective or practical criteria. Follows's (2000) attempt to use her tacit knowledge of children's learning in order to identify a fair(er) form of assessment is an area that begs the use of criteria that can access the somatic, non-verbal quality of attention that is based on a recognition of kinship, which Heshusius (1994) called a participatory mode of consciousness.

I think research in educational leadership and management should be practical. I think that intervention in my own leadership and management practice to bring about improvement is extremely practical. This does not mean that my research is concerned merely with technical matters. I view practical research in terms of the practical ethic discussed by Adelman (1989), where educational purposes and means are addressed together making for informed, committed action (praxis). For me, practical does not exclude theoretical, but locates theoretical in a practical context of ongoing professional evaluation and action.

I want my research to be authentic so that other educational managers are able to recognise it for what it is and empathise with my underpinning values. I dislike deception and manipulation of others. I see my emphasis on the importance of co-researching rather than treating others as respondents or informants as related to my wish to empower others in the research relationship. I like to enable others to speak for themselves rather than interpreting their positions for them, although I am happy to facilitate their understanding where I can.

I think research should be rigorous. I think it is more difficult to work with 'subjective' data than with 'objective' data and therefore educational leadership and management research, with its emphasis on values and action, demands high-level research skills (Lomax, 1994b). This has important implications for the idea of validity, which is about being able to make a plausible case for one's research claims before an 'educated' audience of peers. But we can get too obsessed with the notion of validity and there is a danger in attempting to codify the grounds or criteria for validity too closely because we are likely to lose a sense of our own tentativeness. However, I have included in Table 10.1 some criteria for judging action research that you might like to apply to your own research; you may also look at *You and Your Action Research Project* (McNiff et al., 1996), a blow-by-blow guide to doing action research.

Table 10.1   Criteria for judging action research

Attribute	Outcome	Criteria for judging
Purpose	Action for improvement	• Have I improved my practice so that it is more effective? • Have I improved my understanding of this practice so that it is more just? • Have I used my knowledge and influence to improve the situation at local, institutional and policy levels?
Focus	Doing it oneself, on one's own practice	• Have I taken responsibility for my own action? • Have I looked objectively and critically at the part I played? • Have I learned from my own practice and made changes where necessary?
Relations	Democratic	• Have I incorporated others' perspectives on the action into my explanation? • Have I involved others in setting the agenda of the research and in interpreting the outcomes? • Have I shared ownership of the action research with others?
Aim	To generate theory	• Have I explained my own educational practice in terms of an evaluation of past practice and an intention to create an improvement, which is not yet in existence? • Have I described and explained my learning and educational development that is part of the process of answering the question? • Have I integrated my values with the theories of others as explanatory principles?
Method	Critical, iterative	• Have I monitored what was happening? • Have I found sound evidence to support my claims about action? • Have I made good professional judgements that will inform subsequent action?
Validation	Peer	• Have I tested the strength of my evidence and the validity of my judgements with other teachers and academic peers?
Audience	Professionals, policy-makers, users, academics.	• Have I influenced the situation?

Most important for me is that research should be holistic. As a teacher–educator investigating my own practice, I do not separate my intent to motivate my students from my intent to help them develop their technical competence, from my intent to help them refine their professional judgement. I value respect for the whole person, which I think means treating professional knowledge holistically and giving due weight to the work of practitioners engaged in research.

Finally, I believe that educational research should be influential. I want educators' voices to be heard and I want them to share their values and persuade others about the significance of their work.

References

Adelman, C. (1989) 'The practical ethic takes priority over methodology', in Carr, W. (ed.) *Quality in Teaching*. London: Falmer Press.

Begley, P. (2003) 'In pursuit of authentic school leadership practices', in Begley, P. and Johansson, O. (eds) *The Ethical Dimensions of School Leadership*. London, Kluwer Academic Publishers.

Belenkey, M.E., Clinchy, B.M., Goldberger, N.R. and Tarule, J.M. (1986) *Women's Ways of Knowing*. New York: Basic Books.

Carr, W. and Kemmis, S. (1986) *Becoming Critical: Education, Knowledge and Action Research*. Lewes: Falmer Press.

Eisner, E.W. (1993) 'Forms of understanding and the future of educational research', *Educational Researcher*, 22 (7): 5–11.

Eisner, E. (1997) 'The promises and perils of alternative forms of data representation', *Educational Researcher*, 24 (2): 4–10.

Elliott, J. (1991) *Action Research for Educational Change*. Milton Keynes: Open University Press.

Evans, M. (1995) 'An action research enquiry into reflection in action as part of my role as a deputy headteacher'. PhD thesis, Kingston: Kingston University.

Evans, M. (1997) 'Shifting the leadership focus from control to empowerment – a case study', *School Leadership and Management*, 17 (2): 273–283.

Evans, M., Lomax, P. and Morgan, H. (2000) 'Closing the circle: action research partnerships towards better learning and teaching in schools', *Cambridge Journal of Education*, 30 (3): 405–419.

Follows, M. (2000) 'Looking for a fair(er) assessment of children's learning, development and attainment', *CAKN Newsletter*, No. 2, June 2000.

Fukuyama, F. (1992) *The End of History and the Last Man*. London: Penguin.

Gurney, M. (1989) 'Implementer or innovator? A teacher's challenge to the restrictive paradigm of traditional research', in Lomax, E. (ed.) *The Management of Change*. Clevedon: Multi-Lingual Matters, pp. 13–28.

Hang, F. (1987) *Female Sexualisation: A Collective Work on Memory*. London: Verso.

Hargreaves, A. (1995) 'Beyond collaboration: critical teacher development in the post modern age', in Smyth, J. (ed.) *Critical Discourse on Teacher Development*. London: Cassell.

Heshusius, L. (1994) 'Freeing ourselves from objectivity: managing subjectivity or turning towards a participatory mode of consciousness', *Educational Researcher*, 23 (3): 15–22.

Kekale, J. and Pirttila, I. (2006) 'Participatory action research as a method for developing leadership and quality', *International Journal of Leadership in Education*, 9 (3): 251–268.

Koshy, V. (2005) *Action Research for Improving Practice: A Practical Guide*. London: Paul Chapman.

Linter, R. (2001) 'Research at the policy and practice interface: the experience of a teacher governor', PhD thesis, Kingston: Kingston University.

Lomax, P. (1994a) 'Action research for managing change', in Bennett, N., Glatter R. and Levačić, R. (eds) *Improving Educational Management through Research and Consultancy*. London: Paul Chapman with the Open University.

Lomax, P. (1994b) 'Standards, criteria and the problematic of action research', *Educational Action Research: An International Journal*, 2 (1): 113–125.

Lomax, P. (1999) 'Working together for educative community through research: towards evidence-based professionalism', *Research Intelligence*, 68: 11–16.

Lomax, P. and Evans, M. (1996) 'Working in partnership to implement teacher research', in Lomax, P. (ed.) *Quality Management in Education: Sustaining the Vision through Action Research*. London and New York: Routledge/Hyde.

Lomax, P. and Whitehead, J. (1998) 'The process of improving learning in schools and universities through developing research-based professionalism and a dialectic of collaboration in teaching and teacher education, 1977–1978', *Journal of In-Service Education*, 24 (3): 447–467.

Lomax, P., Whitehead, J. and Evans, M. (1996) 'Towards an epistemology of quality management practice', in Lomax, P. (ed.) *Quality Management in Education: Sustaining the Vision through Action Research*. London and New York: Routledge.

McNiff, J., Lomax, P. and Whitehead, J. (1996) *You and Your Action Research Project*. London and New York: Routledge/Hyde Publications.

McNiff, J. and Whitehead, J. (2005) *Action Research for Teachers: A Practical Guide*. London: David Fulton Publishers

Middlewood, D., Coleman, M. and Lumby, J. (1999) *Practitioner Research in Education*. London: Paul Chapman.

Schon, D.A. (1983) *The Reflective Practitioner: How Professionals Think in Action*. New York: Basic Books.

Schon, D.A. (1995) 'The new scholarship requires a new epistemology', *Change*, November/December 1995.

Scratz, M. and Scratz-Hadwich, B. (1995) 'Collective memory work: the self as a re/source for re/search', in Scratz, M. and Walker, R. (eds) *Research as Social Change*. London: Routledge.

Van Manen, M. (1995) 'On the epistemology of reflective practice', *Teachers and Teaching: Theory and Practice*, 1 (1): 33–50.

Wai Shing Li, Wai Ming Yu, Tak Shing Lam and Ping Kwan Fok (1999) 'The lack of action research: the case for Hong Kong', *Educational Action Research Journal*, 7 (1): 33–49.

Whitehead, J. (1993) *The Growth of Educational Knowledge*. Bournemouth: Hyde Publications.

Whitehead, J. (1999a) 'Educative relations in a new era', *Curriculum Studies*, 7 (1): 73–90.

Whitehead, J. (1999b) 'How do I help you to improve your learning? Spiritual, aesthetic and ethical contradictions in my discipline of education', in 'My discipline of education'. PhD thesis, University of Bath. See also the Living Theory section of www.actionresearch.net

Wildman, P. (1995) 'Research by looking backwards: reflective praxis as an action research model', *ARCS Newsletter*, 13 (1): 20–38.

Recommended Reading

Koshy, V. (2005) *Action Research for Improving Practice: A Practical Guide*. London: Paul Chapman.

Lomax, P. (ed.) (1996) *Quality Management in Education: Sustaining the Vision through Action Research*. London and New York: Routledge.

McNiff, J. and Whitehead, J. (2005) *Action Research for Teachers: A Practical Guide*. London: David Fulton Publishers.

Middlewood, D., Coleman, M. and Lumby, J. (1999) *Practitioner Research in Education*. London: Paul Chapman.

11

Practitioner research and leadership: the key to school improvement

David Frost

Practitioner research of one sort or another has an increasing band of devotees. Since the mid-1970s in the UK, it has been championed enthusiastically by the university schools of education through their award-bearing CPD programmes for teachers. Accounts of these activities indicate a flourishing of a variety of academic programmes which seek to support teacher and school development (see, for example, Dadds, 1995; Frost et al., 2000; Handscomb and MacBeath, 2004; Middlewood et al., 1999). More recently practitioner research has been promoted by the National College for School Leadership through its Networked Learning Communities initiative (Dadds, 2004; Street and Temperley, 2005) reflecting the recognition that it has significant potential to contribute to school improvement. It is perhaps somewhat paradoxical however, that even within the context of institutional improvement, the links between practitioner research and educational leadership have been underplayed. I want to argue here that it is not just that practitioner research can be used to improve the practice of leadership, but that practitioner research and leadership are really two sides of the same coin and they are both vital dimensions of the process of improving schools.

So what does practitioner research have to offer? The large number of Masters dissertations to be found in university education departments' libraries testifies to the fact that practitioner research can be life-changing for those who engage in it. The following comments made by a graduate of a practitioner research based MEd. are not untypical.

> It's completely changed the way I think about my teaching, the way I approach my teaching, the way I look at the kids, the way I look at their learning ... I realise now that I don't think the same about anything. I don't even think the same about the way I think about things. And I think that the change has been that radical, very very fundamental, ... I don't think about anything at school the same any more. I think about things in a totally different way. (quoted in Frost and Durrant, 2002: 152)

The opportunity to engage in research as part of a Masters degree is highly valued because, as illustrated above, it involves intense reflection which is something that is normally squeezed out by the relentless pressure of teaching and managing schools. Engaging in research can also enable individuals to become more confident and articulate in discussing educational issues. This tends to give them a stronger voice in the running of their schools and an enhanced sense of professionalism. Perhaps more obviously relevant to school improvement is the suggestion that engaging in research can also lead to improvements in classroom practice. This is, of course, one of the defining characteristics of the action research tradition (as described in Chapter 10 of this volume) which occupies a particular place within the more generic category of practitioner research.

> The fundamental aim of action research is to improve practice rather than to produce knowledge. The production and utilisation of knowledge is subordinate to and conditioned by this fundamental aim. (Elliott, 1991: 49)

The emphasis on the commitment to action for improvement is not necessarily to the fore in other forms of practitioner research and even where accounts draw on the action research literature it is sometimes evident that the impact of the project in question is limited to the professional development of the individuals directly involved. Where this is the case improvements tend to be small-scale and unsustainable because colleagues have not been sufficiently involved in the process and the innovations have not become embedded in the fabric of the school. Arguably, this problem can be attributed to what Elliott called 'academic imperialism':

> Action research and the 'teachers as researchers' movement are enthusiastically promoted in academia. But the question is: are the academics transforming the methodology of teacher-based educational inquiry into a form which enables them to manipulate and control teachers' thinking in order to reproduce the central assumptions which have underpinned a contemplative academic culture detached from the practices of everyday life? (Elliot, 1991: 14)

The argument hinges on the question of who is the audience for the research. In her important review of action research for the British Educational Research Association, Bridget Somekh drew attention to the problem that arises when the audience for teachers' case studies is the university rather than the school (Somekh, 1995). This can have a distorting effect because the discourse that the practitioners are enticed into is heavily influenced by academics who are not themselves practitioner researchers.

In the academic world, judgements about validity tend to be derived from models of research that are not concerned primarily with immediate improvement, but with generalisations. In spite of the broadening of methodological approaches in the social sciences, so called 'positivistic' ways of thinking about research tend to permeate the literature. Positivism is influenced by the world of the physical sciences where it is assumed that the world has an objective reality in which patterns, trends and causal relationships can be observed or otherwise discovered (see Carr and Kemmis, 1986 for a detailed account). Such revelations can allow us to predict the effect of this or that action. This view of research has some relevance where the research is carried out by professional researchers with the aim of producing generalisable claims that contribute to our publicly accessible knowledge base (Bassey, 1999), but it is unhelpful for practitioner researchers.

In contrast, the action research literature emphasises the complexity and uniqueness of the contexts in which educational practice takes place. It promotes the ethical commitment to the improvement of that practice which is immediate, direct and integrated into the process of inquiry (Somekh, 1995). The action research literature almost uniformly puts forward a model in which there is a cycle such as the one represented in Figure 11.1.

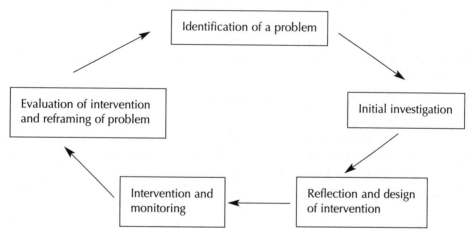

Figure 11.1   Action Research model

This model clearly has the potential to support change and improvement, which is why it is popular. However, in practice a great deal of practitioner research, while making a token nod towards the action research literature, proceeds along quite different lines. I suggest that the obstacle to school improvement in these cases is a mindset that we might call 'the QIFI mindset', where QIFI stands for Question, Inquiry, Findings and Implementation. In this way of thinking the teacher identifies an interesting *question*, carries out *inquiry*, produces *findings* and then reports these to the leadership team with the expectation that the head (or some other senior person) will take responsibility for *implementation*. Let me try to explain what is wrong with this way of thinking in the context of practitioner research.

What's wrong with questions?

In the QIFI mindset research *questions* come first. For example, researchers at the Scottish Council for Educational Research are very clear about this.

> Research questions are the vital first step in any research. They guide you towards the kinds of information you need and the ways you should collect the information. They also help you to analyse the information you have collected. (Lewis and Munn, 1997: 7)

While this may make good sense to an academic researcher, it is quite misleading for the practitioner researcher who is likely to be more interested in school improvement. Rather than posing questions out of academic curiosity the practitioner researcher begins with a purpose or concern that arises in the normal flow of professional reflection, deliberation and discussion. This is most likely to be a pragmatic one that centres on the effectiveness of a practice/strategy or the fairness/justice of a situation. It may be, for example, a concern to:

- Develop a particular aspect of practice
- Develop a culture conducive to learning
- Raise standards of attainment for students currently performing below predicted levels

The title of Lewis and Munn's pamphlet 'So You Want to Do Research?' suggests the idea of research as something undertaken merely out of interest or for the purposes of achieving a Masters degree, but, if we are truly seeking to improve practice, we need to focus on priorities for improvement and these are a matter of institutional deliberation. Pursuing a part-time Masters degree carries with it a pressure to identify a topic or question that makes sense to the academic supervisor. Understandably, the desire to succeed in the degree may mean that the teacher concerned seeks first to satisfy the supervisor by identifying what seems to them to be an interesting question. This is perhaps following the line of least resistance; more challenging, perhaps, is the identification of a professional concern or purpose. This almost certainly demands that we engage with the rather tricky business of consultation and negotiation with colleagues and other interested parties. Like most organisations, schools are full of complicated relationships, power struggles and patterns of vested interest (Hoyle, 1986, 1999) so anyone wishing to initiate a process of inquiry and development will have to exercise skilful leadership.

The first task then is to work with the structures and processes of the school as an organisation to secure sufficient support for taking action to examine an aspect of practice or a problem. Having achieved a mandate for addressing a concern there comes the challenge of working with colleagues to clarify the issues and questions; these are bound to be contentious. For example, let us suppose that there is sufficient agreement on there being scope for developing the transition from primary to secondary school. For one colleague the question might be: 'How can we ensure that the primary teachers are preparing the pupils for entry into Year 7?'. This question implies that the root of the problem is in the practice of colleagues in the primary schools. If those colleagues were to be consulted they might well want to pose an alternative question such as: 'How can we enable Year 7 form tutors to play a more effective role in supporting new entrants?'. For any Year 7 tutor involved in framing this agenda, the most important question might be: 'How can subject teachers personalise learning so as to reflect the different levels of attainment of new entrants?'. These are all interesting questions but they are closely related to vested interests of the parties concerned and it is the exploration of the tensions between these questions that is necessary to clarify how best to address the concern. The key task here therefore is not to decide on the best question, but to manage the discussion between interested parties so that light can be shed on as many aspects of the concern as possible.

What's wrong with inquiry?

When approaching systematic *inquiry* for the first time practitioners often assume that some kind of questionnaire-based survey is a sound inquiry strategy. For novices the strategy offers the false promise of objectivity. Of course, if done well, it does have the potential to provide fairly reliable data that can reveal patterns of frequency and prevalence. There is no doubt that sometimes this can be useful for school improvement purposes – for example if we want to know students' perceptions about the school as a safe environment for learning or how much time members of staff devote to their various professional duties and tasks. The problem is that the questionnaire is often used inappropriately when what is really needed is deeper understanding and a rich portrayal of what is happening in the classroom rather than superficial data about a whole population. So while it may be helpful, for example, for the senior leadership team to know that 37 per cent of students in the school have felt unsafe at school during the past year, what is really needed is a sense of what a lack of safety feels like, what makes students feel unsafe and what seems to help to combat this feeling. This sort of insight is more likely to be achieved through interviews, focus group discussions and students' logs.

It may be that one of the reasons that questionnaires are popular is that they do not involve any interpersonal challenges. The researcher in this case is removed from the situation; questionnaires can be distributed, completed anonymously, and analysed in a mechanical way (Durrant and Holden, 2006), whereas, interviews and group discussions make personal demands on the person conducting the inquiry. Most of us will find it easier to drop copies of a questionnaire in our colleagues' pigeon-holes than to arrange to sit down with one or more of them to discuss what might turn out to be complex and difficult issues. So, as all the research literature emphasises, it is really important to choose a data-gathering technique that matches the sort of evidence we need, and to think in advance about how the data might be analysed. However, to emphasise these two points can lead to overlooking the aspect of the process that is of crucial importance for school improvement. This is the strategic dimension.

Strategic inquiry

In order to illustrate the nature of strategic inquiry I want now to contrast two alternative approaches to practitioner research. Both approaches may well be seen as valid, but one is more likely to lead to school improvement.

(A) Inquiry for research purposes

Harminder has a school-wide role supporting literacy. She was pursuing a part-time MEd. degree and chose for the focus of her research the technique of teachers modelling writing for students. She wanted to know what teachers were currently doing, how effective this is and what understanding they had of the issues and techniques.

She arranged a series of lesson observations in which teachers intended to model the writing they expected. Her observation focused on a couple of key questions. How did the teacher model the writing task? How did the pupils respond?

After each lesson, Harminder briefly interviewed a small group of pupils to ask them how helpful they found the teachers' modelling techniques. This data enabled Harminder to categorise the various techniques used by teachers. She also drew out of the data a number of issues such as the variance in teachers' ability to talk to the pupils about their own uncertainty and their own thought processes when they write themselves. The data from the small groups of pupils were used to evaluate the various techniques observed. Harminder had tape-recorded the interviews – she listened to the tapes and made a list of positive and negative points.

Harminder then wrote a summary of what good modelling of writing practice looks like and included this in a report to the headteacher. The report included recommendations for whole school implementation.

In Vignette A, Harminder has evaluated a range of practice and has informed herself about the issues, but she has left the business of implementing change to the headteacher. An alternative approach is characterised in Vignette B below.

(B) Inquiry for development purposes

In order to support the development of literacy in the school Harminder wanted to help colleagues develop techniques for modelling writing in their subject areas. She started by consulting the deputy head to identify an opportunity to seek the collaboration of colleagues. She made a presentation in 'staff briefing' about the value of teachers modelling writing tasks and invited all staff to let her know if they would like to collaborate with her in a small-scale project to share and develop practice.

Several colleagues volunteered to participate so Harminder spoke to the deputy head about arranging for these teachers to be available for an hour and a half session during the day. This involved using some supply cover and asking a few teachers to give up a free period. At the meeting, Harminder presented a demonstration of how a writing task could be modelled by the teacher. This involved actually writing on the overhead projector and verbalising the decisions and thought processes involved. Colleagues were asked to share any good techniques they were already using and Harminder made notes. She proposed that they write brief descriptions of a range of techniques and then arrange to try out some of these. Members of the group would observe each other doing this in order to evaluate them in use.

After the meeting Harminder typed up her notes – she described four different techniques and then listed the issues that were mentioned in the meeting. She also suggested a pairing for the classroom observations and produced an observation schedule which indicated how colleagues would record what they saw. Again she consulted the deputy head to get his help in arranging the observations.

The group agreed to meet again after having carried out one observation. The observation records had been typed up and were copied for everyone in the group. There was a very animated discussion which led to more techniques being identified and the ones used already being refined. A range of 'dos and don'ts' was also agreed.

Following this second meeting, Harminder produced a guidance leaflet for the whole staff. It was called 'Techniques for modelling writing in your subject'. She sent a draft to members of her group and asked for critical comments. A corrected version was presented to the whole staff in the monthly 'Learning Forum'.

In Vignette B, Harminder has achieved a lot more than she did in Vignette A. She was clear about her school improvement goals, sought support from the senior leadership team and had a clear mandate to act. Her project began to have impact from the very start because the issue was brought to the attention of the whole staff. Subsequent collaboration ensured that several teachers' practice would be developed in the course of the project. In addition, it is far more likely that the outcomes of the project would be regarded as valid by colleagues because they had arisen from the work of a team. The impact of the project was widened through the presentation of a guidance leaflet.

In Vignette A, we could say that Harminder carried out a research project, whereas in Vignette B we could say that Harminder led a development process. If we were drawing up an action plan for mere inquiry we would want to specify such things as questions and data-gathering techniques, but in a *development process* we would be thinking more strategically about ways to involve colleagues in the enterprise. Below is a list of some of the possible elements in such an action plan.

Elements in the process of development

Consulting colleagues
Sounding out, asking advice, seeking permission, reassuring colleagues, testing out ideas, finding out what has happened before, establishing trust, etc.

Having discussions with colleagues
Clarification of the problem, identifying the issues, reviewing practice, joint planning, agreeing priorities, exploring others' understandings, interpreting data together, etc.

Engaging in systematic reflection
Keeping a diary, thinking it through, reflecting with a mentor (see Consulting colleagues), etc.

Reading
Searching for accounts of similar projects, exploring the research literature, looking up government advice (DfES, QCA, BECTA websites for example), reading relevant internal documents, etc.

Data-gathering
Observing, interviewing, multiple diaries, focus groups, listening to group activities, analysing pupils' work, reviewing documentation, auditing, surveying, etc.

Networking
Visiting other departments, visiting other schools, emailing network members, emailing individuals discovered through reading, etc.

Training colleagues
Running a workshop, providing coaching, arranging mutual observation, making presentations to staff, distributing guidelines, etc.

Joint planning
Planning in a team, making materials together, designing a data-gathering exercise, etc.

Trialling/experimenting
Trying out new classroom activities, experimenting with a new teaching technique, focusing on a particular aspect of classroom activity, etc.

I suggest that it is the optimum combination of such activities together with sensitive and skilful leadership that is most likely to have the maximum beneficial impact on professional practice. This means that, rather than ask teachers and school leaders to become practitioner researchers we might do better to enable them to develop the skills of project management.

What's wrong with findings?

In the QIFI mindset the posing of questions is followed by a process of inquiry which in turn reveals *findings*. This is a curious word. It suggests that there are truths that are somehow just lying there waiting to be revealed. This is a fallacy that has crept into the world of practitioner research on the back of scientific thinking (Carr and Kemmis, 1986). It assumes that the researcher's purpose is to reveal predictable patterns – if we do this sort of thing, that sort of thing will be the result. This way of thinking simply does not apply when we are investigating cases such as classrooms and schools. Patterns might be reliably revealed if we were looking at many classrooms in many schools, taking full account of variables such as the context of the schools and the social and economic background of the pupils, but the practitioner researcher is invariably looking at just one school, one year group or one classroom. The reality is that the outcomes of practitioner research are context-specific and subject to continuous interpretation. The evidence we generate can help us to justify our next steps but such choices have to be provisional.

In any case, if school improvement is our goal, the outcomes of practitioner research need to be a report of actual changes to professional practice together with an account of the development process employed to bring such changes about. Insights about obstacles and issues faced along the way will help colleagues to learn from such accounts and wisdom about innovation can be accumulated.

Another problem with *findings* is that any insights or evaluations that arise from school-based inquiry are inevitably someone's interpretations and, because the inquiry is conducted within an institution with its particular social relationships and structures, such interpretations are bound to be contentious. Some will recognise them as corresponding with their own professional perspective and judgement and some will remain sceptical. So it is pointless to try to claim an overarching validity that sets aside the social relationships of the institution and the multifarious judgements of the professionals within it. It is far better, I suggest, to embrace this institutional reality and draw colleagues into debate about the implications of the evidence.

What's wrong with implementation?

The word *implementation* suggests that a practice is predetermined, designed and fully formed so that all that remains is the faithful performance which can be evaluated against standards. It is a word that sits comfortably alongside 'delivery' and 'roll-out', being part of the McProfessionalism school of thought.

In Vignette A above, Harminder had completely ducked the responsibility of leadership. She had presented her conclusions and expected other people to implement change, which is to say that she believed that it was not her responsibility to provide leadership – that is what the senior leadership team would do. I suspect that this is a commonly held expectation and it is quite unrealistic of course. In spite of all the talk about 'super-heads' and the like, real headteachers know that practice is not improved by senior leadership diktats based on the findings of a teacher's research project. Rather, change comes about via carefully orchestrated deliberation and working with the organisational structures of the school (Gronn, 2003).

In Vignette B, Harminder has embraced the challenge of teacher leadership. This does not depend on a formal position of responsibility within the hierarchy of the school, but is based on the conviction of the individual and their willingness to work collaboratively to move practice forward. Of course, it also depends on the sensitivity of senior leadership to be able to facilitate and encourage such distributed leadership (Spillane, 2006; Spillane et al., 2001). The view of distributed leadership that is operational here is not limited to 'middle leadership' or 'emergent leadership'; it assumes a more inclusive type of teacher leadership. I have argued elsewhere that all teachers can participate in the leadership of learning-centred development work which has three essentially inter-related dimensions, as in Figure 11.2.

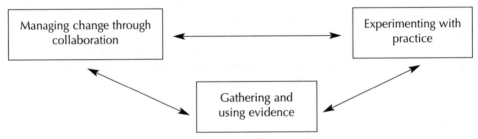

Figure 11.2 The leadership of learning-centered development work (Frost and Durrant, 2003)

If it is school improvement that we are seeking, we have to create organisational cultures within which all members of the school community can contribute to the sort of process represented in Figure 11.2. Inquiry (evidence-gathering, etc.) goes hand-in-hand with practical, classroom-based innovation within a framework of collaboration. In this model, the concept of implementation is redundant. Rather, we see practice being developed through a continuous process of review, evaluation and collaborative development and this requires that leadership is exercised at all levels. It requires both teacher leadership (Frost and Durrant, 2003; Frost and Harris, 2003) and an invitational style of senior leadership. This is what Frank Crowther and his colleagues in Australia refer to as parallel leadership, which:

encourages relatedness between teacher leaders and administrator leaders that activates and sustains the knowledge generating capacity of schools; parallel leadership is a process whereby teacher leaders and their principals engage in collective action to build school capacity. (Crowther et al., 2002: 38)

Cultivating teacher leadership

Enabling teachers to exercise leadership is not a discrete activity but part of the wider business of building a particular kind of professional community (McLaughlin and Talbert, 1993) in which there is a high degree of what Thomas Sergiovanni has called *leadership density*. He argues that a successful school is one in which the maximum degree of leadership is exercised by the maximum number of people, including teachers, pupils, parents, support staff and so on (Sergiovanni, 1992). This clearly relates to the way Mitchell and Sackney talk about schools as communities.

> In a learning community, individuals feel a deep sense of empowerment and autonomy and a deep personal commitment to the work of the school. This implies that people in the school form not just a community of learners but also a community of leaders. (Mitchell and Sackney, 2000: 93)

In a study of the impact of teachers' development work, teachers who claimed to have led learning-centred development processes talked about the conditions that enabled them to do this (Frost and Durrant, 2002). The teachers interviewed emphasised the importance of creating the right conditions within schools to enable them to exercise leadership and maximise the impact of their work. They were in no doubt as to the crucial role that headteachers have in this respect, offering a range of both positive and negative experiences to illustrate their views. Teachers suggested that internal support is needed in the following areas:

Cultural and structural support

Support for planning and research

Extending internal and external networks

Recognition and celebration of leadership and voice

(Frost, 2004)

Since that small-scale study was completed, the schools involved have continued to build the conditions that enable practitioners to lead processes of development. I now feature two of them to illustrate.

The case of Barnwell School

Barnwell School at the beginning of the current decade had been, by its own admission, a struggling school (Johnson, 2006). Attainment levels were low and, in 2001, the numbers of children achieving five or more A*–C grades in their GCSE examinations dipped below 25 per cent. The school thus fell into the DfES category of 'Schools Facing Challenging Circumstances' (SFCC), which brought with it additional resources but also the challenge of frequent HMI inspections. Raising standards in teaching and learning became an urgent priority. Prior to the first post-SFCC inspection, the senior leadership team had already begun to build a professional culture in which reflection, inquiry and, most importantly, risk-taking were prominent features. The 'Teaching and Learning Forum', for example, was one strategy that provided a space for teachers to hear presentations from their colleagues about innovative practice. This was a voluntary, collective activity taking place at the end of the teaching day. All members of staff were invited and nobody was coerced or pressured into attending. The sessions were organised and chaired by the Deputy Head, Paul Barnett. Another capacity-building initiative already established at Barnwell encouraged teachers to engage in action research and drew them into a knowledge-building process through the 'Research and Development Group', which met on a half-termly basis to support their school-based research dedicated to raising achievement by providing guidance and strategies for the whole school. In an interview Paul Barnett explained:

> we'd created a tradition of staff looking at small-scale enquiry ... but impacting on whole school policy. So we'd looked at the attitudes to learning of students, and we'd looked at the role of assessment for learning and comment-only marking. We'd looked at our rewards and sanctions policy over the period of 3 years. And we take a project for a year, and we involve all members of the school community, in the sense of teaching staff, non-teaching staff, the parents, the students, the governors, are all involved somewhere in an enquiry, and their views are sought as to how they feel about a particular element. And then all of that's drawn together and we share it with governors and staff, and out of that will come an amended policy, or a new direction ... the research and development group can typically be 20 members of staff ... a range of responsibilities, a range of experience ... (interview with Deputy Headteacher)

Paul Barnett had responsibility for developing the teaching and learning at that time and, whilst he was pleased with the way these initiatives were contributing to a more reflective culture, he was constantly looking beyond the school for ideas and structures of support. The school had brought in all the usual itinerant gurus but this was not sufficient, as Paul explains in his own account:

I had experienced a sense of frustration at the lack of impact I felt I was able to make in developing sustained improvements in student learning. I had been responsible for many successful 'training day' presentations and activities ... these had reinforced in me the view that INSET is an event whereas school improvement is a more organic process to be engaged with over time (Stoll and Myers, 1998). The HMI inspection also awakened in me an awareness of a synergy in my role between leadership, school improvement, professional development and learning. The central thread for me became the link between leadership and learning. (Barnett, 2004: 2)

Paul Barnett operated on the belief that 'ideas are out there' (Fullan, 1993: 85), but this needed to be more than the acquisition of bought-in experts. The headteacher, Richard Westergreen-Thorne, was also aware of the need to reach out and make use of a range of external structures of support. He had been one of the few headteachers to attend a presentation at the LEA professional development centre to examine the potential of the 'Herts. MEd in Teaching and Learning' to contribute to development activities in schools. This programme had been created through a partnership between the local educational authority (Hertfordshire) and the University of Cambridge specifically to support school improvement (Frost et al., 2003). The deputy headteacher had also enrolled as a student on the programme and had committed himself to an investigation focused on 'leadership for learning' (MacBeath et al., 2005). This was just the beginning of a trend that saw the signing up of a further nine teachers on the Masters programme and even more than that on the linked Teaching and Learning Certificate programme. The number of teachers engaged in professionally focused inquiry was rapidly approaching critical mass.

The case of Sir John Lawes School

In contrast to Barnwell, Sir John Lawes started the decade from a position of strength. An Ofsted inspection graded 85 per cent of lessons as good or better and the quality of support for professional development was significant in securing the specialist *training school* status. Levels of attainment were rising, staff morale was high and the new headteacher was able to adopt a style of leadership which encouraged innovation and risk-taking. Discussion within the senior leadership team focused on the headteacher's desire to 'de-centre' leadership and develop as a knowledge-creating school (Hargreaves, 1999). Assistant headteacher Jo Mylles wrote about the school's decision to establish a Teacher Led Development Work (TLDW) group in the school:

At Sir John Lawes, the impetus to establish a teacher-led development programme was also provided by a successful Ofsted inspection in 2003. The report highlighted the excellent leadership provided by the headteacher, praised the quality of teaching and learning and described the school's programme of leadership and professional development opportunities as excellent. However, given the spotlight on pupil attainment as a measure of a school's success, it was imperative that the school maintain its momentum. Although the school was flush from its success there was uncertainty about how best to move forward. There was a mixture of excitement and trepidation about how to create further capacity for improvement and success. One strategy which emerged was to develop the collegiate and collaborative work at the school as a way of further empowering staff to engage in development activities to innovate and make a difference. (Mylles, 2006: 5)

The TLDW group was only part of the picture. The school has been developing what they refer to as 'personalised learning for staff' (Mylles and Santos-Richmond, 2006), which involved establishing traditions such as 'the breakfast brain gym' and 'learning lunches' where colleagues are invited to eat together and engage in focused discussions on pedagogical themes. Annual residential conferences for the whole staff were planned and led by the staff, the most recent one featuring a keynote address not from one of the well-known and expensive speakers that we see so often at such events, but from one of the school's own newly qualified teachers.

The TLDW group scaffolds teacher leadership in which teachers undertake development work that is documented in a portfolio of evidence leading to academic certification up to Masters level. The group sessions provide support for group members' inquiry-based development work, helping them to design a range of improvement initiatives that will have direct impact on the quality of teaching and learning in the school. Group sessions are led jointly by Jo Mylles, Assistant Headteacher, and Maria Santos-Richmond, Head of the Humanities Faculty, in collaboration with myself. These sessions give teachers the opportunity to clarify their vision, values and professional concerns and plan for maximum impact. The process is supported by occasional visits to the university Faculty of Education library, occasional participation in county-wide networking events and online research. According to Jo Mylles, 'The aim is to help the teachers to build their "agency" so that they can act strategically to make a real difference to professional practice and to pupils' achievement' (Mylles, 2006: 4).

Support for practitioner researcher in educational settings is provided by a number of university Masters-level programmes in England, and there is evidence (see page 173) that practitioner research has the potential for institutional improvement. However, I belive that, in order for that potential to be fully realised, we need to focus more explicitly on ways to foster distributed leadership.

Conclusion

There is no doubt in my mind that practitioner research plays an essential role in school improvement. However, I believe that we have to guard against the persistence of unhelpful positivistic thinking that can undermine the moral purpose of educational innovation (Fullan, 1993). One way we can do this is to adopt a critical view of the QIFI mindset and the fallacy that objective analysis of data will lead to research findings that can be used to justify the implementation of new practices by all-powerful headteachers. Instead we need to build a climate in which practitioners can collaborate to raise questions about practice, experiment with better practice, evaluate practice and develop practice. This is as much about discussion, reflection, review and deliberation as it is about data-gathering. Data is of marginal use unless colleagues are prepared to engage in the discourse through which we learn to practise differently and this requires the skilful exercise of leadership on the part of all members of learning communities.

References

Barnett, P. (2004) 'Leadership for learning: empowering heads of department as leaders of learning'. Unpublished MEd. thesis, University of Cambridge.

Bassey, M. (1999) *Case Study in Educational Research Settings*. Buckingham: Open University Press.

Carr, W. and Kemmis, S. (1986) *Becoming Critical: Education, Knowledge and Action Research*. London: Falmer Press.

Crowther, F., Kaagan, S., Ferguson, M. and Hann, L. (2002) *Developing Teacher Leaders: How Teacher Leadership Enhances School Success*. Thousand Oaks, CA: Corwin Press.

Dadds, M. (1995) *Passionate Enquiry*. Lewes: Falmer Press.

Dadds, M. (2004) *Teacher Researchers: Perspectives on Practitioner Research*. Cranfield: NCSL Networked Learning Communities.

Durrant, J. and Holden, G. (2006) *Teachers Leading Change: Doing Research for School Improvement*. London: Paul Chapman.

Elliott, J. (1991) *Action Research for Educational Change*. Buckingham: Open University Press.

Frost, D. (2004) 'What can headteachers do to support teachers' leadership?', *Inform No. 4*. Occasional papers published by 'Leadership for Learning: the Cambridge Network', August 2004.

Frost, D. and Durrant, J. (2002), 'Teachers as leaders: exploring the impact of teacher led development work, *School Leadership and Management*, 22 (2): 143–161.

Frost, D. and Durrant, J. (2003) *Teacher-Led Development Work: Guidance and Support*. London: David Fulton Publishers.

Frost, D. and Harris, A. (2003) 'Teacher leadership: towards a research agenda', *Cambridge Journal of Education*, 33 (3): 479–498.

Frost, D., Durrant, J., Holden, G. and Head, M. (2000) *Teacher Led School Improvement*. London: RoutledgeFalmer.

Fullan, M. (1993) *Change Forces*. London: Falmer Press.

Gronn, P. (2003) *The New Work of Educational Leaders: Changing Leadership Practice in an Era of School reform*. London: Paul Chapman.

Handscomb, G. and MacBeath, J. (2004) 'Professional Development through Teacher Enquiry', *Professional Development Today*, 7 (2) (Spring): 6–12.

Hargreaves, D.H. (1999) 'The knowledge creating school', *British Journal of Educational Studies*, 47: 122–144.

Hoyle, E. (1986) *The Politics of School Management*. London: Hodder & Stoughton.

Hoyle, E. (1999) 'The two faces of micropolitics', *School Leadership and Management*, 19 (2): 213–222.

Johnson, J. (2006) 'Using Learning Preference Profiling to develop teaching and learning across the school', *Teacher Leadership*, 1 (1): 33–40.

Lewis, I. and Munn, P. (1997) *So You Want to Do Research? A Guide for Beginners on How to Formulate Research Questions*. Edinburgh: SCRE.

MacBeath, J., Frost, D. and Swaffield, S. (2005) 'Researching leadership for learning in seven countries (The Carpe Vitam Project)', *Education Research and Perspectives*, 32 (2): 24–42.

McLaughlin, M. W. and Talbert, J.E. (1993) *Contents that Matter for Teaching and Learning*. Stanford: Center for Research on the Context of Secondary School Teaching, Stanford University.

Middlewood, D. Coleman, M. and Lumby, J. (1999) *Practitioner Research in Education: Making a Difference*. London: Paul Chapman.

Mitchell, C. and Sackney, L. (2000) *Profound Improvement: Building Capacity for a Learning Community*. Lisse, Netherlands.: Swets and Zeitlinger.

Mylles, J. (2006) 'Building teacher leadership through Teacher Led Development Work groups', *Teacher Leadership*, 1 (1): 33–40.

Mylles, J. and Santos-Richmond, M. (2006) 'Teacher-led Development Work'. Presentation to the National Union of Teachers 'Teacher-led Enquiry' Conference, London, 9 June 2006.

Sergiovanni, T. (1992) *Moral Leadership: Getting to the Heart of School Improvement*. San Francisco, CA: Jossey-Bass.

Somekh, B. (1995) 'Action research and improvement in social endeavours', *British Educational Research Journal*, 21 (3): 339–355.

Spillane, J. (2006) *Distributed Leadership*. San Francisco, CA: Jossey-Bass.

Spillane, J.P., Halverson, R. and Diamond, J.B. (2001) 'Investigating school leadership practice: a distributed perspective', *Educational Researcher*, 30 (3): 23–28.

Street, H. and Temperley, J. (eds) (2005) *Improving Schools through Collaborative Enquiry*. London: Continuum.

Recommended reading

Dadds, M. and Hart, S. (2001) *Doing Practitioner Research Differently*. London: RoutlegeFalmer.

Durrant, J. and Holden, G. (2006) *Teachers Leading Change: doing research for school improvement*. London: Paul Chapman.

Katzenmeyer, A. and Moller, G (2001) *Awakening the Sleeping Giant: Helping Teachers Develop as Leaders* (2nd ed). Thousand Oak, CA: Corwin Press.

12

Interviewing leaders: penetrating the romance

Peter Gronn

In this chapter, I take as my departure point for a consideration of interviewing with, and about, leaders, the late James Meindl's idea of the 'Romance of Leadership' (RofL) and its implications (see Note, p. 203). The RofL was his short-hand means of referring to a predilection of the members of some societies and eras to reverence leaders and leadership. Based on my own experiences as a researcher over more than two decades in this field, this chapter outlines a variety of ways in which interviewing may be advantageous for investigating educational leadership, having regard to perception and information processing by subjects, informants and the interviewer him or herself. Recent advances in understanding the human perception and encoding of information have highlighted the importance of proto-typing leaders. A prototype mediates an individual's search for and interpretation of current and subsequent leader-related information (Lord and Maher, 1993: 7). This claim implies that research evidence of leaders and their work runs the risk of informant perception and attribution bias. For this reason, the chapter shows how (via the RofL) informant cognition influences interviewing, so that it is not a neutral data-gathering mode.

I begin the chapter by elaborating some key assumptions which undergird the field of leadership. I then review the work of Meindl for he, perhaps more than anyone, has alerted leadership scholars to the dynamics and significance of cognitive attribution. In the light of the RofL I then reflect on my experience of interviewing established, prospective and former leaders, from which others engaged in interviewing leaders about leadership may draw lessons.

The later writing of Meindl (e.g., 1990, 1993, 1995; Meindl et al., 1985) was less concerned with the perceptual apparatus by which individuals process leader-related information than with the social and cultural formation, reproduction, diffusion and influence of leader prototypes. For Meindl, the RofL privileges leadership in explaining social and organisational causation. Thus, in an analysis of the popular business press in the United States, he noted how leadership was the favoured explanation for unanticipated firm behaviour (Meindl, 1990: 164):

189

Extremely poor performances were as likely as extremely positive performances to be associated with indications of greater reliance on leadership
factors, possibly to explain, make sense out of, and otherwise come to
terms with such performance levels.

In follow-up experiments, participants also invoked leadership ahead of alternative factors to account for similar kinds of performance variations. Meindl et
al. (1985: 79) concluded that the RofL represented a deep-seated: 'faith in the
potential if not in the actual efficacy of those individuals who occupy the elite
positions of formal organizational authority'.

Constructing leaders

The conventional language of leadership distinguishes between two well-rehearsed
categories of agents: 'leader' (sometimes 'leaders') and 'followers'. The reasons
why this binary has been taken up need not detain us, except that its adoption
reflects the early and enduring influence of social psychological writings on the
development of the leadership field, and the fascination of a pioneer generation of
researchers with the dynamics of behaviour in small group formations. The
attempts of these writers to track and measure influence flows gave rise to an a
priori imposition of this idealised template of a leadership–followership division
of labour in a range of settings (for example, peer groups, gangs, clubs, classrooms, work groups). When in the mid-1970s scholars shifted their attention from
small groups towards organisation-wide leadership, their favoured earlier terminology was retained and it automatically migrated its way in focus, scale and
scope to the upper echelons of organisations, without (in many cases) any overt
justification for doing so. By such means, a discursive orthodoxy took root. The
connection between the agents in this idealised relationship is generally thought of
as causal and might be represented as: leader > followers, with the sign '>' denot-
ing both the direction and preponderance of influence, meaning that a leader is
presumed to succeed in getting followers to do what they might otherwise not
have chosen to do.

There are all kinds of problems with this dualistic way of construing reality.
These problems provide potential pitfalls for students of leadership. For a start,
expressing the leadership relationship singly (as in 'leader–followers') is to
make presumptions about number and source of influence. Expressing that
same relationship in plural terms (as in 'leaders–followers') is still presumptu-
ous in respect of both these dimensions of influence, but at least it represents
an incremental advance on the former view in that expressing relations in this
way allows for possible multiple sources of influence. These numerical distinctions suggest that students of leaders and leadership have some important
research decisions to make: do they endorse one or the other of these binaries
and try to work within them, or do they reject them outright? Additional difficulties are that commentators who take either of these dualistic templates for

granted rarely, if ever, make clear how it is that leaders get to be leaders and followers get to be followers. The normality of each category is simply taken for granted. Moreover, the qualitative difference in status between what it means to be a leader and what it means to be follower is unclear. Thus, Thody (2003: 147) found that terms usually employed as descriptions of leaders, such as 'effective', 'independent' and even 'entrepreneurial', are also used by some writers to distinguish follower personality types. Finally, if a person is labelled as a 'leader' or a 'follower', does this mean in each case that the individual in question is always and forever confined to one or the other role? If, on the other hand, movement backwards and forwards between the two categories is allowed for, in what circumstances and by what process does this membership migration occur? Implicit in these last two important questions is the element of time, so that there may be a presumed period for which such relations of 'leader–followers' or 'leaders–followers' apply, although this is rarely stated as commentators in their analyses tend to pay lip service to time. The effect of this elision is the artefact of 'presentism': the casting of the relations between leader(s)–followers in a kind of atemporal immediacy.

Romanticising leaders

The prior assumptions about leadership just highlighted apply, regardless of one's nominated data-gathering techniques (for an elaboration see Gronn, 2004). Despite his quest for an alternative to the prevailing leader-centrism, Meindl retained the traditional categories for capturing it that have just been queried, except that he gave the connection between them an apparent new twist. (The reason for 'apparent' will be clear shortly.) Meindl de-centred leaders in his analyses by adopting what he termed a follower-centric approach. It was this which provided the psychological foundation for the causal force of the RofL. What, then, did he mean by follower-centrism and what are the implications of this idea for informant interviewing?

With follower-centrism, Meindl proposed reversing the normal relationship, so that followers > leader(s), with the sign '>' meaning that persons become leaders by virtue of followers attributing them with that status. This new equation begged the question of who these presumed 'followers' were, although what Meindl was doing, in effect, was nothing more than taking literally the adage that 'there can be no leaders without followers'. This is one reason for my previous use of 'apparent'. The other is that Meindl's proposed reversal of agency relations seems to be a re-statement of Weber's (1978: 242) claim about the basis of charismatic authority and leadership (that is, that: 'the recognition of those subject to authority [is] decisive for the validity of charisma') and its application to all types of leadership. Meindl (1990: 185–187) was influenced here by the resurgence of interest in charismatic and transformational leadership amongst organisational theorists which he termed the 'so-called new look'.

191

For him (Meindl, 1993: 99), leadership was a state of mind that emerged in the consciousness of followers, in which case leaders come into being (that is, persons are constituted as leaders) as the outcome of group members' thinking 'about their relationships to one another and to their tasks'. In this cognitive process of leader construction, provided an individual's directly observable and indirectly reputed behavioural and performance cues match existing prototypes or implicit theories of leadership in the minds of observers, then there was a strong chance of the individual in question being attributed with leadership (Meindl, 1993: 100).

Clearly, Meindl was attempting to capture the idea that leadership is an emergent phenomenon. He promoted his perspective as an antidote to the renewed 1980s interest in the traits of charismatic and transformational leaders. That is, he was addressing an aspect of the problem of category migration highlighted earlier, as part of which he was drawing heavily on psychological theories of attributional reasoning (for example, Meindl, 1990: 162–164). In this switch, his stance was not one of anti-leadership (Meindl, 1995, p. 330), for it complemented leader-centrism (Meindl, 1990: 198), but it also meant that he shifted his focus from groups to numerically larger collectivities. Here he drew extensively on Weber's phenomenon of charisma to illustrate how attributions of leadership travelled, both rapidly and as a result of mass arousal. This process of leadership diffusion he likened to social contagion. Here, he sought to expand the focus of scholars beyond the interpersonal processes and dynamics privileged by the concern with small groups to: 'the output of social psychological forces operating among followers, subordinates and observers' (Meindl, 1990: 188). The implications of his revisionism entailed a renewed emphasis on the social networks of followers and related settings in which they negotiated and constructed their images of leaders, with the composition and density of such networks determining the strength, variation and consistency of the range of 'leader' constructions. For these reasons, the very stuff of leadership comprised the manipulation and analysis of impressions, image, spin, performance cueing, reputation and the like (Meindl, 1995: 333–335), along with an understanding of the emotional arousal levels required to trigger the contagious diffusion of particularly appealing versions of leadership (Meindl, 1990: 190–197).

Interviewing leaders

There are some important methodological implications of these claims about how leaders get to be leaders and the RofL assumption that leaders: 'do or should have the ability to control and influence the fates of the organisations in their charge' (Meindl et al., 1985: 96). One possible response may be to dismiss the claims as suspect and unhelpful, and simply to take at face value the common sense categories discussed above as well-rehearsed and reliable. Numerous commentators do this, except that 'leader' then runs the risk of being equivalent in meaning to such formal positioned-based terms as 'manager' and 'superior', with 'follower' equivalent to 'subordinate'. While this synonymous usage may apply in some contexts, it will be inappropriate in others. On the other hand, with the approach advocated so far there is less risk of researchers becoming unwitting accomplices in perpetuating the leader-centric attributional processes described by Meindl.

As I reflect back on my research interviewing, it is apparent that two key factors have influenced the likelihood that I might romanticise leaders. These are status and age (of both myself and my informants), neither of which figures specifically in Meindl's explanation of his RofL. In my case, however, they have combined to affect me as an interviewer and my interviewees (including leaders themselves or informants about these leaders) in four main ways. First, I have been aware of something like Meindl's RofL whenever I have interviewed high social and political status (that is, elite) informants, especially when they are also or have been prominent public figures. The corollary of this is that in instances where I was conscious of relatively less evidence of these features, my inclination to romanticise my informants was generally much weaker. As I hope to show, the elite status of an informant helps to sustain a leadership persona and reputation. Second, the effects of informant status (and the RofL) have been mitigated by age. That is, the effect of status as a barrier to understanding persona and reputation has tended to be stronger when the informant has been older and in their mid- or late careers, although weaker for people in their early careers. This is probably because younger and inexperienced informants are much less likely to have acquired the leadership 'savvy' that comes with a well-developed persona and reputation. Third, with accrued career experience as an interviewer I have become far less likely to romanticise leaders and to be deferential towards leadership informants than earlier on as a young researcher. Fourth, with the elevation of my own formal academic rank over a period of two decades or more, informants have tended to become correspondingly more deferential towards me.

I now describe the interplay of these factors for my informants and myself by reference to the following examples of interviewing:

1 High profile, well-established leaders
2 Informants about high-profile, well-established leaders
3 Prospective leaders
4 Former leaders

These four instances are meant to be illustrative, rather than exhaustive, possibilities. There is a cautionary tale here. It is that, while interviews can be powerful and compelling in their verisimilitude and may convey the sense that one is, as it were, succeeding in penetrating the consciousness of an informant, the difficulties I canvass (particularly in relation to instances 1 and 2) suggest that use of interviews as sole data sources should probably be treated with scepticism.

Interviewing high-profile, well-established leaders

'High profile' and 'well-established' may seem to be arbitrary descriptions. This is because in light of the earlier discussion of attributions they beg the question of who decides about the justification for established or not so established, and for high or low profiles, and because the evidential bases of these kinds of judgements are uncertain.

In reality, a number of factors can operate in a researcher's favour in deciding who counts as a well-established leader. Usually, the reputations of high profile and well-established leaders precede them. Indeed, they may often be legends in their own lifetime. This was certainly true of Informant #1. In his case, the aim of my project was to write a biography of his life and work. I had no difficulty in identifying #1, for he was a prominent Australian with an extensive entry in *Who's Who?* and whose views were regularly sought by the print and visual media. He had been headmaster of a well-known Australian boys' school and, following his retirement, he had held a succession of advisory roles and public offices. In 1988, as part of the Bi-Centenary, he was also recognised officially by the Australian government for his contribution to education. When I commenced my research, the writings, speeches and addresses of #1 were widely available, and he had already published his memoirs. This information suggests there may have been little point in my writing an account of his life, except that there were a number of unanswered questions in his published recollections of his career. Later, it became apparent that there were also episodes in his life that he had glossed over or ignored in his autobiography. For these reasons, I then developed a healthy scepticism (which I retain) about the value of autobiographical forms of life writing as the (or even a) preferred source of learning about leadership (see the recent debate between Shamir et al., 2005, Gronn, 2005 and Shamir, 2005).

When I began interviewing #1, we fell quickly into a regular pattern of approximately fortnightly mid-morning conversations. I prepared a schedule of flexibly worded and sequenced questions based on different sections and chapters of his memoirs, my aim being to obtain additional background and personal details, and to have #1 reflect on the significance of particular events and the influence of key individuals in his life. This strategy of using interviews as devices for extracting information proved to be only moderately successful. There were a number of reasons for this. One was that my feelings towards #1 influenced my perceptions of his work and contribution. Early on, I gave a paper to a symposium on biography at the annual conference of the Australasian Political Studies Association. During question time, a graduate student asked me how I was dealing with the phenomenon of 'transference' – Freud's term for the unconscious feelings communicated between analyst and analysand when they engage with one another as surrogates for other roles – particularly during interviews with #1. I recall fumbling my way through an answer. In fact, even though at that time I was not yet aware of Meindl's idea of romanticising leaders, in anticipation of the issue raised by the questioner, I had already begun documenting some of my 'internal conflicts' in a diary. Shortly afterwards, I tried to articulate these tensions in two sets of feelings (Gronn, 1987): those concerned with self–other relations (that is, tensions between a researcher and an informant) and those between sense of self and ideal self (that is, tensions within a researcher).

I learned many valuable lessons in this extended period of interviewing. The first lesson (which I acknowledged in a letter to his family that I wrote shortly after #1's death) was that it is almost impossible when engaged in prolonged and intense interviewing with a high profile informant for that person not to become a mentor. The experience of interviewing such persons changes an interviewer. In my case, the influence on me was not so much that I started to absorb #1's values or world-view, but that by trying to pin down the details of his outlook, along with its origin and justification, I began to query (and even abandon) some of my own cherished nostrums. The second lesson was my discovery that interviews can be factually notoriously unreliable. The effect on me was to become less positively inclined to the oral history interviewing approach that had risen in research popularity during the 1970s. For this reason, archival records started to become my primary and preferred source for information and my interviews tended to supplement this avenue of inquiry. Another lesson was my realisation that interview informants build up a very limited mental stock of illustrative incidents and examples concerning their own lives. The details of events with which I was familiar from #1's writings, for example, were often quoted back to me almost verbatim in answers to my interview questions. Finally, there was an important lesson about responsibility. Because numerous details about an informant's life come into an interviewer's possession, there is a very real sense in which he or she comes to assume the role of 'keeper of the record'. This observation relates back to the earlier suggestion about status. The point is not so much that one experiences this mantle as a burden, nor that it bestows a spurious sense of power and control, nor even a sense of having intruded on an informant's privacy. It is, rather, that an interviewer is obliged to strive for accuracy and fidelity in representing the informant's life, regardless of the particular informant's persona and reputation. As a consequence of this responsibility, the description and analysis of that life and its mode of representation (for example, in the form of a biographical article) may result in a de- or less romanticised view of a leader. If one strives to achieve a 'forensic' analytical standpoint in relation to data, as I did, then scales begin to fall from one's eyes. I regard this kind of outcome as inevitable, unless, of course, interviewers see it as their role to assume the stance of a leader's acolyte.

Interviewing informants about high-profile, well-established leaders

As is evident from the wording of the heading, I have resisted the temptation to think of this category of informants as 'followers'. In no sense, for example, did any of the people to whom I spoke about #1 follow him. This word is simply too gross or blunt as a category of informants and it makes no allowance for the distinctive quality of those informants' relations with the subject, for differences in the status of those informants, nor for shifts over time in their status. The people whom I interviewed in the course of my biographical work on #1 included eminent judges and doctors, eight English and Australian professors and seven Englishmen and Australians with knighthoods (two of whom had been heads of government). While most of these people had long ago been impressionable young schoolboys and they each attested to the early formative (and, in some instances, subsequent) influence of their erstwhile headmaster on their lives, their admiration was reserved for a 'father figure' who was also a mentor, and who later became a personal friend to whom they felt a strong bond of loyalty and a sense of indebtedness.

When I began interviewing #1, I was vaguely aware of the milieu or circles in which he moved. A number of the informants who were members of his circle had achieved public eminence in a variety of ways, I discovered, with the result that they were not the kind of persons with whom to trifle. As busy people, I could not afford to waste their time. For this reason my questions had to be extremely well informed and rehearsed. Here, the RofL operated in a number of unforeseen and unintended ways. For a start, to be granted an interview as a budding young researcher at the time felt like I imagined the experience of being accorded an audience with royalty. Then, to be admitted into the privacy of an informant's home or office was equivalent in some instances to being 'ushered into the presence' of a dignity. While this entry did not entail the calculated reduction to the 'paralyzing despondency' achieved by Hitler's favoured architect, Albert Speer, with the 60 feet of distance between the double entrance door and the desk of the Führer to be negotiated by unwary visitors (Fest, 2003: 104), I often found the experience to be intimidating (depending on the informant's age, seniority and situation). The reason for this is that all kinds of unknown and anticipated social niceties applied in these high-status circles. (To Marxists, these people would have qualified as 'ruling class', and yet I was a mere unassuming lad from lower middle-class, eastern suburban Melbourne.) Thus, even though one may have the requisite ticket of entry, so to speak (in the form of a letter of introduction from the subject of the interview and/or a formal letter affording institutional ethics clearance), and thereby have acquired status as someone worthy of being taken seriously, one is still very much at the mercy of such high status informants.

This point prompts me to think back to some basic research texts for postgraduates which highlight the disproportionate power of interviewers in relation to informants and, frankly, I am staggered by the unreality of the claim. I vividly recall being shouted at angrily over the telephone by a retired high-ranking army officer, for example, when I tried to re-negotiate an appointment. Clearly, he was on a short fuse and he must have thought that I was mucking him around. I also remember feeling rather crestfallen soon after I arrived to interview an ageing and slightly deaf Australian politician, and was motioned to sit opposite him in the blanket-covered armchair normally reserved for his Golden Retriever. Not being accustomed to disputing the wisdom and the ways of an ex-prime minister, I obeyed (stupidly), so that when I left his house I was almost completely covered in dog hair. On the other hand, there were occasions when I caught a re-assuring glimpse of the real person behind a high-status informant's public persona. One interview with a prominent public intellectual was interrupted by a series of phone calls which he insisted on taking in an adjacent room. My growing exasperation was relieved somewhat when he put the phone down after one call, sent a small table flying and, believing he was out of earshot, screamed 'Bugger!' as he tripped himself up.

The main advantage this leadership circle offered me as an interviewer was a ready-made snowballing network of informants. I soon learned, however, that this possibility could be two-edged. I now know that the pool of potential information that awaits one from this source has to be offset against two other factors. First, an interviewer very quickly encounters a collectively defined level of esteem in which a leader is held within the circle of intimates. This is not intended as a conspiratorial claim. Meindl is by no means the sole commentator to highlight the cultural tendency to canonise leaders and leadership. During the early part of my research with #1, for example, I knew of the emblematic Hodgkinsonian assertion that: 'The term "leadership" is an incantation for the bewitchment of the led' (Hodgkinson, 1983: 228). Later, I discovered historical evidence of how various expert professionals in the public realm (often from within the circle of a leader) are susceptible to pressures to contrive public appearances in the face of the facts of private realities (Kucharski, 1984). In some instances, the durability and extent of the collective esteem around a leader may warrant its description as a myth or legend. In my case, there was a high degree of reverence for #1. Secondly, I quickly found out that the eagerness of the circle of intimates to be interviewed was disproportionately matched by the mostly poor quality of the information that they provided me. While it was never my intention deliberately to seek out negative views about #1, I encountered an extraordinary reluctance to say anything even mildly critical of him. Did this represent a collective desire to be protective? Admittedly I was asking informants to delve back a long way into their lives, but as a general rule they displayed a singularly poor recollection for vital information and details. On the other hand, there was no shortage of 'colour' in the anecdotes and stories they recounted to me. These were proffered as indicative of the man and his character, and as being (presumably) self-evidently worthy of reproduction in whatever I planned to write.

At the time I was firmly of the view that the attributions of leadership in the minds of these first two sets of informants were associated, however vaguely, with notions of greatness. These assumptions were rarely made explicit, although they were not hard to sense in the informants' many remarks about accomplishments, inspiring deeds and individual worth. I remember discussing leadership during my first interview with informant #1. As we were farewelling each other, he told me, motioning with both hands towards his chest, that leadership came from within. This, I suppose, was his way of saying that leadership was an inherent trait or essence, and something with which one was born.

Interviewing prospective leaders

A different view from this one about leadership being something one is born with, of course, is that leadership can be learned and that the status of 'leader' is not inherent but can also be acquired. These kinds of assumptions are especially evident in my recent research with my colleague Kathy Lacey on Australian government school sector principal recruitment. The contrast between the milieu just described and that of the prospective principals we have interviewed could not be starker.

Interviewing aspiring principals represents a complete change of gear. Whereas established leaders are highly likely to have confronted and to a substantial degree have learned to master their emotional vulnerabilities – so that there may be only minimal evidence of these for an interviewer to detect – the content of interview talk with aspirants tends to be heavily emotionally saturated. This contrast has arisen in our investigations partly as a result of our different research purposes and our study design, for with principal aspirants we have been focusing explicitly on the developmental work which senior teachers experience in managing their professional identities while they review their possible future career options and pathways. In these instances, from the interviewer's side of the research relationship, there is remarkably little of the 'fog' of leadership romance or mystique to be worried about. Moreover, any notion of 'followers' is irrelevant to would-be leader informants as none of them conveys any sense of having built a following among colleagues and peers or that this is even a necessary priority. At this point in their leadership trajectories they tend to be self-preoccupied. On the other hand, Meindl's leadership romance is exactly the personal challenge with which our informants have to get to grips. It tends to confront them in the guise of the exceedingly high leadership expectations that have been built up around the school principalship – which Copland (2000) refers to as the myth of the super-principal – whether these hopes and expectations sit easily with them, and whether they 'have what it takes' to be able to perform the role. The contrast between the two interview sets (that is, established and aspiring leaders) is also due to the effects of the factors identified earlier, namely status and age. Thus, younger mid-career teachers are wrestling with what it means to acquire an identity as educational leaders and with their capacity to cope with the stresses that they are aware of from observing their own principals and that they may encounter in their own future roles.

Two factors in particular have stood out in our aspirant interviews. First, we have been struck by the way in which research designs produce unanticipated outcomes. In one project, we deliberately structured our one-on-one and focus group interviews with the intention of obtaining our informants' perspectives on their own work and career experiences. We succeeded in that goal, but what has also happened is that these fora have provided the aspirants with a kind of haven or space which offers them sufficient security to verbalise their personal anxieties about possible future professional role exposure in a climate of high stakes accountability. In some instances, the level of personal detail and depth of feeling relayed to us have been striking. This is an intriguing phenomenon: here is a group of highly competent professional people, who are positioning themselves in their own minds (with varying degrees of ambition and intensity of focus) for a role that is often associated with the 'loneliness at the top' syndrome, and who are dealing with the possibility of entry into this psychological zone, so to speak, by relying on the research as a surrogate vehicle of support. Whether our interviews have been conducted face to face or by telephone hook up (with several teachers located in remote geographic regions of the country) has not really mattered, for the responses we have generated to our questions disclose a willingness to reveal, if not quite 'all' then a significant depth of feeling. And yet (with the exception of one person), neither of us knows any of our informants personally or professionally and we have met only one or two of them previously, and then only very briefly. Nonetheless, the rapport and trust we have established has been almost instantaneous. What this tells me is that these are people who perhaps have nowhere else to go in their professional lives to confide their fears and misgivings. Yet the interviews with us, it would appear, seem to provide them with a listening post. To be fair, our use of e-journals alongside interviewing in one of our projects (Gronn and Lacey, 2004) has probably been the spur for our informants' depth of introspectiveness, which helps reinforce the earlier point I made regarding the inadvisability of using interviews in leadership research as sole sources of data procurement.

The second thing we have noticed is the tightness of the interview dialogue and density of the informants' comments. What I mean here is that we have generally managed to achieve what (in my experience) university lecturers typically urge upon their graduate research students as a preferred interview model. That is, avoid wordiness and try to obtain extended informant responses with short sentence-length questions, so that as an interviewer you might have the luxury of your follow-up questions defined for you by being able to seize on something said in the preceding response. Although there have been some exceptions, interview after interview transcript reveals a similar pattern of extended frank and fulsome answers. A good illustration is evident in the aspirants' highly ambivalent feelings about principal selection and appointment processes (Gronn and Lacey, 2006a). Contrast this candour with the earlier experience I recounted of having to 'squeeze hard', so to speak, in order to extract any worthwhile information from my high-status informants. In emphasising this point about frankness, I am not trying to convey the impression that interviewing becomes something that one does not have to work at with such forthcoming informants, for the fact is that a few of our interviewees have been taciturn while in other instances we have had to curb their garrulousness. Rather, my point is that the informants' willingness to talk (and to trust us) in the anonymity of the interview situation is a sure sign of the amount of internal psychological effort involved in the 'working through' of anxieties that has to be engaged in by those who are contemplating leadership. For this reason, what we may be tapping into here is a phenomenon that is similar to Archer's (2003: 33) idea of internal conversation as 'reflexive deliberation', in which our informants are externalising their self-talk for us in response to our questions. That is, at this stage in their leadership careers these principal aspirants are engaged in the kind of 'identity work' that is part of the anticipatory socialization accompanying the process of identification with a new role, and in our interviews with them they have been relying on us to assist in smoothing their transition to what will be expected of them.

Unlike the two previous categories of experienced leader informants, the frankness of the revelations of this group of 'wanna-be' leaders occurs because as a cohort its members have virtually nothing about which to be defensive, and little or nothing by way of reputation and prestige (outside of their current workplaces) to lose. On the other hand, while the role challenge confronting this group differs markedly from that of the next example of former leaders who, by comparison with their younger confreres, have a lot to lose, the latter sample has been equally as forthcoming with us when we have interviewed them.

Interviewing former leaders

The openness in interviews of former principals has taken a slightly less confessional form than that of the aspirants. (We wanted them to tell us why they vacated their roles when they did and to describe for us the circumstances of their departures.) By this point I mean that the recently departed group displays a more 'existential' understanding, in the sense of being willing to reflect on the overall balance of burdens and joys they experienced in their previous role incumbencies. This characteristic is evidence of the career challenge confronted by former principals known as divestiture (Gronn, 1999: 39–41).

There are two elements to divestiture. The first is the psychological requirement, now that one inhabits changed sets of circumstances (following retirement, resignation, etc.), to de-identify with a previous occupational role. The second is the need to adjust to the loss of leader status. This loss occurs because the strength of the 'leader' attributions of previous role set members and colleagues diminishes or even disappears altogether. On the other hand, the reality of this loss may be only temporary given that some former leaders re-invent themselves or move on (as I indicated that Informant #1 did) to new roles and relationships (Day and Bakioğlu, 1996). Of the four categories of interviews I have been discussing in this chapter, this is the one in which there was least explicit evidence of leadership mystery or romance. In the absence of transcribed excerpts to which to refer, this is not an easy point to convey meaningfully; however a clue to the reality of it for our informants is found in the earlier citation from Meindl concerning faith in the efficacy of elites. As interviewers we have been struck by the starkness of the role reality our informants have described for us. The safest overall generalisation to be made about efficacy on the basis of our data analysis (which is still in progress) with this group of 30+ ex-principals who departed earlier than they originally expected (Gronn and Lacey, 2006b), is that roles let people down, rather than the reverse. That is, our informants took the opportunity provided by our interviews to try to position themselves favourably in their war stories in relation to what their previous principal roles had demanded of them and what they were able to accomplish as incumbents. Thus, when our informants said that there were achievements in their school that had taken place on their 'watch', this tended to be because, they claimed, *they* had made them happen or they had enabled others to make them happen, and not because the role itself had been instrumental in their success. When, on the other hand, there was a lack of achievement or there were fewer achievements than they had anticipated, or there were disappointments, these were because the role had *failed them*, not because they had failed the role.

Because we have not probed individuals' responses further than one-off interviews with each of them, it is difficult to pursue in any detail this inference I have drawn about maintenance of leader potency and to confirm its validity. Nonetheless, amid all their negative tales of mental and emotional stress, sense of abandonment, occasional experiences of panic attacks, complaints about work–life imbalance, bodily indisposition, sense of loneliness and so on, as well as their positive ones, their determination to appear to be efficacious is part of the construction of self which they sought to project. My point here is not dissimilar from that of Ebaugh (1988: 213) who, in her study of the role exit of ex-nuns, claimed that: 'during the course of an interview, information-seeking questions and therapeutic consequences often co-exist'. The desire to be reconciled to what has happened in their working lives, as distinct from retaining a sense of bitterness and an inability to let go, is the likely clue to the former principals' need to see themselves, and to be seen as, efficacious. This mirroring of self-esteem through the vehicle of an interview provides a source of self-confirmation, and a means of maintaining self-image and reputation. Interviews, for informants as much as for researchers, constitute a performance in which each party is on show before the other. In fact, while I wrote these words they brought to mind the occasion when the reality of the performative nature of interviewing began to hit home, in a way that contrasts so markedly with the robustness that I have just described. One of my most disarming research experiences occurred in a life history interview that I conducted with an experienced and well-regarded secondary principal. This event was very early in my academic career. To my horror, about half way through my questions she burst into tears. On this occasion my informant was one of a number of principals who had agreed to talk to me about how and why they became principals. With me scarcely able to believe what was happening before my eyes, she apologised and then insisted that her outburst was not my fault, because displays of tearfulness on her part were a quite normal feature of her personality. Horrified by this apparent distress or sadness, I was not at all convinced by this attempted reassurance. Thankfully, nothing remotely comparable with that experience has happened to me since then.

Conclusion

In this chapter I have tried to draw a series of contrasts between experiences of interviewing leaders at different points of their careers. There were three instances (1, 2 and 4) in which the interviews, which were intended as a straightforward means of obtaining information, also provided informants with an opportunity to clarify their deeds and accomplishments, along with those of others, and for conveying a sense of winding down in a leadership role. The remaining instance (3) was one in which prospective leaders were yet to accomplish the kinds of outcomes typically associated with leadership, but were gearing up to be able to do so. Here I drew on Meindl's arguments about the cultural preference attached to leadership in the causal explanation of actions and event outcomes, which he derived from his revisionist follower-centric approach to leadership. The overall purpose in doing so was to show how some dimensions of this cultural preference to romanticise leadership about which Meindl wrote intrude into the dynamics of interviewing, and how awareness of their unintended intrusion might facilitate a more sensitive understanding of research interviewing and the significance of interview-derived leadership research data. It might well be possible for interviewers to accomplish these purposes or even to understand how informants' implicit assumptions about leadership impact on leadership research projects, particularly as these come to light in interviews, without having prior knowledge of Meindl's ideas. This certainly happened in my own case (because it was not until after much of what I described above had taken place that I read his work). On the other hand, research is an activity in which the cliché to be forewarned is to be forearmed does genuinely apply, in which case heightened sensitivity about common discursive constructions and ways of thinking about leadership may be sufficient to bring about improved interviewing and to yield better quality research outcomes.

Note

James R. Meindl, Donald S. Carmichael Professor of Organization and Human Resources, School of Management, State University of New York at Buffalo, died suddenly and unexpectedly in 2004.

References

Archer, M.S. (2003) *Structure, Agency and the Internal Conversation*. Cambridge: Cambridge University Press.

Copland, M.A. (2000) 'The myth of the superprincipal', *Phi Delta Kappan*, 82 (7): 528–533.

Day, C. and Bakioğlu, A. (1996) 'Development and disenchantment in the professional lives of headteachers', in Goodson, I.F. and Hargreaves, A. (eds) *Teachers' Professional Lives*. London: Falmer. pp. 205–227.

Ebaugh, H.R.F. (1988) *Becoming an Ex: The Process of Role Exit*. Chicago, IL: University of Chicago Press.

Fest, J. (2003) *Speer: The Final Verdict*, (transl E. Osers and A. Dring), Orlando, FL: Harcourt.

Gronn, P. (1987) 'Notes on leader watching', in R.J.S. Macpherson and H. Sungaila (Eds), *Ways and Meanings of Research: An Introduction for Students of Educational Administration*. Armidale, NSW: University of New England Press. pp. 99–114.

Gronn, P. (1999) *The Making of Educational Leaders*. London: Cassell.

Gronn, P. (2004) 'Methodologies of leadership research', in Goethals, G.R., Sorenson, G.J. and MacGregor Burns, J. (eds) *Encyclopedia of Leadership*, Vol. 3. Thousand Oaks, CA: Sage. pp. 995–1000.

Gronn, P. (2005) 'Questions about autobiographical leadership', *Leadership*, 1(4): 481–490.

Gronn, P. and Lacey, K. (2004) 'Positioning oneself for leadership: feelings of vulnerability among aspirant principals', *School Leadership and Management*, 24 (4): 405–424.

Gronn, P. and Lacey, K. (2006a) 'Cloning their own: aspirant principals and the school-based selection game', *Australian Journal of Education*, 50 (2): 102–121.

Gronn, P. and Lacey, K. (2006b) 'Burden and joy: school principals' decisions to exit their roles', (in preparation).

Hodgkinson, C. (1983) *The Philosophy of Leadership*. Oxford: Blackwell.

Lord, R.G. and Maher, K.J. (1993) *Leadership and Information Processing: Linking Perceptions and Performance*. London: Routledge.

Kucharski, A. (1984) 'On being sick and famous', *Political Psychology*, 5: 69–82.

Meindl, J.R. (1990) 'On leadership: an alternative to the conventional wisdom', in Staw, B.M. and Cummings, L.L. (eds) *Research in Organizational Behavior*, Vol. 12. Greenwich, CT: JAI Press. pp. 159–203.

Meindl, J.R. (1993) 'Reinventing leadership: a radical, social psychological approach', in Murnighan, J.K. (ed.) *Social Psychology in Organizations*. Englewood Cliffs, NJ: Prentice–Hall. pp. 89–113.

Meindl, J.R. (1995) 'The romance of leadership as a follower-centric theory: a social constructionist approach', *Leadership Quarterly*, 6 (3): 329–341.

Meindl, J.R., Ehrlich, S.B. and Dukerich, J.M. (1985) 'The romance of leadership', *Administrative Science Quarterly*, 30 (1): 78–102.

Shamir, B. (2005) 'Leaders' life stories are social reality: a rejoinder to Gronn', *Leadership*, 1 (4): 491–500.

Shamir, B., Dayan-Horesh, H. and Adler, D. (2005) 'Leading by biography: towards a life-story approach to the study of leadership', *Leadership*, 1 (1): 13–29.

Thody, A. (2003) 'Followership in educational organizations: a pilot mapping of the territory', *Leadership and Policy in Schools*, 2 (2): 141–156.

Weber, M. (1978) *Economy and Society*, Vol. 1 (ed. and transl. Roth, G. and Wittich, C.). Berkeley, CA: University of California Press.

Recommended reading

Day, C. and Bakioğlu, A. (1996) 'Development and disenchantment in the professional lives of headteachers', in Goodson, I.F. and Hargreaves, A. (eds) *Teachers' Professional Lives*. London: Falmer. pp. 205–227.

Gronn, P. (2005) 'Questions about autobiographical leadership', *Leadership*, 1 (4): 481–490.

Gronn, P. (2004) 'Methodologies of leadership research', in Goethals, G.R. Sorenson, G.J. and MacGregor Burns, J. (eds) *Encyclopedia of Leadership*, Vol. 3. Thousand Oaks, CA: Sage pp. 995–1000.

Gubrium, J. and Holstein, M. (eds) (2002) *Handbook of Interview Research: Context and Method*. London: Sage.

Part C
Research Tools

13

Interviews in educational research: conversations with a purpose

Peter Ribbins

Over the past 30 years, in a wide variety of projects and contexts, I have used most of the main methods available to those who engage in social research. Of these, for me and for many of my students, interviewing in all its many forms has usually been the most fun and, with observation, also the most fruitful. However as an approach to research, whilst it can seem the easiest to start, it can be among the most difficult to finish. But what is it to interview and what kinds of topics are best studied using this approach? Dexter (1970) describes the interview as a 'conversation with a purpose' (p. 123). For Guba and Lincoln (1981), 'of all the means of exchanging information and gathering data known to man ... interviewing is perhaps the oldest and certainly one of the most respected of the tools that the inquirer can use' (p. 154). When, in the 1970s, studying for a Masters' in educational administration, I first planned such conversations I saw few difficulties. I soon discovered that an ability to talk and listen did not ensure good interviews. In what follows, I will say something about what I have learnt and in doing so will draw mainly on the studies of educational leaders in which I and some of my Doctoral students have been involved. Most recently these have included studies of headteachers (Davies, 2002; Pascal and Ribbins, 1997; Pashiardis and Ribbins, 2003; Rayner and Ribbins, 1999; Ron, 2004; Zhang, 2004), college principals (Woolford, 2004), top civil servants (Sherratt, 2004), middle leaders in schools (Ribbins, 2007), and ministers of education (Ribbins and Sherratt, 1997). From this I hope to offer practical advice to those about to engage in interview-based research which might also have something to say to those with experience of this but who wish to explore, perhaps even question, what they already 'know'.

Writing a short chapter on so complex a topic means being highly selective, I will focus on how interviews can produce rich and relevant data. Readers seeking more detailed help can turn to the *Handbook of Interview Research* (Gubrium and Holstein, 2002) and its 44 chapters by a host of distinguished authors. For my part I will discuss: (1) why we interview and how to go about this; (2) the main interview forms and how interviews can be undertaken, and (3) the conduct of research interviews and of interview-based projects.

Why interview?

For Dexter (1970: 11), 'interviewing is the preferred tactic of data collection when ... it appears that it will get *better* data or *more* data *at less cost* than other 'tactics'. For me the purpose of interviewing is to find out what is in somebody else's mind but not to put things there. We interview people to explore their views in ways that cannot be achieved by other forms of research and report our findings in as near as we reasonably can their own words. Hence the liberal use of quotations made in most reports of research of this kind. Such accounts should seek to convey to the reader the views of those interviewed faithfully. But there are many ways to be untruthful. It is possible to misrepresent the views of interviewees by claiming they have said something when they did not (*faking*) but also by selectively reporting their words to suggest they have said something they did not intend. This can be done by deleting text from a quotation in a way that changes its meaning (*misrepresenting*). But even reporting without omission does not guarantee that an interviewee is not misrepresented. This can happen when a quote is taken out of context or patently does not square with the thrust of an interview as a whole. To do this is to *raid* as Silver (1977: 17) elegantly terms this practice. It is to 'use' data to serve the purposes of the interviewer rather than to represent the authentic view and voice of the interviewee.

If interviewers have a duty to report honestly, they must also provide a framework within which those interviewed can respond appropriately. Two precepts shape my attitude. First there are no bad interviewees, only bad interviews. If people fail to talk about themselves candidly the fault usually lies with the interviewer, although an exception may be 'reluctant respondents' (see Adler and Adler, 2002). They are being asked to talk about themselves; what can be more interesting? Second interviewees from educational settings are more likely to respond positively if treated with respect than disdain. As Sherratt and I, in a study of the lives of Secretaries of State for Education, put it, 'our intention [was not] to go out of our way to ... hector or badger them ... We feel such a strategy can produce accounts ... more revealing than those achieved using a more brutal approach' (Ribbins and Sherratt, 1997: 5).

Being respectful does not mean suspending critical judgement. On the contrary, since the interview is a setting to which those involved bring different expectations and interests anything an interviewer hears is potentially suspect. Those who research must still evaluate the reliability of what they are told by an interviewee: in doing so they can compare and contrast what is said within a single interview and, better still, across repeat interviews.

Much of my research has involved discussions with educational leaders about how *they* describe their professional lives. But what they tell me and what they actually think, and do, might not be consistent. Checking requires triangulation, which means at the data-collecting stage seeking further evidence including talking to relevant others, studying documents and observing action (Bush, 2006). I stress triangulation as a form of validation in data collection, but as Cohen et al. (2000) note, this is just one facet of issues on the reliability, validity and generalisability of data from interviews (pp. 120–126). Following Kvale (1996), they argue, surely correctly, that such validation should take place at every stage of an interview-based study from initiation to reporting (p. 286). For such reasons, Guba and Lincoln (1981) argue that '[r]esearch … based solely on interviews may be sabo-taged and crippled … triangulation of methods is the best means of ensuring that one will be able to make sense of data collected through interviews' (p. 155). Even this needs qualification. Some topics can be studied using interview data alone – claims about what people *say*. Others cannot – claims dealing with what people *do*. I will now turn from the why of interviewing to the how.

Ways of interviewing

Three issues seem especially relevant: What are the main forms of interview? How can they be conducted? How should they vary according to the type of interviewee?

Types of interview

I find it helpful to think of interviews in terms of four broad types, varying according to how structured or planned they are, and who controls them and how. Seen as a continuum at one pole are 'verbal questionnaires', followed by 'interviews', then 'discussions' and at the other pole are 'chats'. Each has its defining characteristics, strengths and weaknesses.

Verbal questionnaires

The fundamental objective of qualitative interviewing is to provide a framework within which respondents can express their views in their own terms. This means avoiding supplying the predetermined responses necessary in quantitative research. Given this I deal with 'verbal questionnaires', sometimes termed 'struc-tured interviews', only for the sake of completeness. At best they represent, as in much market research, a closed response interview – in this, although a conversa-tion with a purpose may seem to be taking place, all questions and possible responses are pre-specified by the 'interviewer'. There are advantages to this, the data are very easy to analyse, but its key disadvantage is that it entails 'reality being hammered into shape' by the interviewer – it may be trying to find out what is in the interviewee's mind, but in doing so it is putting far too much there.

Interviews

This is almost certainly what most people have in mind when they think about conducting a research conversation with a purpose. It entails the researcher broad-ly controlling the agenda and process of the interview, whilst leaving interviewees free, within limits, to respond as they best see fit. This means the production of a 'semi-structured' interview schedule largely determined in terms of sequence and wording. I have used such schedules in numerous projects, notably studies of headship in many countries (Pashiardis and Ribbins, 2003: 11–12; Rayner and Ribbins, 1999: 51–53). For some the schedule must be rigorously adhered to; any departure risks increasing the likelihood of interviewer bias and diminishing the possibility of rigorous response comparison. I am more pragmatic – for example in responding to a question, an interviewee might jump to a later question; to interrupt them in full flow is likely to be disruptive and annoying, and may reduce their ability and willingness to speak freely later. In such a context, the schedule can be used by the interviewer to respond flexibly to the interviewee whilst still keeping track of what has been covered and what remains to be considered. Broadly, the strengths of this type of interview is that compared with the forms discussed below, it substantially reduces the possibility of interviewer bias and increases the comprehensiveness and comparability of interviewee response, facilitating final data analysis. However, it is less flexible, its relevance from the perspective of the interviewee may be diminished, and it increases interviewer bias in agenda-setting. On a practical note, I have taken the view in my own work that if it is possible to undertake only a series of one-off interviews in a research project, this semi-structured format is the best approach to adopt.

Discussions

A 'discussion' is a planned meeting between an interviewer and one or more interviewees in which the former guides the conversation working, usually, to a highly flexible and open agenda. Some find it helpful to think of this as a 'guided interview'. This approach can be especially beneficial early in a research project, when the researcher is uncertain about the significance of key concepts and activities relating to topic and setting, and when more than one interview with an interviewee is planned. It entails pre-identifying a rough agenda of topics, leaving the exact sequence and phrasing of questions to the interview. Usually I note a few trigger words on a card which I use to get a conversation started and to keep it going. I hope to say as little as possible – the assumption being that the topics the interviewee raises are more likely to reflect their real concerns than any agenda I could devise. This can work well – early in my study of pastoral care I asked a headteacher to tell me what this meant for him. He responded passionately, clearly, at length and almost without interruption. I have rarely enjoyed such an informative couple of hours. But this approach does not always work as well, and in any case is less justified in follow-up interviews. However, it is more flexible than an interview and more comprehensive than a chat, and since the interviewer usually has some control over the issues considered, it is normally less hard to analyse. Conversely, a series of discussions can throw up a very wide variety of topics and the nature of responses from one discussion to the next can be very different. This can make for major problems when comparing the findings of the whole set of such discussions, especially when large numbers have been recorded.

Chats

A 'chat' is an (apparently) serendipitous interview. It occurs when a researcher seizes a chance, for example making coffee in a staff room, to have an 'unplanned conversation' with a subject. Opportunities for such chats are greatest when an external researcher spends a good deal of time within a research setting, for example in an ethnographic study, or where an internal researcher is engaged in an investigation of some aspect of her or his own workplace. I have noted 'apparently' above in parenthesis because it is quite possible for a researcher to plan for a chat by creating the opportunity and preparing for it in advance. Indeed those being studied sometimes do this as well. More usually chats have no pre-arranged agenda and are unrecorded. If it becomes obvious to subjects that they are being interrogated or if the researcher begins to record things, then the rules of the game change and the interaction will be regarded as an interview. Chats can be highly flexible and highly relevant. People will tell interviewers things in a chat they might not in a formal interview. But for a variety of reasons they need to be employed with care, there are traps for the inexperienced or unwary. They can vary very greatly in quality and reliability, are hard to record and, if a great deal of the data of a research project takes this form, hard to analyse. They can also present the researcher, especially those studying aspects of the institution within which they are working, with tricky ethical problems. In particular, careful thought will need to be given to what substantial use of this method means for the notion of 'informed consent'?

If you intend to use a chat as part of your data collection, record it as soon as possible after it has taken place. I try to do this immediately but if I fail to do so within 24 hours I discard it: much of what is 'remembered' after this is likely to be fiction. Various techniques can help to enable recall. First, I am very selective in what I try to remember in detail. The longer the conversation the more important this is. Second, as the chat proceeds I make a mental note of key words as triggers to flesh out subsequently a record of the chat – even so much of this account will be glossed. Third, I try to identify and remember exactly whole sentences likely to be strong candidates for future quotation. Only those blessed with an eidetic memory can hope to reproduce many of these. Fourth, it is possible to improve. From time to time, having taped an interview I try to reproduce a part of this relying solely on memory. This can then be checked against the tape. It helps to practise.

Forms of interviewing

Interviews can be conducted in various ways. Drawing on my research and that of my students, I will consider four forms, noting some advantages and limitations of each.

Face-to-face

In its simplest, most usual, form this involves one interviewer and one intervie-wee. Joint interviewing, if costly in terms of resource, can be worth considering. If an interviewee refuses to be tape-recorded the presence of two interviewers means one can talk whilst the other takes notes. It also allows members of a team of interviewers to monitor each other in order to ensure a level of consistency between them. Finally, it can offer opportunities for less experienced interviewers to work with more experienced colleagues and in doing so develop their inter-viewing skills. Joint interviewing can work successfully but can be difficult. Some interviewees, faced with two interviewers, might be intimidated and so respond less openly, honestly and frankly than they might otherwise have. There can be problems for interviewers. Joint interviewing works best when the interviewers have broadly similar interviewing styles and worst when they do not.

Face-to-face interviews can be undertaken between one or more interviewers and one or more interviewees. Focus group interviews have become a common research tool in recent times. Morgan (2002) defines this as 'a research technique that collects data through group interaction on a topic determined by the researcher' (p. 141). This is a 'broad definition that includes most forms of group interviews, with the exception of observing naturally occurring conversations in ongoing interaction' (p. 141). This last may be an important source of data, but I believe it should be regarded as an observation and not as an interview. For me a focus group is to be distinguished from other forms of group interview by the role of the 'interviewer' and the notion of 'group interaction'. At the risk of over-simplification, in 'normal' group interviews interviewers are concerned mainly with the nature of their relationship with the members of the group as individu-als. In a focus group, the job of the 'moderator', as the interviewer is usually termed, is 'to keep the discussion on the topic while encouraging the group to interact freely … Following group discussion, it is usually the moderator's job to do the analysis and prepare the research report' (p. 146). As such, the key objec-tive of a focus group interview is to achieve an accurate representation of the views of the group as a whole in interaction whereas in other forms of group interviews what is more usually sought are faithful accounts of the views of the individuals who constitute the group.

My experience of interviewing groups has largely been of the latter kind, usu-ally with pupils in primary and secondary schools. It has its advantages – I have, for example, found that pupils tend to be more forthcoming in groups than when interviewed on their own. It can offer an economic way of canvassing the views of a larger number of people. Disadvantages include the possibility of some regression to the mean in the views expressed, and it can be difficult to avoid the assertive dominating the discussion. Finally, group interviews are far harder to record than one-to-one discussions. I rarely interview a group of more than eight; my limited experience with bigger numbers has not often been satisfactory.

Telephone

I have conducted few such interviews. In doing so I have felt the loss of most non-verbal signals frustrating and so use this method only if there is no real chance of face-to-face discussion or if the cost is prohibitive (Shuy, 2002). Such considerations have led some of my Doctoral students to this approach. Zhang (2004), in a study of the lives of secondary headteachers in mountainous and rural western China, planned his research in two main phases. The second phase was to take the form of two face-to-face interviews with each of the 25 headteachers involved. Finding visiting them in their schools for the first round of face-to-face interviews entailed a great deal of difficult even dangerous travelling, he decided to undertake the second set by telephone. Sherratt (2004), in a study of six successive Permanent Secretaries at the Ministry of Education, managed with difficulty to get them all to agree to be interviewed face-to-face. Like Zhang, he wanted a follow-up discussion but knew the most he could hope for was a telephone interview. Sherratt and Zhang believed these interviews worked well enough, but felt this was so only because the earlier round had been face-to-face. In passing, there are now simple devices that allow reliable recording of such interviews. The same can be said of the next form of interview.

Email

Studies relying on computer-assisted (Couper and Hansen, 2002) and Web-based (Mann and Stewart, 2002) interviewing are becoming commonplace. Their impact has been greatest in survey interviews but they have also begun to be used in qualitative studies – usually as email interviews. Two of my Doctoral students have used this approach. One wished to study the views of selected secondary principals of international schools and the other wanted to explore the possibilities of Web-based, action research for enabling the personal support and professional development of primary headteachers in Israel.

Using this approach in the first study was justified because the geographical spread of these schools meant undertaking face-to-face interviews in worthwhile numbers was all but impossible. Since he wished his study to be interactive, he rejected using written interviews. A pilot study comparing telephone and email-based approaches convinced him of the merits of the latter – it was more reliable technically and less demanding practically. This was so not least because email interviews produce a record as they proceed, whereas telephone interviews require transcription. Given its Web-related theme, the use of email interviews was probably even more appropriate in the second study. In this the researcher used, in part, an interactive email approach which allowed her to corresponded with all her subjects and they with her and each other and in doing so to produce a series of on-going transcripts which constituted a substantial aspect of her final data base (Ron, 2003).

Written

Whilst email-based studies are proliferating, written interview research is rare. Mortimore and Mortimore (1991a, 1991b) asked seven primary and nine secondary heads to write to a set of issues including 'the background of the headteacher and the school; the head's personal philosophy of education; organization and management of the school; organization and management of learning; relationships; and personal reflections on headship' (1991a: ix). They claim the heads responded frankly. They certainly wrote thoughtfully, often passionately. But how far the text represents their authentic voice is hard to tell because little information is presented on the methods used to construct these accounts or on the editorial role the researchers played in this. In a second such study, Zhang (2004) in Phase One of his research distributed a written interview to all 158 junior secondary headteachers' in Chuxiong. Despite the support of the principal of the local teachers' college, only 27 responded. Zhang (2004) offers various reasons for this response, concluding 'it is relatively easy to talk, it is much harder to write … It could be … I tried to include too many questions' (p. 92). Whatever its merits this approach has some serious limitations. As he notes, it can be seen by interviewees, with some justification, as more demanding than alternative forms. He also suggests that it 'may be less suitable as a method of probing difficult and complicated questions' (p. 92) in part because it is less interactive and spontaneous. Conversely, it can enable the study of those who are difficult to access and it does produce ready-made transcripts. As such it is less resource-demanding than other methods, but in what sense it allows for meaningful conversation or offers an effective way of getting at what is in other people's minds is more doubtful.

Responding to different categories of interviewee

Few believe there can be a one-size-fits-all approach to interviewing. At the very least interviews must have regard to the needs of different types of interviewee and the context in which they take place, an issue thoroughly examined in Gubrium and Holstein's edited volume (2002) in chapters on children and adolescents (9), men (10), women (11), race (12), the old (13), elites (15), the ill (16) and the reluctant (25).

Had I more space, an issue I would have discussed at greater length is that of cultural relativity and its implications for those who engage in interview research. This has been a concern in my personal research into headship in other cultures and in managing research projects, even when working with teams composed mainly of local researchers, in other countries (see Ribbins, 1999). Those who wish to pursue this issue can do so in this publication, in a helpful chapter by Ryen (2002), and in the contribution by Dimmock to this book (see Chapter 4).

Managing interview-based research

Research in education relying, in whole or in part, on interviews has to be managed at the level of the individual interview and of the whole project.

Interview management

Producing rich and reliable data from interview-based research requires managing effectively at least four key things: what is asked and how, the interviewer and the interviewee, recording and transcribing.

Managing what is asked

This is about schedules and questions: it is about knowing what you, as interviewer, wish to find out and asking the right questions, in the right way, at the right time and in the right order to encourage the interviewee to tell you. What is apposite varies according to the type of interview and person being interviewed – themes for a 'chat' or 'discussion' must be kept to a minimum; the former conceived as specific issues to be raised if an opportunity occurs, the latter thought of in broader terms. Schedules for 'interviews', especially when one-off, must be thought through in detail. Thus, for example, the Rayner and Ribbins (1999: 51–53) schedule contains 14 main questions and numerous sub-questions. This was feasible only because the interviews were to be quite long, between 120 and 180 minutes, and with highly practised talkers.

In this context, I have often been asked by my students how many issues and questions they should cover in an interview. There is no simple answer. Much depends on context and circumstance and on the answers to the following kinds of question: What are you trying to find out? How complicated and sensitive is this? Who are you interviewing? Are you planning one-off, or do you anticipate follow-up interviews? How long do you expect the interviews to be? Broadly, I have found that inexperienced researchers producing first draft interview schedules almost always hope to cover far too many themes in the time available – this is compounded by a desire to ask long questions and to raise multiple sub-themes. In producing my own schedules, and in advising students on theirs, I begin by trying to list all the things I could ask and then reduce this to the things I must ask. The second list is almost always much shorter than the first.

If good schedules make for good interviews so do good questions. Effective interviewers use questions that enable interviewees to tell them what is in (or on) their minds and avoid those that put things there. *Closed* questions seek factual information (*How long have you been a head?*), require a yes/no answer (*Is this your first headship?*), or specify possible responses (*How do you feel about being a head – very happy, happy, or unhappy?*). *Open* questions are at the core of qualitative interviewing and have many possible answers (*How do you feel about being a head?*). *Follow-up* questions come in various forms. Some *probe* for detail (*When did you first apply for a headship? What happened?*), others seek to *check* something directly (*Does this mean you were the only internal candidate*) or by *reflecting* back (*Did I hear you say* – repeat this, pause ...), or by *recapitulating* (*Can we summarise what you said on why you became a head as follows ...?*).

Some questions should be avoided – notably those that *lead* interviewees to a particular answer (*Headship has become much more demanding, how and why?*). This would be acceptable if asked in two parts – *Has headship become more demanding?* Those who agree will usually go on to explain how and why, those that don't can be asked.

Managing the interviewee and the interviewer

Skilful interviewing requires interviewers to manage themselves and those they interview effectively. It entails *getting the questions right.* Complex questions, particularly those raising multiple themes, can be discouraging and confusing. Lengthy questions can mean the interviewer spends far too much time talking and the interviewee too little. Too many questions risks harrying and antagonising interviewees. Obscure questions, expressed in a language that is not readily accessible to interviewees, invite misunderstanding.

It also entails *getting the relationship* right. Normally interviewers should try not to let their values shape their relationship with interviewees. Try to establish *rapport* (a stance *vis-à-vis* the person) and *neutrality* (a stance *vis-à-vis* what they are saying). The former means making clear you value the person you are talking to and are glad to hear what they tell you. The latter means they can tell you anything without risking your disfavour. There are ways in which this can be established. When phrasing a question let the person know you have heard it all before: the good and bad. You are not interested in the sensational but in his/her views and what his/her experience has been like. When asking difficult questions I sometimes provide a simulation (*Suppose I was at the next senior team meeting, what usually happens?*).

It is important to offer support and recognition: use verbal and non-verbal signals to let the interviewee know how the interview is going. Positive reinforcement is vital but directive feedback can be necessary. The enthusiastic or fixated can be difficult. Stock phrases have worked for me: *Can I stop you for a moment? Before we go on can I make sure I fully understand something you said earlier?* (I then steer things back to my agenda.) But remember that what at the time seems irrelevant to you, might not be to the interviewee or, in the final analysis, to your research project.

Managing recording

This raises two questions: Why is recording necessary? How can it be done? The answer to the first is simple: in interview studies, recording generates data, without data there is no research. The answer to the second is more complicated. It deals with the forms of recording and their merits. For written and email interviews recording is a by-product of the process. Regarding the other forms, four types can be located along a continuum in terms of how reliable, comprehensive and intrusive they are, with memory located at the low pole, then taking notes, then tape-recording, and with videoing at the high pole. This last has advantages.

For example, it enables non-verbal signals to be recorded. However, such data is subject to high researcher bias and as a method it is formidably intrusive. It is also very time-consuming to analyse.

Teaching interviewing I have found a role-play exercise helpful. The class is divided into groups of four. The group's first task is to identify a research project and agree key items of an interview schedule. Its second task is to select a person to act as interviewee, a second to interview and record using written notes, a third to tape the discussion, a fourth to observe what takes place, making notes on this. The interview is time-limited (20 minutes), at the end of which the class takes a break. On returning, I ask them to spend 30 minutes writing up as quickly and as fully as possible the discussion drawing on memory (interviewee), notes (interviewer and observer) and tape (recorder), and then a further 30 minutes comparing their accounts. Various lessons are usually learned, including: how unreliable memory is; how demanding it is to simultaneously conduct and record an interview; and, how much less reliable and comprehensive memory is than notes, and notes than a taped record. I try to use such a session for a number of other purposes; for example, by ensuring across the whole class that different kinds of tape recorder (varying in size, quality and sophistication) are used. Although warned of the need to get to know their recorder, there are still often problems – the recorder is not properly set up, there is not enough tape, the recorder has been placed poorly and so is hard to hear when transcribing – these things can happen even to the experienced.

Interviewing Kenneth Baker, Home Secretary and before that Secretary of State for Education, with a sophisticated new recorder, I noticed a red light appear. I had no idea what this meant. Checking in a panic after the interview, I found no problem – but this was not good enough. I should have familiarised myself with the machine and checked it was working. There are occasions when it is well worth considering using two tape recorders – this might well have been one of them. It is important to prepare and practise carefully before engaging in a real-time interview. There are two more lessons those new to interviewing soon learn – how difficult it can be to write up a conversation from memory or notes, and how time-consuming it is to transcribe a taped discussion. How can this last problem be minimised?

Critical to this is the quality of the recording (Modaff and Modaff, 2000). This means using the right kind of machine and locating it where it is best placed to record. To minimise intrusivity, I used to believe the smaller the recorder the better but came to resort to larger machines, often with an external microphone, because: (1) this produces a better recording; and (2) most interviewees soon forget about the recorder. In the rare cases they did not, I switched, ostentatiously, to taking hand-written notes. Recent developments in technology now make this problem redundant. Tiny, robust, reliable and sophisticated digital recorders are now available that record well, and in doing so greatly facilitate transcription and the preparation of audio data for qualitative analysis (Stockdale, 2003).

Managing transcribing

Those who engage in interview-based research must decide how best to produce their data in order to facilitate its analysis and writing up. However the interview has been recorded this means some form of transcription. Email and written interviews necessarily produce such a text, thus obviating the need for any form of transcription. The same might be said of interviews recorded in written notes. In my experience, this view is misguided. Unless the interviewer happens to be skilled in the use of shorthand, at best notes can only give a very partial record of the interview. However, if such notes are written up as soon as reasonably possible after an interview, the interviewer will be able to use this as an opportunity, drawing on her or his memory, substantially to enhance the record of the discussion that took place. For such reasons, and for others I have discussed above, it is even more important to produce a text of a discussion in which the only record the interviewer has available is memory (as with a chat), and to produce this pretty well immediately. What of taped interviews? On this, I am aware that not all who tape-record transcribe, relying instead on listening to the tape or tapes several times. I have serious doubts about this approach. First, whilst it might be manageable in small-scale projects, it is far less so in studies which involve multiple interviews. Second, given its highly selective way of identifying 'useable' quotes, it is liable to data 'raiding'. Third, without transcripts stored on a computer, it is not possible to make use of the increasingly helpful software programmes that are available for the analysis of qualitative data (Seale, 2002).

It is one thing to make a case for transcription, another to do it. For a discussion of the possibilities and perils of transcriptions see Poland (2002); for some 'heresies' see Nisbet (2006). This raises issues, most obviously in the case of taped interviews, on (1) what is to be transcribed and (2) how to go about this. The first focuses on how much of an interview should be transcribed. To this there is no one answer; much depends on the purpose of the research and how this might best be achieved. If the purpose is to investigate the patterns of speech of a target group, the transcription must replicate the syntactic and linguistic imperfections found in their talk. But an examination of most reports of educational research will show that few believe this always necessary. I believe that a balance has to be made in which I edit transcriptions to make them intelligible to the reader whilst remaining faithful to what the interviewee has said. The second has to do with determining how much of an interview is to be transcribed. When doing my own, I make ongoing judgements about what to include and leave out. Interviews vary in quality and relevance – in a 'good' interview I expect to transcribe almost all of it, in a 'poor' interview much less. When I have decided to omit a large part of a discussion I usually note this in the text. I do so because experience has taught me that what may seem 'irrelevant' at one stage of a research project can become highly relevant later. If this happens I can return to the tape and transcribe the discussion dealing with this. To be able to do this it is necessary to retain the tape; I now keep all tapes until a project has been completed and reported. So much for substantive matters, what of more technical considerations?

Anything that eases transcribing is worth doing, but a major benefit of producing one's own texts, especially in multiple interview projects, is that this enables the generation of a level of knowledge of their content unmatched by any other method. Such knowledge comes into its own when analysing and writing up the study.

Project management

In planning an interview study, for a funded project or a student thesis, Kvale's (1996: 88) seven-stage procedure, as elaborated by Cohen, Manion and Morrison (2000: 273–287), is illuminating (thematising, designing, interviewing, transcribing, analysing, verifying and reporting). Even so, I find it helpful to collapse this into three main phases as follows.

In the *first phase* of a project researchers must determine what to study, why this is worth doing, and how to go about it.

Phase two focuses on setting the project up, determining its scope and identifying who is to be involved under what terms. In many of my interview-based studies, typically a group of heads were selected and invited to take part. It was not intended that they would represent the views of heads as a whole in the sector being studied. Rather, as Rayner and Ribbins (1999) describe it, the research involved ten heads drawn from 'special schools serving different types of special need along with some from mainstream schools [who] we expected to be interesting, who had different life experiences, who were at a variety of points in their careers and who were drawn from across England and Wales' (p. 2).

A key issue in planning such research, something I have often been asked by inexperienced researchers, is how many interviews should I undertake? Like the earlier query of how many issues can be raised in an interview, this is a variation of the 'How long is a piece of string?' question. In short, there is no one fully satisfactory answer since much depends on considerations of purpose and circumstance. Some things are clear. For example, that less is expected of those engaged in Masters' level studies than those involved in Doctoral studies. In this context 'less' normally means some combination of fewer and/or shorter interviews. Similarly, less will be required, in extent and perhaps scope if not in quality, of EdD as against PhD students. Different tutors and courses will have varying views on such matters. On the EdD course in educational leadership at Birmingham University, my colleagues and I advised our students that, other things being equal, they should normally consider undertaking between 10 and 20 substantial interviews.

With regard to the PhD studies, I have already said a good deal about Zhang's research of headteachers and headship in China and its range of interviews amounting in total to some 70. This is an unusually high number, even for a PhD study, but only about a third of them involved substantial face-to-face interviews. A ground-breaking study by Sherratt (2004) was even more ambitious. It set out to examine the extent to which, and how, the six Permanent Secretaries who held office at the Department of Education between 1976 and 2002 influenced policy. He interviewed each of them face-to-face and then by phone, along with many other influential education policy-makers at a national level. In doing so he conducted many more interviews than the 33 interviews used in his thesis. Reflecting on my experience, many years of supervising interview-based research at a Doctoral level has taught me that initially students tend to overestimate what is possible regarding the scope of their project and underestimate the amount of interviewing that will be required.

Phase three involves doing the field research, analysing it, writing it up and publishing it having regard to the terms agreed with respondents. It is important to be scrupulous on this. In most of my portrait-based headship studies all were interviewed for between two and three hours each. All but two of the interviews took place at their schools, almost always in their offices. Whilst interruptions were not uncommon, these circumstances are close to ideal and may be more difficult to achieve with others. It is important to be adaptable – people promise to see you and forget, or are ill, or called away and you have a wasted journey. Make another appointment, and return. In most of my research in England and Wales, although not usually elsewhere, those who took part knew it was to be 'on the record'. Most interview studies offer to protect the identity of their interviewees. The practical, and even legal, difficulties of doing this fully successfully can be very complex (Wenger, 2002). Interviews were taped and transcribed. Censorship was restricted mainly to the deletion of libels, of which there were fewer than in anonymised discussions. Each respondent was sent a transcript and invited to propose corrections. The letter of contact guaranteed they could pull out at any time, but very few have. It also stressed, should their interview be published, that this would be in a form which had regard to their wishes. A few made much use of their right to propose revisions, most very little.

I have been involved in similar, anonymised, research (Pashiardis and Ribbins, 2003; Ribbins and Zhang, 2005). These were reported as posopographies – group biographies. What of their relative merits? An advantage of on-the-record research is that the reader, and interviewee, is well placed to contest researcher claims. Its disadvantages are that interviewers might be more tempted to protect respondents from the consequences of frankness than they should be and, interviewees may be less open in what they say than they could be. The latter will depend partly on how skilfully interviews are managed.

Reflections

In this chapter, drawing on the literature and my own experience, I have considered how researchers using interviews can produce rich and reliable data on which to base their analysis and final report. Summarising, I would offer those new, or even those not new, to such research three pieces of advice. First, good interviewing does not come naturally. For most it must be learned. This entails reading, thinking, watching others and practising before undertaking interviews in real time. Second, even the skilled and experienced can be better. It is important: (1) to consider what went well and what did not and to learn from this; and (2) to try new ways of working. Third, try to remember as you toil through a difficult interview or struggle with a mountain of 'rich and reliable' data, that research should be fun, serious fun, a controlled adventure as Goffman (1968) has memorably described it.

References

Adler, P. and Adler, A. (2002) 'The reluctant respondent', in Gubrium, J. and Holstein, M. (eds) *Handbook of Interview Research: Context and Method.* London: Sage. pp. 515–537

Bush, T. (2006) 'Authenticity – reliability, validity and triangulation', in Briggs, A.R.J. and Coleman, M. (eds) *Research Methods in Educational Leadership and Management* (2nd edn). London: Paul Chapman.

Cohen, L., Manion, L. and Morrison, K. (2000) *Research Methods in Education* (5th edn). London: Routledge/Falmer.

Couper, M. and Hansen, S. (2002) 'Computer-assisted interviewing', in Gubrium, J. and Holstein, M. (eds) *Handbook of Interview Research: Context and Method.* London: Sage. pp. 557–577.

Davies, M. (2002) *The Headmaster Tradition Revisited*, EdD Thesis, University of Birmingham, (unpublished).

Dexter, L. (1970) *Elite and Specialized Interviewing.* Evanston, IL: North Western University Press.

Goffman, E. (1968) *Asylums.* London: Penguin.

Guba, E. and Lincoln, Y. (1981) *Effective Evaluation.* San Francisco, CA: Jossey-Bass.

Gubrium, J. and Holstein, M. (eds) (2002) *Handbook of Interview Research: Context and Method.* London: Sage.

Kvale, S. (1996) *Interviews.* London: Sage.

Mann, C. and Stewart, F. (2002) 'Internet interviewing', in Gubrium, J. and Holstein, M. (eds) *Handbook of Interview Research: Context and Method.* London: Sage. pp. 603–629.

Modaff, J. and Modaff, D. (2000) 'Technical notes on audio recording', *Research on Language and Social Interaction*, 33 (1): 101–118.

Morgan, D. (2002) 'Focus group interviewing', in Gubrium, J. and Holstein, M. (eds), *Handbook of Interview Research: Context and Method.* London: Sage. pp. 141–161.

Mortimore, P. and Mortimore, J. (1991a) *The Primary School Head.* London: Paul Chapman.

Mortimore, P. and Mortimore, J. (1991b) *The Secondary School Head*. London: Paul Chapman.

Nisbet, J. (2006) Transcribing interviews: some heretical thoughts, *Research Intellegence*, 97, 12–14.

Pascal, C. and Ribbins, P. (1997) *Understanding Primary Headteachers*. London: Cassell.

Pashiardis, P. and Ribbins, P. (2003) 'On Cyprus: the making of secondary school principals', *International Studies in Educational Administration*, 31 (2) 13–34.

Rayner, S. and Ribbins, P. (1999) *Headteachers and Leadership in Special Education*. London: Cassell.

Ribbins, P. (1999) 'Producing portraits of leaders in education: cultural relativism and methodological absolutism?', *Leading and Managing*, 5 (2): 78–99.

Ribbins, P. (2007) 'Middle leadership in schools in the United Kingdom: improving design – a subject leader's story', *International Journal of Leadership in Education*, 10 (1): 13–30.

Ribbins, P. and Sherratt, B. (1997) *Radical Educational Policies and Conservative Secretaries of State*. London: Cassell.

Ribbins, P. and Zhang, J. (2005) 'Headteachers and their exits: moving on and moving out in Chuxiong in rural China and elsewhere', *International Studies in Educational Administration*, 33 (3): 74–89.

Poland, B. (2002) 'Transcription quality' in Gubrium, J. and Holstein, M. (eds) *Handbook of Interview Research: Context and Method*. London: Sage. pp 629–651.

Ron, T. (2003) 'An account of a mainly Web-based, action-research programme and its effects on the professional development of a group of primary school principals in Israel'. PhD Thesis, University of Leicester (unpublished).

Ryen, A. (2002) 'Cross-cultural interviewing', in Gubrium, J. and Holstein, M. (eds) *Handbook of Interview Research: Context and Method*. London: Sage. pp. 335–355

Seale, C. (2002) 'Computer-assisted analysis of qualitative interview data', in Gubrium, J. and Holstein, M. (eds), *Handbook of Interview Research: Context and Method*. London: Sage. pp. 651–671.

Sherratt, B. (2004) 'Permanent Secretaries and educational policy'. PhD Thesis, University of Birmingham (unpublished).

Shuy, R. (2002) 'In-person versus telephone interviewing', in Gubrium, J. and Holstein, M. (eds) *Handbook of Interview Research: Context and Method*. London: Sage. pp 537–557

Silver, H. (1977) 'Nothing but the past, or nothing but the present?', THES, 1 July, 17.

Stockdale, A. (2003) *An Approach to Recording, Transcribing, and Preparing Audio Data for Qualitative Analysis* (available on www2.edc.org?CAEPP/audio.html).

Wenger, C. (2002) 'Interviewing older people', in Gubrium, J. and Holstein, M. (eds) *Handbook of Interview Research: Context and Method*. London: Sage. pp 259–279

Woolford, P. (2004) 'Changing times for FE leaders'. EdD Thesis, University of Birmingham, (unpublished).

Zhang, J. (2004) 'A study of the lives and careers of selected secondary head teachers in Rural China'. PhD Thesis, University of Birmingham (unpublished).

Recommended reading

Cohen, L., Manion, L. and Morrison, K. (2000) *Research Methods in Education* (5th edn). London: Routledge/Falmer Press.

Gubrium, J. and Holstein, M. (2002) (eds) *Handbook of Interview Research: Context and Method*. London: Sage.

Kvale, S. (1996) *Interviews*. London: Sage.

14

The trouble with questionnaires

Judith Bell

The trouble with questionnaires is that, sometimes, they seem like a very easy way to get hold of a great deal of information quickly (no need to decide what to do with the responses until they arrive) and any fool can devise one in the time it takes to drink a cup of coffee. Wrong on all counts. They are fiendishly difficult to design and should never be considered by anyone who believes that 'anyone who can write plain English and has a modicum of common sense can produce a good questionnaire' (Oppenheim, 1992: 1). Of course, the ability to write plain English is always a help and common sense is a commodity which is good to add to the research armoury, but before any method of data collecting can be considered, decisions have to be made about *precisely what it is you need to find out*. Sounds obvious, but that is the stage which is so often hurried or even overlooked completely and this omission can result in the selection of entirely inappropriate data-collecting instruments which produce useless responses. So, we had better start at the beginning.

Begin at the beginning

Let's say that you have recently taken over responsibility for the Diploma in Forest Management in your college, and though you are fairly confident that most aspects of the diploma programme are sound, you have reservations about others. You have just heard that in six months' time the college is to receive a visit from a team of external assessors who will require evidence of the college claims for quality provision. The only evidence you have is examination results, and they have tended to be ... well ... variable. That is probably not surprising because college policy has always been that if employers are willing to release their employees for the three years of the part-time diploma, then students are accepted. Some want to come; others don't. Some want to work; others won't. You discover that there are no records of student feedback, nor of any curriculum discussions between college-based and forestry management placement staff. It's clear that the diploma needs a thorough spring-clean.

Let's also say that you are half way through a Masters course and that the dissertation looms. Subject to the approval of the college principal and the dissertation supervisor, here was an opportunity to kill two birds with one stone by carrying out an investigation into the quality of the Diploma in Forestry Management.

It is easy to select a topic in general terms but the hard work begins in moving from the general to the specific. You will have your own ideas about the particular aspects which should be considered but you also need to consult colleagues and students about what they consider to be vital elements in the programme. Their views might be different from yours. The first-thoughts top-of-the-head shot at identifying priorities might include:

- Something on the curriculum
- Quality of teaching in the college and on placements
- Quality of student support
- Quality of supervision, particularly on placements
- Relevance of the college course to the work of forestry management
- Balance of theory to practice
- Relationship between college and placement staff
- Students' views about all the above – and anything else they consider important
- College social and sports facilities
- Effectiveness of the tutorial system
- Library access
- Study facilities
- Assignment feedback to students
- Overall quality of the programme

Some or none of these might be selected as being of prime importance but whichever are selected will form the framework for the study. How much time will you have for this investigation? Which items are absolutely essential and which merely desirable? Time has to be spent on this stage of the research, but it's easy to lose sight of the key issues. Punch (1998: 36) reminds us that at this crucial stage in the research planning it's good to remember the 'What are we trying to find out?' question. He warns us that:

> The focus on this question almost always shows that there is 'much more here than meets the eye'. The topic expands, and many questions are generated. What perhaps seemed simple and straightforward becomes complicated, many-sided and full of possibilities.

Quite so, but a word or warning. Boundaries have to be set because, if they aren't, you could go on expanding the topic for ever. External assessors would come and go; reports would be produced; blame and praise allocated in equal measure; courses closed and others opened and you would still be at the stage of deciding what the focus of the study should be. Not everything can be done, so decisions have to be made about what is essential, what is merely desirable and what can be done in the available time.

It would be impossible to include all the items on the first-thoughts list, so let's say you decide to consider students' views on the following priority areas:

- Quality of teaching, support and supervision of students in college and on placements
- Relevance of the college diploma programme to the work of forestry management
- Balance of time spent on theory of forestry management and practice
- Students' overall satisfaction with the diploma programme

What is the best way of obtaining students' views on these topics? You know what information you require and you now have to decide how best to obtain it. Only when you have considered *precisely* what you want to find out and why, will you be able to decide on which data-collecting instrument will be best for your purposes. If you decide on a questionnaire, work can start on question wording – and that is not as easy as it sounds.

The importance of precise wording

Concepts to variables

All questionnaire items have to be worded in ways which will be absolutely clear to students and which can be *measurable*. Let's start with the most difficult item in the list of priority areas, namely 'students' satisfaction with the diploma programme'. If students are asked 'Are you satisfied with your course?' responses might well be on the lines of 'No', 'Yes', 'Sort of', 'It's all rubbish'. It might be argued that if all the researcher needed was information about the numbers of students who said they were satisfied, the question would be perfectly all right. But what does 'satisfaction' mean? Might it mean 'it's a darn sight better being warm and dry in college than working in a freezing forest in the pouring rain' or might it mean 'this is the best course I've ever known, the teaching is excellent, the placements and the balance of theory to practice just right', etc, etc.? The Yes/No type of response is of no real value because you need to know more and to discover what 'satisfactory' and 'satisfaction' actually mean to the students. Ways have to be found to overcome this dilemma.

Satisfaction is a concept and we can't actually observe or measure concepts but we can probably think of ways in which individuals indicate or demonstrate satisfaction. Take time to think about it. Talk about it to colleagues. Brainstorm it. Produce flow charts with ideas because somehow or another ways have to be found to move from the unobservable to the observable.

Rose and Sullivan provide some useful examples of ways in which the concept of 'class' might be observable.

226

If we wish to understand something about class (a concept and therefore ... not observable), what can we observe in the real world which manifests class? That is, what indicators can be used for class so that we can obtain data about class? This is the essence of the measurement problem and when we link an unobservable concept with an observable indicator we are producing *operationalizations*. (Rose and Sullivan, 1996: 12/13; emphasis in orignal)

They define 'measurement' as being 'simply a way of saying that, in respect of some variable, one case is *different* from another – not bigger or smaller, better or worse, but only different' (p. 17) and 'operationalization refers to the rules we use to link the language of theory (concepts) to the language of research (indicators)' (p. 13). They suggest that 'employment' or 'social class' might serve as indicators of 'class', so what indicators might there be of 'satisfaction'? This is quite tricky and you may need several attempts at producing indicators, so once again, ask colleagues and friends for their views, build up a flow chart, focus the mind and get back to basics and the '*What do I need to know?*' question.

Ambiguity, imprecision and assumption

If you were to be asked what you meant by 'curriculum' you would, I'm sure, be able to provide a clear, succinct and comprehensive definition but are you absolutely sure all your colleagues would give the same definition? Ask a room full of people, some concerned with education, some not, and in all probability you would get a variety of responses. Ask students and they might tell you it meant syllabus, subjects or something to do with the course. In other words, you cannot assume they will all have the same understanding of 'curriculum' nor that their understanding is the same as yours. Other wording has to be found which will make it clear what is meant.

Leading and presuming questions

It is surprisingly difficult to avoid leading questions. If the wording is on the lines of 'Do you not agree that there is insufficient time spent on forestry practical work?' then that's obviously a leading question but other questions like 'Does the college make adequate provision for counselling?' may be harder. What is 'adequate'? There's a presumption here that respondents know that a counselling service exists, what it does and whether or not the provision is adequate. In its present form, the question is invalid and if you really want to know something about students' opinions of the service, you will need to work harder to produce wording which will enable respondents to give a clear answer.

Double (or even triple) questions

'Has the science component of the programme helped your understanding of pest control and planting techniques?' Well, perhaps it helped my understanding of pest control but not planting techniques. If information is required about both, then separate questions are needed.

'Is the quality of teaching, support and supervision in college and on placements good?' You would not put a question like that, of course; the wording here is just your reminder about what you want to find out. It is a very complex question and would need to be broken down into separate components, with explanations about the meaning of 'support' and 'supervision'. However, it is pretty common to come across questionnaires with double questions, particularly in hotel 'feedback' questionnaires such as:

The management is always looking for ways of improving the service to guests. We should be grateful if you would circle the appropriate number below and return the form to reception.

How would you rate the service and cleanliness of the hotel?

Excellent	Very good	Good	Satisfactory	Less than satisfactory
1	2	3	4	5

I found this in the bedroom of a large chain hotel and all the following questions followed a similar format. They certainly believed in stacking the odds to emphasise the positive, with only one negative item, but that's the least of it. The double question is obvious but there are multiple features of both. You might consider that the service was good in parts. Pleasant, helpful personnel at reception, efficient chamber maid who did a great job, but the porter was surly and the waiters in the dining room were downright disagreeable. As far as cleanliness was concerned, the bedroom was spotless and most public areas were fairly clean except the toilet in the foyer, which was filthy.

It's easy to mock and far more difficult to produce flaw-free questions, but this example is poor in another way. You often see 'excellent' and 'very good' on questionnaires, but it's a fine line between the two and I've never seen an explanation of the difference. Usual practice is for hotels, travel companies and others to group responses. In this case, I don't have much doubt that 'excellent', 'very good' and 'good' would be grouped and the summary of guest comments would be that '80% of guests rated everything under the sun as good or better'.

Memory and knowledge

Your respondents will only have about half an hour to complete the questionnaire and so questions need to be worded in a way respondents can answer without much hesitation. For example, 'What marks did you get for pest control in your first year?' sounds straightforward enough, but if the students are in their third year they may not remember. They would need to check and there's no time to check, so either they will not answer or they will guess. Similarly, what if you were to ask 'Do you think you will be able to obtain a sufficiently high mark for the final diploma examination to be awarded a pass?' Well, in the first place students may not know or may not remember what the pass mark is, and what's the point of asking a question like this anyway?

Checking again and considering word order

Question selection and precision wording are likely to require a good many drafts before final versions come up to standard. Eliminate any item that doesn't comply with the *what* rule. There is neither the time nor the space to fill the questionnaire with irrelevancies in case they come in handy. You want every single item to be worded in such a way as to ensure that all items are necessary, that respondents understand what you mean, are able to provide an answer on the spot and are not offended by your wording or assumptions. You may change your mind several times about the order of questions so it's probably a good idea to write questions on cards or separate pieces of paper. Cards are easier to handle and to sort but anything will do. As soon as the sorting and eliminating is done, you will be ready to move on to issues of appearance and layout – apart from one last check. Go through each question or item and ask yourself once more:

- Is there any sign of ambiguity, imprecision or assumption?
- Are there any items which require memory or knowledge which respondents may not have?
- Are there any double, leading, presuming, offensive or sensitive questions?

Questions or statements?

It's not all over yet, because even though you know what you want to find out, the way the questions are worded will influence the usefulness of the responses. Go back to the item relating to the quality of students' supervision while on placements. It wouldn't really be enough to have responses like 'Good', 'Non-existent' or 'Bad' would it? Wouldn't you want more detail? You might decide that ranked items would be likely to produce a greater degree of discrimination and that a Likert scale would be better than straight questions. It would be up to you to decide which approach is best, but let's look at what a scale might look like.

Likert scales ask respondents to indicate, usually by circling a number, rank order of agreement or disagreement with a statement. There is generally a three, five- or seven-point range, though researchers frequently prefer an even number of items, as in the following example, mainly to avoid the neutral central point.

229

In my view, the supervision provided for forestry management practical work is good.

Very strongly disagree	Strongly disagree	Disagree	Agree	Strongly agree	Very strongly agree
1	2	3	4	5	6

The statement could equally well have begun with 'Very strongly agree', and researchers will frequently change the order during the course of the question-naire in order to make sure respondents are awake. Of course, that means that you also have to be awake and to remember what you are doing when you come to score the responses. That also means that you need to decide not only how you are going to score and but also what the scores will mean *before* ques-tionnaires are distributed.

We need to be careful about what we can deduce from Likert scales. They certainly arrange individuals or objects from the highest to the lowest but the intervals between each may not be the same (Cohen et al., 2003). We cannot assume that the highest rating (6 in the above case) is six times higher than the lowest (which is 1). All that can be said is that 'the data in each category can be compared with data in the other categories as being higher or lower than, more or less than, etc., than those in the other categories' (Denscombe, 2003). In spite of these limitations, Likert scales can be helpful and as long as the instructions to respondents are clear, useful information can be obtained.

So, you take your pick. Questions or statements?

Question order and appearance

If you are satisfied you have done everything possible to ensure that the word-ing of questions is as clear as you can make it, it will be time to decide on the order in which they are to appear on the questionnaire. There should not be any complex or sensitive questions, but if one or two have slipped in, it is best to place them well down in the order. The last thing you want is for potential respondents to take offence or decide the questionnaire is too hard – and to throw it into the nearest bin.

Appearance is important. I have no doubt we have all received scruffy question-naires, particularly those which have been distributed to friendly households as part of a school project, but this isn't a school project and it has to look good. Remember that in all probability you will be the one who is required to carry out the analysis of responses and to produce a report of findings, so it becomes rather important to be able to see and record responses without having to search for them in irregularly positioned boxes or circled numbers which are all over the place.

Respondents' rights

You are asking respondents to do you a favour, even if they are students and you are the boss. They are entitled to know why they are being asked to complete your questionnaire and what you are going to do with their responses. Unless you or a colleague plan to distribute the questionnaires in person, and explain the 'why' and the 'what' on the spot, a letter is required. Be honest and don't promise anything you can't deliver. Many investigations promise anonymity and confidentiality but, occasionally, both have been variously and to my mind damagingly interpreted. Sapsford and Abbott (1996: 319) provide what is a helpful definition of anonymity and confidentiality. They write that

> As we are using the term, *confidentiality* is a promise that you will not be identified or presented in identifiable form, while *anonymity* is a promise that even the researcher will not be able to tell which responses came from which respondent.

So if anonymity is promised there is no question of numbered questionnaires and a record kept of which number applies to which respondent; no tricks such as numbers or symbols on the back of the questionnaires. It means there is no possibility of reminder letters. If the forestry management questionnaires were to be distributed in class, then any blank returns would mean that the students declined to participate and that would be that. If the questionnaires are distributed via internal mail or by post, then you have to accept whatever returns you get.

There can be some difficulties over confidentiality. If in your report you say that 'the Director of Resources was of the opinion that ...', you are identifying him/her if there's only one Director of Resources. If your description of a school or department is too explicit, then everyone who works in that area will immediately know which school or department you are talking about. No one minds if the report is complimentary but if your school happens to have poor examination results and high truancy rates, you might be less joyful about the world knowing about it. Sapsford and Abbott (1996: 318) make their views perfectly clear when they write that 'a first principle of research ethics – to be found in all the various codes of conduct imposed by professional and academic organizations – is that the subjects of research should not be *harmed* by it' and, sad to say, there have been cases where individuals and organisations have been harmed. The subject of ethics in research will already have been covered in Chapter 5 of this book but the dangers of loose interpretation of 'anonymity' and 'confidentiality' are worth reinforcing here (see Bell, 2005: 57–58; 167–171).

Piloting the questionnaire

You may feel everything is now done and dusted and you are ready to distribute the questionnaires, but there's another important step to take yet. No matter how busy you are, all data-collecting instruments have to be piloted. You may have consulted everybody about everything, but it is only when a group similar to your main population completes your questionnaire and provides feedback that you know for sure that all is well. If you cannot find a similar group, then ask friends, colleagues, anyone you can get hold of. There is another very good reason why you absolutely have to carry out a pilot exercise and that is that so far you have not considered how you will record and analyse the returns and once the 'real' questionnaires are returned, you need to know what to do with them. Even if this is to be a straightforward descriptive study which only requires frequencies (the number of items in each category) and frequency distributions (how often each item occurs), trial analyses need to be made and methods of presentation considered. As Youngman (1978: 3) rightly reminds us:

> At the risk of disillusioning many readers, the first truth of research analysis is that it does not start the day after the last item of data is collected … the analytical strategies must be planned early in the research processes … Deciding upon the actual research procedure will determine the precise nature of the practicable analyses.

It might be that for the purpose of the college study, frequencies and frequency distributions will be enough, but your Masters dissertation may well require more sophisticated analysis and that will need to be tried out *before* questionnaires are distributed. If a computer statistical package is to be used for analysis, then you will need to be absolutely sure which package will be appropriate, what will be involved in keying in the data and in understanding what the printout means. So once again back to *precisely what do I need to find out* and *which statistical strategies will be necessary in order to provide me with that information*. Best to find out before you are finally committed to the wording of your questionnaire.

Distributing the questionnaires

At last it's time to distribute the questionnaires to your respondent group. It would obviously be best if you or your colleagues were able to distribute and explain the purpose of the study in class time, but that's not always easy to achieve. For a start, not all colleagues will be overjoyed at losing their class time and even if you have permission from the college management, you may not be top of the popularity poll with your colleagues unless you have asked them and obtained their agreement beforehand. If they say, 'Definitely not. We need every minute we can get if these students are to pass the exam' you might be able to pull rank, but that approach will generally be unwise. If you insist and even show the letter in which the principal gave permission, you might be saying goodbye to any possibility of collaboration, assistance or support from the protesting colleagues in future. It's best not to rock the boat too much.

If class completion fails, you might be forced to distribute the questionnaires via the internal mail system, but the rate of return will inevitably be lower and you really do need as many completions as possible if the study is to mean any-thing. Whatever approach is selected, or forced on you, do your utmost to avoid postal distribution. In the first place, you or the college would have to provide a stamped addressed envelope, which is expensive. More seriously, the rate of return for postal questionnaires is generally poor. What to do then? Well, you could try being exceptionally nice to your colleagues before crisis time. You will already have consulted them about which topics are essential and will have asked their advice about questionnaire wording. They know why the study is being carried out and though they may think the entire quality exercise is a waste of time and an annoying additional task when there is already insufficient time to do the job, they are likely to be more responsive to a request for help with distribution if they have been participants in the exercise.

Producing the report or dissertation, looking for themes, groupings and patterns

If you were carrying out this study as part of a Masters dissertation, you would already have carried out a review of the literature. As you read, themes would have begun to emerge together with valuable insight as to how others planned their research. In any investigation, we are always looking for patterns and groupings. If all you did was to provide a list of every student's response to each question, you would be left with pages of lists which meant very little and few readers would have been willing to spend the time necessary to search for groupings themselves. All data need to be interpreted and if patterns do emerge, they will require particular comment, though *take care not to make claims which cannot be substantiated*. Decide which methods of presentation will best illustrate the data: tables, charts, histograms – and what else? (see Chapter 12 of Bell, 2005: 203–228).

Your aim will be to produce a clear, informative report of the findings which, you hope, will contribute to the college understanding of students' perceptions of the Diploma in Forestry Management *and/or* be one worthwhile component of the Masters dissertation.

If your preparation has been sufficiently thorough, all will be well. Your questionnaires will be clear and well designed; the comments from your pilot exercise will have been considered and any appropriate changes made; appro-priate methods of analysis will have been tried out before distribution of the questionnaire; your report will be well written and will make no unsubstanti-ated claims – and you will be able to congratulate yourself on a job well done.

Checklist

1) Select a topic which really interests you and is likely to be worth all your time and commitment.	If you have no interest in the topic, you will quickly become bored and lose interest.
2) Spend time refining and focusing your topic and never lose sight of key issues.	Set boundaries. You cannot do everything. Decide which aspects of your investigation are essential and which are merely desirable.
3) Make sure you have permission to carry out the study.	Never assume everything is bound to be all right because there might be regulations about research being carried out in your institution.
4) Consult colleagues about the topic. They may have good ideas and different points of view from you.	They may know about useful sources of information – and you may well need their help throughout the research so it is as well to recruit them as participants.
5) Are you sure a questionnaire is the best way to obtain the data you need?	Always refer back to 'What am I trying to find out?'
6) Take time over question wording.	And remember that responses need to be measurable.
7) Concepts are abstractions and so cannot be observed or measured.	Ways have to be found to link concepts to indicators.
8) Are any of your questions ambiguous or imprecise?	Are you making any assumptions?
9) Do you have any leading, double or presuming questions?	If you are not sure, ask colleagues what they think.
10) Are you asking respondents to remember something that happened some time ago?	Are you assuming they have knowledge which they may not have?
11) Take care over question order.	If you have any complex or sensitive items, do not put them early on in the questionnaire.

12) Make sure the appearance and layout of the questionnaire are good.

A scruffy appearance will do nothing to encourage responses.

13) Respondents have rights and they are entitled to know why they are being asked to complete your questionnaire and what you are going to do with the responses.

They are doing you a favour by completing the questionnaire, so they should be fully informed – and thanked.

14) If you promise anonymity and/or confidentiality make sure your respondents know what you mean.

Make sure *you* know what you mean. If you promise either or both, you must honour that promise.

15) Always pilot questionnaires.

Make changes to wording if necessary and try out methods of analysis with the pilot returns.

16) Decide on methods of questionnaire distribution.

Try to negotiate distribution and completion in class time if possible. Avoid a postal questionnaire unless you are desperate.

17) If your trial recording and analysis has been well done, you should know beforehand exactly where and how you intend to record responses.

As you record, you will be looking for patterns and recurring themes.

18) In an ideal world, it would be good to wait until all returns were in before beginning the recording process.

But we don't live in an ideal world and you will inevitably be short of time, so start recording as soon as returns start to come in.

19) Make sure your report is clear, to the point and highlights key issues.

And *never* make claims which can't be supported by your evidence.

20) Thank everyone who has assisted you with the research.

You may need their help again some time.

References and recommended reading

Bell, J. (2005) *Doing Your Research Project: A Guide for First-Time Researchers* (4th edn). Maidenhead: Open University Press/McGraw-Hill. (Chapter 8 deals with designing and administering questionnaires.)

Bell, J. and Opie, C. (2002) *Learning from Research*. Maidenhead: Open University Press. (Parts 1 and 2 consider the approach to research, and in particular the questionnaire design adopted by two postgraduate students. Might be useful to consider the hurdles they faced – and the ways those hurdles were successfully overcome.)

Cohen, L., Manion, L. and Morrison, K. (2000) *Research Methods in Education* (5th edn). Abingdon and New York: Routledge/Falmer. (Chapter 4 on Sampling and Chapter 5 on Validity and Reliability are well worth consulting).

Denscombe, M. (2003) *The Good Research Guide for Small-scale Social Research Projects* (2nd edn). Maidenhead: Open University Press/McGraw-Hill. (Everything in this book is worth consulting, but in Part II (Methods of Social Research), Chapter 9 'Questionnaires' is particularly helpful.)

Oppenheim, A.N. (1992) *Questionnaire Design, Interviewing and Attitude Measurement* (new edition). London: Cassell. (Chapters 1, 2 and 3 provide guidance about survey design and Chapters 7, 8 and 9 cover questionnaire planning, questioning wording, basic measurement theory – and much more. An excellent book to keep for reference.)

Punch, K.F. (1998) *Introduction to Social Research: Quantitative and Qualitative Approaches*. London: Sage.

Rose, D. and Sullivan, O. (1996) *Introducing Data Analysis for Social Scientists* (2nd edn). Buckingham: Open University Press.

Sapsford, R. and Abbott, P. (1996) 'Ethics, politics and research', in Sapsford, R. and Jupp, V. (eds) *Data Collection and Analysis*. London: Sage. Ch. 13.

Youngman, M. (1994) 'Designing and using questionnaires', in Bennett, N. Glatter, R. and Levačić, R. (eds) *Improving Educational Management through Research and Consultancy*. London: Paul Chapman with The Open University. Ch. 17. (This chapter is a revised edition of M.B. Youngman (1982) *Analysing Questionnaires*, Rediguide 12, Guides in Educational Research, University of Nottingham Rediguides. It is an excellent chapter which deals with the importance of planning, question specification, questionnaire design, distribution and return.)

15

Observation as a research tool

Janet Moyles

Observation as a tool for the leader/manager can be powerful, flexible and 'real'. It is not dependent, like survey methods, on respondents' personal views but seeks explicit evidence through the eyes of the observer either directly or through a camera lens. 'Because observed incidents are less predictable there is a certain freshness to this form of data collection …' (Cohen et al., 2000: 305). Observation is often part of ethnographic research and leads to a description of people, events and/or cultures: it is then a holistic approach concerning the observation of 'everyday' events and the description and construction of meaning, rather than reproduction of events (Robson, 2002). However, as the teaching profession has been opened up to scrutiny, observation in school, particularly of meetings and of classrooms, has become somewhat imperative. Observation also plays a part in mentoring and appraisal.

This chapter will examine a range of issues relating to our understanding of observation as a research process and tool. Using examples from my own educational research in various settings, and drawing on others' research in wider leadership and management arenas, it will explore:

- Observation as a 'natural' process and in educational research
- Two main forms of observation with brief ethical considerations
- Various ways of supporting observational research
- Some ways of analysing and interpreting observational data
- Reliability and validity issues in relation to observational data

Observation as a 'natural' process

It is something of a natural instinct for many of us to be observers. Whether we are on a beach watching others enjoying the outdoors or scrutinising the weather through our windows, we look at, see and interpret what is happening. Our everyday observation skills function very much alongside our purposes for observation and are often determined by what we *think* or *hope* we are going to see. Whatever it is we observe and want to understand undergoes significant *interpretation*. However, in the process of interpretation, we cannot divorce our underpinning values and beliefs from the ways we ourselves perceive a situation or what we *expect* to occur. So it is in educational research, particularly from the perspective of those within education as leaders and managers, who will have certain 'views' and expectations of school systems and classroom practice.

Herein lies a significant challenge for educational researchers, especially those stepping 'outside' their role for a short period, who want objectively to observe educational phenomena. Interpreting what is observed, from the potential wealth of data that may be gathered, especially in field work, is a key feature of observational research, although a majority of the interpretation, if we are trying to be objective, needs to occur directly from the data gathered (not as easy as it sounds). It is difficult always to be wholly objective. What we can try to do is to acknowledge and overcome our personal interpretations by a variety of means, not least of which is using our professional knowledge as researchers to ensure clarity of concepts, purpose and method both before and after observational data-collection.

When we make decisions about *what* to observe, we first need to be clear about what are our *purposes*. This means ensuring that our conceptualisation of the research question is as clear as it can possibly be (Robson, 2002). What is it we want to study and why? For example, in order to make staff meetings more equitable and encourage participation in issues from a wider group, leaders may simply want a clear picture of:

• How many teachers make a contribution to discussions in staff meetings?
• How many of these contributions last longer than five seconds?
• How many of these contributions are questions?
• How many of these questions add to the debate?

In classrooms, leaders may want to see how often individual (target) children interact with the teacher and what is the basis of this interaction:

• How many times does a teacher interact with a particular child(ren)?
• How many of these interactions extend beyond one exchange?
• How many open-ended questions are posed within these exchanges?
• Does the response involved show evidence of children using thinking skills?

Or leaders may want to establish how the culture of the school is projected by those within it. Beare et al. (1989) suggest that culture is expressed in three ways: conceptually or verbally (use of language); behaviourally (through rituals, ceremonies, rules); and in visual or material mode (through equipment, mottoes, crests and uniforms). This might mean observing:

• How do staff and pupils talk about the school?
• What do the everyday activities and actions of staff and pupils (e.g. in assemblies, sports days, prize-givings, etc.) reflect of their perceptions of, and attitudes towards, the existing culture?

- How do displays and public areas around the school reflect the culture of the school as you, the leader/manager, perceive it?
- Does the environment of the school show a general culture of care and respect?
- Do pupils appear to wear their school uniforms with pride, resentment, dignity?

We can only gain much of this information by observation (and through recording); if we ask teachers and others for such information, they may find it difficult to divorce feelings from 'facts'. Their perceptions of events may be clouded, for example, by whether they felt more concerned about getting home before the rush hour than attending the staff meeting at that time, concerns about the deleterious effects of the target child's behaviour on other pupils, or worries about whether discussion of cultural aspects will deflect from important teaching and assessments. To find out what actually happens it is necessary to observe and, of course, to interpret expertly from our reading, knowledge and understanding. For example, in a project investigating reception class practices, one target child was observed every two minutes for an entire day: every activity in which that child was engaged was recorded as field notes. When the results of this were analysed, a clear picture emerged of just how much (and how little) time this target child spent on particular activities and how much time was spent in contact with adults (Adams et al., 2004).

Observation is a very useful research tool for leaders/managers because it can:

- Give direct access and insights into complex social interactions and physical settings
- Give permanent and systematic records of interactions and settings
- Be context-sensitive and ecologically valid (Denscombe, 2003)
- Enrich and supplement data gathered by other techniques (allowing triangulation and thus increasing reliability)
- Use very varied techniques, yielding different types of data and with the potential to be widely applied in different contexts
- Be used to address a variety of types of research questions.

Leaders/managers and others in education who embark upon research using observational methods need, however, to be aware of some of its challenges. For example, it places high demands on time, effort, resources and on sustained commitment. The wealth of data gathered has to be categorised and analysed. There are often unknown effects upon the subject(s) of the observation, which can impact upon the data gathered and it is susceptible, as we have seen, to observer bias and underlying assumptions. These can all affect the reliability of the data (see Chapter 6 in this book). Different forms of observation will be more or less susceptible to these factors, as we shall see.

Forms of observation

We can observe using 'naturalistic' approaches (Guba and Lincoln, 1987) or more 'formal' approaches (Croll, 2006). In the former, the researcher is drawn in as a participant in specific events and contexts either overtly or covertly. It may involve becoming a 'complete participant' (LeCompte and Preissle, 1993: 93) – that is, one with an insider role within those being studied who may know (overt) or may not know (covert) they are being observed. Or it may involve being a 'participant-as-observer' – a more likely role in schools and classrooms where leaders/managers are likely to be participants in different aspects of school life when undertaking observations. (For more details on participant/non-participant observation, see Cohen et al., 2000: Ch. 17.)

In formal approaches, the researcher is non-participatory and often uses systematic observation tools as a means of data-gathering. These pre-determine the focus of the observation and can be quantified, for example, by noting the number, frequency or timing of particular events. In the case of the questions in the previous section, leaders as researchers would be observing frequencies of events, event sampling and duration from a primary data source (Anderson with Arsenault, 1998).

Both participant and systematic observation are common in educational research, an example of the former being the research of Woods (1996). The forerunner of most classroom observation instruments was that developed by Flanders (1970) which is known as the Flanders Interaction Analysis Category (FIAC) system. (For full information on FIAC see Wragg, 1999; for examples of systematic observation of meetings, see Williams, 1994.)

Systematic observation

The benefit of well-conceived systematic observation schedules to leaders/managers is that they offer the opportunity for replication and comparison of data over time, which is extremely important for monitoring overall development and improvement in schools. The writer and colleagues, for example, used the ORACLE teacher observation schedule (see Galton et al., 1980, 1999) to establish whether the type and level of teacher interaction in primary classrooms has changed since the advent of the National Literacy Strategy and the Literacy Hour approach to teaching and learning (Moyles et al., 2003). The results indicate that teachers had increased their levels of interaction with pupils but that variation existed between KS1 and KS2 teachers in the level and type of demands made of pupils through questioning. This would have been problematic to determine without the opportunity for comparison which the well-established teacher observation schedule permitted.

The difficulty with systematic observation for those new to research is the development of the observation instrument itself. Even if one utilises an existing instrument there is the challenge of learning how to use it effectively (if it is used

	Boys	Girls
Teacher 1	𝍷𝍷𝍷𝍷 𝍷𝍷𝍷𝍷 𝍷𝍷𝍷𝍷 𝍷𝍷𝍷𝍷 𝍷𝍷𝍷𝍷 II	𝍷𝍷𝍷𝍷 𝍷𝍷𝍷𝍷 𝍷𝍷𝍷𝍷 II
Teacher 2	𝍷𝍷𝍷𝍷 𝍷𝍷𝍷𝍷 𝍷𝍷𝍷𝍷 II	𝍷𝍷𝍷𝍷 𝍷𝍷𝍷𝍷 𝍷𝍷𝍷𝍷 IIII

Figure 15.1 Number of times two different teachers made direct response to (a) boys and (b) girls during a (20-minute) lesson

in any way other than that for which it was designed, the findings will be invalid). Clearly leaders could design some relatively simple instruments which serve a given purpose. For example, a simple tally, as shown in Figure 15.1, can usefully show the number of times two different teachers make a direct response to (a) boys and (b) girls during a lesson. What this cannot tell the leader/manager is the duration or content of the observations but, for example, it is interesting to see that one teacher makes more direct responses to boys whilst the second teacher shows more balance in the responses. Finding out why this may be so could be established either by developing a much more sophisticated instrument or by, for example, video-recording and analysing the observed lessons. Similarly, Figure 15.2 shows the interactions between participants in two minutes of a staff meeting. What this reveals, readers can decide for themselves.

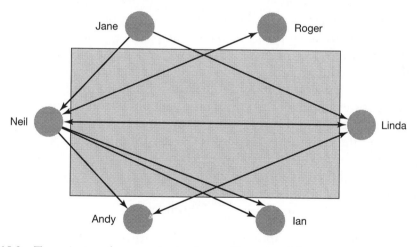

Figure 15.2 Two minutes of communication in a staff meeting. Who communicates with whom?

These kinds of instruments can be made more sophisticated by adding layers of information related to the content of the interactions under investigation (who asked 'open' and 'closed' questions, about what area of interest were the questions asked) or to the antecedents and precedents of any observed events (at the point of misbehaviour or disagreement, what was previously said and what followed). Another way is that used in the Exeter Schedule (see Wragg,

1994: 43–49) in which the researchers decided on a list of child behaviour characteristics (for example, noisy or illicit talk, physical aggression to another pupil, defiance of teacher) and also on a list of how teachers might deal with that behaviour (for example, order to cease, get into close proximity to child, humour). All the categories had to be agreed in advance by the group of observers. These two lists (after piloting and inter-rater reliability measures) then formed the basis of a series of schedules which were used on segments of lessons to monitor how teachers manage pupil misbehaviour. (One of my own examples of a semi-structured observation schedule with an explanation of its purpose is given at the end of this chapter.)

Participant observation

Participant observation is the most likely form to be used by leaders/managers as it allows the researcher to be part of the 'natural' setting and to 'become' part of it (often with no pre-determined view about what findings will emerge or how they will be interpreted). For example, leaders may well be overt participant observers in a governors' meeting with the aim of reviewing how the governing body operates. Participant observation involves making field notes and/or recording events using audio-visual means in a relatively unstructured way. In covert participant observation (unlikely to be used by leaders/manager), the researcher joins the subjects and acts and reacts as they do, recording observations at a later time. This kind of covert operation happens when, for example, researchers want to find out how particular groups live. Television and newspaper journalists occasionally use this method in developing work for documentary programmes by, for example, joining groups of homeless males or football hooligans and living life as they do. One of the classic examples of this is the participant observation recorded in Whyte (1981). Covert research of this type raises many ethical issues, particularly in relation to whether the ends justify the means (Foster, 1996; Hitchcock and Hughes, 1997). It is very unlikely to be used by leaders/managers because of the sensitivity associated with children as direct or indirect research participants and issues of informed consent and negotiation of access (Bell, 2005). You can read more about the ethics of such research in Chapter 7 of this book.

Non-participant and semi-participant observation

Non-participant observers usually enter the 'scene' of the research with knowledge of what they want to observe and why. In many observations in educational research, it is probably true to say that whilst much of it is non-participant, the context of practitioner-based research, in which many researchers are themselves teachers, makes it very difficult for the researcher not to be an 'informed', semi-participant observer, particularly leaders/managers. This raises some difficulties (like getting too 'involved') but is also useful because the leader/manager already has 'insider' knowledge to bring both to recording important events and to analysing the data gathered through field notes. Being non-participant involves the leader/manager in aiming to be 'invisible, either in fact or in effect (that is, by being ignored)' (Walliman, 2001: 241). It is possible, although difficult, to be a 'fly-on-the-wall' in classrooms. This is more likely if the leader/manager (a) spends considerable time in meetings or in the classroom with their research equipment (for example, camera, audio recorder); and (b) takes particular measures, such as avoiding eye-contact with teachers and children and wearing unobtrusive ('chameleon') clothing. As a non-participant it is also necessary to turn a 'blind eye' to occurrences in the classroom that are not part of the research – the child who is misbehaving can become an embarrassment to the teacher with the head-teacher present as an observer – whereas a semi-participant can, if the teacher chooses, share the experience at the end of the observational session. Clearly there are challenges in this situation to retaining objectivity, particularly for a leader/manager. Fortunately, combining and triangulating methods allows some reduction of this in interpreting findings.

Combining methods

Counting or monitoring observed events in the ways outlined above clearly falls short of giving a holistic picture. Even with complex systematic observation schedules, the frequency or duration of observed events can only give a certain picture of what is happening and this often requires interpretation alongside further knowledge of the context. For this reason, many researchers combine the use of systematic observations with other forms of observation, for example, with a classroom non- or semi-participant researcher taking field notes, with video/audio recordings or with interviews or prior surveys (see final section of this chapter).

Observer effects

It is difficult to realise the effects the researcher, particularly a leader/manager, may have on a meeting or classroom/school situation but these may include the following – and many others:

- Concern on the part of those being observed and, therefore, their not behaving normally (some people will admit to this in follow-up interviews as, for example, did the headteacher who said that he always provided wine for end-of-term staff meetings but felt he should not do so when the meeting was being observed).
- Particular foci, for example, of the teaching or meeting, being avoided at the times of observation because they are not felt to be appropriate. (I had an experience in a nursery where the teacher felt it more appropriate to show herself in a direct instruction situation rather than in a play and learning situation with children even though the project was focusing on play and learning.)

- Wanting to be seen to be like others who may also be observed (for example, perhaps wanting to be seen to be conforming with what is 'required', yet not necessarily having considered what that might be).
- Concern that those observed may respond adversely to being observed (for example, children may 'play up' because the headteacher is in the classroom – a case to be made here for being a semi-participant).

See Delamont (1992) for other considerations.

Observer bias

Whilst all researchers will try to remain as objective as possible, observer bias is difficult to avoid totally, particularly for leaders/managers researching in their own institutions (there is no such thing as value-free data-gathering!). Observational biases occur because of:

- *Selective attention.* Our sensory mechanisms (as we saw above in relation to looking, seeing and interpreting) are themselves subject to bias. We both select what we 'want' to see and then interpret this from our own perceptions and values.
- *Selective encoding.* The leader/manager will have certain expectations of what is likely to be seen and, in interpreting data, will make unconscious and subconscious judgements about them. Surfacing these whenever possible through discussion with others is vital to ensuring the validity of outcomes.
- *Selective memory.* Especially in observations using field notes, it is vital that, if not written contemporaneously, notes are written up as soon afterwards as possible. It is also necessary that all observations are clearly contextualised (see section on recording observations).
- *Interpersonal factors.* Whilst the non-participant leader/manager is trying to obtain a distance between her/himself and the subjects, being in the same room or setting as those observed inevitably raises relationship (and power) issues. The leader/manager as participant–observer may find that personal likes and dislikes can surface when getting a feel for the culture and ethos of the individual context.

Awareness of both effects and bias takes us part-way to generating counter-measures. For example, it is helpful and necessary wherever possible to have someone else's opinion on instruments or procedures. It is also useful to check your own potential biases against what others have written in relation to research of a similar kind, hence the advisability of reading any research similar to your own as well as literature on research methodology.

Ethical issues

For both ethical and objectivity purposes, it is vital to ensure that those being observed are absolutely clear about their rights to an explanation of aims, procedures, purposes, the consequences of the research, publication possibilities and the right to refuse to take part or withdraw at any stage. The subjects need to be competent to make these decisions, acting voluntarily and making their decisions on the fullest possible information. Particularly because of the potential power relations, the leader/manager as researcher needs to be clear that subjects fully comprehend the nature and outcomes of the research and that they will be assured anonymity and confidentiality (McNamee and Bridges, 2002).

There is also the issue of turning a 'blind eye' in order to respond appropriately to incidents during observational research (Maykut and Morehouse, 1994), as we saw earlier.

Various ways of supporting observations

Various means of recording can be used to support data collection as we have seen, from making relatively unstructured field notes by hand or directly on to a laptop, through to using very defined and pre-determined structured and systematic observation schedules. The content of 'live' recording – that is, the field notes taken directly by the observer that have their origins in anthropological research – is, at the point of gathering, entirely the observer's choice. He or she decides what to gather and when to gather it, with an emphasis on meanings and explanations growing explicitly from the context. Both participant and non-participant observations must be contextualised and both can benefit from technological support through video and audio recordings, provided that both the observer and equipment effects are considered.

Contextualising observations

Observational data should always be contextualised: details of the context and circumstances in which the observation took place must be collected alongside the observational data. It is vital to retain information about:

- The context of the observation – meeting, classroom, playground, staff development session
- The overall environment of the observation (e.g., classroom, meeting room) – make an accurate plan to aid memory
- How many subjects were involved at different points – subjects may come and go from view dependent on the context of the observation
- The roles of the subjects involved – chairing the meeting, presenting papers, listening to the teacher
- The time of day at which the observation occurred – this can be very significant in relation to the subjects' responses and behaviours

- The seating arrangements – in classrooms, whether the children were in groups (and of what size); and in meetings who sat where
- The timetable of events – what happened at the start, in the middle and at the end of the observation (time this for your own purposes later)
- The point at which any critical incidents occur as this may be useful information later

Other information will depend on the purposes for the observation and the methods used.

Video recordings and photographs

While both video recordings and photographs will need to be sampled and coded, they are useful for highly focused study or examining fine-grained behaviours such as non-verbal interaction (see Prosser, 1998). They are particularly useful because moving and still images can be revisited to provide exact replicas of earlier data gathered or sequences of events which are being analysed. I have also used video in observational research to play back to teacher subjects a video sequence of a lesson or activity (pre-selected by them) for their comment and analysis, thus including the teacher as a research partner in observational research. These 'video-stimulated reflective dialogues' appear to provide an effective means by which teachers can reflect on practice and consider potential and relevant changes to practice (Moyles et al., 2002, 2003) – all as a result of observation! The use of such visual data could be particularly helpful to leaders/managers as it allows practitioners who have been observed to step outside their own practice whilst simultaneously providing an opportunity to review, draw awareness and reflect upon action as precursors to meaning-making methods (Fletcher and Whitehead, 2000; McNamara et al., 2000). Whilst most observation is non-interventionist, this is an example where the outcomes of the observation (deriving both qualitative and quantitative data) could be used to develop further observations and improve both practice and reflection on practice.

Video-recording classroom events or meetings, or taking photographs around the school, can be useful in capturing the essence and culture of the whole context but there are downsides: the focus range of the camera or the particular 'fix' used by the person operating the camera can skew the data. As was indicated earlier, the mind-set of the observer can determine what is 'seen' and what is therefore video-recorded. For this reason, in my research, which focused directly upon the teacher's role, the camera was fixed almost exclusively on the teacher so as not to be drawn to child participants (Moyles et al., 2002). One can argue that this does not then capture the whole pedagogic process but, as with any method, decisions have to be made as to what will give the best 'fitness for purpose' for required outcomes. In this case, a focus on children could mean that actions, reactions and other behaviours of the practitioner would be missed whilst the camera pans to children.

Digital photographs, particularly those taken in timed sequence, can be useful for recording the progression of events in a classroom or meeting. They can help to identify otherwise difficult aspects such as who is attending or who is apparently on task at any point within the sequence and can also offer a record of several different contexts in which observations were conducted by leaders/managers and be used as memory-joggers for follow-up interviews.

The images obtained from digital video/cameras can also be manipulated; for example, video recordings can be taken and sequenced still images extracted from them which can then be used as discussion points with research subjects. Images can be re-presented immediately following events and can readily be electronically forwarded to distant colleagues for further analysis. Digital images can also be anonymised by the blurring of faces in order to protect the subjects from identification and to encourage participants to make inferences or judgements about 'missing' information.

Semi-structured observation

In many ways this is a misnomer: observation is either structured or unstructured. However, for a number of reasons, the leader/manager might wish partly to structure the observation but also leave opportunity for informal data-gathering. For example, in research attempting to establish the roles in the classroom of teaching assistants (TAs), I found it helpful to track – using a semi-structured schedule – each TA's broad, overall tasks in classrooms (for example, the areas of curriculum in which they were engaged, whether working with individuals or groups of children), whilst at the same time, making audio recordings of conversations with children and taking field notes of the context of the work (another example of combined methods). No attempt was made in the semi-structured schedule to determine the finer points of the role as these were available through the other means.

Another example of semi-structuring observations might be in relation to the rating scales occasionally used by researchers. These are seemingly objective measures but are subjectively determined. For example, the leader/manager engaged in observation of a staff development session might rate the overall setting according to a number of criteria which operate on a scale from excellent to poor in terms of content, presentation, audience participation and so on (Williams, 1994). Meetings can be observed and ranked on a Likert-type scale from business-like to dysfunctional, or classrooms ranked on a scale from well-organised to chaotic. Such scaling does need accurate measures of inter-rater reliability to be of value, however, and that reliability itself depends on the criteria previously determined for rankings such as 'business-like' or 'well-organised'. These measures (classed as high inference) require considerable subjective judgement to be made by the leader/manager, where more structured schedules require 'low inference' judgements in that they require the observer merely to record whether or not something happened.

Shadowing procedures

Shadowing is not always perceived as observational research but to my mind, clearly stands in that category. It is often semi-participatory, requiring ongoing field observations in very close proximity to the subject, as would be the case for a head-teacher shadowing another head or a member of the senior leadership/management team. For this reason it carries certain conditions which need to be met, not least of which is that the subject must feel wholly at ease with the leader/manager in constant attendance. Therefore, the process needs careful setting up and considerable non-shadowing trial time so that the person being shadowed, as far as possible, feels both comfortable and is able to ignore the researcher if the outcomes are to be valid. The process can reap significant benefits, especially if repeated over time, because it can give a total picture of a particular role. I have used such methods on a number of occasions, mainly in matching the expectations of a role with the actual daily fulfilment of that role, in one case in terms of the teaching assistant's role. The intention was to find a match (if one existed) between the TA's job description and the role actually undertaken. The potential disparity only became visible when the tasks undertaken over time and in proportion to the day were matched against the role as described and required by the school. This could equally apply to any role within the institution which carries a job role description. The kind of analysis undertaken from the results of shadowing is quite straightforward, but that is not always the case.

Analysing and interpreting observational data

It will be necessary to consider the following when analysing and interpreting the two principal forms of observational data:

- *Structured observations*. These take longer to conceptualise and prepare and are behaviourist in origin. Structured observations allow comparison, are discrete, have little overlap and categories are (and must be) mutually exclusive.
- *Informal observations*. These are based on an interpretive paradigm and are quicker to prepare but are likely to take much longer to analyse outcomes. There can be much overlap and categories may evolve rather than be pre-determined.

As has been said previously, it is possible that one may inform and feed on the other.

It is important to know what type and level of analysis you intend to employ *before* collecting your data because the amount of transcription and analysis required is likely to be greater than anticipated. In a project called Effective Leadership and Management in the Early Years (ELM) the researchers predetermined the outline content of the typology of leadership and management behaviours from the relevant literature and analysis was then undertaken of the additional data gathered against the outline typology and what might be subtracted or added (Moyles, 2006).

Tools for analysis and data presentation

Somehow, gathering data seems more productive than analysing it and inexperienced researchers often use the process as a bulwark against potential failure. By far the best advice is that given by Silverman (2004) – to analyse your own data as they are gathered. The first session of field observation, or the first batch of completed schedules, alongside your initial analysis of existing data and concepts through the literature, can provide sufficient data to allow analysis to begin. It also gives an indication of how much analysis and interpretation can occur from a relatively small amount of data. This is the point at which it is necessary to check your original analytical intentions and, having made a few forays into it, check that what you decided is still appropriate to your research requirements. For example, do your categories now seem to fit the data gathered? Which concepts look like being the most productive in terms of quantity of related data?

The analysis of transcriptions, as Silverman (2004) suggests, depends upon the generation of a research problem from a particular theoretical orientation, hence the need for having considered carefully and at the outset a clear conceptualisation of the problem under investigation.

There are straightforward, manual ways of categorising and ordering the data gathered: see Cortazzi (1993), Coffey and Atkinson (1996), Dey (1993), Huberman and Miles (1994) for both theoretical and practical examples. These entail various means by which the data are reviewed and main concepts highlighted (usually with a highlighter pen). In addition, there is a now a well-established range of useful computer-based analytical tools such as ATLASti and NVivo (website addresses are given at the end of this chapter). It is important to remember that these tools are only as good as the person who programs in the categorisations, so an initial manual run-through is still vital. The technique or computer program chosen will depend on the skills of the leader/manager and his/her own views as to what will give the most effective and reliable outcomes. All these methods need the observations or field notes to be transcribed into text – easier if done with a digital dictaphone. Computer-based programs require that data are imported in various structures into the program, often by means of Word documents.

Excel and similar spreadsheet packages support the ultimate presentation of quantitative data through charts, tables and graphs to give ready visual access to data but the data must be input in coded format. Coding observation schedules at the point of data-gathering is a must. The power of SPSS in handling statistical data effectively and efficiently is well known in the research world (see Bryman, 2004). It can provide a range of statistical tests which can be applied to data thus securing a range of reliability measures, for example, analysis of variance across subjects or fields or correlations between items (for a straightforward guide, see Coolican, 2004).

Electronic storage is neater and data more quickly retrieved, allowing potentially more time for analysis. It can also add rigour, for example, to counting frequencies, and can offer more confidence in the patterns that data analysis may reveal.

Observation and reliability/validity measures

Observation, as already emphasised, is probably most effective when combined with other forms of data-gathering, for example, interviewing or questionnaire survey, because of issues of interpretation of what is observed and of potential observer bias, identified at the start of this chapter. Used in combination with other methods, it offers the opportunity for findings to be validated through triangulation (see Chapter 6 of this book). Validity is also concerned with the credibility of the means and tools by which the data is collected (Simpson and Tuson, 2003).

Determining reliability is highly dependent upon the range of factors which were discussed earlier, namely (in the case of structured observation) the quality of the research instrument and the number of observations undertaken – the greater the number, the more reliable the outcome is likely to be. A measure of inter-rater/coder reliability is important here: different researchers should be able to achieve highly correlated results by use of the same instrument. In the case of informal observation, measures of reliability relate mainly to 'blind' coding of transcribed data, that is, the transcriptions being given to different researchers who need to achieve similar outcomes from the categories determined. At the extreme – and if there's time and interest – giving another leader/manager the data gathered and allowing them to code on the same principles would be an interesting and informative way of checking both reliability and validity.

Piloting observations

Piloting of observations, whether systematic or informal, should always be undertaken to evaluate the reliability of the instrument in use and in the latter case to get a feel for the validity of different types of field notes. Piloting can also act as a meaningful training for the leader/manager and it should also show whether it is possible to collect data using another's instrument(s) and achieve inter-observer reliability.

Conclusion

Observation is a useful and interesting tool for all researchers, including those involved in leading and managing schools and colleges. Is it the 'best' method? If your purpose is to 'see' what happens and what is enacted then the answer is 'Yes!' Evidence-informed practice is now prominent in educational thinking, practice and policy-making. Observation is a key means for leaders/managers to obtain both 'hard' and 'soft' evidence about the institution and well-conceived structured and informal observational methods can measure what exists and how this changes over time. It cannot, of itself, produce change. Interventionist studies can, however, include the use of video observations to begin the process of change. Observational research can fulfil a range of intentions and be used for a variety of purposes to inform current and future debates in education, of which headteachers are often at the forefront.

References

Adams, S., Alexander, E., Drummond, M-J. and Moyles, J. (2004) *Inside the Foundation Stage: Recreating the Reception Year*. London: Association of Teachers and Lecturers.

Anderson, L. with Arsenault, N. (1998) *Fundamentals of Educational Research*. London: Falmer Press.

Beare, H., Caldwell, B. and Millikan, R. (1989) *Creating an Excellent School: Some New Management Techniques*. London: Routledge.

Bell, J. (2005) *Doing Your Research Project: A Guide for First-Time Researchers* (4th edn). Maidenhead: Open University Press/McGraw-Hill.

Bryman, A. (2004) *Social Research Methods*. Oxford: Oxford University Press.

Coffey, A. and Atkinson, P. (1996) *Making Sense of Qualitative Data*. London: Sage.

Cohen, L., Manion, L. and Morrison, K. (2000) *Research Methods in Education* (5th edn). London: Routledge/Falmer Press.

Coolican, H. (2004) *Research Methods and Statistics in Psychology*. London: Hodder Arnold.

Cortazzi, M. (1993) *Narrative Analysis*. London: Falmer Press.

Croll, P. (2006) *Systematic Classroom Observation*. London: RoutledgeFalmer.

Delamont, S. (1992) *Fieldwork in Educational Settings: Methods, Pitfalls and Perspectives*. London: Falmer Press.

Denscombe, M. (2003) *The Good Research Guide for Small-scale Social Research Projects* (2nd edn). Buckingham: Open University Press.

Dey, I. (1993) *Qualitative Data Analysis: A User-Friendly Guide for Social Scientists*. London: Routledge.

Flanders, N. (1970) *Analysing Teaching Behaviour*. Reading, MA: Addison–Wesley.

Fletcher, S. and Whitehead, J. (2000) 'The "look" of the teacher: using digital video to improve the professional practice of teaching'. Paper presented to BERA annual conference, 7–9 September, University of Cardiff.

Foster, P. (1996) 'Ethical issues in observational research', in Foster, P. *Observing Schools: A Methodological Guide*. London: Paul Chapman.

Galton, M., Hargreaves, L., Comber, C., Wall, D. and Pell, A. (1999) *Inside the Primary Classroom: 20 Years On*. London: Routledge.

Galton, M., Simon, B. and Croll, P. (1980) *Inside the Primary Classroom*. London: Routledge Kegan Paul.

Guba, G. and Lincoln, Y. (1987) 'Naturalistic enquiry', in Dunkin, M. (ed.) *The International Encyclopaedia of Teaching and Teacher Education*. New York: Pergamon.

Hitchcock, G. and Hughes, D. (1997) *Research and the Teacher: A Qualitative Introduction to School-based Research* (2nd edn). London: Routledge.

Huberman, A. and Miles, M. (1994) 'Data management and analysis methods', in Denzin, N. and Lincoln, Y. (eds) *Handbook of Qualitative Research*. Thousand Oaks, CA: Sage.

LeCompte, M. and Preissle, J. (eds) (1993) *Ethnography and Qualitative Design in Educational Research*. London: Academic Press.

Maykut, P. and Morehouse, R. (1994) *Beginning Qualitative Research: A Philosophical and Practical Guide*. London: Falmer Press.

McNamara, O., Jones, L. and Van-Es, C. (2000) 'Evidence-based practice through practice-based evidence: the global and the local'. Paper presented to BERA annual conference, 7–9 September, University of Cardiff.

McNamee, M. and Bridges, D. (2002) (eds) *The Ethics of Educational Research*. Oxford: Blackwells.

Moyles, J. (2006) *Effective Leadership and Management in the Early Years (ELM)*. Maidenhead: Open University Press/McGraw-Hill.

Moyles, J. and Suschitzky, W. (1997) *Jills of All Trades? Teachers and Classroom Assistants Working Together in Key Stage 1*. London: Association of Teachers and Lecturers/University of Leicester.

Moyles, J., Adams, S. and Musgrove, A. (2002) *SPEEL: Study of Pedagogical Effectiveness in Early Learning*. London: DfES, Research Report No. 363.

Moyles, J., Hargreaves, L., Merry, R., Paterson, A. and Esarte-Sarries, V. (eds) (2003) *Digging Deeper Into Meanings: Interactive Teaching in the Primary School*. Buckingham: Open University Press.

Moyles, J., Suschitzky, W. and Chapman, L. (1998) *Teaching Fledglings to Fly? Mentoring in Teacher Education*. London: Association of Teachers and Lecturers/University of Leicester.

Prosser, J. (1998) *Image Based Research: A Sourcebook for Qualitative Researchers*. London: Falmer Press.

Robson, C. (2002) *Real World Research: A Resource for Social Scientists and Practitioner-researchers* (2nd edn). Oxford: Blackwells.

Silverman, D. (2004) *Doing Qualitative Research*, (2nd edn). London: Sage.

Simpson, M. and Tuson, J. (2003) *Using Observations in Small-scale Research: A Beginner's Guide*. Edinburgh: Scottish Council for Research in Education Centre.

Walliman, N. (2001) *Your Research Project: A Step-by-step Guide for the First-time Researcher*. London: Sage.

Whyte, W.F. (1981) *Street Corner Society* (3rd edn). Chicago, IL: University of Chicago Press.

Williams, G.L. (1994) 'Observing and recording meetings', in Bennett, N., Glatter, R. and Levačić, R. (eds) *Improving Educational Management through Research and Consultancy*. London: Paul Chapman with the Open University.

Woods, P. (1996) *Researching the Art of Teaching*. London: Routledge.

Wragg, E. (1999) *An Introduction to Classroom Observation* (2nd edn). London: Routledge.

Recommended reading

Cavendish, S., Galton, M., Hargreaves, L. and Harlen, W. (1990) *Observing Activities*. London: Paul Chapman.

Cohen, L., Manion, L. and Morrison, K. (2000) *Research Methods in Education* (5th edn). London: Routledge/Falmer Press. Ch. 17.

Croll, P. (2006) *Systematic Classroom Observation*. London: RoutledgeFalmer.

Denzin, N. and Lincoln, Y. (2000) *Handbook of Qualitative Research*. Thousand Oaks, CA: Sage.

Prosser, J. (1998) *Image Based Research: A Sourcebook for Qualitative Researchers*. London: Falmer Press.

Robson, C. (2002) *Real World Research: A Resource for Social Scientists and Practitioner-researchers* (2nd edn). Oxford: Blackwells.

Shostak, J. (2000) *Understanding, Designing and Conducting Qualitative Research in Education*. Buckingham: Open University Press.

Simpson, M. and Tuson, J. (2003) *Using Observations in Small-scale Research: A Beginner's Guide*. Edinburgh: Scottish Council for Research in Education Centre.

Williams, G.L. (1994) 'Observing and recording meetings', in Bennett, N., Glatter, R. and Levačić, R. (eds) *Improving Educational Management through Research and Consultancy*. London: Paul Chapman with the Open University.

Websites

ATLASti: www.atlasti.com/

NVivo: www.qsrinternational.com/products/productoverview/product_overview.htm

Semi-structured observation schedule – frequency of predetermined types of adult/child interaction (teaching assistant and/or teacher)

FREQUENCY CHART:		*Type of adult/child interaction*						

Date	Time	School	Round	1	2	3	4

Context/Activity	Main resources	Size of group
		same/different

Category[1]	Type	Tally	Code	Other or Comment
SOCIAL	attention		1	
	name		2	
	social		3	
	joking/comment		4	
BEHAVIOUR	encourage		5	
	praise		6	
	reprimand		7	
	negotiate		8	
QUESTION	for information		9	
	elicit understanding		10	
	prompting		11	
TEACHING MODE	suggest		12	
	explain		13	
	instruct – content		14	
	direct – admin		15	
	describe		16	
	remind		17	
	inform		18	
LISTENING	silence		19	
	response		20	
	reflect back		21	
	ignore		22	

[1] These categories were either too broad to identify small differences or teachers and teaching assistants (as we concluded) operate very similarly in the classroom, probably because TAs model their behaviour on the teacher. (See Moyles and Suschitzky, 1997.)

Source: Association of Teachers and Lecturers/University of Leicester: reproduced with permission

Schedule for post-observation video coding

The following schedule from Moyles et al. (1998) was devised for post-observation analysis of video-taped interactions between student teachers/newly qualified teachers and their school-based mentors. Categories were devised from the main literature on mentoring which were then categorised into Role Dimensions and Strategies. The video itself then provided Action categories and examples which, in turn, supported analysis of the video and inter-observer reliability measures.

Role Dimensions	Strategies	Code[1]	Actions	Code	Examples
PROFESSIONAL					
Supporter	To support	A	praising (general)	1	'good'
	To accept	B	praising (specific)	2	'that was good'
	To reassure	C	listening positively	3	nodding, 'yes', 'u-huh'
	To encourage	D	listening negatively	4	still, closed body posture
	To protect	E	offering practical support	5	'I'll take a group'
	To confirm	F	offering professional support	6	with parents, backing up
			prompting	7	
			waiting	8	anticipatory silence
			telling/stating	9	'you should ...' 'do this...'
			neutral comment	10	'Oh well' ... laugh... repetitions
			sharing professional perception	11	of children, school ...
			sharing professional knowledge	12	'I've done ...' 'I think ...'
			empathising	13	'I understand/remember'
			allaying doubts	14	'don't worry'
Trainer	To coach	G	suggesting	15	'you could ...'
(procedural)	To review	H	reminding	16	'do you remember when ...'
	Identify needs	I	explaining (procedural)	17	'this is because ...'
	Clarify needs	J	explaining (rationale)	18	reasoning behind actions
			criticising constructively	19	'this didn't work ... that did'
			criticising negatively	20	'it didn't work'
			modelling (suggestion)	21	'you could do it like this'
			modelling (expectation)	22	'do it like this ...'
			modelling (arrangement)	23	'I'll do it on Monday'
			questioning (open)	24	'how do you feel it went?'
			questioning (closed)	25	yes/no answer

			questioning (prompt)	26	'what about that group?'
			questioning (open but limiting)	27	could you do this … or this …?'
			questioning (rhetorical)	28	'shall we …?'
			giving background info	29	about children/school
Educator	To perceive needs	K	generalising	30	about context
	To analyse needs	L	extending (suggestion)	31	'That would be good to do in assembly'
	Encourage reflection	M	extending (expectation)	32	'you can do the assembly'
	To challenge	N	setting targets (suggestion)	33	'you should concentrate on …'
	To action plan	O	setting targets (expectation)	34	'so you will concentrate on …'
	To evaluate	P	setting targets (NE)	35	'decide what you will concentrate on'
Assessor	To assess	Q	formalising	36	written outcomes/ assessment (summative)
PERSONAL	To counsel	R	chatting	37	small talk, jokes, etc.
	To befriend	S	informing	38	about school procedures
			arranging	39	to speak to someone, to introduce, etc.
STRUCTURAL	To induct	T			
	To accept	U			
	To facilitate	V			
	To negotiate	W			
	To promote	X			

[1] Both alphabetic and numerical coding were done to facilitate analysis, e.g. L24 = Educator role, analysing needs through open-ended questioning.

Source: Association of Teachers and Lecturers/University of Leicester reproduced with permission

16

Making use of existing data

Shirley Dex and Anna Vignoles

Sole researchers in educational leadership and management are likely to neglect the possibility of making use of existing data sets, and yet for those concerned with levels of academic achievement or social and economic changes which might impact on their institution the analysis of such data can provide valuable insights. The investigation of existing data may also be particularly appropriate for those who wish their research to be unobtrusive.

In this chapter we examine the use of data that has already been collected by someone else or by another organisation. In some cases, it is possible to get hold of a data set that is just ready and waiting to be analysed. In other cases, work has to be done to assemble the data before it can be analysed and, in a sense, therefore, you as researcher will need to create or assemble the data set. We consider both these alternatives and give a few examples of data sources that are available. In practice, there are huge numbers of sources of data that are waiting to be assembled by the researcher. The advent of the Web has proliferated these sources of data and statistics and made them more accessible.

One further distinction to bear in mind is that data can be at the micro or macro level. Micro data usually have individuals as the unit of analysis, although other common examples of micro data include data on firms or schools. When the units of analysis are macro data, there has been some aggregation process over a set of individuals or a set of schools. Examples of macro data might be about the country as a whole, or the Local Authority; for example, the percentage of private schools in an area or the number of faith schools. Data are available nationally and internationally. In this chapter the examples of national data all relate to England, but similar national data sets are likely to be accessible through other government websites.

In the rest of this chapter we will consider first the type of analysis that makes use of existing data, along with some definitions about the types of data possible. We then consider the general ways of constructing, assembling or accessing statistics and data.

Secondary data analysis

Carrying out analysis on existing data is called *secondary data analysis*. Since someone has already collected the data, or at least decided on the categories under which the data are stored, the researcher has to work within these categories. They may not always be exactly what the researcher would like to work with but at the most basic level, this is not alterable. Sometimes it is possible to modify data definitions by constructing new variables out of the existing ones. This might be done by aggregating more than one variable, or taking only some codes of the old variable. This is only possible where you can obtain an electronic copy of the data set stored inside a statistical package like SPSS (you will need to have access to the same software on your own PC in order to read the data and manipulate and analyse it). Secondary data analysis is also described below under the sub-heading 'Ready-made data'. Some examples are provided below.

EXAMPLE 1: Childcare while mother is at work

Millennium Cohort Study Sweep 1 Question: *Does anyone look after *Jack <child's name> while you are at work?* Tick all that apply. (18 specific codes)

1	Respondent looks after	11	Friends and neighbours
2	Husband/partner	12	Live in nanny/au pair
3	Child's non-resident father	13	Other nanny/au pair
4	Your mother	14	Registered childminder
5	Your father	15	Unregistered childminder
6	Your partner's mother	16	Workplace/college nursery – crèche
7	Your partner's father	17	Local Authority day nursery – crèche
8	Child's non-resident father's or mother's mother	18	Private day nursery – crèche
9	Child's non-resident father's or mother's father	95	Other (Specify)
10	Other relatives		

You might be interested in defining 'Formal childcare use'. This could be done by combining codes to make a new variable 'Formal care' coded '1' when any of the following codes were used (12), (13), (14), (15), (16), (17), (18), and otherwise zero. However, if you wanted to investigate 'Out of the home formal care', you would not include codes (12) or (13).

EXAMPLE 2: Importance assigned by parents to education
How important do you think it is for your child to have a good education?

1 Very important
2 Quite important
3 Do not have a strong view
4 Not very important
5 Very unimportant

Here you might create a new variable 'Important' out of people who gave either code (1) or code (2).

However, there is an important caveat to bear in mind before you start creating new variables. You need to check the frequencies of the existing variables before you start to combine them. In Example 2, you may have found that 70 per cent of people gave code (1) as their response and a further 20 per cent gave code (2). If this were the case, you would not be advised to combine them because, by then, nearly all of your sample would be covered, and this would leave you with no variation to examine or analyse. For the same reason, you would not want to analyse a single code (for example, code (1) from Example 2 above), if 85 per cent or more of the people surveyed gave the same, one response. This would indicate the question was not useful for distinguishing between people and offered little prospect for analysis.

So, the first stage to any secondary data analysis is to give a thorough examination to the data that have already been collected, before you start to alter anything or analyse it. This means you should first print out, for all the variables you are interested in, the frequencies for each of their codes. By so doing, you may discover that some variables of interest are be unable to be analysed.

For further information about carrying out secondary data analysis, a good reference book is Hakim (1982a, 1982b). You may also like to refer to Chapter 19 in this book.

Cross-sectional, longitudinal or time series data

An important distinction to bear in mind about data is whether they were collected at one point in time or over a period of time.

A *cross-sectional* data set or survey refers to one point in time. This is like a snapshot photograph. It captures the subject once. Cross-sectional data can allow the researcher to compare subjects within the time period it refers to. So, for example, a survey which contained pupils' Key Stage 1 or 2 scores in 2000 alongside some of their characteristics, for example, their age group, ethnic group, parents' education levels, would allow an investigation and identification of whether there were statistical correlations between Key Stage scores and ethnic origin, or Key Stage scores and parents' education level. It does not allow you to infer that parents' education level causes the child's Key Stage score. In order to get closer to identifying causal relationships, as close as it is possible to get in social science, you generally need to have longitudinal data to analyse.

Longitudinal data are like the cine or video camera moving picture, as opposed to the cross-sectional snapshot. Longitudinal data follow the same subjects as they age and develop over time. For example, linking up the yearly test scores of a pupil as they progress, year by year, through a school creates a longitudinal data set about them. The analysis can be richer if you have some more personal information about the pupils, as well as their outcome data. For example, parental characteristics can be useful, as can the pupil's sex, whether they have any health problems or disability and other characteristics that might affect their learning. Having this over-time record about an individual, when you have sufficient sample sizes of such data, allows you to start to unpick causality; for example, to answer the question about what factors affect a child's outcome in life. One interesting study found that the extent to which parents express interest in their child's education when the child was in early primary school (age 5 and 7), was an important determinant of their educational achievement at age 16. In fact, parental interest in their child's education was more important in determining the child's educational achievement than other parental variables, such as socio-economic status of the parent (Feinstein and Symons, 1999).

A hybrid between these two types of data is the *repeat cross-section* data set. This is where you have a regular sample survey which collects data from individuals at a cross-sectional point in time, and then goes back to collect data at a later cross-section in time using the same questions. However, the repeat data collection is based on a new sample and it is not the same individuals telling you about themselves each time. However, the regularity of such surveys does start to offer greater possibilities for examining change than the one-off cross-sectional survey. For example, a random probability cross-sectional sample of headteachers in 1995 could give you a picture of headteachers' pay and conditions in 1995. And if done again on an annual basis, even though asking a different random probability sample of headteachers, it would provide information about the changes over time in headteachers' pay and conditions.

As well as offering insights into change, repeat cross-section surveys, where they use the same questionnaire, can be pooled to create more cases for analysis. In this way, a smaller sample size for any one cross-section can become bigger by pooling, and allow analysis of groups that would be too small in size for robust analysis in any one survey. An example of this could be pupil cross-section surveys that wished to focus on separate minority ethnic groups, or disabled pupils. However, the latter group are so small in number that pooling over a number of cross-sections would still not produce sufficient sample sizes, without some over-sampling procedure for disabled people being employed.

One example of a repeat cross-section survey is the government's Labour Force Survey. This asks adults about their labour market participation and employment, but also about their qualifications. Studies of the relationship between qualifications and employment status for minority ethnic groups are contained in Lindley et al. (2004, 2006) by pooling four annual cross-sections of these data.

Time series data are similar to repeat cross-sectional data. They consist of statistics or data over time, one per time period, which most often is per year. However, it is aggregate, or macro data, rather than micro data. For example, the proportion of children who receive primary education in every year from 1982 to 2000 in a developing country would create a time series of data. These could be put together for a number of countries, alongside the fertility rate and the Gross National Product (GNP) for that country and that year. It would then be possible to look for statistical relationships between the extent of education and GNP, or education and fertility. Because there is a time reference to the data, it is possible to analyse the effect of education in year t with the outcome of GNP in year $t+1$, or $t+2$, etc. It is also possible to subtract one year's data from another year (1999 GNP–1998 GNP) to produce a difference (or percentage growth) that can be analysed. In this way, again, it is possible to get closer to testing out hypotheses that are causal; for example, the hypothesis that an increase in the percentage of the country's population that have primary education will cause growth in its GNP, or changes in the fertility rate.

Having set out above the main types of data and the analyses they offer, the rest of this chapter charts some of the resources that are available with some examples of how they have been or could be used to research particular topics.

Ready-made micro data sets

These data are already collected in large-scale surveys and are available in electronic form in a statistical package from a Data Archive (most often in social science this is SPSS). The UK Data Archive is housed at Essex University (www.data-archive.ac.uk/) and offers a search facility as well as ability to investigate some data sets for descriptive statistics on line. Data sets can be downloaded after registration and permission is granted, and are free to access for academic use, but there is a charge for other users.

Once one gets a copy of the data and the appropriate software, it is a fairly quick route to carrying out an analysis. However, learning about the statistical package will slow down the process. But many standard statistical packages can offer a transfer write-out of the data into an Excel (or other regular) spreadsheet. The data can then be manipulated and many standard analyses carried out in Excel.

A set of existing, ready-made data sets and their contact details are listed in Table 16.1 at the end of the chapter Some examples of potential analyses of ready-made data are:

- The relationships between pupils' educational attainment and their earlier educational and family background experiences: National Child Development Study (NCDS), British Cohort Study (BCS), National Pupil Database/Pupil Level Annual School Census (NPDB/PLASC).
- The educational attainment of pupils from different minority groups by gender: Universities Statistical Record, Higher Education Statistics Agency data; NPD, NPDB/PLASC.
- The economic value of gaining a degree or other educational qualification: Labour Force Survey, NCDS, BCS, various Graduate Surveys commissioned by the Department for Education and Skills, General Household Survey (GHS) – a number of these surveys were commissioned by what was the Department for Education and Employment.
- Who gets involved in lifelong learning: National Adult Learning Survey, International Adult Literacy Survey (IALS).
- Whether educational attainment varies by region: GHS.
- The relationship between quality assessment grades awarded by the Office for Standards in Education (Ofsted) and the area of the school (Ofsted data).
- How pupils' test scores vary across countries with different educational systems, and ages at which children start school: Programme for International Student Assessment (PISA), IALS.
- The effects of types of child care used in infancy on the child's later development: the Effective Provision of Pre-School Education (EPPE) Project, Millennium Cohort Study.
- How children's scores in maths vary by country and whether these relate to economic indicators; or whether they relate to spending on education or to pupil–teacher ratios. PISA data, which are downloadable from OECD, contain the pupil scores on maths across countries, and other international organisations provide data on the other macro educational measures (see below).

Assemble your own micro data set

In some cases, researchers are stimulated to research a particular topic about which there is no existing data set. For example, it might be interesting to know, as a teacher, whether children's assessments have changed over successive generations; or whether the intake into your school or other education institution has the same sort of socio-economic profile and how this relates to their examination or assessment scores. This may suggest the only way to proceed is to try to collect new data, for example, as a one-off, or repeat survey. But it is always worth considering first what data are already available in administrative records. Administrative records will usually provide information and can be reasonably complete. However, even if they are not complete, you can be sure that you will never get a 100 per cent response rate (or even 40–50 per cent) to a one-off survey of your own, and you may find it hard to achieve a reasonable sample size. Also, if you wanted more than one year of data, there would be a long wait to assemble sufficient data in order to be able to analyse change. So even though the administrative records may not contain all the data you would like, it is often worth compromising to get (often) better quality and more systematic data than a lone researcher could start to collect for themselves. This point would not be true about a large-scale government survey where millions of pounds are usually spent and an army of fieldwork agents are employed to obtain good quality representative survey data on a topic.

PLASC is an annual pupil-level census of schools. These data provide quite detailed information on the teaching resource input into individual schools and on some pupil characteristics (age, gender, ethnicity, eligibility for free school meals and pupils with SEN). The teaching resource variables include the ratio of qualified teachers to pupils, as well as the ratio of support staff to pupils. Prior to PLASC, this kind of data was available at school level from what was known as 'Form 7'. There is, therefore, a long time series of school-level data (one can aggregate PLASC to school level) which researchers can analyse in a number of different ways. Your school will have an electronic version of its recent PLASC submissions and may hold data from its earlier Form 7 submissions. Assembled into a spreadsheet they would offer the opportunity to do some simple descriptive analyses of changes in your school over time. PLASC data for all schools can be obtained from the Department for Education and Skills and, when combined with National Pupil Database (NPD) information on pupils' Key Stage scores, enable various kinds of analyses, particularly value-added analyses. For example, one could undertake an investigation of how the value-added across different schools varies with the level of resource inputs.

PLASC and the National Pupil Database now provide extremely comprehensive individual level data on pupil attainment, pupil characteristics and indeed school characteristics. However, well before the advent of PLASC/NPD, some schools had been collaborating and pooling data to provide schools and indeed researchers with data on all schools in a particular area. At least one such scheme was initiated by the headteacher of Harrogate Grammar School in 1995 as a data set exchange and it is still going on. It now includes comparative expenditure data, income information and staffing cost data on more than 60 secondary schools (Mayston and Jesson, 1999). It is also possible to do this, one school at a time, from the DfES website, entering schools and their postcode and the data you require (www.dfes.gov.uk/inyourarea/). The data can be obtained for KS2, KS3, GCSE and several other statistics or scores currently for 2004 and 2005. The DfES website also offers downloadable performance tables (www.dfes.gov.uk/performancetables). Another alternative is that you obtain national educational statistics from the DfES website, and you collect the data for your own school and present it in the context of the national profile. Where your school differs you could investigate why this might be the case. One possible analysis (available from the Office of National Statistics website at www.statistics.gov.uk) is to examine the sick leave rate at your school and see whether staff in your organisation have sick leave absence rates that are the same, lower, or above the national or regional average.

Macro data, existing data enhanced by collating

In the same way that a researcher can assemble a micro data set, it is also possible to assemble a macro data set. This has got easier since the advent of websites with downloadable material. But there have, for many years, been books of statistical data which can be drawn on and entered into a spreadsheet for analysis. Collecting the data points (statistics) from books can be more laborious than analysing an existing electronic data set already entered into a statistical analysis package, but it is still not usually as time-consuming as collecting new data by carrying out your own survey using a questionnaire.

The DfES website offers time series data on a large number of statistics (www.dfes.gov.uk/rsgateway/DB/TIM/). These are downloadable. Currently some are not very long time series, but they will gradually increase over time. They include the following, among a larger number of topics:

- Average salaries of full-time teachers
- Total teachers in maintained schools
- Initial teacher training available places
- Revenue funding per school pupil
- Number of schools in England in January of each year
- Pupil–teacher ratios
- Primary class size data
- Secondary class size data
- Spending per pupil in real terms
- Spending per pupil in cash terms
- UK educational expenditure per pupil as a percentage of Gross Domestic Product

Just using these data it would be possible to examine whether there are correlations over time with spending per pupil in real (or cash) terms and pupil–teacher ratios, for example.

EXAMPLE 3: The beginnings of a time series spreadsheet containing some example data.

	% pupils achieving LEVEL 2 in KS1 Maths	% pupils achieving LEVEL 2 in KS1 Reading	Average class size (Primary and secondary school)	Average salaries (£) FT primary teachers	Expenditure (£) per pupil in real terms (Primary and Secondary Schools)
1995	79	78		20,860	2920
1996	82	78		21,370	2880
1997	84	80		22,080	2840
1998	84	80	27.1	22,700	2770
1999	87	82	26.5	23,570	2800
2000	90	83	25.8	24,550	2930
2001	91	84	25.2	26,210	3130
2002	90	84	25.2	27,590	3410
2003	90	84	25.2	29,290	3380
2004	90	85	25.7	30,510	2620
2005	91	85			
....					

Source: Collated from separate series in www.dfes.gov.uk/rsgateway/DB/TIM/

It would also be possible to construct a model of whether an increase in average salaries year on year is associated with a change in the achievement rate of pupils in the following years. This involves creating explanatory variables that are lagged in time behind the dependent variable. In this case, you would also need to be calculating the change in any variable from year to year (see Example 3).

However, it would also be possible to go to other sources and supplement the data. Annual aggregate statistics on many areas are available from the General Household Survey and *Social Trends*, dating back to the 1970s. These are available in large libraries, especially university libraries, as annual volumes. It would be possible to trawl through these volumes year by year to construct a time series of variables which could then be examined to see how they were correlated. But such time series are also available, in some cases, on websites – for example, from the Office of National Statistics (ONS) website (www.statistics. gov.uk/StatBase). The areas covered by these volumes include economy, crime, education and training, employment, sick leave, social welfare and information on families, among other subjects. Some sample time series statistics from the education and training section which are also available on the ONS website include:

- Children under 5 in schools as a percentage of all 3 and 4 year-olds, UK
- The percentage of teachers who are new teachers, by type of school
- Year 11 attainment levels of pupils who have been truants

EXAMPLE 4: A spreadsheet format for the beginnings of a cross-sectional 1993 data set

	Adult literacy rate (%)	Combined primary, secondary and tertiary enrolment ratio (female)	% seats in parliament held by women	Real GDP per capita (PPP$)	Life expectancy at birth (years)
Canada	99.0	100.0	18.0	20,950	77.5
USA	99.0	98.3	10.4	24,680	76.1
Japan	99.0	77.2	6.7	20,660	79.6
... etc.					
Brazil	82.4	71.3	7.1	5,500	66.6
Seychelles	88.0			4,960	71.0
Ecuador	89.0	71.1	4.5	4,400	69.0
... etc.					
Kenya	75.7	54.6		2,200	55.5
Ghana	62.0	38.8	8.0	1,400	56.2
India	50.6	46.4	8.0	1,240	60.7
Zambia	76.2	44.9	6.7	1,100	48.6
Rwanda	47.2		4.3	740	47.2
Niger	46.7	10.8	3.6	790	46.7
... etc.					

Source: Adapted Table 1 (pp. 135–137) and Adapted Table 4 (pp. 141–143) selected statistics from 'Human Development Report 1996' by United Nations Development Programme (1996). By permission of Oxford University Press, Inc.

In addition, there are other international organisations (e.g. United Nations, UNICEF, UNESCO, World Bank, International Labour Office/ILO, OECD, Eurostat) with similar annual volumes that cover international statistics, one per country per year which could be assembled in the same way (see Example 4 and the box below, which lists useful publications in book volumes). However, again, more and more statistics are becoming available on websites. For example, UNESCO's website (www.unesco.org) offers a range of annual statistics for a minimum of 50 countries on such measures as:

- Expected duration of schooling
- Indicators of teaching staff resource levels and quality
- Demographic indicators
- Economic indicators
- And many other educational measures

See http://stats.uis.unesco.org/)

Useful publications in book volumes

OECD
Education at a Glance is an annual report providing a full range of education statistics for most OECD countries.

United Nations
One annual publication is the *Human Development Report* (see, e.g., United Nations, 1996 in Example 4). Over time, however, its title has changed. See also:
United Nations, *Demographic Yearbook* 1998
Yearbook of the United Nations 1998, Volume 52
Economic Survey of Europe 2000, No. 1

World Bank
One annual publication is its *World Development Report* (see, for example, World Bank, 1996) which has a statistical appendix.

International Labour Office
Yearbook of Labour Statistics 2000 – International Labour Office.

Eurostat
See *European Social Statistics Demography*, 2000 edition
Europe in Figures 2000
Eurostat Electronic Library
Eurostat Yearbook 2001: A Statistical Eye on Europe, 6th edition

These publications are available in large libraries and for purchase from The Stationery Office (formerly HMSO). Some of them are purchasable as a CD-Rom.

Social Trends
An annual volume of official statistics published by HMSO/The Stationery Office. From 2000 onwards the full copy is downloadable www.statistics.gov.uk/StatBase

General Household Survey (GHS)
The General Household Survey (GHS) is a continuous multipurpose national survey of people and has been carried out continuously since 1971, published by HMSO and the Office of National Statistics. Volumes and data since 1995 are downloadable from www.statistics.gov.uk/StatBase

---

The Office of Economic Cooperation and Development (OECD) offers a range of downloadable macro level educational and other statistics from its website (www.oecd.org). These statistics are presented by country and include comparisons over a range of more developed countries, which are internationally comparable. For example:

- Educational personnel per country
- Educational expenditure by funding source
- Foreign student enrolments
- Graduates by age
- Total population by age and sex
- Students enrolled by age and by type of institution
- Total instruction time for students in primary school and secondary school
- Class sizes and ratios of students to teachers
- Age and gender distribution of teachers
- Teachers' salaries

Your job may still involve collating these separate statistics and series into a data set that can be analysed. Often this involves a bit of data manipulation and interrogation of the website or published data to get a series that overlaps in time, for the same years, with all the data points from all the various variables you are interested in. There are sometimes inconsistencies or gaps in the series; also definitions of variables and measures frustratingly can change over time. It is possible to handle some of these problems in the analysis; for example, one can handle changes in variable definition in regression analysis by entering a dummy variable to show where the definition of your dependent variable changed (this is done by creating a zero 1 dummy which takes the value '1' in years from the change in definition onwards, but zero in the years before the change). In other cases you may have to miss out the year that does not have full information on all of your variables, or enter the mean for cases that are missing.

In the case of higher education, the Observatory on Borderless Higher Education website has pages on Education Statistics which have drawn together information on the main national and international data sources and data sets under its Key Resources section and also offers some downloadable data sets (www.obhe.ac.uk/).

Conclusion

There is no shortage of data, and accessible data sources are multiplying through the ease of website access. It is important to remember that data assembled by the researcher, while needing time to be assembled, is usually a much quicker route to analysis than collecting primary data via a survey. For those involved with issues of educational leadership and management, accessing and interrogating existing data sets can be an important and instructive research method.

References

Carey, S., Low, S. and Hansbro, J. (1997) *Adult Literacy in Britain*. London: The Stationery Office, London.

Dex, S. and Joshi, H. (eds) (2004) *Millennium Cohort Study First Survey: A User's Guide to Initial Findings*. London: Institute of Education, University of London.

Dex, S. and Joshi, H. (2005) *Children of the 21st Century: From Birth to Nine Months*. Bristol: The Policy Press.

Dolton, P.J. and Makepeace, G.H. (1992) *The Early Careers of 1980 Graduates, Work Histories, Job Tenure, Career Mobility and Occupational Choice*. Department of Employment, Research Paper 79.

Dolton, P.J. and Vignoles, A. (2000) 'The incidence and effects of over-education in the graduate labour market', *Economics of Education Review*, 19: 179–198.

Feinstein, L. and Symons, J. (1999) 'Attainment in secondary schools', *Oxford Economic Papers*, 51: 300–321

Ferri, E. Bynner, J. and Wadsworth, M. (eds) (2003) *Changing Britain, Changing Lives*. London: Institute of Education, University of London.

Hakim, C. (1982a) *Secondary Analysis in Social Research: A Guide to Data Sources and Methods with Examples*. London: Allen and Unwin.

Hakim, C. (1982b) 'Secondary Analysis and the Relationship between Official and Academic Social Research', *Sociology*, 16 (1): 12–28.

Lindley, J., Dale, A. and Dex, S. (2004) 'Ethnic differences in women's demographic, family characteristics and economic activity profiles, 1995–2002', *Labour Market Trends*, 112 (4): 153–165.

Lindley, J., Dale, A. and Dex, S. (2006) 'Ethnic differences in women's labour force participation: the role of qualifications', *Oxford Economic Papers*, 58 (2): 351–378.

Mayston, D. and Jesson, D. (1999) *Linking Educational Resourcing with Enhanced Educational Outcomes*. Department for Education and Employment, Research Report 179.

OECD (1997) *Literacy Skills for the Knowledge Society*. Paris: Organization for Economic Cooperation and Development.

United Nations (1996) *Human Development Report*, 1996. New York and Oxford: Oxford University Press for the United Nations. Published annually.

World Bank (1996) *From Plan to Market*. World Development Report. New York and Oxford: Oxford University Press for the World Bank. (Published annually.)

Recommended reading

Earl, L. and Fullan, M. (2003) 'Using data in leadership for learning', *Cambridge Journal of Education*, 33 (3): 383–394.

Goldstein, H. 'Using pupil performance data for judging schools and teachers: scope and limitations', *British Educational Research Journal*, 27 (4): 433–442.

Leithwood, K. Aitken, R. and Jantzi, D. (2006) *Making Schools Smarter: Leading with Evidence*. London: Sage.

Table 16.1 Some examples of ready-made data sets

Data name and references	Description of main topics covered	Sampling procedure	Method of data collection	Type of data/how to get access
The Careers Service Activity Surveys DfES (1999)	These surveys provide information on the early career choices made by young people in England, after compulsory schooling. The surveys give background information on pupils (e.g. gender, ethnicity) as well as jobs and training options chosen by school leavers	No sampling used Census, if it were complete	Careers Service database Repeat cohorts transition from school to work	Micro Very short longitudinal Access via the DfES
Database of teacher records Statistics of education, published annually by The Stationery Office	Individual records of each teacher recognised as qualified in England and Wales, from the date of award of QTS. Contains their pay, qualifications, QTS, age, sex, length of service, current service, school and LEA	Census, if it were accurate	Annual returns from employers to Teachers' Pension Scheme. Some employers do not provide all records	Micro Partly longitudinal **Open access:** Summary statistics can be accessed via the DfES research and statistics gateway at www.dfes.gov.uk/rsgateway/
The General Household Survey (GHS) GHS (annual dates) for – annual report	GHS is an annual sample survey. It contains socio-economic data on a wide range of topics, providing a long time series of data on educational attainment. Limited information on vocational training. Considerable amount of information on employment (income, hours, tenure, industry, occupation, union membership). For information see www.statistics.gov.uk/ssd/surveys/general_household_survey.asp	Stratified random probability sample based on postcodes	Face-to-face interviews	Micro Repeat cross-section **Open access:** Data Archive, Essex University www.data-archive.ac.uk

	Description	Sample	Method	Type / Access
Eurostat Continuing Vocational Training	Covers cost of vocational training, hours spent, training systems, participation rates, apprenticeships and details of participants. Same data available across a number of EU countries	Random sample of enterprises	Surveys	Micro enterprise Repeat cross-section **Open access:** Eurostat http://epp.eurostat.ec.europa.eu/
Graduates' data sets Dolton and Makepeace (1992) Dolton and Vignoles (2000)	A series of three sample surveys to track the employment experiences of people who graduated in 1960, 1970 and 1980 for 6 years after they graduated. The questions are the same in each survey	Random samples	Postal survey	Micro Repeat longitudinal cohort **Restricted access:** Apply via the DfES
International Adult Literacy Survey (IALS) OECD (1997) Carey et al. (1997)	Survey carried out in 12 countries (including Britain). Each respondent undertook tests to assess their literacy and numeracy skills. Other data are available about the respondents; employment status, wages, job characteristics, education, parents, vocational training. For more information see: www.statistics.gov.uk/ssd/surveys/european_adult_literacy_review_survey.asp	Different in each country. Clustered, stratified probability sample in GB based on postcodes	Face-to-face interviews and self-completion of tests	Micro Cross-sectional **Open access:** www.nifl.gov/nifl/facts/IALS.html
Labour Force Survey (LFS)	LFS collects quarterly data on employment, unemployment and inactivity as well as a range of personal characteristics including all educational qualifications, household income and demographic indicators. For more information see: www.statistics.gov.uk/ssd/surveys/labour_force_survey.asp	Quarterly random probability sample survey of households	Face-to-face interviews for first interview, with telephone follow-up in next quarters	Micro Repeat cross-sections (also partly a short 5-quarter panel) **Open access:** Data Archive, Essex University www.data-archive.ac.uk

Table 16.1 Continued

Data name and references	Description of main topics covered	Sampling procedure	Method of data collection	Type of data/how to get access
National Adult Learning Survey (NALS)	Survey of people's experiences of and attitudes towards learning, intended to provide a basis for future monitoring of adult learning (including vocational and non-vocational learning), costs of learning, problems experienced and perceived benefits and barriers. This survey followed three earlier surveys covering some of the same topics, but is not repeat cross-section		Face-to-face interview	Micro Cross-section **Open access:** Data Archive, Essex University www.data-archive.ac.uk
OFSTED database Details of publications using the data are at: www.ofsted.gov.uk/publications/	This contains information from the Headteacher's Form and Statement, and from the inspector's judgement recording the grades for the inspection. It contains data for all schools inspected in a given year. Hence each school only appears on the database approximately every 4 years. Includes data on pupils on the roll, pupil background (at school level), inspection grades since 1996, expenditure data, staffing numbers, pupil attitudes/disaffection, and the school level of pupil outcomes	Schools selected for inspection on a 4-year cycle but more often if performance is not satisfactory. Includes all state schools	Data collected through inspection and entered by Ofsted, mostly complete with a few missing values	Micro for school unit Cross-section but in principle could be linked up to be longitudinal Census over 4 years. **Restricted access:** Contact Ofsted www.ofsted.gov.uk/

	Description	Method	Type / Access
Programme for International Student Assessment (PISA)	The PISA study is organised by OECD and started in 2000 in 32 countries. It aims to assess 'literacy' domains of reading, maths and science. Students carry out tests in these areas and there is a school questionnaire collecting limited data, plus country	Face-to-face interviews plus tests	Micro Repeat cross-section **Restricted access:** Some years of data available in downloadable excel chart from OECD website www.oecd.org or http://pisaweb.acer.edu.au/
Universities' Statistical Record (USR) (HESA)	The USR consists of records of all undergraduate and postgraduate students on courses of one academic year or more; and academic and related staff holding regular salaried appointments and finance data for all universities. Background variables on students include age, sex, marital status, country of birth, occupation of parent, last full-time school attended, GCE A level and other entrance qualifications. Educational information includes degree subject, institution of study, normal duration of course, type of course, year of course, date of enrolment, method of study, qualification obtained, class of degree, date of leaving, reasons for leaving	Full population census survey Administrative records submitted to HESA database	When students have passed through university a longitudinal micro record is provided of their HE **Restricted access:** Apply to HESA www.hesa.ac.uk/

273

Table 16.1 Continued

Data name and references	Description of main topics covered	Sampling procedure	Method of data collection	Type of data/how to get access
Pupil Level Annual School Census (PLASC)	Individual pupil records, including the pupil's name and 'unique pupil number' (UPN), are collected with additional aggregated information on exclusions, teacher numbers, pupil activities and post-16 courses of study annually in January. The submission by schools of a PLASC return, including a set of named pupil records, is a statutory requirement under section 537A of the Education Act 1996 The following fields of information were collected for each pupil on roll: UPN, Name, Gender, Date of Birth, Free School Meal eligibility, English as an Additional Language, Special Educational Need (SEN) Action Stage, SEN Type, ethnicity, pupil postcode and whether a child is in care	Full population census survey	Administrative records submitted to LEAs who submit to central government	Once a pupil has enrolled in a school they are issued with a UPN. Every UPN is recorded on the day of PLASC **Restricted access:** Some summary statistics can be accessed via the DfES research and statistics gateway at the following address: www.dfes.gov.uk/rsgateway/
National Pupil Database (NPD)	The National Pupil Database (NPD) is a census of all pupils in England in LEAs maintained schools. It includes attainment and other pupil-level information in the Pupil Level Annual Census (PLASC)	Full population census survey	Administrative records submitted to LEA who submit to central government	Micro Longitudinal **Restricted access:** The data are available from DfES, subject to their authorisation

274

National Child Development Study (NCDS) www.cls.ioe.ac.uk/ Ferri et al. (2003)	The NCDS was a census of babies born in a certain week in 1958 who have been followed up for the rest of their lives, now on a 4-year cycle, although in the past there were longer gaps between contacts It is a multi-domain survey covering the topics of child and adult education, health, lifestyle, citizenship, household, family, economic activity and income. The questionnaires changed as the child aged and became an adult. The latest data are for age 46 at 2004	Census of babies born in one week	Mixture of face-to-face and postal surveys plus tests of ability on children and administrative health data merged in. Each survey is a separate data set	Micro Longitudinal **Open access**: Data Archive, Essex University www.data-archive.ac.uk www.cls.ioe.ac.uk/
British Birth Cohort (BCS) www.cls.ioe.ac.uk/ Ferri et al. (2003)	The BCS was a census of babies born in a certain week in 1970 who have been followed up for the rest of their lives, now on a 4-year cycle, although in the past there were longer gaps between contacts It is a multi-domain survey covering topics of child and adult education, health, lifestyle, citizenship, household, family, economic activity and income. The questionnaires changed as the child aged and became an adult. The latest data are for age 34 at 2004	Census of babies born in one week	Mixture of face-to-face and postal surveys plus tests of ability on children and administrative health data merged in. Each survey is a separate data set	Micro Longitudinal **Open access**: Data Archive, Essex University www.data-archive.ac.uk www.cls.ioe.ac.uk/

Table 16.1 Continued

Data name and references	Description of main topics covered	Sampling procedure	Method of data collection	Type of data/how to get access
Millennium Cohort Study (MCS) Details of the study are at: www.cls.ioe.ac.uk/ Dex and Joshi (2004, 2005)	The MCS is a cohort study of children born between September 2000 and December 2001 across 4 UK counties, followed up at age 9–10 months, 3 and 5 years and with plans for age 7 It is multi domain survey covering topics of child development and health and parents' education, health, lifestlye, citizenship, household, family, economic activity and income. The questionnaires change as the child age. The latest data are for age 5 at 2005	Clustered and stratified random probability sample based on 1998 wards, with over-representation of wards with high minority ethnic populations and other disadvantaged wards, and non-English wards in UK.	Mixture of face-to-face and postal surveys plus tests of ability on children and administrative health data merged in. Each survey is a separate data set	Micro Longitudinal **Open access:** Data Archive, Essex University www.data-archive.ac.uk www.cls.ioe.ac.uk/
British Social Attitudes Surveys (BAS)	This is an annual survey carried out on a random sample of the population asking about a range of attitudes alongside basic characteristics of the respondents. Some attitude questions are asked every year. Others rotate and are asked at intervals. Modules of questions on particular topical subjects are added from time to time	Random probability sample		Micro Repeated cross-section for some questions **Open access:** Data Archive, Essex University www.data-archive.ac.uk

| **Youth Cohort Study (YCS)** | The YCS is a series of longitudinal surveys that contacts a sample of an academic year-group or 'cohort' of young people in the spring following completion of compulsory education and usually again one and two years later. The survey looks at young people's education and labour market experience, their training and qualifications and a range of other issues, including socio-demographic variables | Random sample of young people in year 11 who have birthdays on particular dates in any month | Micro Longitudinal **Open access:** Data Archive, Essex University www.data-archive.ac.uk |

277

17

Documents and documentary analysis: reading between the lines

Tanya Fitzgerald

Documents litter the worlds in which we live and provide evidence that narrates the details of our personal and professional lives. Birth certificates, school attendance records, examination results, passports, drivers' licences, bank statements, insurance policies, correspondence and wills contain numerous personal details that assist in building a portrait of an individual. Similarly, employment and tax records, curriculum vitae, committee minutes and institutional records contain the minutiae of the professional work and contribution of individuals. As leaders and managers in education, documents such as employment applications, teacher registration, performance management records, curriculum books and statements, school inspections, institutional website data, policies, meeting agendas and minutes, letters to parents, written feedback to pupils and colleagues, memoranda, speeches and media interviews all form part of the public professional record. Documents from schools, colleges and universities therefore can provide valuable information about the context and culture of these institutions and frequently provide another window for the researcher to read between the lines of official discourse and then triangulate information through interviews, observations and questionnaires. For example, a researcher interested in the image a school might wish to portray to its community might carry out a content analysis of keywords that appear in official information such as the prospectus, website and other publicity material. In the second stage, other tools such as observation and interviews could be employed to determine whether what the school publicly says about how it operates is embedded in the culture of teachers and students.

At the macro level, documents such as education policy, speeches of politicians, official websites (such as the Department for Education and Skills, Office for Standards in Education in England, Ministry of Education and the Education Review Office in New Zealand), league tables, official statistics, regulations and legislation can provide another level of public narration. These documents can be examined to determine the extent to which policy and practices at institutional level reflect the agenda of these established bodies. For example, a researcher wanting to examine the impact of appraisal policy in schools and colleges could undertake a content analysis of official policy and examine how, if at all, institutional documents are aligned with national policy and how this is played out in teacher practices.

Our identities are recorded in the official records that we generate. To read between the lines of these official and public narratives, knowledge about the individual personal lives can be generated from private letters, photographs, diaries, emails, blogs, poetry, songs, oral histories, paintings, video and/or DVD recordings, obituaries and reminiscences. Documents can therefore be public or private, written or unwritten and may be stored in a range of locations and in different forms. Accordingly, documents should be examined and interpreted against a backdrop of the relevant personal, social, political, economic and historical factors present at the point of production. For educational leaders and managers in particular, documents offer a lens to interpret events in order to gain insights into the relationship between the written and unwritten, spoken and virtual, public and private, and past and present.

In this chapter, I will examine the uses of documents and documentary research, nature and types of educational documents that can be used for research and offer a framework for the interpretation and analysis of documents. I would also like to stress that documentary research is only one form of qualitative inquiry and I would encourage researchers to consider how aspects of documentary research might be adapted and adopted within other approaches. For example, documentary analysis can be one of the tools employed in a case study approach, in an ethnographic study or as a tool to triangulate data gathered from interviews, questionnaires/surveys, focus groups and on-site observations.

While I cannot provide an exhaustive discussion of all the types of documentary sources that I have outlined above, it is my intention to overview the range of educational documents that researchers might examine. Where feasible, I have made reference to examples for readers to draw on and relate to their own particular circumstances. To assist researchers further, I have offered suggestions as to possible ways in which to access educational documents, outlined a range of possible analysis tools and techniques and have compiled a list of additional theoretical and methodological sources that can be consulted. This chapter examines how the plot lines of individual and institutional records can be developed and how to read between the lines to produce a narrative that renews our understanding of the world and the connection between the social, political, economic and historical factors.

Documents and documentary research

Documentary analysis is a form of qualitative analysis that requires readers to locate, interpret, analyse and draw conclusions about the evidence presented. For students and researchers in the field of educational leadership and management, documentary research might form part of a historical research project or contribute to aspects of case study research. Documentary research allows for sufficient data to be collected for researchers to be able to:

- Identify the significant features of a particular event, activities or case
- Establish a plausible interpretation and explanation
- Test for the credibility and validity of these interpretations
- Construct an argument based on these interpretations
- Relate the argument to policy trends, current practice or other relevant research
- Create a convincing narrative for the reader
- Provide an audit trail that offers other researchers opportunities to challenge the interpretation or construct alternative arguments

Research is a creative, critical and systematic activity that progresses through a series of stages that shape the process of enquiry and contribute to the trustworthiness of the findings. In similar ways to case study research, documentary research offers researchers opportunities to devise and design their own methods of data collection and analysis. In a later section of this chapter, I have outlined possible ways these activities might be undertaken.

One of the advantages of documentary research is that documents have been produced and preserved as a record of the past; but documents, in the main, are not produced specifically for the purposes of social research. This is not to suggest that documents are any less time-consuming or easier to deal with than data from interviews, questionnaires or a focus group. It takes considerable skill to locate elusive documents and considerable interpretative skills are required to uncover the meaning of the contents. Accordingly, researchers need to ask critical questions to evaluate the document, its author, its place in the public record and be mindful of the fact that documents are written so that an author can record his/her view of what occurred. In terms of research in the field of educational leadership and management, at times it is less difficult to establish the accuracy and credibility of documents as researchers are able to contact and/or interview authors.

Scott (1990) cautions researchers to adopt the position that documents cannot be regarded as objective accounts. Documents are required to be examined and interrogated in the context of other sources of data. Data from documents can be used to highlight a range of perspectives on a particular event, activity, group or individual and can be further utilised to determine the representativeness of such a document. For social science researchers, documents offer a form of voice; a voice on past events and activities that provides a level of insight for the reader into these events, activities and participants. Irrespective of the way in which documents are 'read', interpretations may vary as researchers engage in their work with different and differing epistemological and ontological frameworks. This is true of all social science data whereby conclusions are derived from particular interpretations of data.

Documentary research is a form of interpretative research that requires researchers to collect, collate and analyse empirical data in order to produce a theoretical account that either describes, interprets or explains what has occurred. In terms of data collection, this involves transferring significant quotations from documents to either a notebook or computer; each item or quote is a data item and while it may appear tedious, each data item must be correctly labelled with its source location (both library and collection – this is discussed further in the section titled 'Collating Data').

Researchers must therefore engage in systematic activities to ensure the reliability of their evidence and conclusions. This will involve the following ten stages:

1 Identify the research problem or issue.
2 Devise a list of possible aims and research questions.
3 Identify the relevant theoretical and methodological frameworks.
4 Develop a list of key words or themes from the literature.
5 Locate physical (library, archives) and electronic documents.
6 Classify documents.
7 Collect and collate data.
8 Identify emerging themes from the data.
9 Interpret evidence and link with research questions and literature themes.
10 Structure and write report.

Bear in mind too that this process can be applied to other forms of inquiry, in particular case study research. There are endless variations as to how these 10 steps might be applied; what is important to note is that researchers should be systematic about their data collection activities. (I suggest in the section on collating data that date, time and place are important components to record as these form part of the case record.)

As indicated in Table 17.1, there are several advantages and limitations to documentary research. The following sections provide an overview on the types of documents that can be consulted, possible *locations* of documents, *how* data might be collected and *analysed* and provide a list of critical questions to interrogate documents.

Classifying documents

Documents are texts that can be published or unpublished, written, oral and visual and may reside in either the public, private or virtual domains. In all aspects of our lives we leave a permanent record of our existence and activities that can be valuable and useful for researchers.

Table 17.1   Advantages and limitations of documentary research

Advantages	Limitations
Allows researcher to gather data from the words of the participant	Documents can be subjective
Can be accessed at a time convenient to the researcher	Documents can be protected, unavailable for use or not catalogued correctly, or at all
Contain facts that may not be readily available – for example names, dates. Specific event details	Can be difficult to locate, may be stored in several places geographically distant, may be difficult to access
Can provide access to information that may be difficult to gain via interview	May not be accurate and have been created to present a particular view of events, activities or individuals
Use of electronic tools to store and analyse data can provide ease of use for researcher	Can be time-consuming and require methodical analysis

As a general rule, the majority of documents are written and available in the public domain (libraries, archives, museums, institutional holdings). These sources might be further classified as primary or secondary, that can predetermine ways in which analysis might occur. There is considerable debate, however, as to whether these two binaries are appropriate or adequate (McCulloch and Richardson, 2000), as not all documents 'fit' these classifications. Accordingly, there is no rigid distinction between primary and secondary sources and the kinds of questions asked to 'read between the lines' are of critical importance. There is not the space here to provide an overview of the methodological debates surrounding 'primary' and 'secondary' sources and researchers are urged to consult the literature that traverses these debates, some of which are listed in the section titled 'Additional Sources' at the end of this chapter. While I am not suggesting a rigid classification here, primary sources can be regarded as data in much the same way as interview or focus group transcripts because these sources contain raw (that is, not yet interpreted) data. Secondary sources, on the other hand, can be generally regarded as literature as they have been subjected to a level of interpretation and analysis.

The major difference between 'primary' and 'secondary' sources lies in the question of authorship. Primary sources are usually first-hand accounts produced by a witness to a particular event. For example, this might include notes taken from a committee meeting or attendance statistics; records that are produced close to an event, depending on the type of record, may be easy or difficult for researchers to locate. A primary source would not contain any analysis of an event whereas secondary sources provide an interpretation of that event. In both cases, there is potential for bias not only in terms of what was recorded but what was omitted and the particular epistemological view of the author. In recent years, methodological debates across the humanities and social sciences have raged concerning what 'counts' as a primary source (see, for example Burton, 2001; Fitzgerald, 2005). This has expanded the range of primary sources that now include but are not restricted to:

- Rare documents
- Official letters and correspondence
- Parliamentary debates
- Public submissions to the policy development process or reading of Bills
- Select Committee hearings
- Government reports
- Policy documents
- Institutional documents such as school rolls, strategic plans, staff lists
- Minutes of meetings
- Personal letters and diaries
- Newspaper articles, cartoons, letters to/from the editor, editorials, or advertisements
- Maps
- Stories, genealogy and cultural artefacts (particularly important for Indigenous groups)
- Autobiographies
- Photographs
- Posters
- Pamphlets
- Newspapers (advertisements, letters to the editor are useful sources for social context)
- Virtual documents

These sources contribute to what Samuel (1994) refers to as the theatre of memory. That is, they assist in the re-production of past lives and events that can be interpreted in the present. Primary sources are not necessarily free from bias as they may be subject to inaccurate or selective recall. Sources such as autobiographies can be classified as either primary or secondary sources depending on the uses that the researcher makes of this material. For example, autobiographies may function as a record of the lived experiences of an individual but might also serve as a secondary account of their school experience, their work as a teacher and their contribution to education. I am reminded here of the autobiography of Sylvia Ashton-Warner (1908–1984), *I Passed This Way*, that provides primary details of her work as a teacher and activist yet simultaneously offers a secondary account of clashes between Maori and Pakeha (European), urban and rural New Zealand, children and adults against a backdrop of changing educational priorities by the state.

Secondary sources, on the other hand, are usually published documents, the most common of which are books, journal articles, book chapters and student theses. These sources use primary material to interpret events, problems, issues or individual accounts and forward an interpretation of this material. For example, the educational reform agenda sweeping through countries such as England, Canada, Australia, the United States and New Zealand in the late 1980s provided the stimulus for extensive academic debate and scholarship that analysed, in the main, the role of the state (for example, Codd, 2005), the nature and impact of these reforms (for example, Apple, 2001; Blackmore, 1999), the policy borrowing agenda (for example, Thrupp, 2001) and the modernisation of schools (for example, Gunter, 2005). These secondary sources suggest new theoretical perspectives and analyses of contemporary educational problems and can be used to scaffold the reading between the lines that primary sources require. Researchers in the field of educational leadership and management have a number of secondary sources available that chart the intellectual development of the field. The works of George Baron, William Taylor and Thomas Greenfield, for example, are influential texts and provide a theoretical framework for contemporary debates and scholarship.

Locating documents

Documents are reasonably convenient records to locate and access, particularly in the digital age. Library catalogues are available online to all users, irrespective of geographical location, and contain bibliographic and archival sources. Similarly, records offices, such as the Public Record Office in England (www.pro.gov.uk) and the National Archives in New Zealand (www.archives.govt.nz), and archival institutions, such as the main research libraries that house extensive collections of documents, museums and repositories connected with organisations and churches, have online catalogues and/or published catalogues of their main collections. In addition to the print and electronic catalogues, also look for indexes to the microfiche collection. A number of organisations such as the DfES in England (www.dfes.gov.uk), the Ministry of Education in New Zealand (www.minedu.govt.nz), Ofsted (www.ofsted.gov.uk) and ERO (www.ero.govt.nz) have policy documents, media releases, speeches, statistics and research reports published on their websites that can be easily accessed. The National College for School Leadership website (www.ncsl.org.uk) contains research reports, policy documents and information relevant for school leaders and managers. Most documents of the state enter the public domain after a period of time has elapsed, usually ranging from 30 to 150 years, and therefore may not be available for researchers.

Academic journals that publish historical articles frequently offer an index to documents held in various collections or provide a historiography of published material that addresses a particular issue or event. For example, *Women's*

History Review and *History of Education* are two such journals that are useful to consult.

There are a number of reference works, such as:

- Biographical dictionaries (some are available online)
- Guides to parliamentary papers and publications
- Edited volumes of letters
- Published statistics such as the annual official statistics that include education statistics
- Reports of Royal Commissions
- Edited collections of education documents

Most archives and libraries have policies with regard to access to their collections that prevent unauthorised disclosure of private information (such as raw census data).

Analysing documents

It might seem as if documents are reasonably uncomplicated sources of data to locate and analyse. Scott (1990) has suggested that all documents should be assessed according to four criteria:

1 Authenticity
2 Credibility
3 Representativeness
4 Meaning

The issue of *authenticity* concerns the soundness and authorship of documents. One of the first steps is to determine whether the document is an original or a copy. If a copy, it is important to verify that no material has been added, replaced or deleted. The process of reproducing the original by hand, photocopy, scanning or microfilming may have resulted in missing text or unreadable text. It might well be the case too that institutional documents, invariably filed in a variety of places, might not be a complete record, and details such as page numbers, section numbers and reading previous and subsequent Meeting Minutes can point to the existence of other documents a researcher might wish to access.

As well as being sound, it is important to know the author of a particular document. Official policy documents, for example, are produced as a result of a complex administrative process and although the author might not be individually cited, knowledge of this process is critical for reading between the lines of the document. For example, the Treasury produced one of the policy documents that guided the second Labour Government in New Zealand in 1997 (Codd, 2005). The fact that the Treasury produced the Briefing papers (New Zealand Treasury, 1987) points to the suggestion that the fundamental concern of government policy from that point was fiscal efficiency.

Credibility refers to assessing a document for its accuracy. This refers to the factual accuracy of reports and whether they do in fact report the true feelings of the author. All documents are, in the main, selective or distorted as it is difficult to construct accounts that are independent of any particular viewpoint. This is not to suggest that documents are not credible accounts and it is therefore important that information about the author(s) is known. For example, consider how the respective teacher unions reported on the introduction of performance management systems as opposed to how government papers recorded such a policy move or a Local Education Authority (in England) or Board of Trustees (in New Zealand). While differences of interpretation about events are plausible given the respective stance each group adopted, both may have wanted a particular image projected, hence the degree to which their opinions were stated and documented. Documents can be exercises in reputation-building or reputation-restoration and, consequently, researchers are advised to read secondary source material about the specific event or activity as well as about the individual(s) or groups involved. This will assist in establishing a level of credibility.

The *representativeness* of a document is determined by its survival and availability. It might not be the case that a representative sample of documents about a particular policy, for example, might be required but it is important to determine whether the selected documents are representative of the contemporary environment. As indicated in the previous section, there are a range of storage facilities and retrieval mechanisms for documents. This is not to suggest that all documents on a particular issue or problem have either been stored correctly (Fitzgerald, 2005) or not consigned to a shredder. Computerised records are not immune from deletion as current files can be over-written or stored in an unreadable format. Document writing is an activity for the literate and, consequently, there is likely to be bias in terms of authorship. In the main, primary source materials were historically penned by men with the necessary education to record events and activities although this is not to suggest that women did not contribute to historical documents – it is likely that women's letters and diaries have not been passed on to an archive or library as families can assume that these accounts are 'private' and may not offer a contribution to the public account (Fitzgerald, 2005). Selective retention is therefore another issue that researchers need to take into account when making claims about the representativeness of a document.

The *meaning* of a document is its interpretation. This involves, on the surface, the literal or surface reading of the text. It is important to know the accepted definitions of the key words, phrases and concepts and to decipher any handwriting accurately. Once this literal reading has been produced, the next level of interpretation involves both *content* and *textual* analysis. Content analysis (Robson, 1993), a form of quantitative analysis, requires a count of the number of times a particular word/term or image is used. On the other hand, textual analysis (Jaworski and Coupland, 1999) concentrates on deriving an understanding from the qualitative significance of the words/terms and images. Both content and textual analyses require classification of data and reading for embedded meanings. Electronic programmes such as NVivo can assist with the extraction and retrieval of key words particularly if there are an extensive number of documents under examination.

Key questions

Documentary research requires researchers to undertake a systematic interrogation and evaluation of the evidence. This will assist in reading between the lines; uncovering the sub-text or secrets contained in the document, yet not immediately explicit to the reader. In order to reveal the evidence and provide an analysis of the document, it is important to adopt a critical stance. This will involve asking a number of questions about the evidence, such as:

1 Who wrote the document? What is known about the personal and professional biography of the author?
2 When was this document written? What other events were occurring at that time?
3 What prompted the writing of this document? Were there social, political, economic or historical reasons that may have influenced the writer and the contents?
4 What audience was this written for? Does this document set a particular agenda?
5 What are the contents, the language and terms used and the key message(s)? What is the ideological position of the author?
6 What are the omissions? Was this deliberate? How do you know?
7 Are there any sources that can be used as a comparison?
8 Is this document reliable?

While these questions are helpful in analysing documents and extracting data, this is only partial evidence. Documents exist in a social, political and economic context and while they might be representative of that context, documents can contribute to the construction of later contexts. Take for example the range of policies that guided the introduction of leadership training for heads in England and which incrementally contributed to and developed current policies and practices (Brundrett et al., 2006). An understanding of the development of training for headteachers cannot be fully understood unless these policies are all subject to scrutiny.

Collating data

As I have mentioned, documentary research is a form of qualitative research. It involves, in essence, locating underlying themes in materials, analysing these themes and providing an interpretation that augments a theoretical argument.

What is less explicit however is *how* themes are extracted, coded and thus made retrievable.

One strategy for searching for themes in data is to develop a coding system that will readily permit the development of categories that can then be used to formulate conclusions. Altheide (2004) has developed an approach, that he has labelled ethnographic content analysis (ECA), that represents a codification of certain procedures that might be viewed as typical of any kind of qualitative content analysis, although he argues for the constant revision of themes based on data collection activities and emerging interpretations. This is, accordingly, a form of grounded theory in which data are constantly revised to assist with conceptualisation, interpretation and the development of a narrative. This is a useful framework, particularly for case study research that depends on what I term the situatedness of the case and data. Altheide (2004) describes the six steps researchers should undertake:

1 Generate a research question
2 Understand the context in which the documents were generated
3 Read a range of relevant documents
4 Generate categories that will guide the collection of data
5 Test categories by using it to collect and collate data
6 Revise categories

These steps will assist in the development of a grounded theory; the theoretical argument is grounded in the data. In addition, I would suggest that the literature relevant to the research questions may provide initial categories for the researcher to 'test' on the documents. The constant revising of categories is an important element and certainly a strategy I have used in my own work to date.

As an educational historian, I have undertaken research in archives in New Zealand, Australia and England over the past decade. One of these projects examined the contribution of missionary women to the first schools in New Zealand and was based on an initial 'hunch' that the written record of this period (1823–1840) that suggested that missionary men were preachers as well as teachers was incorrect. The documents required here were located in a number of libraries, archives and museums in three countries; they were either original written materials, transcripts or had been microfilmed. To provide an overview of both the depth and range of sources, I had eight file boxes (and later eight electronic folders) that were labelled with the name of each library, museum or archive in which the documents were located. Data collected from documents in each of the locations were then stored in their relevant file box or electronic folder. In order to produce a coherent chronological narrative of events, I then combined information from all eight files into one. This may appear to be tedious but it ensured that I had (1) copies of all the documents according to their location and (2) a chronological file that provided a linear narrative that assisted with analysis and interpretation.

In order to capture the data from the range of libraries, museums and archives, I devised the table shown as Figure 17.1 to assist with interpretation and analysis. Here I will draw on Scott's (1990) four criteria to explain this methodology and data-collation method.

Source	Text	Coding

Figure 17.1   Example of documentary analysis tool

Source: refers to the reference number, location and file name/number. In this column I recorded the archive/library reference number, writer of document, name of intended recipient, date of document and any other relevant material, such as location of writer. Every new document, whether a single letter, one diary entry in a week/month/year, sermon, church record and so on, was 'counted' as a single source. This was of benefit for two reasons: first, it helped to establish the number and range of documents I was dealing with (representativeness) and, secondly, when the archive records from all eight repositories were combined, this informa-tion then provided a level of authenticity. Not every document pertaining to one particular event, individual or group is located in one archive, library or museum. I therefore had eight different tables such as the one above and then combined these to create a chronological record. Had any of the details in column 1 been incorrect, it would have created difficulties retrieving *any* original record. An example from one of these records is reproduced as Figure 17.2.

The year is 1826, and in Column 1 the full reference is provided, date of the let-ter, details of correspondents and I am alerted that this letter is held in the Mitchell Library (ML) Sydney and is part of the Bonwick Transcripts (BT) the relevant col-lection in this library. ML refers also to the relevant folder I created for this library; the numeral 53 refers to the page number. This level of detail then made retrieval of the original quotation less difficult. This was the system I devised; it is impor-tant that researchers devise or adopt their own systems to work with.

Text: Column 2 contains a transcript of the document; no words are omitted, capital letters are retained and the language is unaltered. Any direct quotes used in my analysis and discussion were extracted from Column 2. This is, in essence, the qualitative historical data and, consequently, it is imperative that this text is correctly reproduced from the original. This assists with determin-ing representativeness, meaning and credibility (Scott, 1990).

1826		
ML3 BT 53 Transcripts of records held in the Public Record Office, London Missionary 1824–1829 Samuel Marsden to Edward Bickerseth 2 Feb 1826	[p. 1604] ... I am satisfied that all the female children of the Missionaries at the age of five years should be removed from New Zealand. The scenes which they must daily behold amongst the natives will naturally tend to destroy Female delicacy; which is the strongest Guardian to Female Virtue. I have seen with much pain the effects of young Females been exposed to indelicate Scenes in the Society Islands – the same may be expected to take place in New Zealand while the inhabitants remain in their present state of Degradation. Should the Missionaries [p. 1605] in New Zealand wish to have their children preserved from the unavoidable effects of living amongst Savages, they must have them educated for some time to come in N. S. Wales. [p. 1607] ... It gives me much satisfaction that the Society are sending out persons qualified for their work	Miss. Children Policy Colonisation Females Contact zone

Figure 17.2   Example of documentary analysis

Coding: Column 3 contains the key words or themes that have been extracted from the document text and were devised from multiple readings of similar documents as well as the relevant literature. A list of these key themes was produced on a card and as I was coding each data entry I was ensuring that the same words were used. At the analysis stage, I simply counted the number of examples of each of the words (there was a list of 28 key words) and that provided a quantitative record that assisted with decisions regarding whether the theme was significant. This was a methodical process that assisted with the development of a grounded theory about missionary women, missionary schooling and Indigenous pupils in early nineteenth-century New Zealand.

There might be additional use of a fourth column in this table: to record any questions that arise for a researcher to further check or verify; to make a note of links with possible relevant literature or to assess the document according to Scott's (1990) criteria; and to record the 'count' of key words (content analysis).

As I have mentioned, documentary research is one of the tools that can be employed in case study research. The examples I have used above can be used to collate and analyse case data. In 2005 I was involved in a collaborative research project with a New Zealand school practitioner and an academic colleague in England. Our project examined links between middle leadership and learning and was a case study of two schools in New Zealand and two in England (Fitzgerald et al., 2006). This involved 96 interviews that included the heads/principals, senior managers, middle leaders, teachers, teaching assistants and pupils. In order to provide the contextual background we examined the school prospectus, ERO and

1. How are teachers organised in this school?

Identifier	Comment	Theme
NSH	Basically, they're organised around departments. We've never gone to the faculties in fact which is a disappointment to me. Because to go to faculties you really got to throw all the units away in a basket and re-build. I've watched a lot of schools struggle with the whole Head of Faculty thing so I've stuck with traditional departments and tried to transform them into a co-operative model so that when you make key appointments you make sure they understand the integration that you're looking for in the department and so if we've stuck with traditional departments and we've tried to restructure them so that the whole structure is of a small and interactive with a dynamic team and you say 'Right! You're in this level, use the experiences and responsibilities … anything that you want to have a go at to grow at' … and so they shift the well structured department and shift the responsibilities around in order to grow the whole business of that professional growth the whole dynamics of professional growth. What would you like to grow at? …. responsibilities ... resources … shape it the way we want to so that it's an effective delivery and it's got good outcomes for students. And then pastorally it's quite different because it was the first school in NZ to have Deans and we cherish that. We cherish that for a number of reasons. First of all it does mean we got many (mini) schools we've only got 300 students and when somebody who knows the kids – we've got one person who says, 'These are my kids'. And their knowledge of them is incredible. Their knowledge of the kid, the understanding of them becomes formidable … you are there to care and encourage and grow ... again they're growing.	Structural Co-operative model Shift responsibilities Innovation Risk taking Aligns with website and prospectus content analysis Organisation of teachers commented on in ERO report
ESH	Around learning and teaching. Learning Centres with a Director and Assistant Director and report to leadership group in school of 15. HT, Deputy, Bursar and everyone responsible for an area of learning and whole school responsibility. Teachers attached to Learning Centre. All behaviour, management, guidance and welfare part of Student Services. Leading tutor monitors learning and achievement of pupils. Tutor teams – focus on learning.	L&T the focus Learning focus Responsibility and accountability Aligns with SEF

Figure 17.3   Example of case study analysis

Ofsted reports, websites and had access to the SEF (self-evaluation form). To assist with our analysis, we constructed tables that collated this wealth of data and provided a mechanism to create a plausible and trustworthy account of our findings. One of our research questions was: What is the link between leadership and learning? As mentioned, we interviewed the heads/principals of the four schools and we were particularly interested in how schools organised teaching and learning. One of the first interview questions was: How are teachers organised in this school? Figure 17.3 shows the transcribed responses from the two secondary school heads (ES refers to the English secondary school and NS, the New Zealand school). The third column is an example of our analysis that builds on the literature review and the documentary analysis that occurred in the first stage of the project. The comments noted below the black line triangulate the interview data and assist with the emerging narrative and theorisation of links between leadership and learning. What we were looking for was the 'persistence' of such examples from multiple sources (Lincoln and Guba, 1985), and in this case, the documentary research complemented other forms of qualitative inquiry.

Collecting, collating and analysing data in documentary research is an iterative process that requires checking, re-checking and refining key themes, concepts or ideas. This can be illustrated by the diagram in Figure 17.4.

Research questions lead to raw data ⇒

raw data are stored with relevant location reference and prompt ⇒

reflective thinking about data that leads to content analysis and

⇒ generation of key themes ⇒

that are tested, refined and amended and lead to ⇒

 textual analysis that lead to ⇒

empirical findings and the ⇒

generation of the final report.

Figure 17.4   From research questions to report

Conclusion

This chapter has provided an overview for researchers of the possible ways in which documentary research might be conducted. As I have stressed, it is important to approach research in a systematic, critical and informed way and this may further involve learning new sets of skills to assist with asking questions of the evidence (data), analysing that evidence and formulating conclusions. For those new to documentary research, it is important to read the methodological debates in the field to gain an understanding of the complexities of research, in any form, and at any level. I have provided a number of key questions in this chapter to assist with critical thinking about the research and the evidence and suggested a format for electronically collating and analysing data. In conclusion, I would suggest that whatever documentary research is undertaken that it is manageable within the time available, that the research design 'matches' the questions posed and that an iterative process is employed that subjects the data and conclusions to critical scrutiny. Whatever the strengths and limitations of documentary research, it can be innovative and illuminating and prompt an enthusiasm for research that is infectious.

References

Altheide, D. (2004) 'Ethnographic content analysis', in Lewis-Beck, M., Bryman, A. and Liao, T. (eds) *The Sage Encyclopedia of Social Science Research Methods*. Thousand Oaks, CA: Sage.

Apple, M.W. (2001) *Educating the 'Right' Way: Markets, Standards, God and Inequality*. New York: Routledge Falmer.

Ashton-Warner, S. (1979) *I Passed This Way*. Auckland: Reed Methuen.

Blackmore, J. (1999) *Troubling Women: Feminism, Leadership and Educational Change*. Buckingham: Open University Press.

Brundrett, M., Fitzgerald, T. and Sommefeldt, D. (2006) 'The creation of national programmes of school leadership development in England and New Zealand: a comparative study', *International Studies in Educational Administration*, 34 (1): (in press)

Burton, A. (2001) 'Thinking beyond the boundaries: empire, feminism and the domains of history', *Social History*, 26 (1): 60–71.

Codd, J. (2005) 'Teachers as "managed professionals" in the global education industry: the New Zealand experience', *Educational Review*, 57 (2): 193–206.

Fitzgerald, T. (2005) 'Archives of memory and memories of archive: CMS women's letters and diaries, 1823–1835', *History of Education*, 34 (6): 657–674.

Fitzgerald, T., Eaton, J. and Gunter, H.M. (2006) 'Leadership of learning: Middle leadership in schools in England and New Zealand'. A Report to the National College for School Leadership as part of the International Research Associate Programme. Manchester: Manchester University.

Gunter, H.M. (2005) 'Remodelling the school workforce in England: a study in tyranny'. Keynote address to the annual conference of the British Educational Leadership Management and Administration Society, Milton Keynes.

Jaworski, A. and Coupland, N. (eds) (1999) *The Discourse Reader*. London: Routledge.

Lincoln, Y.S and Guba, E.G. (1985) *Naturalistic Inquiry*. Newbury Park, CA: Sage.

McCulloch, G. and Richardson, W. (2000) *Historical Research in Educational Settings*. Buckingham: Open University Press.

New Zealand Treasury (1987) *Government Management: Brief to the Incoming Government* (2 vols). Wellington: Government Printer.

Robson, C. (1993) *Real World Research: A Resource for Social Scientists and Practitioner-Researchers*. Oxford: Blackwells.

Samuel, R. (1994) *Theatres of Memory: Past and Present in Contemporary Culture*. London: Verso.

Scott, J. (1990) *A Matter of Record: Documentary Sources in Social Research*. Cambridge: Polity Press.

Thrupp, M. (2001) 'School-level education policy under New Labour and New Zealand Labour: a comparative update', *British Journal of Educational Studies*, 49 (2): 187–212.

Recommended reading

This is not a definitive list of texts but offers researchers an abridged list for their guidance.

Internet

Gorst, A. and Brivati, B. (1997) 'The Internet for historians', in Butler L. and Gorst, A. (eds) *Modern British History: A Guide to Study and Research*. London: IB Tauris Publishers.

Methodological debates

Goodson, I. and Sikes, P. (2001) *Life History Research in Educational Settings: Learning from Lives*. Buckingham: Open University Press.

McCulloch, G. (2004) *Documentary Research in Education, History and the Social Sciences*. London: RoutledgeFalmer.

Prior, L. (2003) *Using Documents in Social Research*. London: Sage.

Steedman, C. (1999) *Dust*. Manchester: Manchester University Press.

Photographs and visual sources

Lawn, M. and Grosvenor, I. (eds) (2005) *Materialities of Schooling: Design, Technology, Objects, Routines*. Oxford: Symposium Books.

18

Using diaries in research

Marlene Morrison

Diaries are among a wide and often complex array of documentary materials that may be of interest to researchers in the field of educational management and leadership (see Figure 18.1). While personal chronicling and self-narratives have long and distinguished histories, their use in research is more recent. This chapter is concerned with diary-focused research as a distinctive genre that straddles both quantitative and qualitative approaches. Diary-keepers are researchers or research participants or both. For the purposes of this chapter, diary-keeping is seen, in process and outcomes, as essentially social, even though historic or romantic associations with the term might be to view diaries as intimate or personal (Morrison and Galloway, 1996). Much of the concern in this chapter is given to diary use by research participants, and to diaries that are solicited rather than unsolicited accounts (for the latter, Scott (1990) provides a useful framework). Finally, attention will also be drawn to diaries and portfolios as increasingly popular forms of practitioner research, especially their application as elements of reflective inquiry for 'growing' leaders, and usually undertaken by practitioners rather than by academics.

However, initial attention is also given to the importance of diaries for researchers, especially qualitative researchers, for whom diaries are not simply procedural tools for managing and documenting research stages (important though this is for all research) but are also integral to the production of the analytic record 'that underpins the conceptual development and density' (Strauss, 1987: 5) featured in qualitative accounts of educational experience. The discussions that follow are not exhaustive. Researchers in educational leadership and management, for example, will always need to recognize that the potential contributions of diaries, and roles for diarists, may disguise important differences in meaning and use depending upon cultural contexts, discussed elsewhere in this volume (see Chapters 4 and 17).

Q: *How might primary school managers improve the effectiveness of temporary (supply) teacher use in school?*

Time	Main activities	Other activities
13.00	Children in. Did register. Didn't tally. Incorrect from morning! Took ages to sort out; some children's names difficult to pronounce. Register not very clear. Need to be accurate for swimming.	A mum came with me – an older lady – very nice but not very effective. Very noisy in changing areas. I was dotting from one to the other.
13.20	Eventually set off. Took a while to get there as kept starting and stopping. Worn out when I arrived!	
14.00	Eventually we got there down to the pool instructor. He took the more able group – leaving me alone with 20 children in a small pool. We worked hard but they didn't tire. Changing took ages. Walked back after a great lecture from me. Got back 14.40. Too late for play.	I have never felt so worn out after swimming. Only I had to get out of the water for a short while Miracles never cease.
15.00	I kept them out for 10 min. play while I had a drink. An ESN teacher took a group for reading. I let rest finish off any work then get an activity while I heard readers. Behaviour improving.	Didn't think they'd settle to a story and they hadn't read all week.
15.30	Dismiss children. Write note for teacher.	Dep. wished I was going back as I'd controlled class.

Q: *What was the most demanding task or situation you had to deal with today? Any additional comment on today's activities?*

A. Swimming – very dangerous situation – particularly at the baths. 1:20. Ridiculous.

Figure 18.1   A diary extract: a supply teacher's afternoon
(Morrison and Galloway, 1996: 50; reproduced with permission of Palgrave Macmillan)

Researchers' diaries

Until recently, published references to diaries referred mainly to their importance for researchers (Burgess, 1981, 1984). Diaries kept by researchers are examples of documentary evidence that can be used for a range of purposes. In earlier accounts, distinctions are made between logs, diaries and journals. Holly (1984,

1989) differentiates between a log – a truncated record of information that relates to specific situations, rather like an aide-mémoire – and a diary, which is seen to contain more 'personal' information, and includes interpretation as well as description 'on multiple dimensions' (1984: 5). According to Holly, journals, a third form of research record, are carefully structured to combine both objective notes and free-flowing accounts. As Burgess (1994) suggests, these distinctions are probably more useful analytically than in practice, since the umbrella term 'diary' can frequently comprise substantive, methodological and analytic elements, as in the case of Griffiths (1985), who recorded distinctive elements of his work as 'Diary 1' and 'Diary 2'.

A diary or log serves a range of elementary yet critical purposes for the researcher. It provides a tool for charting both progress and critical research moments. These can be plotted against the planning checklist agreed among the research team, or with the research supervisor. It might, for example, include contact dates with the supervisor or research team, and chart agreement and progress on the tasks and targets for the research.

For the qualitative researcher, the diary performs a range of functions. Burgess (1981, 1984) focused on the principles that are associated with it, raising questions about the recording and categorising of data, and the issue of inclusion or otherwise of diary data in the final account.

Of course, not every researcher has the time, resources, or the epistemological 'will' to record in the depth and detail deployed by Okely (1994), for example. The brief extract below gives some sense of a daily journal that often consumed a whole notebook per day. Her approach is in the traditional anthropological tradition:

> With minimal success, I had combed the anthropological ... literature for guidance and reassurance in the face of increasing scepticism among my employers about non-questionnaire research. Then a chance meeting with the African anthropologist Malcolm Mcleod afforded me the best and only detailed methodological advice I was to find at the outset of fieldwork. From his experience, he suggested 'write down everything you hear, smell, and see; even the colour of the carpets ... Ideally you should fill an exercise book each day.' So I jettisoned my earlier, increasingly unsatisfactory attempts at writing notes under prescribed headings. I had been deciding what was relevant and in the process omitting other details, possibly for ever. My notes took the form of a chronological diary ... Events were written up as soon as possible ... Ideas, tentative interpretations and dominant themes were also written in the text, as the field experience developed ... As both fieldworker and future author, I was free to allow the ideas to germinate in their own time, and through my thinking, not by proxy. Subsequent participant observation and extended contemplation would sort the wheat from the chaff. (1994: 23–24)

This extract raises at least two questions: How structured should the researcher's diary be? And what role will the diary 'jottings' play in the analysis of data and in the final report/dissertation/thesis?

Okely's account appears to be at one end of a diary continuum that extends from a mainly free-flowing account to a highly structured summary of timed events using specific headings. From my earliest experiences as a researcher, I have kept a diary for every project in which I have been involved; a diary whose format and style straddle the middle of the continuum introduced above. Basically, they comprise three columns. Column 1 is a daily record of all events, frequently substantive, sometimes methodological, and usually completed at the end the day; column 2 is used for analytic memos, records emerging themes and ideas, and poses questions; while column 3 is used for retrospection and introspection (what I call the R and I column). This provides an opportunity to note and refine ideas and thoughts after time has elapsed from the original diary entry. The diary with its columns was kept in an exercise book but it is now stored as a computer file. Most recently, software packages for qualitative data analysis provide further opportunities for the enthusiastic diarist. None of the above is meant to imply that the diary is ever a complete record, or a neutral medium of production, or that it will remain unaffected by other writing and reading that is part of the qualitative research process (see also Atkinson, 1992).

Miles and Huberman (1994: Ch. 4) sound a note of caution for researchers new to qualitative studies, and argue strongly against allowing any data, including diary data, to accumulate over weeks and months without engaging in early analysis of that data:

> Some qualitative researchers put primary energy into data collection for weeks, months, even years and then retire from the field 'to sort out their notes'. We believe this is a mistake. It rules out the possibility of collecting new data to fill in the gaps, or to test new hypotheses that emerge during analysis. It discourages the formulation of 'rival hypotheses' that question a field-worker's routine assumptions and biases. And it makes analysis into a giant, sometimes overwhelming, task that demotivates the researcher and reduces the quality of the work produced. (1994: 50)

Researchers' diaries have been utilised as important elements of action research, where the diary may be seen as an important tool for reflection and as a vehicle for the provocation of personal and professional change, as, for example, in Walker (1988), a study of general practitioner trainees. In combination with other forms of data such as interviews, photographs, and video records, etc., diary data can also make an important contribution to ethnographic accounts of educational experience.

For example, Burgess and Morrison (1998) conducted a project between 1993 and 1994 that investigated the ways in which adults, children and young people in English primary and secondary schools experienced food and eating. It formed part of a larger ESRC programme entitled *The Nation's Diet: The Social Science of Food Choice* (Burgess and Morrison, 1998). Recommendations were for educationists (policy-makers and practitioners), nutritionists and sociologists, and the methodological approach was ethnographic. As the principal researcher, Morrison (1995) spent a term in each of four schools, observing the institutional dynamics of food and eating in a range of formal and informal settings for teaching and learning: classrooms, dining halls, playgrounds, school corridors, journeys to and from school, neighbouring ice-cream vans and chip shops. Events were recorded daily in diary form and some diary extracts were published, both in the final report and subsequently. In the following example, the data from the diary is used illustratively to inform readers about lunch-time eating experiences in a school.

Monday

Today 365 £1 purchases have been recorded by the canteen supervisor. Am told by several members of staff during first break that it's like a zoo in there [the dining hall]. First day's observation supports that impression. Children are literally herded to the hatch in groups. When queuing gets unmanageable students are sent outside and return when it appears to be quieter. Dinner ladies' role appears to be one of gatekeeping: keeping out, letting in in batches. Food eaten is a nutritionist's nightmare. Most children eat cake and chips. The most popular combination is cake, chips, and a packet of tomato ketchup.

Thursday

Those in receipt of FSM [free school meals] are not checked to see what they purchase, so chips in combination with three or four cakes is not uncommon. There is a shortage of knives and forks, and no water. Cheap coloured drinks are very popular. Latest habit appears to be to ignore the straw supplied with drinks, turn the carton upside down, suck plastic carton, tear into with teeth, and suck contents from the resultant tear. Interesting noises! Some pupils leave the dining hall with half eaten purchases. Two observed with bags of chips in coat pockets. (1995: 246)

In such ways, ethnographic accounts using diaries illustrated ways in which schools are important arenas for assessing the ambiguities and contradictions of food consumption which are features of adult populations, and which, for a variety of reasons, Morrison found replicated in learning environments.

Having introduced aspects of the usefulness of diaries for researchers, the chapter now turns to diary-keeping by research informants as tools for data collection and analysis.

Research informants' diaries

As do all personal accounts, diaries exhibit the strengths and weaknesses of information that is solicited from research informants: 'they are partial, and reflect the interests and perspectives of their authors' (Hammersley and Atkinson, 1995: 165). In educational research, where there may have been a tendency to privilege both the 'oral' and the 'observed' – what people say they do and what they are observed doing – over the literate, diaries provide an interesting counterpoint, since diarists are invited to write what they do and/or think. Whether or not this is because we tend to assume that 'the spoken account is more "authentic" or "spontaneous" than the written account' (1995: 165), diaries have specific uses in 'picking up' the minutiae of vicarious educational experience in ways which the other major form of solicited written information, questionnaires, do not. However, even this brief introduction suggests a view of diaries as rather traditional, paper-bound instruments. Diary research now links to recent literary styles of development and advances in recording diary information, such as audio-visual, or through developments in the use of electronic diaries (Saris, 1989), and schema for coding sensitive information (Coxon et al., 1992). Further technological developments include qualitative software packages that have allowed diary data to be considered alongside other forms of data analysis. Diaries are used in a wide variety of contexts, formats and styles; they can also be both large-scale and highly structured (Gershuny et al., 1986).

Whatever forms diaries take, a number of fundamental assumptions about diary-keeping need to be considered.

- Diaries rest on the view that research informants are in especially advantageous positions to record aspects of their lives and work. Such a perspective does more than extol the virtue of self-report. Implicit in this statement are interpretive ideas discussed in the second chapter of this book, namely, that participants in education are social actors who, through personal logs and reports, make available 'inside' information that might not otherwise be available or visible to the researcher.
- Diaries allow researchers access to evidence that may not be otherwise available to the researchers, whether on *logistical* (researchers cannot be everywhere) or *ethical* (researchers should not be everywhere) or *pragmatic* (researchers need to be elsewhere) grounds. The extent to which diary data constitutes 'substitute observation' (Morrison and Galloway, 1996) might be seen as a challenge for diary design and use (see below).
- Combined with other forms of data collection and analysis, diaries are based on a premise, shared by both qualitative and quantitative research, that the researcher can collect, aggregate, collate, and analyse diary records, in order to produce a wider and/or deeper picture of what educational experience means to groups, as well as to individuals.

- Diary accounts have the potential to produce large amounts of data. Researchers need, therefore, to convince themselves, as well as potential diarists, that the activity is worthwhile and for specific educational purposes, and to reach agreement with diarists about which aspects of individuals' lives will be open to public scrutiny, and in what forms. Simultaneously, researchers need to be very clear about *why* they are inviting diary participation; from the planning stage, this extends to knowledge about how the data are going to be analysed and includes how, and when, analytic categories and codes are to be assigned.

Diary designs

Diaries can be used qualitatively and quantitatively to illuminate a range of educational issues. For interpretive as well as 'action' researchers, who may be encouraged to complete diaries as personal accounts, reflections, or confessionals about daily experience, the notion of 'designing' diaries might be seen as counter-intuitive. Yet, researchers need to design diaries that maximise their usefulness in relation to the research topic and the main questions to be addressed. Formats might, therefore, include different styles and booklets of various kinds, with instructions of types and lengths depending upon the age and background of the diarist, for example, and the interests of the researcher and the research. Diary designs have a number of hidden costs: time needed to access potential diarists, brief them and then remind them (sometimes again and again!) of the need to complete diaries.

Some published guidance on the use of diaries appears to narrow the focus to specific, limited uses. For example, Bell (1999) asserts that diaries:

> are not records of engagements or personal journals of thoughts and activities, [Why not?] but rather logs of professional activities ... Do you really want to know that someone had a cup of tea, paid the milkman, or had a bath [You might need to ... it depends on the research problem], or are you only interested in professionally related activities [perhaps]? (1999: 148–149; the insertions are mine)

Surely the key issue is the need for clarity about the research problem addressed, and its relation to diary use? If the core intention, for example, is to examine the ways in which school departmental and faculty heads manage time for professional activities (Earley and Fletcher-Campbell, 1989), then the use of a timed weekly log of professional activities seems apt. But if the purpose of the research is to investigate the ways in which managers, teachers and/or students make connections between the public and private spheres of their lives, then the times afforded to personal hygiene, refreshments and shopping might take on a specific significance, and should therefore be included.

Part of the rationale for using diaries proposed (Galloway and Morrison, 1993 discussed in Morrison and Galloway, 1996: 35) in a project entitled

'Supply teaching: an investigation of policy, processes and people', was 'to make connections between private and public aspects of supply teachers' lives which showed infinite variation'. Earlier, Morrison had used diaries as a way of exploring how mature women students, who entered a college of education after a lengthy period of non-participation in education, managed to 'juggle' study with paid and unpaid work such as child-rearing, and with leisure activities (Morrison, 1996: see below).

Design challenges

Diarists are usually invited to complete diaries over specified time periods. Because diaries are time-consuming, instructions to accompany diaries, and the layout and appearance of the diary 'booklet', may take on a specific significance. Ultimately, diaries have the potential to become onerous; tendencies to non-completion are, therefore, only partially overcome by meticulous attention to cosmetic appearance and clear instructions.

Large-scale time budget studies have used diaries in leisure research, and the investigation of household work strategies and the sexual division of labour. Diary surveys feature in studies of food purchase and consumption choices and in investigation of income and financial matters among individuals and households. The period covered is usually either one or seven consecutive days; but two-to-four non-consecutive day diaries and part-day diaries are also possible. For both qualitative and quantitative purposes 'time slots' in the diary can be open or fixed and activity categories, precoded or open. Gershuny et al. (1986) describe the 'Szalai' system devised in the 1960s (with 190 activity codes) as a *de facto* standard for time budget surveys (Szalai, 1972).

The choice of format is rarely straightforward. A large-scale, one-day survey of the distribution of activities in a population might be very useful descriptively, but less useful interpretively than diary surveys over a longer period. Researchers have used seven-day time frames, aware that 'time budget researchers who wish to improve the quality of their estimates have an alternative to increasing their sample size; they can increase the period covered by the research instrument' (Gershuny et al., 1986: 18).

Large-scale designs of this kind are clearly not an option for the single-handed researcher. But some of the challenges remain similar. Objections to diaries of longer duration are that agreements to participate become more difficult to secure, and the quality and rate of response may vary and/or decline. The propensity to respond may vary at different times in the day/night, and the gap between the event and its record and interpretation by the diarist may widen. All this suggests that research design for small- or large-scale use of diaries must accommodate practical constraints. Earley and Fletcher-Campbell (1989) used weekly diaries to investigate educational management but, recognising how these encroached on time, excluded diary-writers from other elements of their research.

Illustrative examples

Studying time

Researchers have used diaries as an instrument for investigating time, to locate individuals 'in time' and to pursue experience and the passage of time, specifically during *transitions* in the life, work, or study cycles of educators and students. Bradley and Eggleston (1976) used diaries in their study of probationer teachers who were asked to keep weekly diaries on three separate occasions during the term. Such an approach might be adapted for studies about the professional activities of newly appointed heads or those aspiring to headship, for example, or in studies of transitions from careers in educational leadership to retirement.

As introduced earlier, Morrison (1996) used informant diaries to study the gendered experience of mature women returning to study in a college of further education after a long period of absence. The resultant analysis formed the basis for recommendations to college managers about how qualitative improvements in the experience of study time at college, that was, for students, part of an ongoing negotiation between study, work, family and leisure time, might improve both student retention and examination success rates. Diaries were based on a similar format to that shown as Figure 18.1 at the beginning of this chapter. The three columns in the format used denoted 'Time', 'Main activities' and 'Other activities' respectively. The time column addressed the 'When?' question; this included the timing of daily activities (from 7 am to 10 pm for up to 10 days) and the sequencing in which activities occurred. Responses in the two remaining columns addressed, in part, the 'What?' question; in other words, the diarists' descriptions of the activities in which they were engaged. As importantly, these two columns were also designed to address a thematic issue that was emerging from the preliminary data, namely women students' repeated references to the need to 'juggle' time. Thus respondents were asked to describe what they considered to be the main activity of the time period, and to give a description in 'their own terms' about what activities, if any, they considered to be 'other or supplementary during that period'. Findings revealed that 'studying' activities occurred simultaneously with activities like cooking, ironing, loading the washing machine and listening to children read. It was possible to plot the times when study was considered to be the main or only activity (usually on college premises), when it was combined with other activities and the priority given to study (or not) at specific times of the day, or on specific days. Instructions to answer the question 'What?' were not infrequently extended by the diarists to address the question 'Why?'; this supports earlier comments about the mixing of description and interpretation (Holly, 1984) that the act of diary-writing often evokes. This provided added insights about how mature women students defined 'wasting', 'worrying', and 'waiting' time(s). Unexpectedly, the diary also revealed a range of understandings about what the word 'study' meant; for some students, 'reading' was relegated as a study activity which lacked status because it did not entail the act of 'doing'; open-ended suggestions from tutors 'to read', for example, could be construed as 'wasting' time when there were 'more important' things to do, like writing an essay, cooking dinner, or collecting children from school.

A 'substitute' for observation

Researching supply teaching, diary accounts were used by Galloway and Morrison to investigate supply work in schools, a phenomenon that is both ordinary (occurring frequently, if irregularly), and extraordinary, in that it sometimes brings into schools teachers who are total strangers to the pupils for whom they are fleetingly responsible (Galloway, 1993). Explaining the mechanics of diary use, they comment:

> Seventeen supply teachers completed diaries, enabling experience to be tracked in detail. The selection did not purport to be a representative sample; rather they exemplified a range of different situations pertaining to individuals doing supply work *that went beyond what researchers could observe given the practical constraints affecting the field work*. In total, diaries provided data on eighty days to support that being obtained elsewhere. However, unlike interviewing (where self-report sometimes occurs over a lengthy time span), daily accounts would add an immediate and alternative dimension to verbal accounts of experience. (Morrison and Galloway, 1996: 37; emphasis added)

Previous writers have used diaries as an 'observational log, maintained by subjects which can then be used as the basis for intensive interviewing' (Zimmerman and Wieder, 1977: 481). Not only do Morrison and Galloway (1996) give detailed attention to the extent to which 'writing about experience adds an element of artificiality and superficiality to already complex features of data recording in "natural settings"' (1996: 41), they also caution against simplistic assumptions about diary data as a substitute for observation by the researcher. On occasion, diary accounts *were* at variance with observations recorded by researchers. (In other circumstances, Oppenheim (1966) has noted the tendency either for diarists to record what they think researchers will wish to read, or amend 'usual' behaviour during the recording period.) In this sense, diaries share the strengths and weaknesses of all forms of self-report. In the supply teaching example, in place of statistically representative information, the semi-structured diary method provided the research informant with opportunities to represent varied experience, and, for the research team, afforded 'glimpses of the infinite variety of life as the stop-gap teacher' (1996: 45).

Pupils' diaries

So far, all examples of diary use have considered diary accounts solicited from adults. In studying food and eating in schools, Burgess and Morrison (1995; Burgess, 1994) designed diaries to be used by primary school pupils. It was important for Morrison, the principal researcher, to talk with pupils about what needed to be done and to design a booklet that was both appropriate and attractive to children. Diary-keeping was restricted to one week, including a weekend, and a cover letter inside the diary, signed by the researcher, was addressed personally to each child (Figure 18.2).

Dear [name of pupil]

A FOOD AND DRINK DIARY

I hope you will help me. I am a researcher who would like to know more about what children eat and drink. If you write in this diary, it will help me to know more.

So, next MONDAY, TUESDAY, WEDNESDAY, THURSDAY, FRIDAY, SATURDAY, AND SUNDAY, please write in your diary. It may help you to write if you think about answering these questions:

WHAT DID YOU EAT AND DRINK TODAY?

WHEN DID YOU EAT AND DRINK TODAY?

WHERE DID YOU EAT AND DRINK TODAY? (at SCHOOL, HOME, SOMEWHERE ELSE?)

DID YOU GO ON A VISIT and EAT THERE?

DID YOU ENJOY A CELEBRATION? (like BIRTHDAY or ANNIVERSARY)

DID YOU LIKE WHAT YOU ATE AND DRANK?

PLEASE WRITE ABOUT HOW YOU FELT.

Thank you very much for your help. Please return the diary to school after seven days.

Yours sincerely

Marlene Morrison
Research Fellow

Figure 18.2   Diary instructions: sample letter
(Burgess and Morrison, 1995: Appendix)

As Bell (1999: 150) comments: 'diarists must be at a certain educational level to understand the instructions, let alone complete the diary'. The method poses questions about the capacity of a mixed ability group to articulate a written record at similar levels of detail. Yet, the main challenge of the approach pertained to the wide variety of responses evoked. In Figure 18.3 two extracts (also noted in Burgess, 1994) illustrate how two pupils (among 60 respondents) interpret the instructions for diary use differently.

Diary extract 1 21/6/93
Today at dinner time I ate sandwiches, a chocolate, crisps and drank some Coke. In the morning I drank some tea. When I came back from school I ate rice pudding, chappati and curry. Then later some fruit. I ate in the morning and in the afternoon and at night. I ate at Birmingham museum and at home. At dinner time I ate with my friends, and in the morning and at night I ate with my family. I went on a visit and ate there. No, I did not enjoy a celebration. Yes I did like what I ate and drank today. I felt very hungry today.

Diary extract 2 Monday 21st June 1993
1)   Today I ate 2 turkey batches, crisps and a bottle of pop.
2)   I ate and drank at dinner time.
3)   I ate and drank somewhere else.
4)   I ate with my friends.
5)   Yes.
6)   Yes.
7)   I liked what I ate and drank.
8)   I enjoyed eating and drinking.

Figure 18.3   Children's diaries: sample entry
(Burgess,1994)

Qualitatively, 60 diaries produced a rich source of data about children's lives, but as the extracts suggest, they also presented challenges. The first diary entry is a kind of free-flowing account; the second treats each of the questions raised in the introductory letter from the researcher as topics to be answered, albeit briefly, and maintains this style throughout the week. In particular, the extracts illustrate challenges in comparing data across diaries, an important issue if the research intentions are to trace the use of time for eating, for example; or the extent to which children exercised 'choice' in the selection of foods they record as having eaten. Readers might also wish to consider the extent to which diaries pose ethical issues in terms of the level of intrusion into the lives of the diarists and their families; in this case, as for all diary-keeping, intentions and purposes for use needed to be clear. Ethical issues for research are also featured in Chapter 7.

Critical incidents, problem portfolios and new possibilities: the 'shared' diary

Of key interest to researchers of educational leadership and management is the need to understand effective ways of managing. Understanding needs to extend beyond the use of time for professional activities on a daily or weekly basis, and to include interest in how managers decide what is more (or less) important for them to give their attention (or time) to. Bell (1999: 151–153) records a range of approaches that have been applied in the area of educational management.

An investigation by Oxtoby (1979) focused on the ways in which heads of department sifted the more significant aspects of their jobs from the more trivial ones. He writes:

> The critical incident approach is an attempt to identify the more 'noteworthy' aspects of job behaviour and is based on the assumption that jobs are composed of critical and non-critical tasks ... The idea is to collect reports as to what people do that is particularly effective in contributing to good performance and then to scale the incidents in order of difficulty, frequency and importance to the job as a whole. The technique scores over the use of diaries in that it is centred on specific happenings, and what is judged to be effective behaviour. (1979: 240)

Marples's (1967) use of 'problem portfolios' that record 'information about how each [management] problem arose, methods used to solve it and so on', is further recommended by Oxtoby (1979) because, he argues, it maximises the usefulness of self-report whilst minimising the 'weaknesses' of the diary method – its 'time-consuming' and 'trivial aspects'. His strong positivist leanings are also apparent; concern about the absence of 'objective quantification' in diaries and 'critical incidents' (Oxtoby, 1979) is partly overcome by the potential for the statistical analysis of problem-solving that 'problem portfolios' provide.

More recently, 'shared' or group diaries have been suggested for research into educational management issues. Burgess (1994) suggests that 'diary groups' at school senior management level offer the potential to share day-to-day practice. For a different purpose, Galloway et al. (1995) employed a hybrid diary/log to investigate the use of interactive video in educational and training institutions, arguing that such approaches might also serve a variety of research purposes. Diary booklets attached to workstations invited users to record date, time and place used, start and finish times, software used, and whether the equipment was used by a group, on a course, or individually. Given space for more qualitative comment on their experience, numerous contributors made entries: some minimal, others more extended reflections.

Diary data analysis

Theoretical emphases affect how diaries are analysed. Diarists are creators of written texts that are open to descriptive or perspective analysis (Purvis, 1984). In the case of descriptive analysis, diary-keepers are 'witnesses' to the educational phenomena of interest to the researcher. But diary data can also be used as representative indicators of the perspectives of the group to which the writer belongs. In descriptive analysis, the diary's accuracy is centrally important; in perspective analysis, its contribution lies less in its 'truthfulness' and more in the representativeness of the category to which the diarist is assigned. Analytically distinct, the two types of analysis are potentially complementary.

Like any document, diaries can be considered in terms of 'authenticity, representativeness, credibility, and meaning' (May, 1993: 144). As with data collection, data analysis can take qualitative or quantitative forms; the balance of concerns may differ between approaches, but the essential components remain the text, the audience and the diarist.

Content analysis may be quantitative or qualitative, with computer analysis of diary records becoming more commonplace, examining, for example, the frequency with which certain phrases and words appear in the diary text. Quantitative analysts derive categories from the data in order to compare and count them. In the context of diaries, research priority goes to what is written rather than the decisions and situations that inform the writing. Qualitative data analysis views diary writing as a process or construct in which diary-writers address potential and actual readers. 'Reading' of the text accompanies consideration of data from secondary sources, interviews and observation. Some research accounts of diaries focus increasingly on complementary use of both quantitative and qualitative approaches (for example, Marsh and Gershuny, 1991) on work history data in a publication that attempts to bridge the quantitative–qualitative divide (Dex, 1991).

Diary design must consider how diaries will feature in the final report. Platt's (1981) advice on the presentation of findings from documents is instructive, especially her suggestion for a clear enunciation of the role of diaries from the outset, and the use of diary extracts as illustrative data for general themes emerging from the research overall. For large numbers, sampling and coding procedures need explanation. In ethnographic and case study research, the sources and reasons for selecting diaries and diarists need to be clearly articulated (Morrison and Galloway, 1996).

Combining diaries and diary interviews

While diary use has been advocated as a means of obtaining information that might not be readily available from an initial face-to-face interview or by means of observation, readers will be also have become aware that diaries are rarely used alone. Rather, diaries are frequently used in combination with interviews. At first sight, this appears to be a rather uneasy combination of a form of 'mute evidence' which 'endures physically and thus can be separated across space and time from its author, producer or user' (Hodder, 1994: 393); and the interview, which might be seen as a more 'spontaneous' form of verbal interaction.

Researchers choose these strategies to gain data that will help understand and explain educational phenomena. Interviews prior to diary-writing explain the purpose of the exercise, reinforcing the agreement to participate. The commitment required of diary-writers *demands* an initial face-to-face approach. Indeed, mid-diary progress interviews may also be necessary in order to maintain momentum and commitment on the part of diarists. Post-diary interviews use diary data to explore issues in greater depth.

Both pre- and post-diary interviews were essential elements in the qualitative study of substitute teaching (Morrison and Galloway, 1996) referred to elsewhere in this chapter. Planned and unplanned meetings in the field probably encouraged diary-writers; scheduled diary-interviews and telephone contact undoubtedly sustained commitment.

Post-diary interviews allow matters recorded briefly, as they happen, to be retrospectively discussed in detail (Burgess, 1984). The extent to which the diary method risks becoming intrusive and/or unduly time-consuming has already been noted: post-diary interviews exacerbate this and important ethical questions also arise. Research compromises balance, breadth and depth of information against the degree of intrusion into private as well as public areas.

Diary accounts stimulate additional explanation and data. Studying counter-culture lifestyles, Zimmerman and Wieder (1977) used seven-day diaries as a basis for individuals to talk about: 'less directly observable features of the events recorded, of their meanings, their propriety, typicality, connection with other events' (1977: 484). The diary method gives some access to events that researchers cannot personally record, whilst post-diary interviews produce even richer data. Combining the two gives informants some control over the information that is given and how it is imparted.

Post-diary interviews allow reinterpretation in an interactive process: the diary-writer can review the original data, even construct a 'new' version of events. They complement the original diary exercise, and one practical research decision is whether or not to share sight of the original text with its author during the interview. Specific details mean that the researcher can address themes that emerge as being important in the diary-writing evidence, or in the research generally; familiarity with diary entries is a preliminary to identifying key issues. 'Questions in mind' helped Zimmerman and Wieder (1977) to find answers but also to sense omissions and to 'probe our informants about the reasons they had not done something' (1977: 492). Post-diary interviews sometimes help verify facts, contribute to 'triangulation' procedures or serve as a channel for interim feedback.

Above all, the diary interview sets side by side the written word and the oral evidence of one person. Interviews may confirm diary accounts but they may not. Finding differences between data, for example, may relate to the nature of each method. Ball (1981) used a combination of diaries and questionnaires (rather than interviews) in his ethnography of Beachside Comprehensive School. Commenting on the pupil data, he notes that:

> The sociometric questionnaires failed to pick up the casual friendships that existed between pupils outside school, and made it appear that they had no such contact. In addition, they failed to pick up cross-sex friendships that were established at this time ... The entries in the diaries that several of the pupils wrote for me did, however, refer to these contacts. (Ball, 1981: 100)

If such dissonances between methods appear, this may provide new directions for analysis. As a research tool, the strengths of diary interviews linked to diary accounts are many. However, some limitations inherent in the diary method extend to diary interviews, since the quality of original diary data partly shapes the success or otherwise of subsequent interviews. Overall, post-diary interviews make additional demands on informants but enrich data collection; it is the combination of oral and written data that makes them exciting.

Not for everyone?

Researchers have tended to request diary information from certain groups, and here culture, power, status and education can play a part. Diary-writers have been predominantly people with adequate writing skills, at ease with reflecting on paper; people with sufficient resources who are stable and/or secure enough to produce coherent accounts; and those whose culture values written rather than spoken accounts.

At first sight, educational managers and leaders seem particularly well suited as diary-writers. However, the method has been seen as less appropriate for very 'busy' people with 'limited time'. This depends on whose interpretation of busy-ness is accepted, of course. It is possible to argue that managers are no 'busier' than other educational research participants from whom diary assistance has been sought and frequently obtained; moreover, at senior levels, the principles and practices of diary-keeping are central to daily work schedules, overseen and monitored by secretarial guardians of 'the diary'. One recent example of the use of diaries with secondary heads monitored the impact of their values on their daily work (McEwen et al., 2000). Such approaches have tended to remain relatively uncommon, and it may be that potential research informants with the most power and status to resist them may continue to do so, but perhaps decreasingly so than in the past (see below). Others, notably women, children and young people may see them as empowering.

The rise and rise of practitioner research

A number of descriptors might be used to describe the form of practitioner research undertaken by principals, senior or middle managers, teaching and non-teaching staff in schools, departments or classroom settings. A variant of this is described as 'action research' (see Chapters 10 and 11 in this volume.) Overall, core purposes are seen in terms of bringing about changes to researcher practitioners' own practices whether in relation to classroom, department, school and/or leadership. Whilst this form of research is not without its detractors on both epistemological (Hammersley, 1993) and practical grounds (Huberman, 1996), it is an approach that has grown in importance, not least because of its potential for professional development, and for 'growing' leaders. Increasingly, keeping diaries and portfolios are viewed as key components of such developmental activity, inviting a focus upon critical incidents (Tripp, 1993) and reflective practice. Advocacy of such approaches is not always accompanied by cautionary comment, a notable exception being Robson (2006: 96), who notes the problematic tendency for the term 'critical reflection' to have 'become a meaningless adage', especially when it excludes careful consideration of the 'underlying structures of power in educational settings' or fails to question 'established assumptions and practices'. Moreover, the qualitative research significance of recording critical incidents (that is, the practitioner's *own* interpretation of an event as critical) 'may well depend on how friendly the culture is towards what ... [Brookfield (1995)] ... calls the "reflective life"' (Robson, 2006: 100). At best, diary use in practitioner research adds value to our understanding of practitioners' knowledge and skills. At worst, and devoid of context or understanding of the power regimes in which they are located, the end product can become a time-consuming compilation of practitioner writings and collections of materials that owe more to the 'magpie principle' (Robson, 2006: 99) than to rigorous, critical research.

Conclusion

Six key points should be borne in mind about the use of diaries in educational research.

- *Point 1: Clarity* It must be clear to participants what sort of views and/or activities need to be recorded in the diary and (if appropriate) what period of time needs to be sampled and recorded in it.
- *Point 2: Ease of completion* It is quite likely that the completion of a diary or a log is going to be an added burden for the participant. If they are already busy (perhaps because of the nature of the experience you are asking them to record) it may be particularly important that the diary should not take too much time to complete.
- *Point 3: Flexibility* It is one of the great advantages of diaries that they are able to be used not just to record what happened, or what people did, but also some of the vital contextual information that relates to these events and people's reactions to them.
- *Point 4: Purpose* While the researcher's ambitions must be clear, they are not enough in themselves to convince someone to participate in the project. Ask yourself what the participants are likely to get out of the process for themselves and attempt to enlist their support on that basis.
- *Point 5: Format* The most common formats for diary research are paper-based. But what are the advantages in collecting the information on laptops, tape recorders or by video? What are the disadvantages of such methods?
- *Point 6: Analysis* Consideration must be given from the outset to how the material generated by research diaries will to be analysed. How much precoding is appropriate in the diary in question? How open and responsive can the analytic categories afford to be before they become random stories collected from vague areas of people's experiences?

Diaries can be used qualitatively and quantitatively to illuminate a range of educational issues. This is an essentially interactive genre: writing, reading and interpreting are complex processes involving several parties. New directions in diary research attend equally to the interpretation of diary accounts and to methodological concerns, not least of which are the structural conditions in which such writings take place. Some limitations have been noted of diary-writing as a research tool. But as diaries are increasingly used to gain insights into current patterns of educational life, the need for clarity among researchers about their design and fitness for purpose with a wider range of participants becomes increasingly important.

Acknowledgement

I would like to record my thanks to Dr Sheila Galloway, Principal Research Fellow at the Centre for Educational Development Appraisal and Research, University of Warwick, a long-time colleague and friend with whom I have shared valuable and formative insights about the intentions and purposes of diaries in educational settings.

References

Atkinson, P. (1992) *Understanding Ethnographic Texts*. Qualitative Research Methods Series 25. London: Sage.

Ball, S.J. (1981) *Beachside Comprehensive*. Cambridge: Cambridge University Press.

Bell, J. (1999) *Doing Your Research Project: A Guide for First-time Researchers in Education and Social Science* (3rd edn). Buckingham: Open University Press.

Bradley, H.W and Eggleston, J.F. (1976) 'An induction year experiment'. Report of an experiment carried out by Derbyshire, Lincolnshire and Nottinghamshire LEAs and the University of Nottingham School of Education.

Brookfield, S. (1995) *Becoming a Critically Reflective Teacher*. San Francisco, CA: Jossey-Bass.

Burgess, R.G. (1981) 'Keeping a research diary', *Cambridge Journal of Education*, 11 (1): 75–81.

Burgess, R.G. (1984) 'Methods of field research 3: using personal documents', in *In the Field: An Introduction to Field Research*. London: George Allen and Unwin.

Burgess, R.G. (1994) 'On diaries and diary-keeping', in Bennett, N., Glatter, R. and Levačić, R. (eds). *Improving Educational Management through Research and Consultancy*. London: Paul Chapman with the Open University.

Burgess, R. G. and Morrison, M. (1995) 'Teaching and learning about food and nutrition in school', in *The Nation's Diet Programme: The Social Science of Food Choice*. Report to the ESRC.

Burgess, R.G. and Morrison, M. (1998) 'Ethnographies of eating in an urban primary school', in Murcott, A. (ed.) *The Nation's Diet: The Social Science of Food Choice.* Harlow: Addison, Wesley, Longman.

Coxon, A., Davies, P., Hunt, A., Weatherburn, P., McManus, T. and Rees, C. (1992) 'The structure of sexual behaviour', *Journal of Sex Research*, 29 (1): 61–83.

Dex, S. (ed.) (1991) *Life and Work History Analysis: Qualitative and Quantitative Developments.* London: Routledge.

Earley, P. and Fletcher-Campbell, F. (1989) *The Time To Manage? Department and Faculty Heads at Work.* Windsor: NFER–Nelson.

Galloway, S. (1993) '"Out of sight, out of mind": a response to the literature on supply teaching', *Educational Research*, 35 (2): 159–169.

Galloway, S. and Morrison, M. (1993) 'Supply Teaching in Schools: An Investigation of Policy, Processes and People'. A report to the Leverhulme Trust.

Galloway, S., Budgen, A., Burgess, R.G., Hurworth, R., Pole, C. and Sealey, A. (1995) *School Management Training with Interactive Technology.* Coventry: National Council for Educational Technology.

Gershuny, J., Miles, I., Jones, S., Mullings, C., Thomas, G. and Wyatt, S. (1986) 'Time budget: preliminary analyses of a national survey', *Journal of Social Affairs*, 2 (1): 13–39.

Griffiths, G. (1985) 'Doubts, dilemmas, and diary-keeping', in Burgess, R.G. (ed.) *Issues in Educational Research: Qualitative Methods.* Lewes: Falmer Press.

Hammersley, M. (1993) 'On the teacher as researcher' in Hammersley, M. (ed.) *Educational Research: Current Issues: Vol. 1.* London: Paul Chapman with the Open University.

Hammersley, M. and Atkinson, P. (1995) *Ethnography: Principles in Practice* (2nd edn). London: Routledge.

Hodder, I. (1994) 'The interpretation of documents and material culture', in Denzin, N. and Lincoln, Y. (eds) *Handbook of Qualitative Research.* Thousand Oaks, CA: Sage.

Holly, M.L. (1984) *Keeping a Personal Professional Journal.* Australia: Deakin University Press.

Holly, M.L. (1989) *Writing to Grow.* Portsmouth, NH: Heinemann.

Huberman, M. (1996) 'Focus on research. Moving mainstream: taking a closer look at teacher research', *Language Arts*, 73:124–140.

Marples, D.L. (1967) 'Studies of managers: a fresh start', *Journal of Management Studies*, 4: 282–299.

Marsh, C. and Gershuny, J. (1991) 'Handling work history data in standard statistical packages', in Dex, S. (ed.) *Life and Work History Analysis: Qualitative and Quantitative Developments.* London: Routledge.

May, T. (1993) *Social Research: Issues, Methods, and Process.* St Edmundsbury Press for the Open University.

313

McEwen, A., McClune, B. and Knipe, D. (2000) 'Management and values: the changing role of the secondary headteacher', *Teacher Development*. University of Leicester, No. 2: 222–240.

Miles, M. and Huberman, A.M. (1994) *Qualitative Data Analysis: A Source Book* (2nd edn). London: Sage.

Morrison, M. (1995) 'Researching food consumers in school: recipes for concern', *Educational Studies*. 21 (2): 239–263.

Morrison, M. (1996) 'Part-time: whose time? Women's lives and adult learning', in Edwards, R., Hanson, A. and Raggatt, P. (eds) *Boundaries of Adult Learning*. London: Routledge for the Open University.

Morrison, M. and Galloway, S. (1996) 'Using diaries to explore supply teachers' lives', in Busfield, J. and Lyons, E.S. (eds) *Methodological Imaginations*. London: Macmillan in association with the British Sociological Association.

Okely, J. (1994) 'Thinking through fieldwork', in Bryman, A. and Burgess, R.G. (eds) *Analysing Qualitative Data*. London: Routledge.

Oppenheim, A.N. (1966) *Introduction to Qualitative Research Methods*. London: Wiley.

Oxtoby, R. (1979) 'Problems facing heads of departments', *Journal of Further and Higher Education*, 31: 46–59.

Platt, J. (1981) 'Evidence and proof in documentary research: 2. Some shared problems of documentary research', *Sociological Review*, 29 (1): 53–66.

Purvis, J. (1984) *Understanding Texts*. Open University Course E205, Unit 15. Milton Keynes: Open University Press.

Robson, J. (2006) *Teacher Professionalism in Further and Higher Education: Challenges to Culture and Practice*. London: Routledge.

Saris, W. (1989) 'A technological revolution in data collection', *Quality and Quantity*. 23 (3–4): 333–349.

Scott, J. (1990) *A Matter of Record: Documentary Sources in Social Research*. Cambridge: Polity Press.

Strauss, A. (1987) *Qualitative Analysis for Social Scientists*. Cambridge: Cambridge University Press.

Szalai, A. (ed.) (1972) *The Use of Time*. The Hague: Mouton.

Tripp, D. (1993) *Critical Incidents in Teaching: Developing Professional Judgement*. London: Routledge.

Walker, M. (1988) 'Training the trainers: socialisation and change in general practice', *Sociology of Health and Illness*, 10 (3): 282–302.

Zimmerman, D.H. and Wieder, D.L. (1977) 'The diary: diary-interview method', *Urban Life*, 5 (4): 479–498.

Recommended reading

Burgess, R.G. (1994) 'On diaries and diary-keeping', in Bennett, N., Glatter, R. and Levačić, R. (eds) *Improving Educational Management through Research and Consultancy*. London: Paul Chapman.

Hammersley, M. and Atkinson, P. (1995) *Ethnography: Principles in Practice* (2nd edn). London: Routledge.

Miles, M. and Huberman, A.M. (1994) *Qualitative Data Analysis: A Source Book* (2nd edn). London: Sage.

Morrison, M. and Galloway, S. (1996) 'Using diaries to explore supply teachers' lives', in Busfield, J. and Lyons, E.S. (eds) *Methodological Imaginations*. London: Macmillan in Association with the British Sociological Association.

Scott, J. (1990) *A Matter of Record: Documentary Sources in Social Research*. Cambridge: Polity Press.

Part D
Analysing and presenting data

19

Analysing quantitative data

Anthony Pell and Ken Fogelman

This chapter is intended to serve as an introduction to some of the basic techniques and concepts in analysing quantitative data generated by our research. Its main focus is on inferential statistics – the various tests which we might use to help to assess the confidence we can have in our findings – but equally important is the descriptive and exploratory stage of analysis. This is usually the first stage of analysis, when we might produce the first results in terms of simple distributions and/or summary statistics such as averages and measures of dispersion.

However, it is important to emphasise that this exploratory stage also serves other important purposes such as checking for possible errors in the data or your sample and that your instruments have worked as you would have hoped. Perhaps most important of all is that this early stage should be used to get to know and understand your data, to appreciate both its potential and its limitations. The power of modern computers and software can make it very tempting to proceed straight to the more complex stages of analysis, but most experienced researchers would acknowledge the importance of the exploratory stage – and preferably with some of this analysis done by hand and calculator.

We can then move on to the stage where we are using statistics to inform the inferences we may draw from our data, to begin to answer our research questions. These may be quite complex but they are virtually always some version of questions about differences between groups or about relationships between variables. The nature of the question we want to ask of our data is part of what determines exactly which technique or test we might use, but the other issue we need to take into account is the nature of the data with which we are working. It is this issue which is discussed below.

Types of data

Data collected for educational, and indeed for all research investigations, can be: nominal, ordinal, interval or ratio.

Nominal data simply distinguishes between categories, for example 'yes', 'no' or 'don't know' in answer to some question. A further example would be the use of code numbers, such as 1 or 2, to distinguish between males and females.

Because these numbers are essentially 'markers', it would make no sense to add or multiply them, for example, but there are special statistics, called *non-parametric*, which you can use to study the numbers in each of the categories.

With *ordinal* data, the size of the numbers is meaningful. A headteacher rated 3 on *delegation*, delegates more than one rated 2: a headteacher rated 2 delegates more than a headteacher rated 1. Here the numbers indicate an *order*, whereas nominal data indicates *difference*, only. Again, non-parametric statistics allow you to analyse the implications of this ordered data.

When the differences between adjacent numbers on an ordinal scale are the same, as they would be on a pupil language test marked as percentage scores, for instance, then the data becomes *interval*, and can now be subjected to the usual arithmetical processes of addition, multiplication, etc. More powerful statistics of the *parametric* type (see later) then become available.

However, be warned, the interval scale of the pupils' language test is not made up of equal intervals, because the human abilities and behaviours we try to measure in educational research cannot be recorded with such precision: unlike in natural science.

The natural sciences generate ratio data scales, where the apparent similar differences of the interval scale can be shown to be identical. Thus, on a ruler, 10 millimetres measured from 30 mm to 40 mm is the same as 10 millimetres measured from 70 mm to 80 mm. On, for example, a language test, because language ability cannot be measured in fixed 10% units, the difference between pupils scoring 30% and 40% is unlikely to be the same as the difference between pupils scoring 70% and 80%.

The uncertainties in the measurement of human behaviour limit social and educational research analyses to interval data, at best. Further, it is this uncertainty that limits the interpretation of social statistics. While people generally attribute precision to all quoted figures, which by implication are seen as 'scientific' from ratio-type data, the probable errors brought about by the educational research treatment of mostly interval data has been shown in the past to lead to gross misunderstandings (Shipman, 1972).

Parametric and non-parametric analyses

Parametric tests and analyses are those performed on *ratio* and *interval data*, assumed to be drawn from a wide, *normal population* that has certain special, technical characteristics, which are explained later. Parametric tests use 'distribution-dependent' data. Non-parametric analyses can be performed on simple *nominal* and *ordinal* data, having no particular pattern or distribution, hence the occasional use of the term 'distribution-free' to describe non-parametric statistics.

Non-parametric tests usually treat data, such as continuous test scores, as ranks or orders, whereas the parametric tests operate directly on the raw scores. One advantage of using a non-parametric test is that your conclusion is not qualified by uncertainty about the kind of data you used, and whether it was part of a 'normal' population and so really best suited to the parametric statistic you used. Another important point to bear in mind is that non-parametric tests can work on much smaller data sets, perhaps made up of fewer than ten individuals.

Just a small selection of the wide range of non-parametric statistics are covered in this chapter. You should consult a copy of Siegel (1956), still in print after 50 years, for a more comprehensive treatment.

Non-parametric tests

The chi-square test: the one variable, two-category test

The one-variable chi-square (χ^2) test is a non-parametric statistical procedure, which can be used with 'counts' of individuals falling into two or more categories.

For example, researchers observed 36 primary and 36 secondary teachers working in the classroom. Forty-eight teachers were classified as 'question focused': 32 of the primary teachers but only 16 of the secondary teachers. Do these figures mean that primary teachers are more 'question focused', or were these observations just chance events? The chi-square test gives an answer.

This is what you do.

1 Draw up a contingency table (Table 19.1), entering the number of teachers observed (this is called the *observed frequency*, f_o).
2 As the teachers observed comprised equal numbers in primary and secondary schools, it would be expected (by chance) that equal numbers of each would be classified as 'question focused'. Because 48 teachers were actually observed, it is expected that there would be 24 primary and 24 secondary teachers so classified (these are *expected frequencies*, f_e).

Table 19.1 Observed and expected 'question focused' teachers

Number	Secondary teachers	Primary teachers	All
Observed f_o	16	32	48
Expected f_e	24	24	48
Difference $|f_o-f_e|$	8	8	
$(|f_o-f_e|-0.5)^2$	56.25	56.25	
$(|f_o-f_e|-0.5)^2/24$	2.34	2.34	
$(|f_o-f_e|-0.5)^2/24$		4.68	Chi-square

3 Calculate the difference between f_o and f_e, ignoring whether it is positive or negative.

4 For this simple example, with only *two columns* of numbers for the teachers, we have to make a correction by subtracting 0.5 (Yates' correction) from the difference $|f_o - f_e|$, and then we square the result. (You do not have to use Yates' correction and subtract 0.5 if you have more than two columns or rows of data.)

5 Divide the square you get by f_e, the number expected, 24 in this case.

6 Finally, add your answers for the primary and secondary teachers to get 4.68, which is the chi-square statistic for the observed numbers of 'question focused' teachers.

7 Look in Table 19.2, which shows critical values of chi-square (from Siegel, Table C, p. 249). If your calculated statistic ever reaches or passes these values, you could have a meaningful, non-chance effect. Your chi-square value is then said to be *significant* (this is discussed more fully below).

Table 19.2   Critical values for the chi-square statistic

Degrees of freedom	Critical chi-square value For 5% significance	For 1% significance
1	**3.84**	**6.63**
2	5.99	9.21
3	7.81	11.34
4	9.49	13.28

You can see from Table 19.2 that the calculated value of 4.68 reaches and passes the lower of the two, critical significance levels (highlighted in bold), so the researchers can conclude that 'primary teachers are more question focused in class than are secondary teachers'. So the observed number frequencies are unlikely to be due to chance.

A more detailed explanation of the 'degrees of freedom' column of Table 19.2 is best postponed till after the next chi-square example, but when observed numbers fall into two categories only, in this instance primary and secondary teachers, there can only be *one degree* of freedom. This is because, although the number of 'question focused' teachers, say, can have any value from 0 to 48 (it is 'free'), the number of 'non-question focused' teachers is immediately fixed (at 48 less the number of 'question focused' ones) once the number of 'question focused' teachers is known. Only one of the two categories of question focus is free to have a value.

Introductory note on statistical significance

This term is used frequently by educational researchers and always accompanies statistical tests of research results. Think about this everyday life example:

Imagine a coin is tossed ten times. You would expect to get five 'heads' and five 'tails'. If you found you had six heads and four tails, would this mean that there is something wrong with the coin, or is it due to chance? Your experience tells you that this is just 'chance'. But what if you got eight heads and two tails, or even ten heads? Is something wrong? Is the coin biased?

If a second coin, which you knew was fair, was taken and tossed ten times. And then again for another ten ... and again, and so on for a hundred times, recording the number of heads in each set of ten tosses, you could get experimental evidence for the number of chance appearances of, say, eight heads and two tails. If you have a few hours to spare you could try this for yourself: if not, you will have to take the results on trust. Only in 5 out of 100 sets of ten tosses, would you find eight heads and two tails: this outcome is not impossible, it is just not a very likely chance occurrence.

Go back to the first coin. There is a 5 in 100 chance (said to be 5%) of getting eight heads and two tails just by the natural course of events. This outcome of eight heads and two tails is said to have *statistical significance at the 5% level*.

So in educational research, for measurements of human behaviour with their built in natural variations, by convention an arbitrary critical value is set, and it is actually this 5% we have just met up with. As long as the research results have less chance than 5% of being natural variations, the results are said to be *statistically significant.*

The chi-square test: the two-variable, multi-category test

Here, frequencies of occurrence are cross-tabulated for two variables, and then an extended method used to calculate the chi-square statistic.

In a survey of senior managers in schools, three-point rating scales allowed each individual to be classified on 'leadership' and 'level of professional development'. This allowed a *contingency table* comprising these two variables to be built up, where the data appear in Table 19.3 as the bold numbers for f_o.

To calculate the value of the chi-square statistic:

1 For each of the nine cells in the table, calculate the expected number of individuals by using simple proportion in terms of the 'all' numbers. For cell A,

$$\frac{79}{417} \times 101 = 19.1$$

In general, should the expected frequency, f_e, fall to 5 or below, chi-square should not be used.

Table 19.3 Leadership and professional development

Level of professional development		Low	Leadership rating Average	High	All
Low	f_o	42	28	31	101
$\dfrac{(f_o-f_e)^2}{f_e}$	f_e	A (19.1) 27.4	B (28.6) 0	C (53.3) 9.3	
Average	f_o	34	79	94	207
$\dfrac{(f_o-f_e)^2}{f_e}$	f_e	D (39.2) 0.7	E (58.6) 7.1	F (109.2) 2.1	
High	f_o	3	11	95	109
$\dfrac{(f_o-f_e)^2}{f_e}$	f_e	G (20.6) 15.0	H (30.8) 12.6	I (57.5) 24.5	
All		79	118	220	417

2 For each cell, calculate

$$\frac{(f_o - f_e)^2}{f_e}$$

3 As a formula, $\qquad \chi^2 = \dfrac{\Sigma(f_o - f_e)^2}{f_e}$ [1]

so now add all the values of $\dfrac{(f_o - f_e)^2}{f_e}$ to find chi-square (χ^2). This gives a value of 98.7.

4 Find the degrees of freedom for chi-square by studying the cells in Table 19.3. If you work along the first row, where the total number of individuals is 101, you are free to fill the first two cells as you choose, but the third is then determined for you by the row total of 101. Similarly, when moving down the first column, after the first two cells are filled, then the third is fixed by the column total of 79. This means that, overall, you are free to fill just four of the cells before their composition becomes predetermined: you have *four degrees of freedom*.

In general, the number of degrees of freedom can be found by multiplying the number of rows, less one, by the number of columns, less one.

5 Use the value of chi-square, 98.7, and the number of degrees of freedom to check the critical, significant figures from Table 19.2. You can see that the highest significant figure of 13.28 is easily exceeded, so the researchers can conclude that 'senior managers with the highest level of professional development receive the highest leadership ratings'.

The Sign test

Secondary headteachers attended a national conference to discuss proposals for a substantial change in assessment practice. Prior to the conference, 154 participants completed a series of checklists and rating scales about the proposals. This was the *pre-test* of the research. At the conclusion of the conference, the same headteachers completed a second copy of the checklists and scales. This was the *post-test*.

Table 19.4 summarises the responses on two of the measures:

- valuation of the change proposals, and
- the practicality of the proposals

Table 19.4 Changes in attitudes to an innovation at a conference

Topic	Rating before the conference	Rating after the conference	
		Low	High
Valuation of change	Low	42	31
	High	6	75
Practicality	Low	56	21
	High	14	63

The research questions to be answered are, has the conference:

- improved attitudes towards the proposals, and
- convinced delegates that the changes proposed are practical?

On the valuation of the proposals, 75 delegates expressed positive attitudes both before and after the conference, but for a further 42 the conference confirmed their misgivings. Six delegates actually lost enthusiasm but for 31 the conference had a positive effect.

The practicality of the changes became better realised by 21 of the delegates, but on learning more at the conference, 14 revised their opinions downwards. For the large majority, the conference did not change original conceptions.

The *Sign statistic* can test the responses made before and after the conference to report on whether the changes in the numbers of delegates in each category are random or whether there is a significant pattern. The Sign statistic gets its name from the comparison of the number that respond more positively than expected (that is, show a *gain* in rating, which is indicated by a positive sign +), with those that respond more negatively than expected (that is, *drop back* in their rating, which is conveyed with a negative sign –). Generally, the statistic is most useful when analysing two related samples, as in this case when the same individuals are tested on different occasions.

To calculate the Sign statistic, this is how you proceed for the *valuation of change* scale, first of all.

1 Discard the number of 'no change' respondents, who remain in the same rating group after re-testing. This leaves a total of N = 37 respondents, who are observed to change category from low to high and vice versa.
2 Identify the category with least observations, which is 'drop back' (−) with *x* = 6.
3 Use the sign formula, [2], to calculate the value of z.

$$z = \frac{(x + 0.5) - 0.5N}{0.5\sqrt{N}} \qquad [2]$$

So,

$$z = \frac{(6 + 0.5) - 0.5 \times 37}{0.5 \times \sqrt{37}}$$

$$z = -3.91$$

The negative sign for z has no real meaning here: if the calculation had been done with x = 31, a *z–value* of + 3.91 would have been obtained. Statistical z–tables show significant or critical z–values of 1.96 (5%) and 2.58 (1%) to use with the Sign test when N is 25 or more. (If N is less than 25, the Sign test can still be used but the significance table is different; Siegel, 1956: 250.)

The application of the significance test means that the difference in *valuation ratings* between the 31 who gain and the 6 who fall back has less than a 1% likelihood of being a chance occurrence. The conclusion is that the conference has significantly improved attitudes towards the proposed assessment changes.

Repeating the calculation for the *practicality* ratings gives a z-value of –1.01. This is much less than the lowest critical value of 1.96, so the apparent advantage enjoyed by the low-to-high category is most likely to be due to chance.

Correlation and the contingency coefficient

In the earlier example, the chi-square test showed that senior staff with the highest leadership ratings are those with the highest level of professional development. In statistical terms, it is said that 'leadership rating and level of professional development are positively *correlated*'.

Some researchers eagerly seek correlations as evidence for relationships otherwise hidden away under the surface of their data. If you have found that leadership rating and extensive preparation through professional development go together, you have a strong reason for requiring all candidates for senior management positions to present a coherent professional development portfolio. This is a practical example of using *correlation as a measure of association*. Beware of reading too much into correlation, though. It does not mean, for instance, that attendance on professional development courses *causes* individuals to become good leaders, simply that a self-confident leadership perception often (but not always) accompanies a strong professional background.

Figure 19.1 displays the actual leadership and professional development scores for a sample of 48 senior staff. See how this *scatterplot* shows the positive correlation by allowing us to draw a line sloping upwards, an idea which is further developed later. The degree of correlation is given by a *correlation coefficient*, which can have positive or negative values from zero to one.

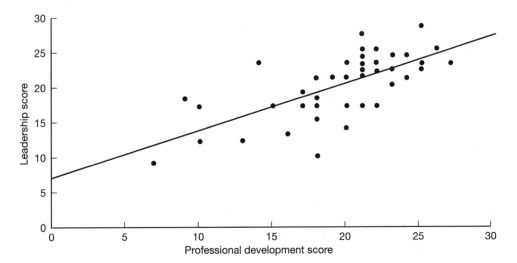

Figure 19.1 Scatterplot of scores showing positive correlation

One of two correlation coefficients you might meet up with in non-parametric statistics is called the *contingency coefficient*, C. It can be calculated directly from chi-square, χ^2:

$$C = \frac{\sqrt{\chi^2}}{\sqrt{N + \chi^2}}$$ [3]

where N is the number of individuals.

In the earlier example of Table 19.3, $\chi^2 = 98.7$ and $N = 417$, so C is calculated to be 0.44, which is a significant correlation for the simple reason that chi-square is itself significant.

If there had been no correlation between leadership rating and level of professional development, C would have been zero. Had there been perfect positive correlation so that high leadership rating *always* accompanied high levels of professional development, C *would not* have been an expected +1.00, which is what you find with other correlation coefficients such as the *Spearman* rank order and *Pearson* ones. The maximum value of C depends upon the size of the contingency table: this value for the 3×3 table is 0.82.

The advantage of using the contingency coefficient is that it can be used for any type of data, including *nominal data*, which otherwise would lack a statistical correlation treatment.

The Spearman rank-order correlation coefficient

From its name, you can deduce that this non-parametric correlation coefficient operates with ordinal data, but it can be used with the higher-level interval data if the parametric Pearson coefficient is felt to be unsuitable. The coefficient, which takes values from -1.00 (perfect negative correlation), through 0.00 (no correlation at all) to $+1.00$ (perfect positive correlation), measures the degree of association between, for example, two sets of scores for a sample of pupils.

Researchers were investigating how college principals rated their own leadership behaviour. Table 19.5 shows the scores for a sample of ten of the Deans on two of the major research scales of 'building a community of scholars' and 'setting direction'.

Table 19.5   College principals' scores of leadership behaviour

Principal	'Building a community' score	'Setting direction' score
A	36	32
B	25	32
C	31	37
D	40	34
E	22	30
F	28	31
G	35	33
H	33	37
I	31	39
J	37	33

To calculate the rank order correlation coefficient, this is what you do.

1 Work out the rank on each scale. If there are any ties, find the average of the two rank places which otherwise would have been used, for example a tie on 'Building a community' with score 31 at rank 6 (and 7) becomes 6.5. Table 19.6 shows the rank orders.
2 For each individual, calculate the difference in the two rank orders (D).
3 Calculate the values of D² and add them all up. This gives 99.50.

Table 19.6 Calculating the rank order coefficient

Principal	Rank order		Difference in rank order, D	D^2
	'Building a community'	'Setting direction'		
A	3	7.5	−4.5	20.25
B	9	7.5	1.5	2.25
C	6.5	2.5	4.0	16.00
D	1	4	−3.0	9.00
E	10	10	0.0	0.00
F	8	9	−1.0	1.00
G	4	5.5	−1.5	2.25
H	5	2.5	2.5	6.25
I	6.5	1	5.5	30.25
J	2	5.5	−3.5	12.25

4 Use the Spearman rank order formula for the correlation coefficient, R for N sets of data, where N = 10 in this case.

$$R = 1 - \frac{6\Sigma D^2}{N^3 - N} \qquad [4]$$

$$= 0.40$$

We have positive correlation between the 'Building a community' and 'Setting direction' scores, which if meaningful, tells us that there is a trend for principals rating themselves highly on relating to others also being purposeful in direction. But, what if the calculated figure of 0.40 is due to chance? We need to use a table of statistical significance to find out the critical value that R must reach before our rank-order correlation can be thought of as other than a chance association. A table of critical values for R appears in Siegel (1956, Table P, p. 284), which shows that the R-value must reach 0.56 to become *significant*. So, despite getting a moderate R-value of 0.40 with the sample of principals, this figure is likely to have arisen by chance. Consequently, principals' leadership ratings of 'Building a community' and 'Setting direction' are not related according to the research evidence of Table 19.5.

Statistical significance re-visited

The college principals' research study can be used to introduce a more severe test of statistical significance, this time at the *1% level*. In Table 19.7, you can see that the principals have been separated according to their type of college. Scores on the scale of 'Building a community of scholars' have been used to allocate each principal to a 'high' or 'low' category according to whether they scored above or below the mean of the scale. For this exercise, the sample comprises 600 principals, which means that there will be 300 low scorers and 300 high scorers

Table 19.7 Significant differences at two levels

Sample of principals by college type	Observed frequencies		Chi-square	Significance
	Low scorers	High scorers		
Arts and Sciences	75	80	0.10	Not
Business	97	49	15.13	1% level
Education	60	90	5.61	5% level
Nursing	68	81	0.97	Not

The research question posed is: what is the effect of college discipline on the principals' rating of 'Building a community'? If the statistical chi-square, one variable/two category test is used for each of the college types in turn, the chi-square values obtained can be compared with those in Table 19.2. For principals of business and education colleges, the relative numbers of high and low scorers differ significantly. There is a significant bias among principals of business colleges towards low scoring. The reverse is true in education. In Nursing and in Arts and Sciences there is no bias one way or the other.

The business college data is of particular relevance here. The value of chi-square is so high that it even exceeds that of 6.63 needed for significance at the 1% level for one degree of freedom (Table 19.2). This means that the chance of the 97:49 ratio being a random occurrence is less than 1%, which suggests that the negative bias shown by business college principals is even stronger than the positive bias in education, where the significance level is just 5%.

The 'cut-off' figures of 1% and 5% are usually applied, conventionally, for all statistical analysis work, and can appear as decimals of 0.01 and 0.05.

You will appreciate that in social research we can never be absolutely certain that differences are real: there is always a slight possibility that chance is at work, but you will find that if you can obtain differences at the 5% or 1% level, your findings will be seriously received. Having said this, a problem does remain and this is that the significance level depends on the size of your sample. If the sample is large enough, significance can be achieved. To help you interpret significance, you need to estimate the *effect size*, which will be explained later.

Parametric tests

Introducing the normal distribution and standard deviation.

As discussed previously, a large amount of data, probably of the interval type, can make up what is called a *normal population* and a precise *parametric statistic* can be called into play to investigate it.

Here is an example of a normal distribution set of data. Several hundred primary children were tested on mathematics achievement using a 36–item test, where the maximum mark was exactly 36. Table 19.8 shows how the scores were spread out: the scores have been grouped to keep the table a convenient size.

Table 19.8 Distribution of maths scores

Score	Score at mid-interval	Number of pupils (N)
Below 5		0
5/6	5.5	3
7/8	7.5	11
9/10	9.5	29
11/12	11.5	38
13/14	13.5	58
15/16	15.5	85
17/18	17.5	100
19/20	19.5	92
21/22	21.5	78
23/24	23.5	55
25/26	25.5	42
27/28	27.5	19
29/30	28.5	11
31/32	29.5	0
33/34	31.5	2
35/36	33.5	1

The scores are shown graphically in Figure 19.2, where the average score of each pair, called the interval mid-mark, has been used on the horizontal axis. The *frequency* is the name used for the number of children who obtained the scores in each box of the *histogram* chart.

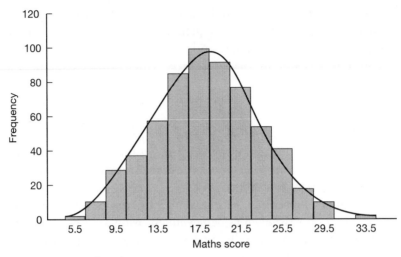

Figure 19.2   Histogram of maths scores

The *mean* of the maths scores is 18.33. This is the sum of all the scores divided by the number of pupils.

The *standard deviation* of the scores, which measures how much the scores are spread out either side of the mean, is 5.06. How to calculate the standard deviation is shown in the next section. In this practical example, about 75% of all the pupils' scores are within one standard deviation of the mean: about 97% are within two standard deviations of the mean.

All the scores follow a near *normal distribution*, which is shown by the smooth, symmetrical curve of Figure 19.2. If the scores were to have a smaller standard deviation than 5.06, then the curve would be narrower with a sharper peak, but the mean would stay at 18.3 (Figure 19.3).

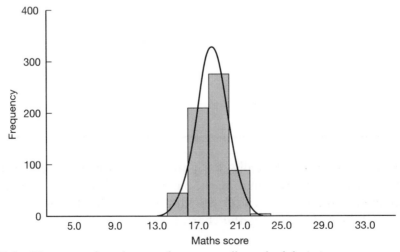

Figure 19.3   Histogram of another set of scores: small standard deviation

A true normal distribution of data always has 68.3% of its values, such as children's maths scores, within one standard deviation of the mean: it always has 95.4% within two standard deviations.

Calculating standard deviations

From Table 19.8, you would probably agree that if you tested a class of children at your primary school, or at a colleague's primary school, on the same maths scale, then because your selected class would be just a small *sample* of a much larger *population*, the mean score for 'your' pupils would almost certainly differ from the value of 18.33 already found. Further, if another primary colleague were also to test his or her pupils, then their sample of pupils would probably differ on mean score from yours as well as from the greater population. This is typical of *sampling* in educational research: the samples selected are likely to have different means, at least, although their standard deviations could be similar. Nevertheless, you can see that means and standard deviations are going to be important in working out *differences* with parametric statistics to see, for instance, if one teaching method is really better than another or whether pupils have improved over the year.

Here is how to calculate the standard deviation from basic principles, using just a few scores from Table 19.8 as an example.

Table 19.9   Calculating a standard deviation

Child	Test mark X	Deviation from mean $(X - \mu)$	Squared deviation $(X - \mu)^2$
A	16	−3	9
B	23	+4	16
C	10	−9	81
D	31	+12	144
E	19	0	0
F	15	−4	16
	---		----
	114		266

1 Calculate the mean (μ) of the marks for the N children from

$$\mu = \frac{\Sigma X}{N} \qquad\qquad [5]$$

$$\therefore \mu = 19.0$$

2 Calculate the *variance* σ^2, and hence the *standard deviation* σ from

$$\sigma^2 = \frac{\Sigma(X - \mu)^2}{N}$$

[6]

$$\therefore \sigma = 6.66$$

The square of the standard deviation, which is the variance, is often used in more advanced parametric statistics instead of the standard deviation.

Sample standard deviations and the standard error of the mean

You will see that the mean and standard deviation of the sample of just six maths scores differ from the values for the population. What will happen if we take lots of different samples? Of course, if we chose a *biased sample*, say from just the pupils who scored between 28 and 34 marks, we would expect a very high mean and a small standard deviation, but what if we chose a *random sample*, which is a selection made from the general population where every member has an equal chance of being chosen, would the mean and standard deviation always be the same?

Table 19.10 shows what happens when forty random samples of six scores are drawn from the original population of maths scores.

Table 19.10 The means and standard deviations for samples of six maths scores.

Mean maths score	Standard deviation	Mean maths score	Standard deviation
17.16	4.72	15.85	1.86
20.04	7.37	21.03	4.33
17.93	2.38	18.29	4.91
19.08	4.84	17.76	6.93
22.56	6.94	15.19	4.89
22.10	4.74	21.57	4.45
19.05	3.02	16.07	3.55
19.33	5.97	18.78	2.96
20.49	4.03	18.25	4.22
18.21	4.33	17.01	6.46
17.77	4.03	17.02	4.87
19.41	2.99	15.50	4.51
19.83	3.22	18.81	6.31
21.39	6.63	20.41	4.43
18.15	6.89	19.31	5.94
18.09	1.97	19.54	6.10
19.46	3.73	19.90	4.53
21.09	3.81	16.97	5.82
19.39	4.33	18.34	5.43
17.29	3.65	16.72	4.50

The mean for these forty samples of six is 18.75, with a standard deviation of 1.79.

You can see that the means of the random samples are certainly not the same; neither are their standard deviations.

The mean of all the sample means, at 18.75, differs a little from the general population mean of 18.33, but there is a considerable difference between the *standard deviation of the sample means* at 1.79, and the standard deviation of the population of scores at 5.06. The spread of sample means shows a very *rough approximation to a normal curve*, but if the size of the samples is increased to 50 random maths scores each, and if the number of samples drawn becomes 80, there is likely to be a closer approximation.

Because sample means are less spread than the individual scores that make up the whole population, the *sample means' standard deviation*, which is named *the standard error of the mean*, is expected to be quite different to the standard deviation of the population.

In general statistical terms, drawing samples of size N from a large population of scores of standard deviation σ results in a standard error of the mean (s.e.m.) given by the standard deviation σ divided by the square root of N.

The population of maths scores has $\sigma = 5.06$, so for samples of size 50,

$$\text{s.e.m.} = \frac{5.06}{\sqrt{50}}$$

$$= 0.72$$

It is by using the s.e.m. that you can test whether your children's test scores are above or below the standards of the population as a whole. Say 'your' class of 32 pupils scored a mean of 17.45. For your sample,

$$\text{s.e.m.} = \frac{5.06}{\sqrt{32}}$$

$$= 0.89$$

With a population mean of 18.33, about 95% of all sample means would be expected to fall by chance within the range of 18.33 + twice 0.89 and 18.33 − twice 0.89 (in other words, between 20.11 and 16.55). Your class mean is within this chance band so it is unlikely to be any different to the average performance. Yet, other colleagues and administrators, unskilled in statistics and education and research, might well judge that you, your children and even your school were 'failing'!

Z-scores: computing standardised scores

With the mean score and the standard deviation having such importance, it is worth introducing a modification to test scores, such as the mathematics set, so that they include this information. This is done by calculating a *z-score* (z) from each raw score (X) by subtracting the mean score (μ), and then dividing by the standard deviation (σ), as shown in equation 7.

$$z = \frac{X - \mu}{\sigma} \qquad [7]$$

Z-scores will have a mean of 0.00 and a standard deviation of 1.00. As an example of the calculation, a maths test score of 26 in the population of scores where the standard deviation is 5.06 has a z-score given by:

$$z = \frac{26 - 18.33}{5.06}$$

$$z = +1.52$$

The z-score is positive because it is above the mean. A score of 15, which is below the mean, has a negative z-score:

$$z = \frac{15 - 18.33}{5.06}$$

$$z = -0.66$$

Table 19.11 shows the percentage of scores in a normal population lying between certain critical z-score values.

Table 19.11 Some critical values of z-score

Z-score range		
Lower	*Higher*	*% of normal population*
−1.96	+1.96	95.0
−2.58	+2.58	99.0
−∞	+1.65	95.0
−∞	+2.33	99.0

The critical values are needed to judge whether results are statistically significant or not. You might recall that a z-score was first encountered in the calculation of the Sign statistic. It has already been used indirectly with the maths scores to see if a class mean score of 17.45 was significantly different to a population of *means* centred on a score of 18.33 and s.e.m. of 0.89. In this case the actual calculation of the z-score is:

$$z = \frac{17.45 - 18.33}{0.89}$$

$$z = -1.26$$

which does not reach the critical value of 1.96 needed for significance at the 5% level.

Once you have a z-score, you can decide whether to set up a new scale without having to use negative values, while selecting a convenient standard deviation of your own choosing. Say you want your new, *standardised* scale to have a mean of 50.0 and a standard deviation of 10.0. To change the z-score of -1.26 that you found above into a standard score, multiply the 1.26 by 10.0 and subtract from 50.0. This gives a *standard score* of 37.4. The advantage of using standard scores is that it allows the relative performance of individuals to be compared even when different tests have been used. Strictly speaking, adding together the marks in school subjects, including 'points scores' for admission to higher education, will be unreliable unless scores have been *standardised* first.

Differences between means: large samples

Researchers are often interested in the difference in the mean scores obtained by two groups or samples that might have been exposed to, say, different teaching methods. Alternatively, you might want to compare the performance of your students with that of others in another school, or perhaps the leadership ratings of principals from different types of institution. In any of these cases, the analysis requires a study of *sample mean differences*. Working from large data sets such as Table 19.10, you find that you get a normal distribution for sample mean differences centred on 0.00, which is shown in Figure 19.4. Critical statistical tails are shown: if the difference of two sample means falls into these areas, then significance is achieved in what is called a *'two-tail'* test.

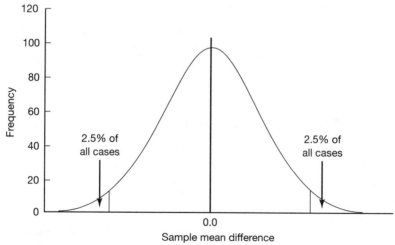

Figure 19.4 Normal distribution of sample mean differences

Taking the example of the college principals' ratings of leadership behaviours, and in particular their scores on 'Empowering others', a sample (n_1) of 220 Arts and Science college principals had a mean score (m_1) on this scale of 16.91 with a standard deviation (s_1) of 4.34. A sample of (n_2) 163 Business college princi-pals had a mean score (m_2) of 18.28 with a standard deviation (s_2) of 4.91.

We now meet up with *hypothesis testing*. In general terms:

> a hypothesis is an educated guess about the meaning of information, which is then to be subsequently investigated with a view to either supporting or rejecting the guess.

The principals' data can provide us with at least two hypotheses:

1 'that there is no difference between the Arts/Science college and Business col-lege means, which is called a neutral or *null hypothesis* (H_o), and presumes that the Arts/Science sample is drawn from a population that has the same mean as the population from which the Business sample is drawn
(so we write H_o: $\mu_1 = \mu_2$)
2 'that the Business college mean is more than the Arts/Science college mean, which is an alternative hypothesis (H_A), and presumes that the Business sam-ple is drawn from a different population to that of the Arts/Science sample; one which has a greater mean score on the 'Empowering others' scale
(so we write $H_A : \mu_2 > \mu_1$).

The difference between the sample means is $18.28 - 16.91$, which is 1.37. If the standard deviation of the distribution of sample mean differences ($\sigma_{m_1-m_2}$) were known, then the z-score for the difference of 1.37 could be calculated.

To find the standard deviation ($\sigma_{m_1-m_2}$), we use equation 8:

$$(\sigma_{m_1-m_2})^2 = \frac{(s_1)^2}{n_1} + \frac{(s_2)^2}{n_2} \qquad [8]$$

This gives:

$$\sigma_{m_1-m_2} = 0.483$$

The z-score for the difference of the means is thus,

$$z = \frac{1.37}{0.483}$$

$$z = 2.84$$

Such a high z-score is beyond the 99% critical value of 2.58 (Table 19.11), which means that such a difference has less than a 1% probability of being a chance occurrence. The *null hypothesis* that the Arts/Sciences and Business prin-cipals have the same mean scores on the 'Empowering others' scale is *rejected* at the 1% level of significance.

Note that when testing a null hypothesis, it does not matter which of the two means is the larger: only the suspicion that they are not the same is under test. This requires a *two-tail test of significance* with 2.5% of 'probability' in each tail at either end of the normal distribution curve. The situation is different when testing the alternative hypothesis that the Business college principals actually score the higher. In this case, a *one-tail test of significance* has the normal curve with its 5% of critical probability all in one tail, so any z-score outside the range of minus infinity to + 1.65 will be statistically significant at the 5% level. As the z-score is 2.84, it can be concluded that *the alternative hypothesis is supported* at the 1% level of significance, where the critical z-value is 2.33, and the Business principals do score higher than colleagues leading Arts/Science colleges.

Differences between means: small samples

If sample sizes fall below 40, the z-score statistic is usually replaced by the more reliable *t-test* for small samples in this range. The t-test has a specific require-ment that the two populations from which the samples are drawn have the *same standard deviation*. If this condition is obeyed then the common population standard deviation for both samples and the standard deviation of the sample mean differences are calculated from the equations below.

The t-test calculation is made clear by taking scores from a survey of principals of primary and secondary principals who were asked to rate their schools on scales of school development activity (SDA) and 'innovative culture'. The data for this example, which appear in Table 19.12, are taken from Midthassel et al. (2000).

Table 19.12 Small samples for a t-test

	Primary principals		Secondary principals	
Scale	Mean score	Standard deviation	Mean score	Standard deviation
School development activity	$m_1 = 1.49$	$s_1 = 0.46$	$m_2 = 1.32$	$s_2 = 0.36$
Innovative culture	$m_1 = 2.73$	$s_1 = 0.42$	$m_2 = 2.36$	$s_2 = 0.33$

Number of primary principals (n_1) = 49
Number of secondary principals (n_2) = 20

Initially, you might think that primary principals give the higher ratings, but then, looking at the standard deviations, perhaps there are no significant differ-ences. These thoughts lead to your two hypotheses for each of the two scales:

1 'that there is no difference between the two sample means', which is the *null hypothesis*: $H_o: \mu_1 = \mu_2$

2 'that the primary principals' mean is greater than the secondary principals' mean', which is the *alternative hypothesis*: $H_A: \mu_1 > \mu_2$.

First, analysing the SDA scale data, the variance σ^2 for the common population of primary and secondary principals is estimated from equation 9.

$$\sigma^2 = \frac{n_1(s_1)^2 + n_2(s_2)^2}{(n_1 - 1) + (n_2 - 1)} \qquad [9]$$

This gives

$$\sigma^2 = 0.193$$

The variance of the population of sample mean differences $(\sigma_{m_1-m_2})^2$ is found from:

$$(\sigma_{m_1-m_2})^2 = \frac{\sigma^2}{n_1} + \frac{\sigma^2}{n_2} \qquad [10]$$

So, substituting $\sigma^2 = 0.193$ gives:

$$(\sigma_{m_1-m_2})^2 = \frac{0.193}{49} + \frac{0.193}{20}$$

$$\sigma_{m_1-m_2} = 0.117$$

The t-score for the difference in sample means is given by an equivalent form of the z-score calculation of equation 7, which becomes

$$t = \frac{m_1-m_2}{\sigma_{m_1-m_2}} \qquad [11]$$

The difference in the means on the SDA scale thus has a t-score of

$$t = \frac{1.49 - 1.32}{0.117}$$

$$t = 1.45$$

The t-score values needed for statistical significance actually depend upon the sample sizes. The number for the *degrees of freedom* (df) has to be calculated from

$$df = (n_1-1) + (n_2-1) \qquad [12]$$

and then the corresponding t-score value is read from a statistical table.

As the combined degrees of freedom for the sample of primary and secondary principals has a value of

$$df = (49 - 1) + (20 - 1)$$
$$df = 48 + 19$$
$$= 67$$

Then, the minimum critical score to test the null hypothesis that the two means are the same is 2.00 for a two-tail test at the 5% level (see Siegel, Table B, p. 248). The calculated t-score of 1.45 falls well short of this value so the *null hypothesis* is retained: the primary and secondary principals do not score significantly different on the SDA scale.

If you repeat the analysis for the data of the second scale of 'innovative culture', you will find that the variance σ^2 for the common population of primary and secondary principals on this scale is:

$$\sigma^2 = 0.162$$

The standard deviation for the population of mean differences is now:

$$\sigma_{m_1-m_2} = 0.107$$

The difference in the means on the 'innovative culture' scale thus has a t-score of:

$$t = \frac{2.73 - 2.36}{0.107}$$

$$t = 3.46$$

As the t-score needed for significance at the 1% level with 67 degrees of freedom is only 2.66 (Siegel, Table B, p. 248), you can see that the difference in mean scores is highly significant this time and the *null hypothesis* is rejected: primary and secondary principals score differently on the 'innovative culture' scale.

Having rejected the *null hypothesis*, we can move on to the *alternative hypothesis* that the primary principals' score is the greater. Although this conclusion might now seem obvious, we have to check our t-score against the *one-tail significance* test value, which is 2.39 (Siegel, Table B, p. 248), to confirm that we can retain the hypothesis that primary principals rate their schools more highly on 'innovative culture' than do secondary principals.

The Pearson correlation coefficient

It is now time to meet up with the widely used Pearson correlation coefficient, which is used with interval data to investigate associations between different variables.

Researchers tested 48 11-year-old girls to compare attainment in maths and reading with feelings about going to school, such as 'enjoyment' of school life and being 'miserable'. Figure 19.5 shows the first of three *scatterplots* of the results. You can see that, generally, the higher the reading score, the higher the maths score. A line-of-best-fit is drawn through the points to 'average out' the variation of the positions. This line slopes upwards, which implies a *positive correlation* between the maths and reading scores. The Pearson correlation coefficient is calculated to be + 0.68 (see below).

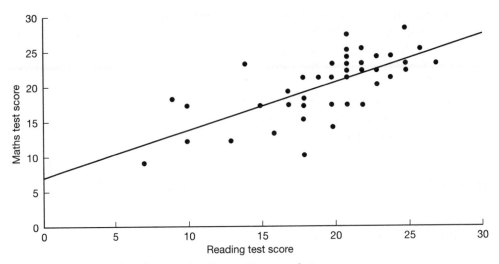

Figure 19.5 Scatterplot of scores showing positive correlation

The scatterplot of Figure 19.6 shows that 'misery' is *negatively correlated* with attainment in reading. The line-of-best-fit slopes downwards. The implication is that the worst readers are more likely to be miserable at school, which is itself an interesting research finding. The Pearson correlation coefficient is −0.40, this time.

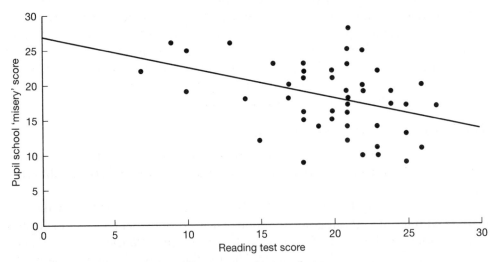

Figure 19.6 Scatterplot of scores showing negative correlation

Sometimes, a scatterplot shows no recognisable trend at all: this is the case with Figure 19.7, where enjoyment of school is compared with attainment in language. The line-of-best-fit appears to be almost horizontal, indicating little correlation. The Pearson correlation calculation gives an insignificant +0.03.

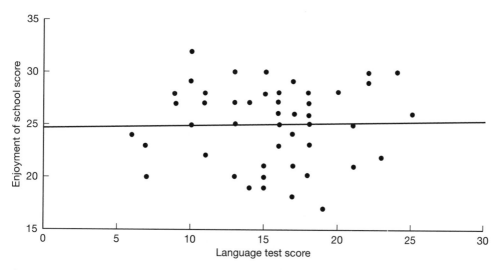

Figure 19.7 Scatterplot of scores showing no correlation

The conclusion has to be that there is no association between language attainment and school enjoyment.

We shall now calculate a Pearson correlation coefficient using an example of pre-test and post-test scores.

Table 19.13 Calculating the Pearson correlation coefficient

Pupil	Pre-test score X	Post-test score Y	$(X-\mu_x)$	$(Y-\mu_y)$	$(X-\mu_x)(Y-\mu_y)$	$(X-\mu_x)^2$	$(Y-\mu_y)^2$
A	26	52	10.8	8.0	86.4	116.64	64.00
B	10	68	−5.2	24.0	−124.8	27.04	576.00
C	16	4	0.8	−40.0	−32.0	0.64	1600.00
D	24	40	8.8	−4.0	−35.2	77.44	16.00
E	4	56	−11.2	12.0	−134.4	125.44	144.00
F	6	32	−9.2	−12.0	110.4	84.64	144.00
G	22	64	6.8	20.0	136.0	46.24	400.00
H	6	40	−9.2	−4.0	36.8	84.64	16.00
I	26	24	10.8	−20.0	−216.0	116.64	400.00
J	12	60	−3.2	16.0	−51.2	10.24	256.00
Sum	152	440			−224.0	689.60	3616.00

1 Find the mean of the X-scores by calculating the sum (152) and dividing by the number of pupils (N = 10):

$$\mu = \frac{\Sigma X}{N}$$

$$\therefore \mu_x = 15.2$$

2 Similarly, find the mean of the Y-scores by calculating the sum (440) and dividing by the number of pupils (N = 10).

$$\mu = \frac{\Sigma Y}{N}$$

$$\therefore \mu_y = 44.0$$

3 Calculate the difference of $(X-\mu_x)$ by subtracting the mean X-score, μ_x, from each value of X.

4 Calculate the difference of $(Y-\mu_y)$ by subtracting the mean Y-score, μ_y, from each value of Y.

5 Multiply $(X-\mu_x)$ by $(Y-\mu_y)$ to get the values in column 6. Then add up the ten products to get

$$\Sigma(X-\mu_x)\,(Y-\mu_y) = -224.0.$$

6 In column 7, square the $(X-\mu_x)$ values from column 4, then add up all ten squares to get

$$\Sigma(X-\mu_x)^2 = 689.60$$

7 To calculate the standard deviation, σ_x, of the X-scores:

$$\sigma_x^2 = \frac{\Sigma(X-\mu_x)^2}{N}$$

$$\sigma_x^2 = 68.96$$

$$\therefore \sigma_x = 8.30$$

8 In column 8, square the $(Y-\mu_y)$ values from column 5, then add up all ten squares to get

$$\Sigma(Y-\mu_y)^2 = 3616.00$$

9 To calculate the standard deviation, σ_y, of the Y-scores:

$$\sigma_y^2 = \frac{\Sigma(Y-\mu_y)^2}{N}$$

$$\therefore \sigma_y = 19.02$$

10 Finally, use the Pearson formula to calculate the correlation coefficient r_{xy} between the pre-test and post-test scores;

$$r_{xy} = \frac{\Sigma(X-\mu_x)(Y-\mu_y)}{N\,\sigma_x\,\sigma_y}$$ [13]

So, $$r_{xy} = \frac{-224.0}{10 \times 8.30 \times 19.02}$$

$$\therefore r_{xy} = -0.14$$

For small sets of data, say with up to 30 pupils, the easier calculations of the Spearman rank order coefficient make it a real alternative to the more reliable Pearson index, even if the interval data has to be ranked first. Whichever of the two coefficients you use, when you have your final value the problem of the *significance* of the correlation has to be addressed

Statistical significance of the Pearson correlation coefficient

The research with the 48 11-year-old girls reported above produced the set of correlation coefficients shown in Table 19.14, which include the three coefficients already considered from the scatterplot diagrams.

Table 19.14   Correlation coefficients: some significant some not

	Pearson correlation coefficient for the pairs of tests (48 pupils)			
Test scale	*Enjoyment*	*Misery*	*Maths*	*Language*
Enjoyment				
Misery	**0.33**			
Maths	**0.28**	**−0.32**		
Language	0.03	**−0.40**	**0.59**	
Reading	0.12	**−0.40**	**0.68**	**0.62**

  Significantly different from zero at the 5% level
  Significantly different from zero at the 1% level

Faced with an array of coefficients, how much weight can you give to the values? If language and reading scores are really correlated because the coefficient is high (0.62), then are language and enjoyment scores not correlated because the coefficient is low? How high must a coefficient be before it ceases to be a chance occurrence and becomes an indicator of a real association?

To answer these questions, you consider the 48 pupils to be just a sample of a broad population of 11-year-old girls who could equally as well have been tested. Some of the critical correlation coefficients appear in Table 19.15.

Table 19.15 Critical values for the correlation coefficient.

Sample size (N)	Correlation coefficient needed to differ significantly from zero (in a two-tail test)	
	At 5% level	At 1% level
1000	0.06	0.08
500	0.09	0.12
200	0.14	0.18
100	0.19	0.26
50	0.26	0.35
48	0.27	0.36
40	0.30	0.49
30	0.34	0.44
25	0.38	0.49
20	0.43	0.54
15	0.48	0.61
10	0.58	0.71
5	0.76	0.88

Critical values for the sample of 48 11-year-old girls

It should now be clear that only the enjoyment-language and enjoyment-reading pairs of tests show no significant statistical correlation. All the other pairs are worthy of further analysis to establish what are the implications for the classroom teacher. Namely, for 11-year-old girls in primary school:

1 Those with high maths scores are likely to be those that enjoy going to school the most.
2 Feelings of misery and inadequacy are associated with low levels of general attainment.
3 There is a strong association between attainment in maths, language and reading.

It would be wrong to say that *because* the child likes being at school, high maths scores will follow. Significant correlation coefficients do not mean that one of the variables causes the other, but, simply, that there is a recognisable trend in the pattern of the two sets of scores.

There is one further point, which must be made: make sure that your correlation sample reflects the known groupings of your pupils. For instance, the practical example we have used has been restricted to 11-year-old girls. This is because the pattern of correlations is not exactly the same for boys of this age. Further, girls at 9 years of age do not show the same pattern as the 11-year-old girls. If you choose a sample that mixes together both girls and boys, as well as different age groups, do not expect a very meaningful pattern: most of the correlation coefficients will be 'not significant', and you may have missed important findings.

As a further example of the above, Midthassel et al. (2000) give a significant Pearson correlation of 0.32 for 81 principals' ratings of school development activity (SDA) and their direct involvement in the same. However, when the data are broken down by type of school, correlations of 0.27 and 0.50 are reported for 49 primary schools and 20 secondary schools respectively. You will see from Table 19.15 that a correlation of 0.25 just fails to reach significance for a sample of 49 but the 0.50 correlation is significant for the secondary principals. The inference here is that secondary principals who rate SDA highly are more likely to be personally involved than their colleagues in primary schools.

Effect size

In this chapter you have met up with the idea of *statistical significance* and hopefully can now appreciate its importance. But this is not the end of the business of interpreting your research results! There is a final hurdle to overcome, which is the *effect size* of any significant differences you find in your research.

As an example, look again at the survey of Midthassel et al. (2000) and in particular the analysis from Table 19.12 for the differences between primary and secondary principals' mean scores on the *innovative culture* scale. The significant difference in the means of (2.73−2.36) indicates that an innovative culture tends to be present more in primary schools. The *effect size* of the difference, d, is found by dividing the difference in means by the common standard deviation of the population for all principals (see equation 9 to get the common variance or standard deviation squared). So,

$$\text{common population standard deviation, } \sigma = \sqrt{0.193}$$

$$\therefore \sigma = 0.44$$

$$\text{and effect size, } d = \frac{(2.73 - 2.36)}{0.44}$$

$$\therefore d = 0.84$$

Cohen (1988) explains about effect sizes at great length. He sees an effect size as *the degree to which a phenomenon is present in a population*. Our example of the principals has produced a *large effect size*, which is defined by Cohen as any d value greater than 0.8 for this test on means. The strength of this phenomenon is equivalent to the difference in average heights of girls of ages 13 and 18 years. *Medium effect sizes* lie between 0.5 and 0.8, equivalent to the difference in average heights of girls of ages 14 and 18 years. *Small effect sizes* lie between 0.2 and 0.5, equivalent to the difference in average heights of girls of ages 15 and 16 years. In most of your research in education, effect sizes will be small because there will be factors at work beyond your control.

If you now look back over this chapter, you can ask yourself whether those significant differences had large or small effect sizes. *The most powerful results in your research will be those with the largest effect sizes.* It will be in these cases that the differences are most likely to show up direct, observable behaviour. Visitors to the primary and secondary schools participating in the Midthassel study could expect to find supporting evidence for the 'innovative culture' in the former schools without too much difficulty. Tests of significance show you where your research results point to likely, non-chance differences, then tests of effect size give the strength of the difference. If you want to follow this idea up, and there is still some controversy, you will find Aron and Aron (1999) very helpful.

In correlation work, *the correlation coefficient is itself a measure of effect size.* Cohen defines a correlation of 0.10 as *small*, 0.30 as *medium* and 0.50 as *large*. Returning to Table 19.14, you can see that the significant correlations cover the range of effect sizes. Effect sizes would not be computed for insignificant outcomes because differences are most likely fluctuations of chance anyhow.

With the parametric Sign test and the chi-square test, reference is best made to Cohen for a full explanation, but in our Sign test the high z-score indicates a large effect size, because such a value of z (3.91) has a probability of occurrence of more than 99% (Table 19.11) and according to Cohen (1988: 147) *the amount above the 50% 'evens' chance is the effect size.* Our Sign test z-score is just more than 49%, which is a large effect size according to Cohen's 25%.

We found the significant chi-square from the one-variable test of Table 19.1 to be 4.68 for the 48 teachers. The effect size of this result is found from the *contingency coefficient* of equation 3, which is calculated to be 0.30. Cohen shows that effect sizes for the contingency coefficient are very similar to those of correlation coefficients in general, so 0.30 indicates a *medium effect size* for the difference between primary and secondary teachers' questioning styles. In a similar way, if you calculate the contingency coefficient in the two-variable example of the senior managers of Table 19.3, you will find a value of 0.82, which points to a *large effect size.*

Conclusion

This chapter has focused on relatively straightforward statistical techniques, concerned with distributions of one variable and relationships between no more than two variables. For more complex situations, where questions relate to relationships among three or more variables, you will need to know about multivariate techniques. If you wish to extend your understanding of statistics you will want to turn to one or more textbooks. Choosing the right book is a personal matter as it very much depends on your starting points and the level of mathematical treatment that you require. Some suggested titles are offered below, but it is desirable to dip into these and some others before deciding which is the most appropriate for your needs. If you find that you have collected more data than you can handle with a simple calculator, then you should try the easy-to-use software package of SPSS (Pallant, 2005), where you will be able to put to work all you have learned from this chapter.

References and Further Reading

Aron, A. and Aron, E.N. (1999) *Statistics for Psychology* (2nd edn). Englewood Cliffs, NJ: Prentice–Hall.

Cohen, J. (1988) *Statistical Power Analysis for the Behavioral Sciences*. Hillsdale, NJ: Lawrence Earlbaum Associates.

Freedman, D., Pisani, R. and Purves, R. (1998) *Statistics*. London: W.W. Norton and Co

Gravetter, F.J. and Wallnan, L.B. (2004) *Statistics for the Behavioral Sciences* (6th edn). London: Thomson–Wadsworth.

Lewis-Beck, M.S. (ed.) (1994) *Basic Statistics*. International Handbooks of Quantitative Applications in the Social Sciences, Volume 1. London: Sage.

Marsh, C. (1988) *Exploring Data*. Cambridge: Polity Press.

Midthassel, U.V., Bru, E. and Idsoe, T. (2000) 'The principal's role in promoting school development activity in Norwegian compulsory schools', *School Leadership and Management*, 20 (2): 247–260.

Pallant, J. (2005) *SPSS Survival Manual* (2nd edn). Maidenhead: Open University Press/McGraw-Hill.

Shipman, M.D. (1972) *The Limitations of Social Research*. London: Longmans.

Siegel, S. (1956) *Non-parametric Statistics for the Behavioural Sciences*. Tokyo: McGraw-Hill.

20

The analysis of qualitative data

Rob Watling and Veronica James

Analysis is the researcher's equivalent of alchemy – the elusive process by which you hope you can turn your raw data into nuggets of pure gold. And, like alchemy, such magic calls for science and art in equal measure. It is understandable, therefore, that the editors of this book chose to place the chapters on data analysis towards the end. It is understandable because the transformation of data into wisdom is often seen as something that can only be done in the later stages of a research project, once the raw material has been safely gathered in. And it is also understandable because the sorts of analysis you do in your project will inevitably depend on the types of research you have been undertaking. You would expect to analyse interview transcripts differently from the notes you make during participant observation, for example. And both of these would be different to the way you would handle the information you find during your literature search. So, of course, some key decisions about analysis will *need* to be taken late on in your project.

But locating these chapters at the end of the book is slightly misleading because analysis is not, in practice, something that *can* only be considered at the end. This is for two main reasons. First, the types of analysis that you are in a position to carry out may determine the types of research you are able to do. If, for example, you do not have the time or resources to analyse 100 in-depth, face-to-face interviews, or to process 1,000 questionnaires, or to use diaries with 25 managers, you had better choose another approach. If you feel that qualitative analysis will be too imprecise for your purposes or too vague to act as the basis for generalisation, or too conceptual to have credibility, you may already have chosen to adopt a more quantitative approach which will require different analytic techniques. So the first point to recognise is that some decisions about analysis may actually *precede* important decisions about methods. But the second point is just as important. With qualitative data in particular (but also with quantitative data as we have seen in Chapter 19), it is simply not possible or desirable to treat analysis as a separate activity which is only done at the final stages of a project. The analysis of data takes place throughout the project. It is an iterative and persistent part of the research process.

Imagine that you are going to conduct a series of interviews with managers at a further education college. In selecting the college that you want to visit you will already be considering some of its key features (its size, its general type, its suitability for your project, and so on). You will certainly do some basic background research about its policies and practice (deciding if it seems to be a forward-looking institution or one which is constrained by local conditions). When you arrive at the college to conduct your interviews you will form some important first impressions of the place, such as the neighbourhood in which it is located, the state of the college buildings, the demeanour of the students, whether it is welcoming to visitors, and so on. Before you start the interviews you may have general discussions with the people you have come to meet, and these are likely to give you more information about the place. By now you will understand quite a lot about the college you have chosen for your research. Indeed, you will have started to analyse some important qualitative data. Throughout the interviews you will be 'reading' the situation – making sense of the interviewees' words and interpreting their body language. You are bound to form judgements, hunches, prejudices, theories, hypotheses and further questions as you go along.

By the end of the day you will have conducted the interviews, responded to the managers' answers in order to get more detail, added a new question to your schedule, formed some key judgements, come to some tentative conclusions about their management style, left the building, reflected on the visit, challenged some of your own assumptions and written up your field notes. You will, in the process, have analysed a huge amount of qualitative data. And that is just in one field visit.

This is a key recognition, that analysis pervades each and every aspect of qualitative inquiry – may even lead, in extreme cases, to the termination of an entire research project (Gummesson, 2000):

> During an interview, I found that a company had engaged an advertising agency to set up a campaign designed to improve the company's image. The media cost of the campaign was expected to be around $300,000. In my judgement the campaign was meaningless; the company lacked business mission, goals, and strategies and hence had no corporate image to communicate. After a brief examination of the project, I got in touch with the chief executive and proposed that the campaign ought to be stopped. It turned out to be possible to cancel the contract with the media. The chief executive was satisfied because he wanted to cut costs.
>
> This example illustrates that information gathering, analysis, conclusions, recommendations, and implementation can take place more or less simultaneously. This contrasts with the stage-by-stage approach (albeit partly iterative) recommended in scientific research. Care has to be taken here, however. There is a considerable risk that without an understanding of the institutional conditions, consultants and researchers may put forward naive, standard solutions. (2000: 127–128)

Whether they realise it or not, all qualitative researchers will have to analyse parts of the data while they are designing the project; when they are conducting their desk-based research; when they are doing their fieldwork; while they are storing, retrieving and handling their records; when they are building and testing theories; and when they are writing up their report. This chapter will consider some of the main ways in which this analysis can take place at any or all of these stages and will encourage you to realise that data analysis is rarely a separate or distinct activity in its own right.

Methods and methodology

As has been pointed out repeatedly throughout this book, researchers are constantly faced with a series of choices and options about research methods. What they are doing when they make these choices is less about making the 'right' choice, than about making the 'best' choice in the particular circumstances in which they find themselves – they are seeking the optimum choice. It is not necessarily 'right' to take a positivist or interpretivist position, to use a standardised measure of literacy or to organise a focus group. The decision needs to be made and justified in the particular context of the research you are undertaking.

The same is true of the approach that you take to analysing your data, whether these data are qualitative, quantitative or – as is far more likely – a mixture of both. The important thing is that you, the researcher, make the decisions thoughtfully, systematically, critically and in ways which can be accounted for. In this way, when you come to defend your work, you will be able to justify your choice of methods (the tools, techniques, instruments and approaches you have adopted) through a clear methodology (a study and an account of the arguments and the philosophical underpinnings of your work).

In the analysis of qualitative research (which is what interests us here) that means making a series of deliberate, critical choices about the meanings and values of the data you have gathered, and making sure that your decisions can be justified in terms of the research, the context in which it was carried out and the people who were involved in it. Nothing less will do.

Denzin and Lincoln (2003) describe this collection of processes as bricolage – 'a pieced-together, close-knit set of representations that are fitted to the specifics of a complex situation' (2003: 5) and go on to look at some of the key skills of the bricoleur – the flexible, creative, intuitive qualitative researcher who seeks to produce an in-depth understanding of complex social phenomena:

> The ... bricoleur is adept at performing a large number of diverse tasks, ranging from interviewing to observing, to interpreting personal and historical documents, to intensive self-reflection and introspection. The ... bricoleur reads widely and is knowledgeable about the many paradigms that can be brought into any particular problem.

The ... bricoleur understands that research is an interactive process shaped by his or her personal history, biography, gender, social class, race, and ethnicity, and those of the people in the setting. The ... bricoleur knows that science is power, for all research findings have political implications. There is no value-free science. ... The bricoleur also knows that researchers all tell stories about the worlds they have studied ...

The product of the bricoleur's labour is a complex, quiltlike bricolage, a reflexive collage or montage – a set of fluid, interconnected images and representations ... connecting the parts to the whole. (2003: 9)

Originality and the six elements of qualitative data analysis

We have already said that data analysis inevitably takes place throughout the entire research process. We have also implied that each piece of research will follow a different route, and that the types of analysis you are engaged in will always depend very heavily on the nature of the project, the people involved and the focus of the investigation. We would also echo Denscombe's (2002) advice that research should contribute something that was not already known, because as he points out, new information, by itself, has limited value as it is about 'what' rather than 'why'. Analysis contributes to originality because the emphasis on 'why' has greater depth and contributes to the generation of knowledge as distinct from information. It identifies the *core elements* of a phenomenon and arrives at the *underlying principles* that explain the phenomenon (Denscombe, 2003: 119).

With all these options, how then can we provide any guidelines for newcomers to research? Are they always on their own, making the best they can of a difficult problem and fearing the examiner who is lying in wait, ready to criticise (and mark down) their choices? It is not that fearful a prospect. There are precedents, both in the general traditions of research and in specific examples of researchers who have looked at similar topics before and identified some of the best ways of operating in different circumstances. The task for the new researcher is to take what he or she can from these past experiences, to adopt the ones that fit their circumstances best, to adapt those that are nearly suitable, and to reject those that are irrelevant or uncomfortable. All these decisions need to be taken critically, and with adequate reflection.

It is wise to realise that there is nothing so unique about the research of educational management and leadership that it will not be raised in the literature relating to educational research in general or in many other aspects of the social sciences. You will find support for your research activity in the writings of teachers, curriculum theorists, local authorities, policy analysts and other educationalists, and you will find relevance in the writings of nurses, lawyers, engineers and social workers who have also decided to adopt a more qualitative approach to their work. Read widely for your research, and develop the fruitful links which are the hallmarks of the sophisticated and mature practitioner. For in many ways, qualitative research is similar to the sorts of process by which we make judgements and arrive at understandings throughout our everyday working lives. But when we call it 'research' we need to be more reflective, more systematic, more critical and more accountable in the ways we proceed.

When we look at other people's research, and at our own, we can identify a series of different stages where analytic processes can be found. For the purpose of this chapter, we have chosen six (though some research projects will have more or fewer than this) and we would like to go through them in turn, suggesting the types of analysis that might occur under any of them (Figure 20.1). We will illustrate our points by referring to writings on educational and social scientific research. What we do not want to imply, however, is that this diagram represents a blueprint for action. This is not designed as a system for moving simply through the research process: you would miss out a number of key stages if you did. Rather, it is a guide to some of the ways in which analysis might be located throughout a qualitative research project, instead of being left till the end of the process where it would loom over you as a final reckoning.

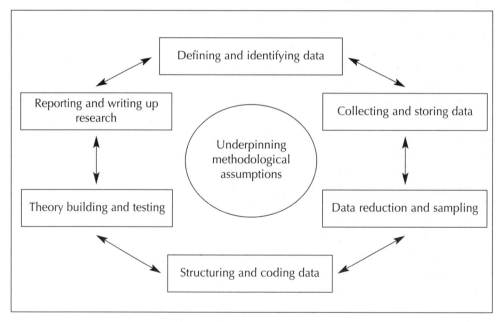

Figure 20.1   Six elements of qualitative data analysis

Defining and identifying data

What do we mean by 'data' – especially in a qualitative study? It is a term with distinctly positivist origins, coming from the Latin and meaning 'things that are given'. It implies a scientific, objective approach to reality in which there is a fixed (a given) world of known and knowable facts for us to discover. It has been argued that with new technologies for qualitative analysis, the practical differences between qualitative and quantitative analysis will diminish (Ryan and Russell Bernard, 2003). However, as we have seen elsewhere in this book, such a view is not always accepted, especially by those who argue that reality is socially constructed and that truths are negotiated by actors in specific contexts:

> Fundamentally, we think that social phenomena exist not only in the mind, but in the objective world as well, and that there are some lawful, reasonably stable relationships to be found among them. The lawfulness comes from the sequences and the regularities that link phenomena together; it is from these that we derive the constructs that account for individual and social life. (Huberman and Miles, 1998: 182)

The qualitative researcher, especially one working within such an epistemological framework, is likely to be searching for understanding, rather than facts; for interpretations rather than measurements; for values rather than information. And the scientific notion of 'data' sometimes sits uncomfortably in such discussions. Some researchers are not happy with the word at all, preferring to write about evidence, information, or material rather than data. For the purposes of this chapter, however, we have retained the term even though it sounds too precise to us.

But whatever you decide to call those things that the quantitative researcher readily refers to as 'data', it is important to acknowledge what you are including in the term. Once you move away from the analysis of given, measurable and objectively verifiable facts, to the analysis of thoughts, feelings, expressions and opinions which are open to debate, there is a clear requirement for you to make justifiable choices about what to include and what to leave out of your account. In doing so you are already involved in a process of analysis – weighing up the value and worth of specific things and deciding whether or not they are likely to 'count' in the research. How much of an interview, for example, will you count as evidence? Is it only the spoken words? Is it also the gestures and body language of the interviewee (Keats, 2000)? Is it also the things people omit to say which you will regard as important?

Even at the design stage we can see that the researchers are weighing up alternatives and making choices about the appropriateness of the people they will be working with and the quality of the data that they are likely to provide. In describing the methods used in their study of English Local Education Authorities (LEAs) and their role in operating teacher capability procedures, for example, Marchington et al. (2004) make a series of points about their sample, all of which we are entitled to presume are relevant to their ultimate analysis:

> First a postal survey of all English LEAs was used to ascertain the numbers of heads and teachers on capability procedures during 1999–2000. Using data provided by the postal survey over 20 LEAs were asked to participate

in a second stage of the project, selected on the basis of usage of procedures, a geographical spread, type of LEA and mix of urban and rural areas. ...

The next stage involved brief structured telephone interviews with head teachers ... Five hundred and twenty telephone interviews were then carried out with a random sample of headteachers in the chosen LEAs. ... Using the data from the telephone interviews, the research team selected case-study schools so as to provide a spread of size and type of school, the type of 'capability' issues, and the outcome for the individual teacher. Fifty-three case studies in 45 schools were carried out, all of which involved face-to-face interviews with the headteacher. Additionally, over 100 further interviews were held with LEA officers, personnel managers and advisors, officials, and representatives of six teacher associations, and with teacher colleges. Finally, seven different LEA capability procedures were itemized alongside several from voluntary-aided schools. (2004: 28–9)

This kind of sampling is inextricably linked to analysis, but it is not only done at the beginning of the project. Finch and Mason (1990) point out, for example, that one of the main differences between qualitative fieldwork and social surveys is the stage at which sampling of people and situations can take place:

In surveys such decisions are made once-and-for-all at the beginning of the project, and follow formalized statistical procedures for sampling. In field-work, such decisions are taken at various stages during the course of the project on the basis of contextual information. To outsiders who are not privy to the changing contextual basis of this project, research decisions can look rather ad hoc. (1990: 25)

It is important to recognise that these preparatory processes of selection involve analysing as well as defining the phenomenon. Drawing on the work of Doyle and Carter (1984), for example, Simco (1995) discusses the difference between academic 'tasks' and 'activities'. This is an important precursor to their study in the classroom – it helps the researcher decide what to observe and how to analyse it:

Essentially 'academic tasks are devised by the answers students are required to produce and the routes that can be used to obtain these answers' (Doyle, 1983: 161). They have a number of elements in their definition ... [and] it is within the precision of the definition of 'task' that the crucial differences between task and activity emerge. Activity is to do with classroom occur-rences within specified periods of time. Tasks are part of activity because they are embedded in it. In essence it is possible to have several tasks and also classroom occurrences which are not tasks but which are part of activity. (1995: 53)

And many other researchers, such as Eslea and Mukhtar (2000), identify what needs to be researched partly by analysing what others have left out of their work:

> The study reported here is an attempt to address some of the problems identified in the bullying and racism research to date. Clumsy definitions, inappropriate questionnaires, white researchers and the unnecessary lumping together of non-white ethnic groups mean that little can be concluded about the real experiences of ethnic minority children in British schools. Any hypothesis must therefore be tentative: experiences of racism and bullying may vary according to country of origin, language, religion, clothing, food, rituals, and so on. On the one hand, one might expect the political tensions between India and Pakistan to be reflected in hostility between children of these nationalities, and on the other hand, that tension between Hindu and Muslim children might be found regardless of nation. Another possibility is that bullying may reflect the relative proportions of different ethnic groups in the local population. This study attempts to begin the process of untangling these possibilities, in order to provide a richer understanding of bullying among Asian schoolchildren in Britain. (2000: 210)

Collecting and storing data

During the collection of qualitative data most researchers will start to form opinions and judgements about it. Let us look briefly at some of Watling's own field notes written after a semi-structured interview with a group of teachers piloting a new curriculum project. He was exploring the extent to which the project was trying to be informative (trying to introduce new areas of knowledge into the curriculum) or transformative (trying to support social change):

> The discussion then moved on to consider some aspects of the distinction between two aspects of the project identified in the interim report as its informative and transformative goals ... During the first few minutes of this part of the discussion, I detected a reluctance on the part of the team to acknowledge a transformative ambition. I was not sure whether to put this down to humility, reservation or disagreement with my basic question.
>
> The team began by suggesting that the pilot was interested first in transforming the teachers and the assumptions of teaching and learning that are inherent in some other subjects. There has also been a transformative element of the work as it is carried out in schools, and this needs to be linked (hopefully) to a wider view of what schools are, how they operate, and what they are 'for'. This, in turn, is linked to the wider aspirations of the current review of the curriculum. (Watling: personal fieldnotes)

We can see that it is *during* the interview itself that theories start to form in the researcher's mind. These theories may be tentative, provisional or unfinished. They may be dispensed with later on or may prove to be key elements of the final analysis. But once again it is important to recognise that they are not left till the end of the research, and that their 'value' needs to be judged by the researcher within the context of the data collection. It is also advisable at times like this to check your analysis by sharing these observations with the people you are working with – whether that is your research and work colleagues, or the participants in your research.

Finally in this section, we would like to encourage you to consider the ways in which you store your data and make them accessible for analysis. Whether your data are on paper, in notebooks, on proformas, on audio or videotape, on computer or anywhere else, you have the opportunity early on to organise them in ways that will be helpful to you later. Some people use card indexes, colour codings, filing systems, photocopies – use whatever works for you and supports the sort of data-retrieval and analysis you need to make. While qualitative data analysis packages are increasingly used, one of the simplest things to do is to print interview transcripts with line numbers (an easy option to select on most word processors) which will make them look like the example of a project transcript below. It will help enormously in identifying specific excerpts from long transcripts:

623 We did some Child Protection stuff recently, and it was very simple, in
624 order to get the message over. We brought out pen portraits of three kids
625 I'd selected to be very, very dire and the pictures on the staff faces told it
626 all. Then I said 'What are you going to do when you have a problem with
627 this kid? Are you going to go eye to eye, nose to nose, scream and shout at
628 him? You can't do that with this kid. This kid has seen worse than
629 anything you can inflict on him. None of them will work – he'll just go
630 and tell you where to go and walk off on you because you can't do
631 anything.' And it had an effect on a number of people, staff have come
632 and seen me since.

Denscombe (2003) offers the following, additional advice:

- As far as possible, get all materials in similar formats (for example, all on A4 size pages or all on record cards of the same size). This helps with storage and when sifting through materials.
- Where possible, the raw data should be collated in a way that allows researchers' notes and comments to be added alongside. So, for example, when taped interviews are transcribed, there should be a wide margin to the right-hand side of the page left blank, so that the researcher can add notes …
- Each piece of 'raw data' material should be identified with a unique serial number or code for reference purposes … (This helps with retrieval, checking, audit trails and preserving anonymity.)
- Make a back-up copy of all original materials and use the back-up copies for any analysis … Because qualitative data tend to be irreplaceable, it is good practice to make a duplicate of any tapes and to photocopy any documents

such as field notes or transcripts. This can prove to be something of a chore. It is time-consuming and can be expensive. But any loss or damage to the material is catastrophic for the research. To save effort it is best to duplicate the raw data as soon as they have been reference coded ... The original should be stored safely – preferably in a location quite separate from the back-up copies, which now become the 'working copies' that the researcher uses for analysis. (2003: 269–270)

Data reduction and sampling

It is highly unlikely that any researcher will use all the data gathered during their project – especially if they are using the sort of qualitative approaches discussed elsewhere in this book which are likely to produce large amounts of rich, deep data.

In reducing the amounts to a manageable size it is possible to use any of the standard sampling techniques. This can be done before any of the data are analysed (in the strict sense of the word). It would be possible, for example, to use a random sampling technique and to analyse only every third paragraph of an interview, or to look in depth at only 50 per cent of the questionnaire returns. But it will usually make much more sense to reduce the data by more purposeful methods – working perhaps on the basis of what you already know to be important or relevant. This may not sound scientific or objective, but researchers are entitled to make sense of the data they are handling – they merely have to account for what they are doing and justify their choices. Your analysis will thus inform the type of data reduction that you carry out. This means, again, that analysis is not something that can always be done at the end of the project. You need to weigh the value of the evidence to your project as you go along, to take informed judgements on its value to your work, to interpret it and to use it as the basis for your understandings and your explanations.

Structuring and coding data

Almost everything that we have considered so far is what we might call *formative analysis*. It reflects the epistemological and ontological aspects of qualitative research projects which seek to provide understandings and explanations, and actively shape the types of data collection that will go on. These perspectives *allow* and *require* the researcher to analyse aspects of their subject iteratively and reflexively. The more-easily recognisable processes of analysis might be thought to begin once the data are safely back in the study (whether this is done during or after the fieldwork). As we listen to our digital or tape recordings, as we read our transcripts or other documents, as we revisit our research journals, we have to start to make some sense of it all. At this listening and reading stage you have a real opportunity to build in the originality of research that Denscombe (2002) refers to. The structuring and coding underpin the key research outcomes, and can be used to shape the data to test, refine or confirm established theory, apply theory to new circumstances, or use it to generate a new theory or model.

The ways of proceeding are varied and often technical, and include indexing, coding, content analysis, discourse analysis and others. Fielding (2002) uses the term 'coding' generically, to cover all these forms when he notes:

'Coding' is fundamental to qualitative data analysis. The corpus has to be divided into segments and these segments assigned codes ... which relate to the analytic themes being developed. Researchers aim for codes which capture some essential quality of the segment, and which apply to other segments too. (2002: 163)

There are tried and tested methods for coding interviews, for example, and the choice of codes may have been pre-determined, or have emerged from the types of data gathered during the research. If we wish, we can use the results of preliminary coding for some simple quantitative analyses – counting responses in a sub-set of the interviews and using the results as the basis for further analysis. (For a discussion of coding and analysis of observations, see Chapter 15 of this book.)

In Arksey and Knight (1999), 178 teachers were asked whether they saw teaching as a profession and if so, why. A sample of responses was selected for coding. Each distinct idea was written down with similar ideas being written alongside each other, and identical responses being tallied. For example, teaching was said to be a profession where teachers:

Wear a suit/neat clothes IIIIII	(g)
Higher education needed III	(e)
Clean shaven IIIIIIII	(g)
Mark work regularly III	(f)
Tidy hair I	(g)
Decide how to teach a topic IIII	(d)

The *full* set of ideas (over a hundred were noted) in the sample of transcripts could be collapsed to form eight main categories, which were:

The public standing of teaching	(a)
Teachers' inter-personal skills	(b)
Teachers' possession of standards and values	(c)
Teachers' autonomy and non-routine decision-making	(d)
The possession of specialist knowledge	(e)
Conscientiousness	(f)
Appearance and self-presentation	(g)
Others	(h)

It can be seen that four of the ideas in the sample above fell into category (d); 3 into (e); 3 into (f) and 8 into (g).

The categories were discussed by all five researchers, who agreed that they were usable and covered all of the data. Definitions of each category were then written to make public their meanings and to enable any member of the team to apply them consistently.

The categories were then used to index the complete set of interviews. (1999:165)

Accounts of such techniques are easy to find in any of the quality research methods handbooks. In the courses we teach we steer students towards guides such as: Bell (2005), Blaxter, Hughes and Tight (2001), Denscombe (2002, 2003), Freebody (2003) and May (2002). But we stress that the techniques you choose to manage your own data are intricately related to the methodological choices you make elsewhere in your work. It is important to use them critically and not just instrumentally.

These techniques include inductive and deductive processes of analysis for which Tesch (1990), in a classic description, devised a complex typology of 26 different kinds of approach arranged into four main groups based on: the characteristics of language; the discovery of regularities; the comprehension of the meaning of text or action; and on reflection. Miles and Huberman (1994), on the other hand, have described a set of 13 'tactics' for generating meaning from qualitative data which they later summarised as follows:

Numbered 1 to 13, they are roughly arranged from the descriptive to the explanatory, and from the concrete to the more abstract: *Noting patterns and themes* (1), *seeing plausibility* – making initial, intuitive sense (2) – and *clustering* by conceptual grouping (3) help one to see connections (between the various pieces of data). *Making metaphors*, a kind of figurative grouping of data (4), is also a tactic for achieving more integration among diverse pieces of data. *Counting* (5) is a familiar way to see 'what's there' – and to keep oneself honest.

Making contrasts and comparisons (6) is a classic tactic meant to sharpen understanding by clustering and distinguishing observations. Differentiation is also needed, as in *partitioning variables*, unbundling variables that have been prematurely grouped, or simply taking a less monolithic look (7).

More abstract tactics include *subsuming particulars into the general, shuttling back and forth between first-level data and more general categories* (8); *factoring* (9) and analogue of a familiar quantitative technique, allowing the analyst to move from a large number of measured variables to a smaller set of unobserved, usually hypothetical, variables; *noting relations between variables* (10); and *finding intervening variables* (11). Finally, assembling a coherent understanding of a data set is helped through *building a logical chain of evidence* (12) and *making conceptual/theoretical coherence*, typically through comparison with the referent constructs in the literature (13). (Huberman and Miles 1998: 187)

Theory building and theory testing

In the accounts from Arksey and Knight (1999) and from Huberman and Miles (1998) above, we can identify an iterative process whereby theories about the data are generated, tested and applied at various stages. Some may need to be rejected, or adapted if they are going to be retained. If there is space in your research report you can describe these changes in your theory base – discussing the alternative viewpoints you have considered and explaining why some of them were not thought suitable. To build and test your theories in this way, as you progress through the research, is one way of showing your critically analytical approach to your work. If you look back through this chapter and at high quality accounts of other people's research, you should be able to identify opportunities for theory building and testing at each and every stage of the research process.

Reporting and writing up research

Some of the 'findings' of qualitative research (again this term has a positivist heritage that not everyone is comfortable with) only really start to emerge when you begin drafting the final report. As you construct an argument based on what you have done, the things you have seen and heard, the people you have worked with, and the data you have handled, some more analysis is not just permissible, it is almost inevitable. The final threading together of the piece, the weight you give to each part of the argument, the elaboration of a line of thought – all these constitute a final round of analysis. Richardson (2003) considers our approach to writing as the final frontier in our efforts to make research come alive to a wider audience:

> I write because I want to find something out. I write in order to learn something that I didn't know before I wrote it. I was taught, however, as perhaps you were, too, not to write until I knew what I wanted to say, until my points were organized and outlined. No surprise, this static writing model coheres with mechanistic scientism and quantitative research. But, I will argue, the model is itself a sociohistorical invention that reifies the static social world imagined by our 19th-century foreparents. The model has serious problems: it ignores the role of writing as a dynamic, creative process; it undermines the confidence of beginning qualitative researchers because their experience of research is inconsistent with the writing model; and it contributes to the flotilla of qualitative writing that is simply not interesting to read because adherence to the model requires writers to silence their own voices and to view themselves as contaminants.

Qualitative researchers commonly speak of the importance of the individual researcher's skills and aptitudes. The researcher – rather than the survey, the questionnaire, or the census tape – is the 'instrument' ... Yet they are taught to conceptualize writing as 'writing up' the research, rather than as an open place, a method of discovery. (2003: 501–502)

Richardson goes on to propose a whole range of creative writing practices that can support analysis in these stages of research, and gives guidance on where to find real examples of the use of 'narratives of the self', fiction, drama, poetry, 'performance science', 'polyvocal texts', 'responsive readings', 'aphorisms', comedy and satire, visual representations and others. She also suggests a series of writing exercises which might encourage you to be more versatile and to adopt new processes for analysis. Our only caveat would be to remind students that their work is likely to be assessed by people who are firmly rooted in the writing traditions she is trying to challenge. It may be a strategy which delivers risk as much as it offers liberation.

Systems and software

Some people are free-thinking, free-floating individuals who can live with the organic mess produced by most qualitative research, and come out at the end with a seamless and well-rounded research report. But most people fall back on systems of one sort or another, whether it be field notes, diagrams, card indexes, or computer packages to turn interviews into descriptive numbers ready for crunching, and, increasingly, to shape thematic analysis. The important thing is to use a system which you understand, which is reliable, safe and which you can justify. There is no room in this chapter to consider them in depth and there will inevitably be different versions and packages available by the time you read this, but they fall into three different groups, as described below.

First, there are simple software packages which can easily be called upon to support the qualitative researcher. Even the simple word processor is capable of helping you to store, retrieve and analyse your data creatively. It can count, tabulate, format, summarise, copy, cut and paste, remove, highlight and annotate. Other, linked, packages such as databases, spreadsheets and presentation software are now much easier to use than they were a few years ago, and it is certainly easier to transfer data between one package and another. Spending time with the software you already know, and exploring it with the help of the many quality manuals now available, can reap benefits.

Also available are packages for specific aspects of literature management. All higher education institutions now have sophisticated search systems for the identification of relevant publications. Along with the Web, these are excellent at identifying otherwise inaccessible literature, but do have the disadvantage that they need training before they can be used proficiently. Available to individuals, as well as being networked in institutions, are the high quality bibliographic software packages such as EndNote, Papyrus and Reference Manager. At its most basic level, this software provides an electronic version of a card index system, allowing users to store and retrieve details of the documentary materials they have used. At its most extensive, it provides a comprehensive system allowing you to import, store, share, manipulate, retrieve and export this data in a wide variety of ways. One of its greatest strengths is its ability to produce detailed bibliographies for academic publications, and to do so in any of the hundreds of styles required by different publishers.

Finally, there is the big growth area that has caused much controversy – a range of software packages tailor-made for handling qualitative research data and supporting the generation and testing of theories. Computer-assisted qualitative data analysis or CAQDAS is now widely used in institutions, taught on methodology courses and easily available to individuals. The packages have been challenged for distorting the epistemological basis of qualitative research, and as Fielding (2002) points out, they could play a significant part in changing the work of the qualitative research community. But many qualitative researchers find that the practical uses, particularly for the management of large quantities of data, far outweigh the disadvantages.

Fielding describes the software packages as falling into three different groups: text retrievers, code-and-retrieve packages and theory building. Text retrievers, such as Metamorph and ZyINDEX, enable users to find and use keywords which appear in the data. For example 'social class', or 'disruptive' can be retrieved, wherever they are in the text and sorted into files, and analytic memos. Code-and-retrieve packages, such as HyperQual and Ethnograph, are designed to enable the division of the text into segments, attaching codes to the segments, and then the retrieval of segments by code or combinations of code. For example, a multiple search might combine females, under 10, in urban schools. The third group, the theory-building software, includes HyperRESEARCH and NVivo. These include both code-and-retreive facilities, which enable numerical counting, and emphasise relationships between the categories. They help users develop higher order themes and categories, and the formulation of propositions which can then be tested.

An overview of the theory, methods and practice of CAQDAS can be found in Weitzman (2003), with some detail of application in Fielding (2002), or precise information in software-specific handbooks, such as Bazeley and Richards (2000). But your final choice will frequently depend on availability, and the time you have available to learn to use the packages. The balance on this final point is between the learning curve that these packages present you with, and the fact that it is often much easier to learn the basics on a small-scale project than on a major piece of research where mistakes and delays can cause serious problems. In a smaller piece of work it is much easier to cut your losses and revert to more traditional (or more radical) systems if you feel out of your depth or constrained by the inevitable limitations of the software. For whichever system you use (and almost every qualitative researcher will use one of these software packages) the important thing is to ensure that the software supports your research, and that it does not dictate your way of working.

Conclusion

We have argued that analysis is an integral part of the whole research process – especially when you are dealing with qualitative data. It informs and responds to the types of research you are able to conduct, it shapes and is shaped by the subject of your work, and it pervades each and every aspect of the research process from project design to the writing of the report. Most importantly, the processes of analysis are inextricably linked to the other methodological choices you make throughout your work. As such they need to be accounted for, justified, critically evaluated and (we hope) celebrated.

References

Arksey, H. and Knight, P. (1999) *Interviewing for Social Scientists*. London: Sage.

Bazeley, P. and Richards, L. (2000) *The NVivo Qualitative Project Book*. London: Sage.

Bell, J. (2005) *Doing Your Research Project* (5th edn). Milton Keynes: Open University Press.

Blaxter, L., Hughes, C. and Tight, M. (2001) *How to Research*. Buckingham: Open University Press.

Denscombe, M. (2002) *Ground Rules for Good Research*. Maidenhead: Open University Press/McGraw-Hill.

Denscombe, M. (2003) *The Good Research Guide*. Maidenhead: Open University Press/McGraw-Hill.

Denzin, N.K. and Lincoln, Y.S. (2003) *Collecting and Interpreting Qualitative Materials*. London: Sage.

Doyle, W. (1983) 'Academic work', *Review of Educational Research*, 53: 159–199.

Doyle, W. and Carter, K. (1984) 'Academic tasks in classrooms', *Curriculum Inquiry*, 14: 129–149.

Eslea, M. and Mukhtar, K. (2000) 'Bullying and racism among Asian schoolchildren in Britain', *Educational Research*, 42 (2): 207–217.

Fielding, N. (2002) 'Automating the ineffable: qualitative software and the meaning of qualitative research', in May, T. (ed.) *Qualitative Research in Action*. London: Sage.

Finch, J. and Mason, J. (1990) 'Decision taking in the fieldwork process: theoretical sampling and collaborative working', *Studies in Qualitative Methodology*, 2: 25–50.

Freebody, P. (2003) *Qualitative Research in Education: Interaction and Practice*. London: Sage.

Gummesson, E. (2000) *Qualitative Methods in Management Research*. London: Sage.

Huberman, A.M. and Miles, M.B. (1998) 'Data management and analysis methods', in Denzin, N.K. and Lincoln, Y.S. (eds) *Collecting and Interpreting Qualitative Materials*. London: Sage.

Keats, D.M. (2000) *Interviewing: A Practical Guide for Students and Professionals*. Buckingham: Open University Press.

Marchington, L., Earnshaw, J., Torrington, D. and Ritchie, E. (2004) 'The Local Education Authority's role in operating teacher capability procedure', *Journal of Educational Management, Administration and Leadership*, 32 (1): 25–44.

May, T. (ed.) (2002) *Qualitative Research in Action*. London: Sage.

Miles, M.B. and Huberman, A.M. (1994) *Qualitative Data Analysis: An Expanded Sourcebook*. London: Sage.

Richardson, L. (2003) 'Writing: a method of enquiry', in Denzin, N.K. and Lincoln, Y.S. (eds) *Collecting and Interpreting Qualitative Material*. London: Sage.

Ryan, G. and Russell Bernard, H. (2003) 'Data management and analysis methods', in Denzin, N.K. and Lincoln, Y.S. (eds) *Collecting and Interpreting Qualitative Materials*. London: Sage.

Simco, N.P. (1995) 'Activity analysis in primary classrooms', *British Educational Research Journal*, 21 (1): 49–60.

Tesch, R. (1990) *Qualitative Research: Analysis Types and Software Tools*. London: Falmer Press.

Weitzman, E. (2003) 'Software and qualitative research', in Denzin, N.K. and Lincoln, Y.S. (eds) *Collecting and Interpreting Qualitative Material*. London: Sage.

Further reading

Bell, J. (2005) *Doing Your Research Project* (5th edn). Milton Keynes: Open University Press.

Blaxter, L., Hughes, C. and Tight, M. (2001) *How to Research*. Buckingham: Open University Press.

Denscombe, M. (2003) *The Good Research Guide*. Maidenhead: Open University Press/McGraw-Hill.

Denzin, N.K. and Lincoln, Y.S. (2003) *Collecting and Interpreting Qualitative Materials*. London: Sage.

Gummesson, E. (2000) *Qualitative Methods in Management Research*. London: Sage.

Huberman, A.M. and Miles, M.B. (2002) *The Qualitative Researcher's Handbook*. London: Sage.

May, T. (ed.) (2002) *Qualitative Research in Action*. London: Sage.

Silverman, D. (2000) *Doing Qualitative Research*. London: Sage.

21

Academic writing: process and presentation

Ann R.J. Briggs

This chapter completes the process which began in Chapter 1 of this book. Having identified our research purpose, chosen an appropriate research approach and design to fit the purpose, constructed and administered the research tools and analysed the data, we are (hopefully) in possession of insights and knowledge which are new and worth sharing. And it is pointless going through this process unless we share our findings as effectively as possible.

> Research in isolation serves no purpose. Effective communication, both to other research workers and to teachers and other educationists, is the essence of good educational research. (Nisbet and Entwistle, 1984: 256)

This chapter is intended as general guidance for those who are new to academic writing, and addresses such questions as:

- Who am I writing for – and how does that affect what I write?
- How do I organise and structure my writing?
- What sort of language should I use?
- How authoritative can I be about my findings?
- How do I present my analysed results?
- How should I further disseminate my research?

You will already have gained insight into the presentation of your research from the other chapters in this book, particularly Chapters 19 and 20. You may find it helpful to use this chapter in conjunction with those which deal with the particular methodology you have chosen.

Audience

One important question to ask before writing up your research is, 'Who am I writing for?' The answer might be among the following:

- Masters or Doctoral degree examiners
- The editor and readers of an academic journal
- Conference delegates
- Senior staff at my place of work

The answer is rarely, simply, 'Myself.'

Each of the 'audiences' listed above has its own expectations, some easy to assess, others less so. All expect to be presented with something new and engaging: new insight into known situations, new concepts or areas of knowledge. The expectations of examiners and academic journal editors can partly be gauged by reading dissertations, theses and journal articles which have received their approval; look again at material of this type that you consulted for your literature review, to seek out and develop an approach to your audience that is appropriate, both for you and for the context in which you are writing.

Other audiences may expect a different focus, and sometimes they necessitate a selective approach to your material. Conference delegates need to be stimulated to think and debate, but within relatively tight time constraints; it may be wise to focus on just one aspect of your research in this context. Choose a research subject that you find particularly intriguing, or that ties in most closely with the theme of the conference, and give a clear presentation of it, rather than trying to present the whole of your research. Indicate to your audience how they can learn about the rest of your findings; if they do not exist in published form, tell people how to contact you.

A different approach to selecting your material is needed for senior staff at your place of work. They probably need a concise and accessible report – written or oral – which summarises all your findings, together with clear recommendations for action. This may mean that months of investigation, analysis and writing must be distilled into 1,000–2,000 words for easy access by a range of staff. If the intended outcome of your research – school or college improvement for example – is to be guided by what you have learned, then a format that motivates the maximum number of people to read (or listen) and respond will have to be chosen. The advice given by David Frost in Chapter 11 about maximising the effect of practitioner research is relevant here.

The findings of a major research project may be presented many times: perhaps in formats appropriate for all the different audiences listed above, as well as in published books or educational newspapers. The heart of the research – its aims, the investigation itself, the analysis of findings and conclusions – must be there in each case, but the balance of what you present to each audience will differ, as will the level of detail you include.

So how do you decide what to include? One approach is to assess how much your audience knows already. In the first three cases given above, the audience will be familiar with the broad concepts underlying your research, and the research traditions into which it fits; they will, however, be assessing your ability to present and engage in those concepts and traditions. They may know nothing of the local context of the research, and may not be specialists in the aspect of education that is the subject of your research. Your senior managers, however, though they may well be 'expert' on the local context and phase of education, may be less familiar with the broad concepts that underpin your research and drive your argument.

In all cases there are areas of information with which you feel your audience are already familiar, and concepts that you feel that they already understand but which are germane to the account you are presenting, and which therefore must be included in your presentation. Even if your audience is familiar with the relevant concepts, people need to know how those concepts fit in with the investigation and analysis that you have undertaken. Whatever your audience's familiarity with the subject, they expect you to be able to explain it, to take it through your train of thought. Remember, your audience has not 'lived through' your research as you have. What you put in or leave out depends upon the required length of the piece, but your writing should be internally coherent – that is, it must not depend upon data or concepts which have not been presented or discussed. This means, of course, that conclusions should be based on what has been presented, not on knowledge which is assumed or 'given'.

Above all, your audience wants to feel that you have the authority to speak or write on your chosen subject. 'The essential feature of any research report is to make a claim to knowledge' (Bassey, 1999: 89). Readers need assurance that the research has been properly carried out; that it recognises and builds upon what has been previously researched and understood; that the data collected have been analysed thoroughly and thoughtfully; and that conclusions bear in mind not only the research findings, but also previous knowledge and the constraints imposed by the scale of the research. This kind of authority can be conveyed irrespective of the length of the written piece: from a thesis of many thousand words to a research abstract of a few hundred words.

Structure

Whatever the length of your written piece, it needs a clear structure; this becomes increasingly important both for you and for your reader in longer pieces of writing. For theses and dissertations, and to a certain extent for articles in academic journals, there are conventions to be followed. If you have been given guidelines for the various sections of your thesis, you would be well advised to follow them, or to make it clear in your writing, after discussion with your supervisor, why you are deviating from usual practice.

Where no format is given for the writing as a whole, think through what your audience needs to know, and the order in which the material needs to be presented, if it is to make sense. You may arrive, predictably, at a presentation sequence such as this:

- The aims of the research and its context
- A review of related research and knowledge
- A description and justification of the chosen research methodology
- A summary of findings
- An analysis of what the findings show
- Conclusions and recommendations

Some contexts allow deviation from this format. In a newspaper article or an internal report, for example, it might be appropriate to catch the reader's attention by presenting the conclusions first: the reader then chooses whether to read on for further detail. The review of related research and knowledge – essential to an academic audience – might be omitted or greatly reduced in journalism or report writing. Writing about your research in a chapter of a book might focus primarily upon the outcomes, with the reader being informed through bibliographical referencing of the existence of fuller accounts of the research.

Developing a good structure for your writing depends also upon your ability to stand outside – or above – your subject, and consider it as a whole. What are the patterns that shape it? Are they your research questions? Are they key issues derived from your literature search? Are they a framework for analysis which you have taken or adapted from other writers, or devised for yourself? Where is the study going, and by what broad routes? Consider this advice from Blaxter et al. (1996: 215) about the themes of your research:

> The *themes* of your report or thesis are the key issues, concepts or questions you identify as being of relevance and interest. These will both inform the research you undertake, so will be evident in your contextual discussion, and help to structure your analysis and findings. They are the aspects of your field or discipline to which your research is contributing.

Within the larger sections of your writing, a consistent internal structure can be achieved by using these themes as a framework of sub-sections. If themes are repeated in successive sections of your writing, the reader will be encouraged to follow routes with which he or she will become increasingly familiar. The structure can be both externally visible – as sub-headings replicated in different sections – and embedded, where the concepts are dealt with in the same order in each section. You may be concerned that this approach will make your writing seem repetitive and unexciting. My response would be that if the structure of your argument is clear, the reader will be 'freed up' to become interested in your findings; if there is no clear 'map' of the pattern of ideas you are presenting, the reader may struggle to follow your train of thought and may not engage with the key points you are trying to make.

Within each sub-section, a finer degree of structuring is also essential. Ask yourself questions such as 'What do the readers need to know next?' and, 'What do they need to know already in order to understand what I am writing here?' to help you to order and organise your writing. Use link paragraphs to act as bridges between sub-sections, and offer summaries to give a chance for the reader – and the writer – to 'take stock' of what has just been presented. Using link words and phrases such as 'but', 'however', 'therefore', 'on the other hand' or 'in addition' helps you to build a cumulative argument, rather than simply presenting a succession of statements, and helps to move your document towards the destination you have in mind.

The flow of your argument can also be either enabled or impeded by the way in which tables and figures are placed. These are a valuable – often essential – part of your presentation, making points which it would be difficult to convey in continuous prose. However, they need clear labelling (with figure number and caption) and thoughtful handling if they are to convey their full impact. Remember that your reader is following the text, and is dependent upon you to 'signpost' to tables and figures appropriately, whether in the text of your report or its appendices, and to draw material from them into the discussion. It is a good idea to distribute evenly throughout the text illustrative material that may lie within it: making the reader encounter a 'brick wall' of tables or figures when trying to follow an argument may not be helpful. Those illustrations that form an essential part of your argument should go in the text; while those that merely support it should be placed in appendices. Text cross-references, both to illustrations in the text and in the appendices, are essential.

The advice given in this section may be hard to apply when you are writing at length for the first time, or after a long break. The proposed length and complexity of your finished document may simply seem too daunting. Remember that a house is built one brick at a time, and it may be necessary for you simply to prepare your bricks (sentences, paragraphs, drafted sub-sections) and lay them out in front of you before you can see how they all fit together in the ways suggested above. Often it becomes clear that a sub-section that was intended to fit in one place will fit better in another – with suitable minor re-wording – once other sub-sections have been written. It is also good practice to ask a colleague or friend to read drafts of what you have written, in order to comment on how well they can follow your argument, and what sections they find difficult to understand. In that way, you can see how easily your reader may follow the structure that you offer.

Language and 'voice'

The effectiveness of your research writing also depends upon your ability to select and adopt a consistent and appropriate stance from which to write. In some areas of ethnographic research, in research which engages in a large degree of self-reflection, and in case study research where a narrative approach is adopted (see Chapter 9) the use of the first person 'I' and 'we' is appropriate. In research where an objective viewpoint is paramount, a neutral third person stance, combined with use of the passive voice, will help to maintain objectivity. This does not mean that the language you use needs to be stilted: the statements, 'Five main-grade teachers were selected for interview' or, 'The college has three main sites' are no more difficult to follow than, 'I selected five main-grade teachers for interview' or 'Our college has three main sites'. If you are not sure which 'person' to use, pay attention to the style of other writing in your discipline, and take advice from academic colleagues. In the end, as Blaxter et al. (1996: 221) comment 'Whether you use the first or third person will depend upon your discipline, your politics, your purpose and your audience.' Look again at Chapters 2 and 3 to re-assess the type of research you have undertaken, and your stance towards reporting it.

Researchers undertaking academic writing after a number of years away from study, or who may not have written formally at length for some considerable time, sometimes incorporate patterns of their own speech into their writing. Whilst this may enable the writer to 'break through' into the writing process, it is important that they move on to a more formal written style. As with gauging the level of presentation needed for your audience, it is advisable to read a range of academic writing in order to adopt a personal style with which you are comfortable, and which is appropriate for an academic reader.

Developing an appropriate viewpoint can merit as much attention as developing an appropriate style. Your viewpoint will be partly influenced by your reading of previous work on related subjects: you undertake a review of the literature in order to set your own work within its intellectual context. As your analysis both of the extant literature and of your own findings develops, you will find yourself developing a critical stance towards previous pieces of research, in order to incorporate them into your themes and arrive at your own conclusions. Taylor (1989: 67) offers a useful checklist of viewpoints which might be developed; these include:

- Agreeing with, acceding to, defending or confirming a particular point of view
- Proposing a new point of view
- Reformulating an existing point of view such that the new version makes a better statement
- Rejecting, rebutting or refuting another's arguments on various reasoned grounds
- Reconciling two positions which may seem at variance by appeal to some 'higher' or 'deeper' principle. (1989: 67)

Note that these stances are developed on 'reasoned grounds', that is, by analysing the available evidence, either from other literature, or from your own findings. Your own critical stance in research, as discussed in Chapter 3, may also influence how you view previous research and the way its findings are presented.

Having carried through your piece of educational management or leadership research, the viewpoint you have reached may lead you to adopt a rather 'imperative' style in presenting the final stages of your analysis and your conclusions, saying that something 'must' be so or 'should' happen. Try very hard to avoid this stance. Think again about the scope of your research, the limitations of your methodology, and the wide range of un-investigated phenomena which may have had an impact upon the researched situation. A stance which balances confidence in making recommendations based upon the data whilst acknowledging the limitations and boundaries of the research is probably a wiser option. Think through the issues presented by Tony Bush in Chapter 6 before asserting your claims too strongly.

Some new researchers ask, 'When can I express my own opinion? Surely that is important?' The simple answer is that your own opinion, unsupported by data, is not valid. The deeper answer is that your own opinion – in the form of your own interests, ethics, values and priorities – shapes the whole of your research: it guides you in choosing what questions to ask, what literature to read, what methodology to adopt, what factors to analyse in your data and what importance to place upon your findings. It may lead you to set up a hypothesis, which your research explores in order to prove or disprove. The complexity for you the researcher lies in your ability to balance your opinion – what you feel is right or fitting – with a 'research attitude' that is prepared to accept a broad range of possible outcomes for the research.

Finally in this section there are some specific features of style to note. You should adopt a consistent model of referencing, both within the text and in your reference list, preferably a model such as the 'Harvard' system with which your readers will be familiar – and which examiners will expect to see. Abbreviations such as 'it's' and 'don't' should usually be avoided, but professionally used abbreviations such as 'SMT' for 'Senior Management Team' are acceptable, provided that they are written out in full and followed by their abbreviation, where they first appear in the text. Specialised terminology – which may include such simple phrases as 'subject leader' or 'homework club' – need at least a brief explanation. Try to avoid using jargon that is very specific to your own institution – terms that may mean little to an outsider. Similarly, if you are writing for an international audience, remember that educational terminology varies from country to country, so it is good practice to offer a brief explanation of specific terms and abbreviations.

Whilst negotiating all these minefields and pitfalls of writing, do not lose sight of your own voice. Your own engagement with the topic investigated, and your own lively interest in it need not be lost in the process – indeed it is these features that will keep your readers engaged. You may choose to research and write from a particular ethical viewpoint or stance: a passionate interest in issues of equity or access to education may underlie your research, and lead you to 'theories and insights [which] can be used to improve [your] corner of the world' (Dadds, 1995: 137). But this does not mean that your investigation will be biased or lack rigour: as any other good research, it should be 'based on sound evidence, tested theory and workable philosophy' (Locke, 1990: 202).

Authority

The previous section has explored some of the factors influencing your choice of language. There are aspects of language which are specifically important in presenting your analysed results. The scope of your investigation and the choice and design of your research tools dictate the limits of the authority with which you can report results. In reporting your research it is important, therefore, that your choice of language matches the scope of your investigation.

For example, a survey which involved all the teachers at one primary school could be reported as: 'Teachers at Sunnymead Primary School thought ...', 'Three-quarters of the teachers at the school agreed that ...' or 'Few of the teachers at the school considered X to be important.' Where the sample comprises the whole population, then, given reliable research tools, the results can be reported as representing the views of the whole population. It may still be wise to acknowledge that there may be personal variations in perception which the sampling design did not enable you to detect.

However, a survey which had sampled lecturers from two faculties of a further education college would be reported differently, for example: 'Half of the respondents agreed with the statement ...', 'All of the staff sampled for the survey reported ...' or 'The overall impression given by respondents from Faculty Y was ...'. If robustly designed probability sampling has been used in your research, then inferences could be drawn for the whole of each faculty, or for a pair of faculties, but not for the college as a whole, unless the two faculties represented a reliable sample of the whole staff of the college.

Where the probability samples are small, or where non-probability sampling is chosen, assertions cannot be made about the whole population. Instead, the perceptions would be presented as a 'snapshot' of opinion, or as elements of a 'rich picture' of part of the school or college. Sampling design is fully discussed in Chapter 8 of this book, and the issues of reliability and validity of data in Chapter 6; both chapters will help you to understand the methodological issues underlying this advice. What is emphasised here is that the choice of words used to describe and present the data must match the parameters set by the research design. Your argument will be more convincing if you stay within the limits of the authority provided by your data. (For further advice on sampling, and its implications for presentation, see Chapter 8 of this book.)

Presenting your analysis

The specific examples discussed in the previous section lead us into a broader consideration of what will be at the heart of what you write: the analysis of the data you have collected. Other chapters in this book, particularly Chapters 19 and 20, will be valuable to you in conducting your analysis; this section focuses on the processes that enable you to present it appropriately to your audience. The rationale for presenting analysed data is rooted in the overall framework of research activity, and a brief recap of the processes that would normally precede analysis may be helpful.

- *Research design.* Here the key questions are developed and presented which the research is to clarify or answer, the context for the research is identified and the broad methodology proposed for the investigation.

- *Literature review*. This sets the investigation within the context of existing research and published information about the phenomenon. It also enables the researcher to understand and discuss the key concepts which underpin the research, and to identify and develop themes and frameworks for analysis.
- *Developing the methodology*. Here the outcomes of the review are considered, together with the key research questions, in order to define the research approach and design the tools to be used. Research methodology texts (such as this one) are used to enable appropriate choices to be made and justified.
- *Collecting the data*. Data are collected which hopefully will provide insight into the research questions, and illustrate the key concepts. Guiding your analysis, therefore, will be both the research questions and the conceptual framework of your research.

The raw data – and you may be faced with a great deal of them, whether stored in notebooks, on tapes or as computer files – will then be subject to two stages of analysis. The first stage enables you to see what the data indicate, and to identify patterns: likenesses, trends, differences and anomalies that are of relevance to the research. You will need to refer to Chapters 19 and 20 for more detailed advice on the analysis process, but your research outcomes may include graphs and charts, summaries of interviews, tables of concepts referred to by respondents, and the output of quantitative and qualitative analytical computer packages. In a thesis or dissertation, much of these analysed data will need to be presented – in the text and in the appendices of your report – in order to describe what you have found. In a journal article or conference presentation, it is likely that only selected data are presented: those that are germane to the argument proposed by the paper.

The second stage of analysis involves considering those discovered patterns – the likenesses, trends, differences and anomalies – in the light of the research questions and the conceptual frameworks derived from the literature. This is the most important part of your research, and it is where your own insight comes into play. At this stage, you are considering what your results 'mean' in terms of the aims of the research, guided by structures of thought which you have already explored in your literature review, and which you will have been turning over in your mind since you started collecting the data.

Whereas the outcomes of the first stage of analysis may seem static – they describe in different ways the research phenomenon that you have investigated – the second stage becomes increasingly dynamic. Arguments are built up which move you towards the 'answers' to your research questions, and to meaningful conclusions about your research area. Unexpected outcomes of your research emerge, and need to be incorporated into your framework of ideas. Along the way you may develop models of the processes you have investigated, or ways of presenting the patterns that you have found, and evaluating their importance. Consider the advice of Huberman and Miles: 'Think display. … Consider what forms of display … are most likely to bring together relevant, transformed data in a way that will permit good conclusion drawing and strengthening of conclusions' (Huberman and Miles, 2002: 396).

Analysis should be rooted in the empirical data, viewed in relation to the research aims and the conceptual framework derived from the literature. It is the interaction of these elements, through the medium of the researcher, that leads the analysis towards new insights and understanding, and produces valid conclusions and recommendations. During this highly dynamic process, as Huberman and Miles (2002) recommend: 'Stay self-aware: be self-critical of your processes of analysis and the findings you produce, and where possible engage "critical friends" who can supportively counter your taken-for granted approaches and suggest alternatives' (Huberman and Miles, 2002: 397).

This second stage of analysis takes time, mental energy – and space on the page. An easy error is to spend most of your time on primary analysis, and most of the analysis section of your writing in simply presenting the results of your research. The real skill is in devising a concise but effective way of presenting those results, by making good use of tables, charts, explanatory comment and material cross-referenced in the appendices, for example, so that the reader has a secure grasp of what you have found, whilst reserving space for a substantial amount of secondary analysis. This part of your presentation, where your data are debated within the framework of your research questions and the key concepts from the literature, lies at the heart of your thesis, conference paper or journal article. It is where you and your reader engage with what is important in your research. Clarity of thought and presentation in this section will influence the confidence of your audience in the validity of your conclusions and recommendations. Presentation of your analytical thinking therefore merits time and care.

Dissemination

I hope that this chapter will have given some guidance on how to undertake the primary task with which you are faced: that of presenting your research. If you are engaged in completing a dissertation or thesis, probably the last thing that you wish to consider is undertaking further writing on the same subject. But consider a moment. Your thesis may be read by close family and colleagues. While a copy may be held in an academic library where other scholars may consult it, on the whole its readership will not be wide; in addition it may well be too long to be read easily. To refer to Nisbet and Entwistle (1984: 256) quoted at the head of this chapter: 'Research in isolation serves no purpose.'

For many practitioner researchers, the main objective of their research is to achieve improvement in practice at their own school or college. As David Frost points out in Chapter 11 of this book, the main way to achieve impact within your organisation is to involve colleagues in your research from the outset. When conducting research on a regional or national basis, a steering group for the research made up of knowledgeable advisers and stakeholders is an invaluable advisory body during the research, and can be a key element in the dissemination strategy. For the research to have impact, the people who are to embed its outcomes need to be involved in the process, or at least to be well informed about it.

When disseminating your research findings within and beyond your organisation, the following media may be appropriate:

- An oral report or developmental workshop based on the research, presented to colleagues and staff from neighbouring educational institutions
- A brief written summary of the research, its findings and recommendations, distributed internally – on paper or via an intranet – to colleagues
- A summary of the research and findings, with explanatory contextual detail, posted on an appropriate Internet discussion group or Web page
- A research paper published on the Internet
- An article submitted to an educational newspaper or magazine
- A paper submitted to an educational or academic conference
- A paper submitted to an academic journal

You will probably be able to think of other dissemination routes, but one important principle is to match the route you choose to the message you are offering, and the other is not to under-rate yourself. If you choose to write a paper for an academic journal or a conference, your writing will be subjected to academic scrutiny before it can be disseminated. Do not let this put you off, even if you do not succeed first time. If the research was worth doing, it is worth disseminating, and if that means a 'lifetime first' of speaking at an academic conference, or of re-drafting your journal article for publication, so be it.

Whatever route you choose, you will probably be surprised at the amount of interest your research generates, and the stimulus you receive to undertake more research. Pushing forward the frontiers of understanding, even in a small way, can be addictive!

And finally ...

If, even after reading all this good advice, you find it difficult to get started with your scholarly writing, don't panic – you are not alone! Even accomplished writers can find the process of writing difficult. There are many useful study guides which will help you to prioritise and plan your work – take from them what advice makes sense to you in your own circumstances. For me, the best advice is the simplest: 'Just write something!' Whatever you write will have to be re-drafted, probably three or more times, so the quality of the first draft is not really important. Once you have written something, and start to look at it critically, you will begin to see what is missing, what is in the wrong place, what needs to be better expressed. It is the engagement with the topic that even a clumsy attempt at writing can produce, that is the key to successful communication.

At some point in the writing process there often comes the moment when, in the words of Blaxter et al. (1996: 229), 'You have become so familiar with a group of ideas or theories that they now appear to you to be no more than common sense.' In other words, you appear to be going through the pointless process of presenting facts and perceptions and conclusions which you feel should be perfectly obvious to anyone. The advice wisely given is: 'Remind yourself of how far you have travelled on your intellectual journey' (Blaxter et al.,1996: 229). Your task in writing is to trace that journey as you write, and engage your reader in it. No one else has handled those concepts and those data in combination before. You, therefore, have a story worth telling.

References

Bassey, M. (1999) *Case Study Research in Educational Settings*. Buckingham: Open University Press.

Blaxter, L., Hughes, C. and Tight, M. (1996) *How to Research*. Buckingham: Open University Press.

Dadds, M. (1995) *Passionate Enquiry and School Development*. London: Falmer Press.

Halsall, R. (ed.) (1998) *Teacher Research and School Improvement*. Buckingham: Open University Press.

Huberman, A.M. and Miles, M.B. (2002) *The Qualitative Researcher's Companion*. Thousand Oaks, CA: Sage.

Locke, M. (1990) 'Methodological reflections', in Saran, R. and Trafford, V. (eds) *Research in Education Management and Policy*. London: Falmer Press.

Nisbet, J.D. and Entwistle, N.J. (1984) 'Writing the report', in Bell, J., Bush, T., Fox, A., Goodey, J. and Goulding, S. (eds) *Conducting Small-scale Investigations in Educational Management*. London: Paul Chapman and the Open University.

Taylor, G. (1989) *The Student's Writing Guide for the Arts and Social Sciences*. Cambridge: Cambridge University Press.

Recommended reading

Blaxter, L., Hughes, C. and Tight, M. (1996) *How to Research*. Buckingham: Open University Press.

Glatthorn, A. (2002) *Publish or Perish – the Educator's Imperative*. London: Sage.

Huberman, A.M. and Miles, M.B. (2002) *The Qualitative Researcher's Companion*. Thousand Oaks, CA: Sage.

Middlewood, D., Coleman, M. and Lumby, J. (1999) *Practitioner Research in Education: Making a Difference*. London: Paul Chapman.

Author index

Subject index